C000125703

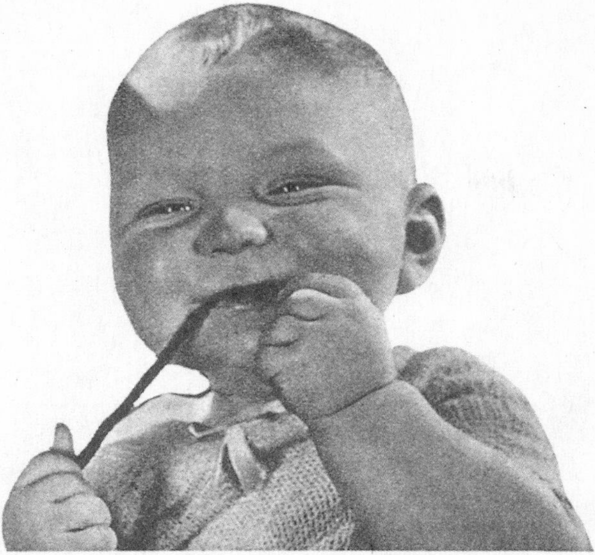

Will you give just one of the million half-crowns needed annually by the N.S.P.C.C. to protect helpless children against cruelty and neglect?

Donations should be addressed to Wm. J. Elliott, O.B.E., Director, National Society for the Prevention of Cruelty to Children, Victory House, Leicester Square, W.C.2

SEND YOUR 'ONE-IN-A-MILLION' TO-DAY

GUIDE TO LONDON

All information in this book comes from a pre-1960 edition
and is current for that time in history.

First published in Great Britain by Ward Lock & Co., Limited
This edition first published in Great Britain in 2008 by Cassell Illustrated,
a division of Octopus Publishing Group Ltd,
2–4 Heron Quays, London E14 4JP

A CIP catalogue record for this book is available from the British Library.

ISBN-13: 978-1-844-03649-3

Printed and bound in China

10 9 8 7 6 5 4 3 2 1

A

Pictorial and Descriptive Guide

TO

LONDON

With Large Section Plans of Central London ; Map of London and Twelve Miles Round ; Railway Maps ; Main Roads out of London ; Hyde Park and Kensington Gardens, and Twenty other Maps and Plans.

OVER ONE HUNDRED ILLUSTRATIONS.

Fifty-Third Edition—Revised.

NOTE—*Our* HANDBOOK TO LONDON, *in superior cloth binding, 5/- net, contains additional Section Street Plans (extending north to Hampstead, south to Denmark Hill) and a complete* INDEX TO STREETS, PUBLIC BUILDINGS, &c. (*about* 10,000 *references*).

LONDON:

WARD, LOCK & CO., LIMITED,

WARWICK HOUSE, SALISBURY SQUARE, E.C.4

AND AT MELBOURNE.

MAPS AND PLANS

* Section Plans I. and IV., comprising North and South London respectively, will be found in the superior cloth-bound Edition, which also contains a complete Index to Streets, Public Buildings, etc.

CONTENTS

THE WEST END.

THE CITY.

SOUTH LONDON.

THE ENVIRONS OF LONDON.

Directory of Hotels, Boarding Houses, Schools, Estate Agents and Business Establishments in Great Britain, *see after p. 16 and at end of Guide.*

INTRODUCTION.

"*When a man is tired of London he is tired of life ; for there is in London all that life can afford.*"—DR. JOHNSON.

DR. JOHNSON'S words are, if anything, more true now than when first written ; for the centuries-old enrichment of London has continued, and it is continuing at such speed that even those intimately acquainted with the trends and movements of the Metropolis can hardly keep pace with its manifold developments. In this Guide we can attempt only to direct the stranger's footsteps so that in a given period he sees all that is most worth seeing of its streets and buildings, and to allude to a few merely of the habits and customs which play so important a part in the life of what Sidney Smith aptly called "The Great Wen." Certainly in no city of ancient or modern days has there been such "fullness of life" as that which crowds the streets of the Metropolis at this period of our history ; and if Dr. Johnson were alive to-day we can well believe that he would enjoy the traditional "walk down Fleet Street" with even more than his accustomed relish.

The Sightseer's London.

Although the Metropolis is so vast that it would take the best part of a lifetime to traverse its 10,000 streets, and another lifetime to know intimately every part of the suburbs, the features of interest appealing especially to sightseers are, with few exceptions, confined to a central area, for the most part north of the Thames, measuring roughly some five miles from west to east, and three from north to south. We are far indeed from saying that there is not anything of interest outside this area ; but we do say that the visitor, however hardy and determined, who has methodically and conscientiously "done" the orthodox sights, and taken a trip or two by way of relaxation to places like Windsor and Hampton Court, will have little heart or shoe-leather left for Islington and Kilburn, and other places in the "Middle Ring," unless the calls of business or of friendship lure him thither. We have accordingly dealt fully with the West End and the City, and outlined all the principal excursions from London; but the reader who is in search of detailed information respecting suburban dormitories and nurseries must, we fear, be referred to volumes of greater capacity. We have done our best to squeeze a quart—ought we not rather to say a hogshead?—into a pint pot, but something has perforce been spilt in the process.

"From the top of a Bus, Gentlemen."

"The way to see London," said W. E. Gladstone in an oft-quoted remark to some American tourists, "is from the top of a bus—the top of a bus, gentlemen." The advice is no less sound to-day. A shilling or two judiciously invested in bus fares will enable all the main thoroughfares to be seen, with a much wider range of view than is afforded by taxi or motor-car, and there are few better ways of appreciating London's very real traffic problems or of viewing the "tide of faces" which fascinated Heine as it fascinates all.

Local Characteristics.

Limitations of space forbid anything like a general survey of London and its various quarters, but the interest of the provincial visitor will certainly be stimulated by remarking that the special aspects of many of the other great towns are reflected here. Thus, the observant will readily discover a commercial Manchester between the General Post Office and the Guildhall, and there is another Liverpool eastward of the Tower; the cathedral towns, with cloisters and closes, deans, canons and choirs, are superbly represented in the City of Westminster; while the Inns of Court, with their "quads" and lawns and stately chapels, are strongly reminiscent of Universities like Oxford and Cambridge.

Certain trades and manufactures are localized, and have been so for many years. The Spitalfields silk-weavers are known all the world over. Clerkenwell is as famous for watch-making as Geneva itself, and the manufacture of jewellery and optical, musical and electrical instruments is almost equally a speciality of that neighbourhood. Lambeth is a rival to North Staffordshire in producing artistic pottery. Southwark is the metropolis of the hop trade; and adjoining Bermondsey tans hides and makes leather for a great part of England. The cabinet-making, French-polishing and upholstering trades have a predilection for Shoreditch, Bethnal Green, and St. Pancras. About Aldgate is clustered the Jewish quarter. In Stepney and Whitechapel large numbers of men and women are engaged in the tailoring and dressmaking trades. Marylebone is another important centre of the same industries. Bootmakers favour Bethnal Green. A considerable settlement of foreigners, chiefly French and Italian, is established about Soho, though they seem to be leaving it for the Charlotte Street quarter, to the north of Oxford Street. Between Farringdon Road and Gray's Inn Road, to the north of the wider part of Holborn, is a large Italian community. The chief markets for tea, corn, wine, and colonial produce are in Mark and Mincing Lanes. The wholesale fruit trade has its headquarters at Covent Garden. The wholesale fish merchants have a natural liking for Billingsgate and its neighbourhood, a liking which other members of the community do not share. Dealers in diamonds collect in the neighbourhood of Hatton Garden and Houndsditch, and carry on a quiet and mysterious trade. Paternoster Row and the British book trade are nearly synonymous terms, although most of the larger publishing houses are now established in other parts of London, notably in the streets adjoining Covent Garden. Fleet Street —" the Street of Ink "—is the centre of newspaper activity, and the adjoining streets and courts are studded with printing-offices. Upper Thames Street is the centre of the paper trade. The financial world of London—bankers, stock and share brokers—for obvious reasons of convenience, finds its centre round the Bank of England and the Stock Exchange, Lombard Street, Prince's Street, Lothbury, and the adjacent thoroughfares being almost literally lined by the headquarters of banks and insurance companies. Other great mercantile and insurance companies and commercial firms are represented in Cornhill, Old Broad Street, Moorgate, King William Street, and other well-known thoroughfares. Shipowners and agents abound near Fenchurch and Leadenhall Streets, with West End agencies at Cockspur Street, Trafalgar Square. Just as naturally, barristers and solicitors congregate in the neighbourhood of the Inns of Court, as we shall see when we come to Lincoln's Inn, Gray's Inn, and the Temple. The Strand, Leicester Square, Shaftesbury Avenue, Covent Garden and St. Martin's Lane are eminently theatrical neighbourhoods; Wardour Street is the centre of the cinema industry; Pall Mall, St. James's Street and Piccadilly are " clubland "; painters, musicians, authors and actors have a liking for St. John's Wood, Bayswater, Kensington, and Chelsea; consulting physicians favour Harley Street, Wimpole Street and Devonshire Street; Great Portland Street, Bond Street and Long Acre are centres of the motor-car trade;

and architects and civil engineers must generally be sought in Westminster, especially Victoria Street.

HOTELS AND TARIFFS.

Several immense new hotels have been opened in London recently, and a considerable number of less palatial establishments, but during the height of the tourist season—July, August, and the early part of September—there is still a shortage of accommodation, and wherever possible rooms should be booked well in advance. It must be understood that the tariffs stated in the following pages are inserted rather as an indication of the grade of the various establishments than as a means of making even an approximate estimate of the cost of a visit. As a further indication of the grade of hotel we give immediately after the name the number of bedrooms. *In all cases inquiry should be made beforehand as to terms.* The list makes no pretence of being exhaustive.

In the following list Private and Temperance Hotels and Boarding Houses are distinguished by an asterisk (*). *Boarding Houses* are principally to be found in the Bloomsbury quarter, but there are many others in the attractive outer suburbs, such as Hampstead, Bayswater, Dulwich, etc. Advertisements of furnished apartments will be found in the daily newspapers.

Hotels, etc., in the Bloomsbury Quarter.

(Plan II, I,K,L., 6 and 7.)

[ABBREVIATIONS: *R.*, bedroom; *b.*, breakfast; *l.*, luncheon; *t.*, tea; *d.*, dinner; *a.*, attendance; *fr.*, from; *temp.*, temperance.]

***Alexandra**, 22, Bedford Place, W.C.1.

Ambassadors (100 rooms), 10, Upper Woburn Place, W.C.1: *R.* and *b.*, fr. 10/6; *t.*, 1/6; *d.*, 4/6.
Boarding terms: fr. 17/- per day.

Bedford (248 rooms), 83–95, Southampton Row, W.C.: *R.*, *b.* and *bath*, 7/9.

***Bonnington** (260 rooms), Southampton Row: *R.* and *b.*, 8/6; *l.*, 2/6; *t.*, 1/-; *d.*, 3/6.
Boarding terms: fr. 13/- per day.

***Connaught House**, 8 and 9, Montague Street, W.C.1.

Cosmo (130 rooms), Southampton Row.

***County** (112 rooms), 5–9, Upper Woburn Place, W.C.1: *R.*, *b.* and *bath*, 5/9.

***Cranston's Ivanhoe** (300 rooms), Bloomsbury Street: *R.* and *b.*, 9/6; *l.*, 3/-; *t.*, 1/6; *d.*, 4/-.
Boarding terms: 15/- per day.

***Cranston's Kenilworth**, Great Russell Street, W.C.

***Cranston's Waverley** (150 rooms), 132, Southampton Row, W.C.1: *R.* and *b.*, fr. 9/6; *l.*, 3/-; *t.*, 1/-; *d.*, 4/-.
Boarding terms: 14/- per day 94/6 per week.

Endsleigh (200 rooms), Endsleigh Gardens, near Euston Station.

Euston (135 rooms) (L.M.S.R.): *R.* and *b.*, fr. 13/-; *l.*, 4/6; *t.*, 1/-; *d.*, 7/-.

Gower (90 rooms), Euston Road, N.W.

Grafton (150 rooms), Tottenham Court Road, W.1.

Great Northern (L.N.E.R.) (83 rooms), King's Cross Station, N.: *R.*, and *b.* fr. 11/6; *l.*, 4/6; *t.*, 1/6; *d.*, 6/6.

Imperial (700 rooms), Russell Square, W.C.: *R.*, *b.*, and *bath*, 9/6; *l.*, 3/-; *t.*, 1/3; *d.*, 4/-.
Boarding terms: 16/6 per day. 105/- per week.

[ABBREVIATIONS: *R.*, bedroom; *b.*, breakfast; *l.*, luncheon; *t.*, tea; *d.*, dinner; *a.*, attendance; *fr.*, from; *temp.*, temperance.]

***Kingsley** (200 rooms), 36 and 38, Hart Street, W.C.1: *R.*, *b.* and *bath*, fr. 8/6; *l.*, 2/6; *t.*, 1/-; *d.*, 3/6.
Boarding terms: 87/6 per week.

***Lincoln Hall** (112 rooms), Upper Bedford Place, W.C.: *R.*, *b.* and *bath*, 6/9.

Montague, 14–16, Montague Street, Russell Square, W.C.1.

National (465 rooms), 38–51, Upper Bedford Place, W.C.1: *R.* and *b.*, 7/9; *l.*, 2/6; *d.*, 3/6.
Boarding terms: 13/9 per day.

Palace (250 rooms), Bloomsbury Street W.C.1: *R.* and *b.*, single, 10/6; *l.*, 2/6; *t.*, 1/6; *d.*, 4/-.
Boarding terms: 15/- per day.

***Premier** (114 rooms), Russell Square: *R.* and *b.*, 6/9.

***Raglan** (135 rooms), Upper Bedford Place, W.C.1.

Royal (790 rooms), Woburn Place, W.C.

Russell (350 rooms), Russell Square, W.C.: *R.* and *b.*, fr. 12/6; *l.*, 3/6; *t.*, 1/6; *d.*, fr. 6/6.
Boarding terms: fr. 22/6 per day.

***Thackeray** (200 rooms), 52–57, Gt. Russell Street, W.C.: *R.*, *b.*, and *bath*, fr. 8/6; *l.*, 2/6; *t.*, 1/-; *d.*, 3/6.

***West Central** (150 rooms), 101, Southampton Row, W.C.: *R.* and *b.*, fr. 8/6; *l.*, 2/6; *t.*, 1/3; *d.*, 3/6.
Boarding terms: fr. 13/- per day.

***White Hall**, Guilford Street, W.C.1; Bloomsbury Square, W.C.1; 4, Montague Street; Bedford Place, etc.

Hotels in the West End.

(Piccadilly, Oxford Street, Bayswater, Kensington, etc.)

Alexander (75 rooms), 35–39, Queen's Gardens Court, W.2.

Almond's, Clifford Street, Bond Street.

Bailey's (180 rooms), Gloucester Road, S.W.

***Balmoral** (120 rooms), 37, Queen's Gate Gardens, S.W.

Batt's (40 rooms), 41 and 42, Dover Street, W.1.

Berkeley, 77, Piccadilly, W.

Berners, Berners Street, W.1 (225 rooms) *R.* and *b.*, fr. 11/-; *l.*, 3/6; *t.*, 1/6; *d.*, 6/-.
Boarding terms: fr. 18/- per day; fr. 126/- per week; 37/6 per week end.,

Bolton Mansions (80 rooms), South Kensington: *R.* and *b.*, fr. 8/6; *l.* 2/6; *t.*, fr. 1/-; *d.*, 3/6.

***British Empire** (80 rooms), De Vere Gardens, W.8.

Burlington, Cork Street, W.1.

Cadogan (75 rooms), 75, Sloane Street.

Carlton, Pall Mall, S.W.

Carter's (30 rooms), 14–15, Albemarle Street, W.

Cavendish (80 rooms), 81, Jermyn Street, Piccadilly.

Claridge's (250 rooms), Brook Street, W.: *R.* and *bath*, 35/-; *l.*, 8/6; *t.*, 2/6; *d.*, 10/6.

Connaught, Carlos Place, Grosvenor Square, W.

Cumberland, Marble Arch, W.: *R.*, *b.*, and *bath*, 12/6.

Curzon (150 rooms), 56–59, Curzon Street, W.

De Vere (100 rooms), 48–50, Hyde Park Gate, and De Vere Gardens, W.: *R.* and *b.*, fr. 12/6; *l.*, 4/6; *d.*, 6/6.
Boarding terms: 21/- per day.

Dorchester (300 rooms), Park Lane, W.

Durrant's (77 rooms), 26–32, George Street, Manchester Square, W.1: *R.* and *b.*, fr. 10/6; *l.*, 4/-; *t.*, 1/3; *d.*, 6/-.
Boarding terms: fr. 17/6 per day.

Fischer's, 11, Clifford Street, W.

Fleming's, 9–10, Half-Moon Street, and 41, Clarges Street, Piccadilly, W.

Ford's (50 rooms), 13–16, Manchester Street, W.

Garland's (50 rooms), 15–17, Suffolk Street, Pall Mall.

Garrick, 3–5, Charing Cross Road.

Great Central (360 bedrooms), Marylebone Station, N.W.

Great Western Royal (150 rooms) (G.W.R.), Paddington Station, W.: *R.* and *b.*, 13/6; *l.*, 3/6; *t.*, 1/6; *d.*, fr. 4/-.

Grosvenor House (500 rooms), Park Lane, W.: *R.* and *b.*, fr. 30/-; *l.* fr. 6/6; *t.*, 2/6; *d.*, fr. 8/6.

Hans Crescent (120 rooms), 1, Hans Crescent, Sloane Street, S.W.

Haymarket (200 rooms), Piccadilly Circus, W.

Hyde Park (250 rooms), 66, Knightsbridge, S.W.

Kensington, Russell Gardens, Kensington, W.

Langham (275 rooms), Portland Place W.: *R.* and *b.*, fr. 17/-; *l.*, 4/6; *t.*, 1/6; *d.*, 7/6.
Boarding terms: fr. 27/6 per day.

***Lexham Court**, Lexham Gardens, S.W.8.

***Linden Hall** (70 rooms), 131, Cromwell Road, S.W.: *R.*, *b.* and *bath*, 8/6.

[ABBREVIATIONS: *R.*, bedroom; *b.*, breakfast; *l.*, luncheon; *t.*, tea; *d.*, dinner; *a.*, attendance; *fr.*, from; *temp.*, temperance.]

May Fair (300 rooms), Berkeley Square, W.: *R.*, single, fr. 27/6; *l.*, fr. 6/6; *t.*, 3/–; *d.*, fr. 8/6.

New Norfolk (40 rooms), 25, London Street, and 2, Norfolk Square, Paddington.

***Orchard** (80 rooms), Portman Street, W.

***Pembridge Gardens,** Notting Hill, W.2.

Park Gate (over Lancaster Gate Tube Station), Stanhope Terrace, W.2.

Park Lane (400 rooms), Piccadilly, W.: *R.*, fr. 14/6; *l.*, 5/6; *t.*, 2/6; *d.*, 8/6.

Park View (45 rooms), Hyde Park Corner, S.W.1.

Phœnix, 19, Prince's Street, Cavendish Square, W.

Piccadilly (300 rooms), Piccadilly and Regent Street.

Portland, 97–105, Gt. Portland Street, W. (114 rooms).

Prince of Wales, 16–18, De Vere Gardens (120 rooms): *R.* and *b.*, fr. 9/6; *l.*, 3/–; *t.*, 1/–; *d.*, 4/–.
Boarding terms: fr. 15/– per day.

***Quebec** (100 rooms), Bryanston Street, W.1: *R.* and *b.*, 11/6; *l.*, 3/6; *t.*, 1/–; *d.*, 5/–.
Boarding terms: fr. 16/6 per day.

Regent Palace (1,119 rooms), close to Piccadilly Circus: *R.*, *bath* and *b.*, fr. 9/6.

Ritz, Piccadilly, W.1.

Royal Court (120 rooms), 8–10, Sloane Square, S.W.

Royal Palace, Kensington High Street.

Shaftesbury (280 rooms), Great St. Andrew Street, W.C.2.

***Somerset** (150 rooms), Orchard Street, W.1.

South Kensington (150 rooms), Queen's Gate Terrace, S.W.: *R.* and *b.*, 10/6; *l.*, 4/–; *t.*, 1/6; *d.*, 6/–.
Boarding terms: fr. 105/–per week.

Splendide (80 rooms), Piccadilly, W.: *R.*, single, fr. 21/–; *l.*, 6/6; *d.*, fr. 8/6.

***Tudor Court,** Cromwell Road, S.W.7 *R.* and *b.*, 9/6; *l.*, 3/–; *t.*, 1/–; *d.*, 4/6.
Boarding terms: 13/6 per day; 84/– per week.

***Vanderbilt** (120 rooms), 76–86, Cromwell Road, S.W.7.

Vandyke, Cromwell Road, S.W.

Washington (120 rooms), Curzon Street, W.

***Westbourne,** Westbourne Terrace, W.2.

White Hall, 92, Lancaster Gate, W.1: *R.* and *b.*, fr. 9/–; *l.*, 2/6; *d.*, 4/–.
Boarding terms: 94/6 per week.

York, Berners Street, W.1.

Hotels in and about the Strand.

(Plan III, K. and L. 8.)

Arundel (80 rooms), Arundel Street, Strand.

Charing Cross (Southern Ry.).

Craven (64 rooms), 43–46, Craven Street, Strand: *R.* and *b.*, fr. 8/6; *l.*, 3/–; *t.*, 1/3; *d.*, 4/6.
Boarding terms: fr. 84/– per week.

***Faulkner's,** Villiers Street, Charing Cross (65 rooms).

Howard (165 rooms), Norfolk Street.

Loudoun (80 rooms), 24 Surrey Street, Strand.

Norfolk (70 rooms), 30–32, Surrey Street, Strand: *R.* and *b.*: fr. 10/6.
Boarding terms: 19/– per day.

***Opera** (33 rooms), Bow Street, Strand.

Savoy, Strand: *R.* and *bath*, fr. 25/– *b.*, fr. 3/–.

Strand Palace, Strand (1,000 rooms): *R.*, *bath* and *b.*, fr. 9/6.

Victoria (300 rooms), Northumberland Avenue, W.C.: *R.* and *b.*, fr. 16/–; *l.*, 5/–; *d.*, fr. 6/6.
Boarding terms: fr. 25/– per day.

Waldorf (400 rooms), Aldwych, Strand: *R.* and *b.*, single, fr. 14/–; *l.*, fr. 4/6; *d.*, fr. 6/6.

York, 80–82, Waterloo Road, S.E.

Victoria and Westminster.

(Plan III, H. I. and K. 10 and 11.)

Goring (100 rooms), Grosvenor Gardens, S.W.1: *R.* and *b.*, 21/–; *l.*, 4/6; *t.*, 1/6; *d.*, 7/6.
Boarding terms: 27/6 per day.

Grosvenor (245 rooms), Buckingham Palace Road, S.W.: *R.* and *b.*, fr. 16/6; *l.*, 5/–; *t.*, 2/–; *d.*, 6/6.
Boarding terms: fr. 27/– per day.

Rubens (150 rooms), Buckingham Palace Road, S.W.1.

Victoria, 46, Buckingham Palace Road.

Wilton (100 rooms), Victoria (opposite Southern Ry. Station): *R.* and *b.*, fr. 9/6; *l.*, 2/6; *t.*, 1/3; *d.*, 4/6.
Boarding terms: fr. 13/6 per day.

City Hotels.

(Plans II and III, M.N.O. 7 and 8.)

[ABBREVIATIONS: *R.*, bedroom; *b.*, breakfast; *l.*, luncheon; *t.*, tea; *d.*, dinner; *a.*, attendance; *fr.*, from; *temp.*, temperance.]

Anderton's (80 rooms), Fleet Street: *R.* and *b.*, 8/6; *l.*, 2/6; *t.*, 1/–; *d.*, 3/6.

Boarding terms: 13/– per day.

Great Eastern (250 rooms) (L.N.E.R.), Liverpool Street Station, E.C.: *R.* and *b.*, fr. 11/6; *l.*, 4/6; *t.*, 1/–; *d.* fr. 5/–.

Boarding terms: fr. 21/– per day.

Manchester (250 rooms), Aldersgate Street, E.C.1.

Three Nuns (70 rooms), adjoining Aldgate Station: *R.* and *b.*, 8/–.

RESTAURANTS.

It may be said of many of the first-class restaurants that they are not so expensive as they look; and humble mortals who are content with a "grill," or other simple dish, will pay little more than they would have to do elsewhere. The numerous establishments of J. Lyons & Co., Ltd., Slaters, Ltd., and other similar companies, supply a fair luncheon or dinner for from 2*s.* to 3*s.* 6*d.*; while fare of a lighter kind can be had at the shops of the Aerated Bread Co., Ltd., J. Lyons & Co., Ltd., Express Dairies Co., Ltd., Messrs. Fuller's, and others. The luncheons and dinners served at some of the restaurants in the neighbourhood of Soho are astonishingly good and cheap.

In addition to the following, there are the restaurants and grill-rooms attached to the principal hotels, which are generally available to the public, and those provided for the convenience of customers at the large stores and drapery establishments.

Boulestin's, 25, Southampton Street, W.C.1.
Buszard, 197, Oxford Street.
Café Marguerite, 171, Oxford Street, W.
Café Monico, Piccadilly Circus.
Café Royal, 68, Regent Street.
Carr's, 265, Strand.
Comedy, Panton Street, Haymarket.
Corner House, Coventry Street, Piccadilly Circus.
Coventry, 7 and 8, Rupert Street, and 13 and 15, Wardour Street, W.
Criterion, Piccadilly Circus.
Fleming's, 68 and 303, Oxford Street.
Florence, Rupert Street, W.
Frascati, 26–32, Oxford Street.
Gatti's, 436, Strand.
Hatchett's, Piccadilly.
Holborn, 218, High Holborn.
Jules', 85, Jermyn Street.
Maison Lyons, Marble Arch, W.1.
Monseigneur, 16, Jermyn Street.
Oddenino's, Regent Street.
Oxford Corner House, Oxford Street.
Pagani's, Gt. Portland Street, W.C.
Pimms, 3–5, Poultry, E.C.2, etc.
Pinoli's, 17, Wardour Street, and 9, Rupert Street, W.1.
Popular, Piccadilly.
Prince's, Piccadilly.
Pritchard's, 79, Oxford Street, W., 13 and 15, Wardour Street, W.1, etc.
Quaglino's, 16, Bury Street, S.W.1.
Regent Palace, Piccadilly Circus.
Reggiori's, opposite King's Cross Station, and 25, Chapel Street, Edgware Road, N.W.1.
Rendezvous, 45, Dean Street, W.
Romano's, 399, Strand.
Rule's, 35, Maiden Lane, Strand.
Scotts, 18–20, Coventry Street, W.1.
Simpson's, Strand.
Sovrani's, Stratton Street, W.1.
Strand Corner House.
Trocadero, Shaftesbury Avenue.
Ye Olde Cheshire Cheese, Wine Office Court, Fleet Street.

The City is noted for old-fashioned taverns, and others with old names but new-fashioned styles. In some a speciality is made of particular dishes on certain days. Luncheon is the speciality of these establishments, which are patronized for the most part by business men.

Vegetarian Restaurants.—Food Reform Association, Furnival Street, Holborn, and others.

GRATUITIES.—The question of the "tip," or, as the French say, the *pourboire*, is certain to cause the inexperienced visitor some perplexity. No hard and fast rules can be laid down, and the whole system is objectionable, but in **Hotels** of medium standing, 2*s.* 6*d.* per person to the waiter or waitress and about half that sum to the chambermaid is sufficient for a stay of a day or two. The "boots" or hall-porter, whose friendly counsel is often of the greatest service to strangers, will also expect to be "remembered." Most experienced travellers calculate tips at about 2*s.* for every pound of the hotel bill.

At **Restaurants** reckon about 1*d.* in the 1*s.* on the bill, with perhaps twice that sum in high-class West End establishments, where waiters frequently have to pay for the privilege of levying toll on the public. Gratuities are forbidden in many of the cheap teashops, but are frequently given.

Railway porters expect from 3*d.* to 6*d.* for carrying a hand-bag or rugs, and from 1*s.* for heavy luggage.

PRELIMINARY INFORMATION.

EXPLANATORY.—In this section, arranged alphabetically, information is given respecting a number of miscellaneous matters of importance alike to visitors and residents.

AIR PORT.—The principal cross-Channel and other air services arrive at and depart from the airport at Croydon, some ten miles south of the metropolis. There is regular motor communication with the West End. For current arrangements apply Imperial Airways, Ltd., Croydon, or any tourist agency. A number of lines linking London with other parts of Britain use Heston Airport, west of London. Another important airport is at Gatwick, between London and Brighton. (See also pp. 67 and 263.)

AMERICANS IN LONDON.—The Hon. J. H. Choate, when American Ambassador, made the following suggestions :—

" An American lately arrived in London should trace out in this great City those memorials and things of interest pertaining to America of which England and London are full. If he lands at Plymouth, his feet rest upon those mysterious figures at the dock, ' 1620 '—the very place where, 300 years ago, our Pilgrim Fathers embarked in the *Mayflower* to try their fortunes in the wilderness, and lay the foundations of the great nation which we now represent. If by chance he lands at Gravesend, in the chancel of St. George's Church he will drop a tear over the tomb of Pocahontas, the American Indian Princess, whose father, Powhattan, was king in Virginia when the great Elizabeth still sat on the throne of England. Coming up to London, if he will allow me to take him ' a personally-conducted tour,' I will conduct him to St. Saviour's Cathedral, in Southwark, where is recorded the baptism of John Harvard. At the Charterhouse will be found associations of Roger Williams, the founder of Rhode Island, and the apostle of toleration."

To this we may add that at the Church of All Hallows, Barking, the entry of the baptism of Wm. Penn (October 23, 1644), who was born on the adjacent Tower Hill, is still to be seen in the registers, and the fact is recorded by a commemorative tablet erected by the Pennsylvania Society of New York. In the same church John Quincy Adams was married on July 26, 1797. The registers of St. George's, Hanover Square, contain the record of the marriage of Theodore Roosevelt (December 2, 1886). In the church of St. Sepulchre, Newgate Street, is the tomb of the redoubtable Captain John Smith, sometime Governor of Virginia. The spire of Christ Church, Westminster Bridge Road, was erected as a memorial of Lincoln, and the stonework in ornamented with the stars and stripes. And lastly, there are statues of Washington and Lincoln in Trafalgar Square and Parliament Square respectively, a bust of Lincoln in the Royal Exchange, and memorial tablets in Westminster Abbey to J. R. Lowell and Walter Hines Page.

AREA AND POPULATION.—The **City,** the London of history and tradition, occupies only a small part of the great Metropolis, 677 acres, to be exact. (For boundaries, see map "London at a Glance.") The night population is small (under 11,000), with a tendency to dwindle still further, but it has been found by actual count that considerably over a million people enter the City in twenty-four hours. The day population has been estimated at about 436,000, "all at work." The administrative **County of London,** the area under the jurisdiction of the London County Council (see p. 24), comprises, exclusive of tidal water and foreshore, 74,850 acres, or 117 square miles, with an estimated population of 4,230,200. The area recognized as **Greater London** includes the City, the whole of the counties of London and Middlesex, and parts of the counties of Kent, Surrey, Essex, and Herts. It is made up of all parishes of which any part is within twelve miles of Charing Cross, or of which the whole is within fifteen miles of Charing Cross. It is 693 square miles in extent, and comprises about 7,000 miles of streets, three-quarters of a million of separate dwellings occupied by over a million families, and has a total population of nearly 8½ millions. Thanks to the suburban railway services and the facilities afforded by trams and buses, the population in this "Outer Ring" has for years been growing at a rapid rate. Within 25 miles' radius of Charing Cross there is a population almost equal to one-quarter of the total population of England and Wales, and about as many as inhabit the whole of Scotland and Ireland. The extent of the built-over area within a radius of twelve miles from Charing Cross may be appreciated from the fact that it exceeds the combined areas of Liverpool, Manchester, Bristol, Leeds, Cardiff, and Swansea, with their suburbs and open spaces. In 1631, when a census was taken by the Lord Mayor at the instigation of the Privy Council, the entire population of London, including the wards without the walls and the old borough of Southwark, was only 130,268.

The rateable value of Greater London is over £96,000,000; that of the City only is nearly £9,000,000.[1] The latter figures give a rateable value of some £13,300 per acre as against £880 per acre for the County of London generally.

The healthiness of Greater London is attested by its remarkably low **Death Rate,** which in a recent year was 11.0 per thousand inhabitants, a record no other capital city can surpass.

BATHS AND BATHING.—Swimming and private baths, maintained by the local authorities, are to be found in nearly every quarter. An open-air swim can be had in the Serpentine, Hyde Park (see p. 139), at the Ponds on Hampstead Heath, and in most of the Parks. There is an up-to-date swimming pool at Earls Court (p. 180). The great Empire Pool (indoor) at Wembley (see p. 154) is the largest of its kind in the world, but is normally only available from May to September.

Of **Turkish Baths** the best known are the *Charing Cross* (Nevill's), Northumberland Avenue; *Imperial*, Southampton Row; the *Hammam*, 76, Jermyn Street, W.; *Broad Street*, Broad Street House, E.C. (Nevill's). In nearly all the charge is reduced after 6 or 7 p.m.

BOROUGH COUNCILS.—These bodies, constituted in 1900, regulate matters of purely local concern, such as street maintenance, lighting, public health, etc. There are twenty-nine Boroughs, or twenty-eight without the City, which was but little affected by the Act. West-

[1] The rateable value of the City of Westminster is still larger—over £11,000,000.

minster, by virtue of its ancient privileges, was also constituted a city. Each Borough has its Mayor, annually elected, with Aldermen and Councillors varying in numbers according to population. Kensington shares only with Windsor and Kingston the honour of being a Royal Borough. The following is a list of the Boroughs, with their area and population at the last census:—

	Area. Acres.	Population.		Area. Acres.	Population.
Battersea	2,163	159,552	Lewisham	7,015	219,953
Bermondsey	1,503	111,542	Paddington	1,357	144,923
Bethnal Green	760	108,194	Poplar	2,331	155,089
Camberwell	4,480	251,294	St. Marylebone	1,473	97,627
Chelsea	660	59,031	St. Pancras	2,694	198,133
Deptford	1,564	106,891	Shoreditch	658	97,042
Finsbury	587	69,888	Southwark	1,132	171,695
Fulham	1,706	150,928	Stepney	1,766	225,238
Greenwich	3,858	100,924	Stoke Newington	864	51,208
Hackney	3,287	215,333	Wandsworth	9,107	353,110
Hammersmith	2,287	135,523	Westminster, City of	2,503	129,579
Hampstead	2,265	88,947	Woolwich	8,282	146,881
Holborn	406	38,860	City	678	10,999 (night) 436,721 (day)
Islington	3,092	321,795			
Kensington	2,290	180,677			
Lambeth	4,083	296,147			

Beyond these Boroughs there are districts equally populous and equally entitled to be considered parts of London, which come within the areas of the Middlesex, Surrey, Kent and Essex County Councils. It is in these suburbs that the rate of growth is most rapid, some of them having doubled their population in a single decade. From time to time the more densely populated extra-London districts obtain charters of incorporation, and there are now 3 county boroughs and 26 municipal boroughs in this area.

BUSES.—See p. 49. **CABS.**—See p. 48.

CHURCHES AND CHAPELS.—In addition to the churches in the City proper, there are about fifty Metropolitan parish churches, and from five to six hundred ecclesiastical parish and district churches and chapels belonging to the Church of England. Of Nonconformist places of worship of every denomination there are upwards of eight hundred; so that we shall not be far wrong in estimating the number of places of worship open every Sunday in the metropolis at between fifteen and sixteen hundred. Owing to the de-population of the City, several of the churches there are closed on Sundays. The midday services during the week are generally well attended, however, and a point of interest is the growing tendency for a church to be associated more or less particularly with a neighbouring large bank, or office, from the staff of which choirs and other officials may be recruited.

The principal churches are described in other parts of this book, while the following list indicates the places of worship most likely to appeal to the visitor whose time is limited. Some of the Saturday daily and evening newspapers give a list of the principal preachers for the following day, with particulars of the music to be rendered, and similar information appears in some of the Sunday papers.

CHURCH OF ENGLAND.

St. Paul's Cathedral.—Sundays, 7.45, 8, 10.30, 3.15 and 6.30; daily, 8, 8.30, 1.5 and 4.

Westminster Abbey.—See p. 104.

Southwark Cathedral.—Sundays, 7.30, 8, 11, and 6.30; daily, 7.30, 8 and 5.

Temple Church.—Sundays, 11 and 3.

Chapel Royal: St. James'—Sundays, 8.30 and 11.15.

Royal Military Chapel, Wellington Barracks—Sunday Parade Service (ticket necessary: apply beforehand to Chaplain), 11; Evening Service, 6.

Savoy Chapel, Strand—11.15 and 6.

Guards' Chapel, Chelsea Barracks, S.W. —Sundays, 8, 11 (parade).

All Hallows, Barking, Great Tower Street, E.C.—8.30, 11 and 6.30.

All Saints', Margaret Street, Cavendish Square—Sundays, 7, 8, 9, 9.15, 10.30, 11.15, 3 and 6; week-days, 7, 7.30, 8 and 5.30; Wednesdays and Fridays, 11.45; Wednesdays, 8.30 p.m.

All Souls', Langham Place—8, 11 and 6.30.

Tower of London, St. Peter ad Vincula—Sundays, 8.15, 11 a.m. and 6.30 p.m.

Holy Trinity, Sloane Street—7.30, 8.30, 10, 11.15, 6.30.

St. Alban's, Brooke Street, Holborn—7, 8, 9.30, 11, 3, 6.30. Daily, 7, 7.45, 8.30 a.m. Mon., Wed., Fri., 6; Tues., Thurs., 8 p.m.

St. Bartholomew-the-Great, West Smithfield—Sundays, 8.45, 11, and 6.30.

St. Anne, Soho—8, 11 and 6.30; week-days, 8.30 a.m.; Wed., 8 p.m.

St. Clement Danes, Strand—9, 11 and 6.30; Wednesdays, 1 and 8; Fridays, 12 (noon) and 1.

St. Dunstan's, Fleet Street—11 and 6.30.

St. George's, Hanover Square—8, 11 and 6.30; week-days, 8 and 6.30.

St. Giles's, Cripplegate—8, 10.30, 3.30, 6.30; week-days (except Saturdays), 10 a.m.; Tuesdays, 7.30 a.m.; Thursdays, 7.30 and 1.15; Fridays, 7 p.m.

St. James's, Piccadilly—8, 11 and 6.15.

St. Margaret's, Westminster.—8.15, 11 and 7.

St. Martin's-in-the-Fields, Trafalgar Square—8.10, 8.30, 10.15, 11.30, 3.30 and 6.15; week-days, daily at 10.15.

St. Marylebone, High Street, Marylebone —8, 11, 12.15 and 7.

St. Mary-le-Bow (Bow Church), Cheapside—11 and 6.30; Tuesdays, 1.15, and Wednesdays, 1 p.m.

BAPTIST.

Metropolitan Tabernacle, Newington Butts—11, 3 and 6.30; Thursdays, 7.30 p.m.

Westbourne Park, Bayswater—11 and 6.30; Wednesdays, 7.30 p.m.

Bloomsbury Baptist Church—11 and 7.

CATHOLIC APOSTOLIC.

Gordon Square—10 and 5; week-days, 6 a.m. (Tuesdays and Saturdays), 10.30 (Wednesdays and Fridays), 5 daily.

CONGREGATIONAL.

City Temple, Holborn Viaduct—11 and 7.

Lyndhurst Road, Hampstead—11 and 7.

King's Weighhouse Chapel, Duke Street, W.—8, 11 and 7.

Westminster, Buckingham Gate, S.W.—11 and 7.

Whitefield's Tabernacle, Tottenham Court Rd.—11 and 7; Tuesdays, 8 p.m.

METHODIST.

Central Hall, Westminster—11, 3.30 and 7.

Wesley's Chapel, City Road—11 and 6.30.

Kingsway Hall—11, 3.30, 9.30.

PRESBYTERIAN.

Regent Square, Gray's Inn Road—11 and 7; Wednesdays, 8 p.m.

Hampstead, High Street, Hampstead, N.W.—11 and 6.30.

Marylebone, Upper George Street, W.—11 and 7; Thursdays, 8.15 p.m.

St. Columba (Church of Scotland), Pont Street, S.W.—11 and 6.30.

Scottish National Church, Russell Street, Covent Garden—11.15 and 6.30.

QUAKERS.

The Friends' House, Euston Road—11 and 6.30.

UNITARIAN.

Rosslyn Hill Chapel, near Hampstead Tube Station—11 and 6.30.

Essex Church, The Mall, Notting Hill Gate—11 and 6.30.

ROMAN CATHOLIC.

Westminster Cathedral, Ashley Gardens, Victoria Street, S.W. See p. 115.

Oratory, South Kensington, W.—See p. 170.

St. George's Cathedral, St. George's Road, Southwark—7, 8, 9.30, 10.30, 12 and 6.30; week-days, 7, 7.30, 8, 10 a.m. and 8.15 p.m.

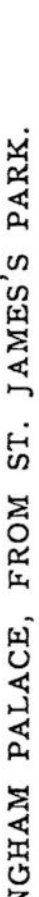

H. Felton,] [London.

BUCKINGHAM PALACE, FROM ST. JAMES'S PARK.

Fox Photos., Ltd.,]

THE THAMES, FROM WES

In the foreground are Westminster Abbey and the Houses o
Waterloo Station beyond. To the left are the Governm

[*London.*

STER TO LONDON BRIDGE.

.rliament, with Westminster Bridge, London County Hall and
)ffices in Whitehall and the Horse Guards Parade Ground.

[Daily Herald.

LAMBETH BRIDGE AND THE HOUSES OF PARLIAMENT.

St. Etheldreda, Ely Place, Holborn—8, 10, 11.15, 4, 7; week-days, 7.15 a.m., except Mondays, daily 8 a.m.; Tuesdays, 8 p.m.; Wednesdays, 1.15; Fridays, 1.15 and 8.

Church of the Immaculate Conception, Farm Street, Berkeley Square, W.—12 and 4; Wednesdays, 8.30 p.m.; Fridays, 3.30 p.m.

St. James's, Spanish Place—7, 8, 9, 10, 11, 12, 4 and 7; week-days 7, 8, 10

CHRISTIAN SCIENCE.

First Church of Christ, Scientist, near Sloane Square Station—11.30 and 7.

JEWS.

Central Synagogue, 129, Great Portland Street—Saturdays, 9.40 a.m.; week-days, 7.30 p.m.

Cathedral Synagogue, Duke Street, Aldgate—Saturdays, 8.30, 2 and sunset; other days, 7.15 a.m.

WELSH.

St. Benet's, Queen Victoria Street—11 and 6.30.

Welsh Presbyterian, Charing Cross Road, W.C.2.

FOREIGN CHURCHES.

Armenian (St. Sarleis), Iverna Gardens, W.8—11 a.m.

Danish (Lutheran), Marlborough House, Chapel—4 p.m., and King Street Poplar—11 a.m.

Dutch, Austin Friars—11 a.m. (except in August).

Finnish, Branch Road, Poplar—7 p.m.

French Catholic, Nôtre Dame de France, Leicester Place, W.C.—8, 9, 10, 11, 7. Daily, 7 and 8 a.m.

French Protestant, 9, Soho Square—11 and 6.30.

French Reformed Evangelical, Monmouth Road, W.—11 and 6.30.

German (Roman Catholic), 47, Adler Street, Whitechapel—11 a.m., 7 p.m.

Evangelische Christus Kirche, Brompton Road—1st, 3rd and 5th Suns. 11; 2nd and 4th Suns. 6.

Lutherische St. Georgs Kirche, 33, Little Alie Street, E.—11 a.m.

Hamburger Lutherische Kirche, Ritson Road, E.8—11 a.m.

Deutsche Reformierte, 3, Goulston Street, E.1—6.30.

Deutsche Wesleyanische, 30, Drayton Park, N.5—6.30.

Greek (St. Sophia's), Moscow Road, W.2.

Italian (Roman Catholic), **St. Peter's,** Clerkenwell Road—7, 8, 9, 10, 11.15 and 7. Daily, 7, 8, 10 and 8.15.

Norwegian (St. Olavs), Rotherhithe—11 a.m.; 6.30 1st Sun. in month.

Russian, Buckingham Palace Road, S.W.1.

Swedish (Lutheran), Harcourt Street, Marylebone, 11 a.m., and 120a, Lower Road, Rotherhithe—7 p.m.

Swiss (Protestant):

French-speaking, 79, Endell Street, W.C.2—11 and (except in August) 6.30 p.m.

German-speaking, 9, Gresham Street, E.C.1—11 and (except July and August) 7 p.m.

CINEMAS.—See p. 65.

CITY CORPORATION.—This famous and dignified body has jurisdiction over the City proper, and maintains an independent police force of eleven hundred officers and men. It can claim an antiquity greatly exceeding that of the "Mother of Parliaments," for a charter granted by William I, still preserved in the City archives, runs (we quote from Bishop Stubbs's translation): "William king greets William bishop and Gosfrith portreeve, and all the burghers within London, French and English, friendly; and I do you to wit that I will that ye be all lawworthy (i.e. possessed of privileges) that were in King Edward's day" (the Confessor). The Norman title of Bailiff was for a while substituted for that of Portreeve. In 1189 Henry FitzAylwin, the first "Mayor," was appointed. He held office for twenty-four years, but on his death a new charter was granted by King John, which directed that the Mayor should be chosen annually. This practice is still followed, though it has frequently happened that the same individual has held office more than once, the most notable instance being that of "Whittington, thrice Lord Mayor of London." The earliest known reference to the chief magistrate as "my Lord Mayor" is dated 1486. The explanation of the title is probably to be found in a misinterpretation of the Latin title *dominus Maior,* which originally meant nothing more than Sir Mayor. In course of time it came to be translated into "the lord the Mayor," whence it was but a step to "the lord Mayor." It was not until 1534 or 1535 that the title "Lord Mayor" came to be generally used. The Lord Mayor of London is one of the five holders of similar offices entitled to be styled "Right Honourable."

In early days the Mayor was elected by a general assembly of the citizens held in St. Paul's Churchyard. Now a Court of Common Hall nominates two aldermen for the office, from whom the Court of Aldermen selects one, usually the senior. The **Lord Mayor** marks his assumption of office by proceeding in state on November 9th to the Royal Courts of Justice, to be presented to the Lord Chief Justice and other judges, and to invite them to the Banquet always held at the Guildhall the same evening. The procession constitutes the famous **Lord Mayor's Show,** a pageant more highly esteemed by "country cousins" than by Londoners themselves. The cost of the "Show" and the Banquet usually amounts to about £4,000, which the Lord Mayor and Sheriffs have the privilege of paying. The Lord Mayor receives a salary of £10,000, but invariably spends far more from his private means. In the City he takes precedence of every subject of the Crown, including princes of the blood royal.

The two **Sheriffs** are appointed annually on Midsummer Day by the Liverymen, in pursuance of a privilege conferred by Edward IV. The **Aldermen,** of whom there are twenty-five, one for each of the wards into which the City is divided, are elected for life or until resignation. The **Court of Common Council** consists of 206 members, elected annually by the ratepayers. The legal and official title of the Corporation is "The Mayor and Commonalty and Citizens of the City of London."

The City revenues in the aggregate are about £2,500,000 pounds a year. The Corporation spends lavishly, extending when occasion arises a sumptuous hospitality to foreign potentates and statesmen. But it also does much solid and useful work for London, especially as regards education, the purchase and maintenance of open spaces, etc. On occasions of national disaster it is usual for the Lord Mayor to open a Mansion House Fund, and by this means large sums are annually raised in support of London hospitals.

CITY GUILDS.—Closely connected with the government of the City are the Livery Companies, or Guilds. There are seventy-nine of these Companies (of which twelve are considered "great"), each with its Master or Warden and Clerk, and many possessing handsome and commodious Halls. Some of the Companies are enormously wealthy, and have devoted large sums to educational and charitable purposes. The origin of the term "livery" in this connection is to be found in the feudal custom of barons and other great lords "delivering" to their retainers badges and liveries known as "Livery of Company."

CLUBS of all kinds—social, political, professional, athletic—abound in London. Admission to the exclusive and luxurious institutions in and around Pall Mall and Piccadilly is almost entirely a matter of social status. In most clubs, however, the duly accredited stranger will find a welcome.

Albemarle, 37, Dover Street, W.1	Ladies and Gentlemen.
Aldwych, 18, Exeter Street, W.C.2	Social; non-political.
Alpine, 23, Savile Row, W.1	Alpine Climbers.
American, 95, Piccadilly, W.1	Americans.
Argentine, 1, Hamilton Place, W.1	
Army and Navy, 36, Pall Mall, S.W.1	Service Officers.

Club	Description
Arthur's, 69, St. James's Street, S.W.1	Social.
Arts, 40, Dover Street, W.1	Artists, Authors, etc.
Athenæum, 107, Pall Mall, S.W.1	Politicians, Authors, etc.
Authors', 2, Whitehall Court, S.W.1	Authors and Journalists.
Automobile Association, Fanum House, Coventry Street, W.	Motoring.
Bachelors', 8, South Audley Street, W.1	Ladies admitted as guests.
Badminton, 100, Piccadilly, W.1	Sporting
Bath, 34, Dover Street, W.1	Social, Swimming, etc.
Beefsteak, 9, Green Street, Leicester Square, W.C.2	Social.
Boodle's, 28, St. James's Street, S.W.1	Country Gentlemen.
Brooks's, 60, St. James's Street, S.W.1	Liberal.
Buck's, 18, Clifford Street, W.1	Social.
Burlington Fine Arts, 17, Savile Row, W.1	Artists, etc.
Caledonian, 33, St. James's Square, S.W.1	Scots.
Carlton, 94, Pall Mall, S.W.1	Leading Conservative Club.
Cavalry, 127, Piccadilly, W.1	Mounted Forces.
Church Imperial, 75, Victoria Street, S.W.	Social, Church of England.
City Athenæum, 9, Union Street, E.C.2	
City Carlton, 24, St. Swithin's Lane, E.C.4	Conservative.
City of London, 19, Old Broad Street, E.C.2	Merchants, Bankers, etc.
City University, 50, Cornhill, E.C.3	
Cobden, 69, Victoria Street, S.W.1	Political.
Conservative, 74, St. James's Street, S.W.1	Political.
Constitutional, Northumberland Avenue, W.C.2	Conservative.
Crockford's, 16, Carlton House Terrace	Bridge Players, etc.
Devonshire, 50, St. James's Street, S.W.1	Liberal.
East India United Service, 16, St. James's Square, S.W.1	Officers and Indian Civil Service.
Eccentric, 9, Ryder Street, St. James's, S.W.1	Social, Drama and the Arts.
Eighty, 3, Hare Court, Temple, E.C.4	Ladies and Gentlemen.
Farmers', 2, Whitehall Court, S.W.1	Agricultural and Social.
Garrick, 15, Garrick Street, W.2	Actors, Authors, etc.
Golfers', 2A, Whitehall Court, S.W.1	Social for Golfers.
Green Room, 46, Leicester Square, W.C.2	Dramatic, Literary and Artistic.
Gresham, 15, Abchurch Lane, E.C.4	Merchants, Bankers, etc.
Grosvenor, 200, Buckingham Palace Road, S.W.1	Social, and at Henley.
Guards', 41, Brook Street, Grosvenor Square, W.1	Guards Officers, Past and Present.
International Sportsmen's, Upper Grosvenor Street, W.1	
Junior Army and Navy, Horse Guards Avenue	Officers, Past and Present.
Junior Carlton, 30, Pall Mall, S.W.1	Conservative.
Junior Constitutional, 101, Piccadilly, W.1	Conservative.
Junior Naval and Military, 96, Piccadilly, S.W.1	Com. Officers of H.M. Service.
Junior United Service, 11, Charles Street, S.W.1	Officers of Army and Navy.
Kennel, 84, Piccadilly, W. 1	Dog Fanciers, etc.
M.C.C., St. John's Wood Road, N.W.8	Headquarters of Cricket.
Marlborough, 52, Pall Mall, S.W.1	Social.
National, 12, Queen Anne's Gate, S.W.1	Protestant.
National Liberal, Whitehall Place, S.W.	Liberal.
Naval and Military, 94, Piccadilly, W.1	Army, Navy and Marines.
New University, 57, St. James's Street, S.W.1	Oxford and Cambridge Men.
1900, 24, Ryder Street, W.1	
Northern Counties, 3, Whitehall Court, S.W.1	Social.
Oriental, 18, Hanover Square, W.1	Social.
Orleans, 29, King Street, St. James's, S.W.1	Ladies admitted as guests.
Overseas League, Park Place, St. James's	Non-party ; Empire.
Oxford and Cambridge, 71, Pall Mall, S.W.1	Oxford and Cambridge Men.
Portland, 9, St. James's Square, S.W.1	Non-political.
Pratt's, 14, Park Place, S.W.1	Social.
Press, St. Bride's House, Salisbury Square, E.C.4	Journalistic.
Public Schools, 61, Curzon Street	Public School Men.
Publicity, 49, Chancery Lane, W.C.2	
Queen's, West Kensington, W.14	Tennis, etc.
Reform, 104, Pall Mall, S.W.1	Liberal.
Rotary, Russell Hotel, Russell Square, W.C.1	

Royal Aero, 119, Piccadilly, W.1	Aviation.
Royal Air Force, 128, Piccadilly, W.1	
Royal Automobile, 89, Pall Mall, S.W.1 . . .	Motorists.
Royal Societies, 63, St. James's Street, S.W.1 .	Members of Learned Societies.
Royal Thames Yacht, 60, Knightsbridge, S.W.1 .	
St. James's, 106, Piccadilly, W.1	Diplomatic Services.
St. Stephen's, 1, Bridge Street, Westminster, S.W.1	Conservative.
Savage, 1, Carlton House Terrace, S.W. . . .	Authors, Artists, etc.
Savile, 69, Brook Street, W.1	Social.
Sesame, 49, Grosvenor Street, W.1	Ladies and Gentlemen.
Sports, 8, St. James's Square, S.W.1	Social, Sports and Athletics.
Thatched House, 86, St. James's Street, S.W.1 .	Non-political.
Three Arts, 19A, Marylebone Road, N.W.1 . .	Music, Art, Drama.
Travellers', 106, Pall Mall, S.W.1	Travellers.
Turf, 85, Piccadilly, W.1	Social.
Union, 10, Carlton House Terrace	Social, non-political.
United Service, 116, Pall Mall, S.W.1	Combatant Officers.
United Sports, 4, Whitehall Court, S.W.1 . . .	Social.
United University, 1, Suffolk Street, S.W.1 . .	Oxford and Cambridge Men.
University of London, 19–21, Gower Street, W.C.	
White's, 37, St. James's Street, S.W.1	Social, non-political.
Windham, 13, St. James's Square, S.W.1 . . .	Social.

LADIES' CLUBS.

Alexandra, 12, Grosvenor Street, W.1.
American Women's, 46, Grosvenor Street, W.1.
Bath, 34, Dover Street, W.1.
Church Imperial, 75, Victoria Street, S.W.1. Social, Church of England.
City Women's, 9, Wine Office Court, Fleet Street.
Cowdray, 20, Cavendish Square, W.1.
Empress, 35, Dover Street, W.
Forum, 6, Grosvenor Place, S.W.1.
Halcyon, 13, Cork Street, Bond Street, W.1.
Ladies' Army and Navy, 27, St. James's Place, S.W.1.
Ladies' Automobile, 76, South Audley Street, W.1.
Ladies' Carlton, 5, Grosvenor Place, S.W.
Ladies' Empire, 69, Grosvenor Street, W.1.
Ladies' Park, Parkside, S.W.1.
New Century, 12, Hay Hill, Berkeley Square, W.1.
New Victorian, 30A, Sackville Street, W.1.
Pioneer, 12, Cavendish Place, W.1.
Three Arts, 19A, Marylebone Road, N.W.1.
University Women's, 2, Audley Square, W.1.
Victoria, 9, Halkin Street, S.W.1.

CONCERTS, etc.—In the season the music-lover may make his choice any afternoon or evening from half a dozen first-class performances. The most important take place in Queen's Hall (now regarded as a "studio" of the British Broadcasting Corporation), Albert Hall, Wigmore Hall, and Grotrian Steinway Hall (the last two are in Wigmore Street). Concerts and orchestral performances are also broadcast by wireless every afternoon and evening.

In many of the City churches midday organ recitals are given for the benefit of workers, and in nearly all the parks, both in central London and the suburbs, there are regular band performances during summer.

COUNTY COUNCIL.—The London County Council succeeded the Metropolitan Board of Works in 1889, and took over the important duties of the former London School Board on the passing of the Education Acts of 1902–3. It has general jurisdiction over the County of London (an area of 117 sq. miles), a county which in 1889 was carved out of the counties of Middlesex, Surrey and Kent. Its expenditure is over thirty-six million pounds per annum, education alone accounting for twelve million pounds. The Council comprises a chairman, vice-chairman, and deputy-chairman, elected annually, the first and the last not necessarily from among its own members ; 20 aldermen, elected for six years, one-half retiring every three years, and 124 Councillors, elected every three years in March. The headquarters of the Council are at the County Hall, an imposing modern building at the east end of Westminster Bridge (see p. 78). The Council meetings (open to the public) are held on Tuesdays at 2.30 p.m.

DOMINION AGENCIES.—The Agencies of the Overseas Dominions are mostly in or near the Strand :—

Australian Commonwealth, Australia House, Strand.
British Columbia, 1, Regent Street, S.W.1.
British India, India House, Aldwych, S.W.1.
Canada, Trafalgar Square, W.C.2.
Crown Colonies, 4, Millbank, Westminster, S.W.1.
Irish Free State, 33, Regent Street, S.W.1.
Malay States, 57, Trafalgar Square, S.W.1.
Newfoundland, 58, Victoria Street, S.W.1.
New South Wales, Wellington House, 125, Strand.
New Zealand, 415, Strand, W.C.2.
Queensland, 409, Strand, W.C.2.
Southern Rhodesia, Rhodesia House, Strand, W.C.
South Africa, Union of, Trafalgar Square, W.C.2.
Tasmania, Australia House, Strand, W.C.2.
Victoria, Melbourne Place, Strand, W.C.2.
Western Australia, Savoy House, Strand.

DRESS.—Visitors from abroad desirous of doing in London as Londoners do may welcome a hint or two under this head, though great latitude is allowed, and all varieties of costume may be seen in the streets. For formal calls and social events of importance a black morning coat and silk hat are *de rigueur*, but City and business men are usually content with lounge suits, and "bowlers" and soft felt hats are generally worn. Evening dress is usual when dining at high-class restaurants, and is compulsory for those who desire to dance (this does not, of course, apply to dance teas). At theatres, evening dress is nearly always worn in the boxes and stalls, and generally in the dress circle.

EMBASSIES and CONSULATES.

America, United States of	Embassy, 4, Grosvenor Gardens, S.W.1. Consulate, 18, Cavendish Square, W.1. Commercial Attaché, Bush House, Aldwych, W.C.2.
Argentine	Embassy, 11, Lowndes Square, S.W.1.
Austria	Legation, 18, Belgrave Square, W.1.
Belgium	Embassy, 103, Eaton Square, W.1.
Brazil	Embassy, 19, Upper Brook Street, W.1. Consulate, Aldwych House, Aldwych, W.C.
Bulgaria	Legation, 24, Queen's Gate Gardens, S.W.7.
Chile	Embassy, 1, Carrington House, Hertford Street, W.1. Consulate, 76, Victoria Street, S.W.1.
China	Legation and Consulate, 49, Portland Place, W.1.
Czecho-Slovakia	Legation and Consulate, 8, Grosvenor Place, S.W.1
Denmark	Legation, 29, Pont Street, S.W.1. Consulate, 7, Norfolk Street, Strand, W.C.2.

Egypt	Embassy, 75, South Audley Street, W.1. Consulate, 26, South Street, W.1.
Finland	Legation and Consulate, 37, Smith Square, S.W.1.
France	Embassy, Albert Gate House, Hyde Park, W.2. (Office 58, Knightsbridge, W.2.) Consulate, 51, Bedford Square, W.C.1 (11 to 4, Sats. 11 to 1).
Germany	Embassy and Consulate, 9, Carlton House Terrace, S.W.1.
Greece	Legation, 51, Upper Brook Street, W.1. Consulate, 7, Park Lane, W.1.
Hungary	Legation, 46, Eaton Place, S.W.1.
Italy	Embassy, 4, Grosvenor Square, W.1. Consulate, 68, Portland Place, W.1.
Japan	Embassy, 37, Portman Square, W.1. Consulate, 15, St. Helen's Place, E.C.3.
Latvia	Legation and Consulate, 87, Eaton Place, S.W.1.
Mexico	Legation, 48, Belgrave Square, S.W.1. 8, Halkin Street, S.W.1.
Netherlands	Legation, 21, Portman Square, W.1. Consulate, 28, Langham Street, W.1.
Norway	Legation, 21–24, Cockspur Street, S.W.1. Consulate, 26, King Street, E.C.2.
Peru	Legation and Consulate, 145, Sloane Street, S.W.1.
Poland	Embassy, 47, Portland Place, W.1. Consulate, 2, Thornhaugh Street, W.C.1.
Portugal	Embassy, 11, Belgrave Square, S.W.1. Consulate, 8, Chester Place, W.2.
Roumania	Legation, 4, Cromwell Place, S.W.7.
Spain	Embassy, 24, Belgrave Square, S.W.1. Consulate, 21, Cavendish Square, W.1.
Sweden	Legation, 27, Portland Place, W.1. Consulate, 329, High Holborn, W.C.1.
Switzerland	Legation, 18, Montagu Place, W.1.
Turkey	Embassy, 69, Portland Place, W.1.

FIRE BRIGADE.—The London Fire Brigade, with new headquarters at Lambeth, is controlled by the County Council. There are about 2,000 officers and men, with stations in all parts of London. The cost, amounting to over £800,000 a year, falls on the rates, except for a contribution of £80,000 from the Fire Insurance Companies and a £10,000 grant from the Treasury. In addition to the London Fire Brigade there is a Salvage Corps, maintained by the principal insurance companies, whose business it is to take charge of the goods and property jeopardized by fire. The gross amount of insurances effected on London property is well over two thousand millions a year, a stupendous sum which, after making every allowance for "cover," gives a fair indication of the material value of the world's greatest and largest city. One of London's little-known sights are the Wednesday afternoon displays at Lambeth H.Q., to which the public are cordially invited.

FREEDOM OF THE CITY.—This privilege—greatly prized—may be obtained by one of four methods: (*a*) by servitude (having been bound apprentice to a Freeman); (*b*) by patrimony (as the son or daughter of a Freeman); (*c*) by redemption or purchase; (*d*) by gift (honorary freedom).

HOTELS and tariffs.—See Introduction, pp. 12–15.

HOSPITALS.—The following are among the principal London Hospitals :

St. Bartholomew's, Smithfield.
Charing Cross, Agar Street, Strand, W.C.2.
Children's, Great Ormond Street, W.C.1.
Elizabeth Garrett-Anderson (Women), Euston Road, N.W.1.
Guy's, St. Thomas's Street, S.E.1.
King's College, Denmark Hill, S.E.5.
London, Whitechapel Road, E.1.
Middlesex, Mortimer Street, W.1.
Moorfields Ophthalmic, City Road, E.C.
Royal Eye, Blackfriars Road, S.E.
Royal Free, Gray's Inn Road, W.C.1.
Royal Masonic, Ravenscourt Park, W.
Homœopathic, Great Ormond Street, W.C.1.
St. George's, Hyde Park Corner, S.W.1.
St. Mark's, City Road, E.C.
St. Mary's, Praed Street, Paddington.
St. Thomas's, Albert Embankment.
University College, Gower Street, W.C.1.
Westminster, near Westminster Abbey.

HOUSES, MEMORABLE.—The following are among the numerous houses associated with bygone celebrities and distinguished by memorial tablets erected by the London County Council, the City Corporation, the Royal Society of Arts, the Incorporated Society of Musicians, or private individuals like the Duke of Bedford and the Duke of Westminster. Many of the houses are more particularly referred to in our descriptive rambles (see Index). In some cases the tablets have been affixed to houses not in themselves noteworthy, but occupying the sites of old houses that have had distinguished occupants.

The City Corporation have affixed a number of plaques, denoting the sites of historic buildings, gates, etc., within their area.

"I ask anybody who is in the habit of taking long walks in London or in other cities, whether it is not an immense relief to come on some tablet which suggests a new train of thought, which recalls to the mind the career of some distinguished person, and which takes off the intolerable pressure of the monotony of endless streets."—*Lord Rosebery.*

Balfe, M. W., 12, Seymour Street, Portman Square.
Banks, Sir Joseph, 32, Soho Square.
Barry, James, 36, Castle Street, Oxford Street.
Beaconsfield, Earl of, 22, Theobald's Road (at birth) ; 29, Park Lane, and 19, Curzon Street, Mayfair (at death).
Blake, William, 28, Broad Street, Golden Square ; South Molton Street, W.
Borrow, George, 22, Hereford Square, Brompton.
Browning, Elizabeth Barrett, 50, Wimpole Street.
Browning, Robert, 19, Warwick Crescent, Paddington.
Burke, Edmund, 37, Gerrard Street, Soho.
Byron, Lord, 24, Holles Street, Cavendish Square (bronze relief bust on modern premises). There is also a bust on 8, St. James's Street.
Carlyle, Thomas, 24 (formerly 5), Cheyne Row, Chelsea, and 33, Ampton Street, Gray's Inn Road.
Chamberlain, Joseph, 40, Princes Gardens, S.W. ; 25, Highbury Place, N.
Chatham, William Pitt, Earl of, Pitt House, North End, Hampstead.
Chesterfield (2nd, 3rd and 4th Earls), 45, Bloomsbury Square.
Cobden, Richard, 23, Suffolk Street, Pall Mall.
Constable, John, 76, Charlotte Street, Fitzroy Square.
Cook, Captain, 88, Mile End Road.
Cruikshank, George, 263, Hampstead Road.
D'Arblay, Madame (Fanny Burney), 11, Bolton Street, Piccadilly.
Darwin, Charles, 110, Gower Street.
De Quincey, Thomas, 61, Greek Street, Soho.
Dickens, Charles, 48, Doughty Street, Mecklenburg Square (now *Dickens Museum*).
Do. Do. 1, Devonshire Terrace, Portland Place (1839–51).
Do. Do. 13, Johnson Street, Somers Town (boyhood).
D'Israeli, Isaac, 6, Bloomsbury Square.
Dryden, John, 43, Gerrard Street, Soho.
Du Maurier, G., New Grove House, The Grove, Hampstead.

Eliot, George, Holly Lodge, 31, Wimbledon Park Road, Wandsworth.
Faraday, Michael, 48, Blandford Street, Portman Square.
Flaxman, John, 7, Buckingham Street, Fitzroy Square.
Franklin, Benjamin, 36, Craven Street, W.C.
Fox, Chas. J., 9, Arlington Street, Piccadilly.
Gainsborough, Thomas, Schomberg House, 80, Pall Mall.
Garrick, David, 5, Adelphi Terrace, and 27, Southampton Street.
Gaskell, Mrs., 93, Cheyne Walk, S.W.
Gladstone, W. E., 73, Harley Street, and 10, St. James's Square.
Goldsmith, Oliver, 2, Brick Court, Temple.
Gray, Thomas, 41, Cornhill, E.C.
Handel, George Frederick, 25, Brook Street.
Hazlitt, William, 6, Frith Street, Soho.
Herschel, Sir John, 56, Devonshire Street, Portland Place.
Hogarth, William, 30, Leicester Square; 119, Fenchurch Street.
Hood, Thos., 17 (now 20), Elm Tree Road, St. John's Wood, and 28, Finchley Rd.
Hunt, Leigh, 10 (now 22), Upper Cheyne Row, Chelsea.
Hunter, John, 31, Golden Square.
Huxley, T. H., 4, Marlborough Place, St. John's Wood.
Do. Do. 88, Paradise Street, Rotherhithe.
Irving, Sir Henry, 87, Newgate Street, E.C.
Jenner, Edward, 14, Hertford Street, Park Lane.
Johnson, Samuel, 17, Gough Square, Fleet Street.
Kean, Edmund, 12, Clarges Street, Piccadilly.
Keats, John (birthplace), 85, Moorgate; (residence) Lawnbank, Hampstead.
Lamb, Charles, 64, Duncan Terrace, Islington.
Leighton, Lord, Leighton House, Holland Park Road, W.
Lind, Jenny (Mme. Goldschmidt), 1, Moreton Gardens, Kensington, S.W.
Lister, Lord, 12, Park Crescent, Portland Place.
Lytton, Lord, 31 (now 68), Baker Street.
Macaulay, Lord, Holly Lodge, Campden Hill, Kensington.
Mill, J. S., 39, Rodney Street, Pentonville, and 18, Kensington Square.
Millais, Sir John Everett, 7, Cromwell Place, South Kensington.
Milton, John, 125, Bunhill Row.
Morris, William, 26, Upper Mall, Hammersmith, W.
Morris, Wm., D. G. Rossetti, and Sir E. Burne-Jones, 17, Red Lion Sq., W.C.
Napoleon III, 1c, King Street, St. James's.
Nelson, Lord, 147, New Bond Street.
Nightingale, Florence, 10, South Street, Park Lane, W.
Page, Walter Hines, 6, Grosvenor Square.
Pepys, Samuel (birthplace), 13, Salisbury Court, Fleet Street; (residence) 4, Buckingham Street, Strand.
Pitt, Wm., 14, York Place, Portman Square (now 120, Baker Street).
Reade, Chas., 70, Knightsbridge.
Reynolds, Sir Joshua, 47, Leicester Square.
Rogers, Samuel, 22, St. James's Place.
Romney, Geo., Holly Bush Hill, Hampstead.
Rossetti, D. G., 17, Red Lion Square (with Wm. Morris and Sir E. C. Burne-Jones).
Ruskin, John, 54, Hunter Street, Brunswick Square.
Russell, Lord John, 37, Chesham Place, Belgravia.
Scott, Sir Gilbert, The Grove, Hampstead.
Shakespeare, William, 13, Silver Street, Wood Street.
Sheridan, Richard Brinsley, 14, Savile Row.
Siddons, Mrs., 27, Upper Baker Street, and 54, Great Marlborough Street.
Smith, Sydney, 14, Doughty Street, Mecklenburg Square.
Stephenson, Robert, 34, Gloucester Square, Hyde Park.
Swinburne, A. C., 11, Putney Hill.
Thackeray, W. M., 16, Young Street, Kensington; 2, Kensington Palace Green 28, Clerkenwell Road; 36, Onslow Square, W.
Turner, J. M. W., 23, Queen Anne Street, and 118, Cheyne Walk, Chelsea.
Walpole, Sir Robert, 5, Arlington Street.

LIBRARIES, READING-ROOMS, etc.—Nearly all the London boroughs maintain **Public Libraries,** where newspapers, magazines and books of reference may be consulted without charge, though only local ratepayers and residents can, as a rule, borrow books. Among public libraries in the central part of London mention may be made of the **Guildhall Library,** Guildhall, E.C.; **Holborn,** High Holborn; the **St. Bride Foundation Institute,** Bride Lane, near Ludgate Circus; the **Bishopsgate Institute,** Bishopsgate Street, E.C., and the **Cripplegate Institute,** Golden Lane, E.C. The **Westminster Public Library** is in St. Martin's Street, Leicester Square.

Visitors who are interested in the history and associations of London should see especially the fine collection of books and prints at the Guildhall and the Bishopsgate Institute. Here, too, may be seen the principal Directories (local and trade) of the world.

At the County Hall (p. 78) is a valuable **Educational Library.**

Technical newspapers and journals are best seen at the **Patent Office Library** (p. 196), which comprises also a valuable collection of technical books and is open, without formality, to all.

A good selection of foreign newspapers can be seen at the Bishopsgate Institute and the Guildhall Library.

Circulating Libraries.—Mudie's, Queen's House, Kingsway, W.C.2, with branches at 27, Old Broad Street, E.C.2, Victoria, S.W.1, 132, High Street, Kensington, etc.; **W. H. Smith and Son,** Kingsway, W.C., with branches in nearly all suburbs; **"The Times" Book Club,** 42, Wigmore Street, and others. **Boots's Book-Lovers' Library** has branches throughout London and suburbs. **London Library,** 14, St. James's Square, W. (p. 127). **Rolandi's,** 43, Berners Street, W. (foreign). The librarians will gladly give particulars as to subscriptions.

British Museum, ticket necessary (see p. 161).

Guildhall, on signing visitors' book (see p. 208).

Dr. Williams's, University Hall, Gordon Square, W.C. On introduction of a minister. Chiefly theological.

Sion College, Thames Embankment, Blackfriars. On introduction. Theological.

Patent Office, Southampton Buildings, Chancery Lane. On signing visitors' book. Technical and scientific.

Lambeth Palace. Valuable episcopal books and MSS.

Science Museum Library, South Kensington. Scientific volumes and periodicals.

Victoria and Albert Museum, South Kensington. Books on art, prints, drawings, photographs, etc. (see p. 174).

Imperial War Library, Imperial War Museum, (see p. 257).

Royal Empire Society Library, daily (Sundays and public holidays excepted) from 10 a.m. to 8 p.m. Non-Fellows may use Library on presentation of a letter of introduction from a Fellow of the Society, or from an educational or other recognised authority.

LITTLE-KNOWN LONDON SIGHTS.—Lovers of the quaint and curious may be glad to have a list of a few London sights and reminders of Old London that frequently escape the attention of visitors who content themselves with the orthodox round of the great show-places. Many others could be named: the following are merely given to indicate the wealth of interest that lies off the beaten track. For descriptions consult Index.

Staple Inn, Holborn, opposite Gray's Inn Road.
17, *Fleet Street*, opposite Chancery Lane.
Panyer Alley, Newgate Street.
Roman Bath, 5, Strand Lane.
St. Etheldreda's Church, Ely Place, Hatton Garden.
Shepherd's Market, between Curzon Street and Piccadilly.

York Gate, Embankment Gardens, near Charing Cross.
Standards of British Lineal Measures, Trafalgar Square and Guildhall.
Chapel of the Ascension and St. George's Burial-Ground, between Marble Arch and Lancaster Gate.
Dogs' Cemetery, Hyde Park (north side).
Royal Academy Diploma Galleries, Burlington House, Piccadilly.
Soane Museum, Lincoln's Inn Fields (north side).
London Stone, St. Swithin's Church, Cannon Street.
London Wall (fragments of), in thoroughfare of same name, and near Tower, and elsewhere in the City (see p. 69).

LOST PROPERTY.—In case of loss of articles in Underground trains, buses, or other vehicles of the London Transport Board, inquire at the Lost Property Office, London Passenger Transport Board, Baker Street Station, N.W.1 (Mons. to Fridays only, 10 a.m. to 7 p.m.); for articles lost elsewhere apply at Police Lost Property Office, Lambeth Road (close to Lambeth Palace: Plan III, L. 10), hours 10 to 4. About half the articles lost annually are restored to owners; those remaining unclaimed after three months are returned to the drivers or conductors who deposited them. A charge of 15 per cent. of the value is usually levied on lost property restored by the police. If luggage is lost in a train or at a station belonging to one of the railways not under the control of the London Passenger Transport Board inform the stationmaster, or if at a terminus, inquire at the "Lost Property Office" there. *Always remove old labels from luggage.* Much loss and inconvenience would be avoided by the observance of this simple rule.

MARKETS.—The great Markets of London, though not so popular a show as the Halles Centrales of Paris, are full of interest to the visitor. The wholesale part of the business, when shopkeepers from all over London come to provide for their customers, is mostly conducted early in the morning, but a considerable retail trade is done all through the day. The following are the principal markets:—

Covent Garden (p. 187) is the principal fruit, flower and vegetable market. Tuesdays, Thursdays and Saturdays are the principal market days.

Smithfield (p. 228). These extensive buildings comprise the London Central Meat Market and the poultry, fish, vegetable and hay markets. They are under the control of the City Corporation. Mondays and Thursdays are the busy days; the market is all but closed on Saturdays.

The **Caledonian Cattle Market,** Islington is one of the largest in the world, covering upwards of 30 acres. Millions of cattle, sheep and pigs are sold here during the year, and it is no uncommon sight to see 30,000 animals of one kind and another in the pens on a single day. Monday is the principal day for cattle and ponies. On Friday afternoon is held a miscellaneous "pedlars' market," which attracts bargain and curio-hunters from all parts of the metropolis. The variety of wares exposed for sale is extraordinary, and the crowd of buyers and spectators hardly less so.

Leadenhall Market, Leadenhall Street, with its vegetables and game, is another interesting sight.

Billingsgate, Lower Thames Street, London Bridge. This is the great fish market, but it cannot be described as attractive.

Spitalfields Market, for fruit, vegetables and flowers is now among the largest and most modern markets of its kind in the world.

Shadwell and Columbia Markets also serve the East of London and the Borough Market the South.

MILITARY.—The only troops usually quartered in London are the Household Cavalry at Knightsbridge Barracks and other cavalry at Hounslow; a Royal Horse Artillery Battery at St. John's Wood and other artillery at Woolwich; the R.A.S.C. at Woolwich and Hounslow, and battalions of the Guards at Wellington Barracks (St. James's Park), Chelsea Barracks, and the Tower of London.

An interesting military spectacle each morning at 11 o'clock is the **Changing of the Guard** at St. James's Palace, or, if the King be in residence, at Buckingham Palace (see p. 121). Gigantic troopers are on sentry duty daily at the Horse Guards (see p. 81), and are rarely without a circle of admirers, young and old, particularly at a little before 11 a.m. (Sundays 10) when the Guard is mounted, and at 4 p.m. when it is dismounted. Each afternoon a detachment of Guards proceeds from Wellington Barracks to the Bank of England, where it is on guard until the following day. The most imposing military pageant in London is that of **Trooping the Colour,** on June 3, the "official" birthday of the King (see p. 81). The **Royal Tournament** (Navy, Army and Air Force), held at Olympia during May, enjoys great popularity, and modern transport facilities make it possible to number among London's military attractions the **Aldershot Tattoo** in June.

MONEY, BRITISH.—Since the War *gold* coins (sovereigns and half-sovereigns) have practically disappeared, being replaced by **Notes** of the face value of twenty shillings (green) and ten shillings (brown). The silver coins are the crown (5*s.*), now very rare; half-crown (2*s.* 6*d.*); florin (2*s.*); shilling; sixpence (half a shilling); and "threepenny bits." Be careful to distinguish between half-crowns and florins; the former are larger. *Bronze,* or copper: penny (1*d.*), halfpenny (½*d.*), and farthing (¼*d.*). Farthings are but little used except at drapers' establishments and in the poorer districts.

Notes are also issued by the Bank of England for sums of £5, £10, £20, £50, and upwards (see also p. 205).

MONEY-CHANGERS.—Foreign money can be exchanged for English at the various branches, in the City and West End, of *Cooks' Tourist Offices*; at *Davison's*, 148, Strand; the *Bureau de Change*, 16, Strand; *Selfridge's*, Oxford Street; *Harrod's*, Brompton Road; *Whiteley's*, Queen's Road; and elsewhere.

MOTOR TOURS.—An agreeable interlude to sight-seeing may be had by taking advantage of the public motor-coach trips from London. These are advertised in the daily papers, and seats can be secured at any of the tourist agencies. It is impossible here to give precise details, but among the runs are those to Buckinghamshire (Milton and Penn Country), and the Thames Valley, Brighton, Margate, Oxford, the Surrey Hills, etc.

Facing King's Cross Railway Station and in Buckingham Palace Road, beside Victoria Station, are important **Motor-Coach Stations,** whence vehicles set out not only for the trips round London but for journeys to all parts of England, and to Scotland and Wales. There are similar stations in the vicinity of Tavistock Square and elsewhere, but these details are subject to alteration.

MOTORING IN LONDON.—See p. 48.

NEWSPAPERS.—Of the many hundreds of newspapers and periodicals published in London, the ordinary visitor is likely only to make acquaintance with the principal morning and evening and the illustrated weekly papers.

Morning Papers.—*The Times, Daily Telegraph, Morning Post, Morning Advertiser* (Licensed Victuallers), *Financial News, Financial Times, Sporting Life, News-Chronicle, Daily Mail, Daily Express, Daily Herald, Daily Mirror* (illustrated), *Daily Sketch* (illustrated).

Evening Papers.—*Evening News, Evening Standard, Star.*

Sunday Papers.—*Observer, Sunday Times, The People, Sunday Dispatch, News of the World, Sunday Referee* (sporting and theatrical), *Reynolds News, Sunday Express, Sunday Pictorial* (illustrated), *Sunday Graphic* (illustrated), etc.

Weekly Illustrated Papers.—*Illustrated London News, Sphere, Sketch, Tatler, Illustrated Sporting and Dramatic News, The Field* (sporting), *Country Life, The Bystander, The Queen* (for ladies), *The Lady*, etc.

Punch is the leading humorous paper, and makes a speciality of political cartoons.

Weekly Reviews, etc.—*Spectator, Time and Tide, The New Statesman and Nation, John O' London, Public Opinion, Times Weekly*, etc. Among the monthly magazines the *Windsor* holds a high place.

Many **Overseas Papers** have offices in London, at which copies of recent issues can be obtained.

PARLIAMENTARY REPRESENTATION.—The metropolis was formerly divided into fifty-eight constituencies, each electing one member, with the exception of the City, which had two members. Under the Representation of the People Act (1918), which extended the franchise to large numbers of women, seats were redistributed. The County of London is divided into sixty-one parliamentary constituencies, each returning one member (except the City of London, which returns two), the total representation being sixty-two. Greater London has more than a hundred members, and can therefore exercise a powerful influence on the national councils.

PARKS AND OPEN SPACES.—No other metropolis possesses so many parks and breathing places as does this huge, overgrown city of ours. But it must be admitted that Londoners require as many "lungs" as they can get. Besides the great parks under the control of the Crown, like Hyde Park, Kensington Gardens, St. James's, Regent's and Greenwich Parks, amounting in the aggregate to nearly 2,000 acres, there are under the management of the County Council considerably over a hundred other parks, gardens and open spaces, totalling 4,800 acres, to say nothing of the numerous small spaces controlled by the Borough Councils, which constitute an acreage of nearly 500. Altogether, therefore, leaving out of account the numerous semi-private gardens, like those owned by the Inns of Court, and the great Squares, we have in the County of London alone over 7,000 acres of parks and open spaces. If the survey is extended to Outer London, we get into touch with such magnificent expanses as Richmond Park, with its 2,358 acres; Bushy Park, with an acreage of 1,100; Putney and Wimbledon Commons, covering over 1,000 acres; Mitcham Common, boasting an area of nearly 500 acres; Hounslow Heath, embracing about 281 acres. Nor does this exhaust the list of London's pleasure grounds, for in this connection we must take into account Epping Forest, whose 5,560 acres have been preserved to the public by the City Corporation; and Burnham Beeches, 492 acres in extent, which was another of the Corporation's gifts to the people of London.

The largest of the public parks in London proper is, of course, Hyde Park, which, with Kensington Gardens, covers 636 acres. If we take as one area (as we fairly may) the chain of open spaces formed by the Horse Guards' Parade, St. James's Park (93 acres), the Green Park

(53 acres), Hyde Park, and Kensington Gardens, we have an area of about 750 acres. It is, in fact, possible by just crossing the road at Hyde Park Corner to walk from the Westminster corner of St. James's Park in an almost direct line for nearly three miles through parks and gardens abounding in magnificent timber and wild bird life.

Of the 101 open spaces controlled by the London County Council, the finest is Hampstead Heath (288 acres), with Ken Wood (195 acres), Parliament Hill (271 acres), Golder's Hill (36 acres) and Waterlow Park (26 acres) adjoining. Blackheath (267), Battersea Park (199), Clapham Common (205), Tooting Commons (218), Wandsworth Common (195), and Peckham Rye (113) are the largest spaces south of the Thames. Bands play in many of the parks throughout the summer on certain evenings and on Sundays, and facilities are provided for bathing, boating, cricket, tennis, bowls, putting, etc. Refreshments can be obtained at moderate prices in most of the parks.

PICTURE GALLERIES.—In the case of public galleries the fees (if any) and hours of admission are given in our descriptive notes (see Index). On certain days of the week a charge of about *6d.* is made for admission to some of these (see later pages); on other days admission is free. For private exhibitions in the galleries of well-known picture-dealers in Bond Street and elsewhere, see advertisements in daily newspapers. The general charge for admission to these is about *1s.*

Dulwich Gallery, Gallery Road, S.E.
Guildhall Art Gallery, King Street, E.C.
Hampton Court Palace.
Imperial War Museum.
Kenwood, Hampstead.
Leighton House, 12, Holland Park Road.
National Gallery, Trafalgar Square.
National Portrait Gallery, ditto.
Royal Academy, Piccadilly. Summer Exhibition, May to August.
Royal Institute of Painters in Water Colours, 195, Piccadilly.
Royal Institute of Oil Painters, 195, Piccadilly.
Royal Society of British Artists, Suffolk Street, Pall Mall East, S.W.
Royal Society of Painters in Water Colours, 5A, Pall Mall East, S.W.
Sir John Soane's Museum, 13, Lincoln's Inn Fields.
Tate Gallery, Millbank.
Victoria and Albert Museum, South Kensington.
Wallace Collection, Hertford House, Manchester Square.
Whitechapel Art Gallery, 81–2, Whitechapel High Street.

POLICE.—Although a large proportion of the offences committed in the United Kingdom take place within the borders of London, a comparatively small number of policemen is found sufficient to protect its inhabitants from the Ishmaelites whose hands are against every man. The **City Police Force,** to whom is committed the protection of that London the evident wealth of which caused Blücher to exclaim, " What a city this would be to plunder ! " numbers only about eleven hundred good men and true; while the **Metropolitan Police,** who take care of Greater London, extending for a radius of 15 miles from Charing Cross, consists of about twenty thousand men of all ranks. There are also a few women police. The City Police Force is under the control of the City fathers, and has its headquarters in Old Jewry; the heads of the Metropolitan Police are responsible to the Secretary of State for the Home Department, no local body having any authority over them. The chief offices of the Metropolitan Police are at New Scotland Yard, on the Embankment. The City Police may be distinguished from the Metropolitan Police by the fact that their armlets are red and white instead of blue and white. Their helmets, moreover, are crested.

The police of London, by their courtesy and readiness to assist strangers, have won a world-wide renown. When in doubt " ask a policeman " is a very good rule in London thoroughfares.

POSTAL.—To facilitate delivery and collection of letters, the metropolis is divided into postal districts, each with its local headquarters, and much prompter delivery of London letters is assured by adding to the address not only the initials of the district in which the receiver resides, but a number indicating the proper office of delivery. The districts are known as E.C., E., S.E., S.W., W., W.C., N.W., and N. Thus the principal Government Departments are addressed "Whitehall, S.W.1," while this Guide is published from "E.C.4." The greater part of the City is E.C. A subtle social superiority is supposed to cling to the letters W. and S.W. The principal delivery is made about 8 a.m., and there are many others during the day.

Post Offices are usually open from 8 a.m. to 8 p.m., but some of the larger offices keep open later. On Sundays and Bank Holidays certain offices are open from 9 a.m. to 8 p.m. The latest time of posting in the Central Districts for the Provincial Night Mails is 5.30 p.m. for Scotland and the Channel Islands, 6.30 p.m. for Ireland, and 7.30 p.m. for England and Wales. Letters may be posted at most of the railway termini, with an additional "late fee" stamp, in a station late fee box, or in a box attached to Mail trains up to a few minutes before the departure of the trains.

Air Mails.—Packets, adequately stamped and marked "Air Mail," may be posted in the ordinary way, or in the special *blue* letter boxes.

On **Sundays** there is no general delivery of letters, but both in London itself and in the suburbs there are evening collections.

Poste Restante.—Strangers without a permanent address in London can have their letters sent to the General Post Office, King Edward Street, E.C., or to any branch office, marked "to be called for" or "Poste Restante." If demanded, proof of identity must be given. Letters from abroad not called for are kept two months; letters from provincial towns a fortnight; at the end of that time they are sent to the Returned Letter Office, Mount Pleasant, E.C., to be returned to senders or destroyed.

Express Letters.—Letters and parcels may be sent (weekdays only) to any part of London and suburbs at a charge of 6*d*. a mile or part of a mile. There are nearly 600 Post Offices transacting Express Delivery services in London.

Telegraph Offices are open as a rule from 8 a.m. to 8 p.m. (some on Sundays and Bank Holidays from 9 a.m. to 8 p.m.). Minimum charge (9 words), 6*d*. The following are **always open**: Central Telegraph Office, St. Martin's-le-Grand, E.C.1; Leicester Square Branch Office, 39, Charing Cross Road, W.C.2; Liverpool Street Station; Marylebone Station; St. Pancras Station; King's Cross (L.N.E.R.) Station. The railway station offices transact telegraph business only, and do not deliver off station premises. Telegrams may be delivered to telephone subscribers by telephone instead of by boy messenger, an arrangement by which a considerable saving of time is effected.

Messages intended for **wireless** transmission overseas may be handed in at any postal telegraph office or at Electra House and Tower Chambers, Moorgate, E.C.2 (always open). There are numerous branch offices of the Cable companies.

Postal Underground Railway.—See p. 212.

Telephones.—Telephones are under the control of the General Post Office. Public telephone call office facilities are provided at many post offices, railway stations and shops; and in kiosks. The minimum charge for the use of a call office is *2d.* Normally, the charge is based upon the radial distance between the exchanges concerned, but details of the charges applicable in London are exhibited in every call office. Trunk (and toll) calls may be effected from practically all public call offices: a call office charge of *2d.* is payable in addition to the appropriate trunk, etc., charge. Reduced rates are charged for trunk and toll calls made between 7 p.m. and 5 a.m. A message may be dictated from a call office to any post office in the United Kingdom which is a telephone express delivery office for delivery by express messenger, on payment of the appropriate telephone fee for the call (including a call office fee of *2d.*) plus a writing-down fee of *3d.* for the first 30 words and *1d.* for each 10 words or part thereof in excess of 30; plus the express delivery charge of *6d.* a mile, or part of a mile, from the office of delivery to the addressee.

(For detailed information concerning postal services, see the Post Office Guide, at any post office; for the Telephone services see the Telephone Directory).

RAINFALL.—The annual average is between 24 and 25 inches.

RESTAURANTS.—See Introduction, pp. 15–16.

ROMAN LONDON.—There are more remains of the Roman occupation (1st to 5th century A.D.) than is generally understood. For sections of the Wall see p. 69. In Strand Lane is a portion of a Roman bath, and many other relics are preserved in the Guildhall, the London and the British Museums. The most extensive recent discoveries have been made at St. Albans (see p. 273).

SEASONS.—The London Season nominally extends from the beginning of May to about the end of July. At this time Parliament is sitting, the Royal Academy and other picture galleries are open, and nearly all the leaders of society are in town. Later, the great migration commences, and every day the roads and railway stations are thronged by jostling crowds, eager to get to the sea and the moors. At the same time the great invasion of "country cousins" and visitors from America, the Dominions and the Continent sets in. The best time to see London is the spring, when the trees in the Parks are just breaking into leaf, the air is still crisp and cool, and the "show places" are not inconveniently crowded.

SHOPS AND SHOPPING.—A fair lady of the eighteenth century, in a letter which has been preserved to us, aptly described London as "an old lick-pocket." The accusation is certainly no less true to-day than it was then. We can hardly accept the delicate responsibility of advising readers where and how to spend their money, but those who are strange to town may be glad of a few general indications.

The best and most attractive shops are in Regent Street, Oxford Street, Bond Street, Piccadilly and the streets adjacent thereto. Holborn, Cheapside, the Strand, St. Paul's Churchyard, and Tottenham Court Road are also much favoured by shoppers. Outside the central district the chief shopping quarters are the Brompton Road, High Street, Kensington, Sloane Street, and Queen's Road, Bayswater.

The great **Stores,** where practically everything may be bought, from parasols to pineapples, include the *Army and Navy Stores,* 105, Victoria Street, Westminster, and the *Civil Service Supply Association,* 425, Strand, and Queen Victoria Street—these were originally co-operative concerns only, but are now open to all; *Selfridge's,* Oxford Street; *Harrod's,* Brompton Road; *Barker's,* High Street,

Kensington; *Whiteley's*, Bayswater; *Peter Robinson's*, Oxford Street; *Waring's*, Oxford Street; *Wallis's* and *Gamage's*, Holborn.

Early Closing.—Shops are compelled by law to allow their assistants a weekly half-holiday. The day of closing varies in different districts, Wednesday and Thursday being the most usual. Nearly all City and West End shops close at 1 on Saturdays.

STEAMBOATS.—A number of steam and motor boats make daily passages during the summer from Westminster Bridge to Kew, Richmond, Hampton Court, etc. Luncheon and tea are served on board at moderate prices. See advertisements in the daily newspapers, etc.

On the higher reaches of the river, the saloon steamers belonging to *Messrs. Salter Bros.* of Oxford make delightful trips in summer through ninety miles of Thames scenery (see p. 274). For full details see the *Guide to the Thames* in this series.

Down the River.—Steamers and motor boats run at intervals during the day from Westminster Bridge to Tower Pier and Greenwich, often doing the trip in less time than would be required by a bus or a tram, and providing close-up views of the shipping, especially below London Bridge.

Starting from the Tower Pier steamers make daily trips down river to Southend, Margate, Clacton, Felixstowe, Yarmouth, etc. See announcements in daily papers.

SUNDAY IN LONDON.—Continental critics have dealt somewhat harshly with the English Sunday. Take M. Taine for instance: "Sunday in London—the shops are shut, the streets almost deserted; the aspect is that of an immense and well-ordered cemetery. The few passers-by in the desert of squares and streets have the look of uneasy spirits risen from their graves. It is appalling. After an hour's walk in the Strand especially, and in the rest of the City, one has the spleen; one meditates suicide."

Much depends upon one's point of view, but things have changed considerably in recent years, and Sunday need no longer be regarded as a *dies non* even by the sightseer. Information as to **Churches and Chapels** will be found on pp. 19–21. During summer large numbers spend the day, or part of it, on the Thames or other pleasure resorts in the vicinity of London, or even by the sea, the railway and motor-coach companies advertising special excursions. Most of the **Museums** and **Picture Galleries** are open on Sunday afternoons; both afternoon and evening there are concerts, and many Cinemas are open. In the evening during summer there are band performances in the Parks and in the open spaces controlled by the County Council.

And if on Sunday mornings the deserted City streets still justify M. Taine's description, we may remind the visitor that there is no such time for making leisurely acquaintance with the highways and byways and quaint nooks and corners of this mighty metropolis, while Sunday mornings provide two of the most interesting spectacles in London—the market in Middlesex Street (see p. 239) and the Church Parade in Hyde Park.

VIEW-POINTS, NOTABLE.—All the bridges over the Thames afford fine views. Wordsworth's lines on **Westminster Bridge** at daybreak, commencing "Earth has not anything to show more fair," are well known. An even better view-point (though the fence obstructs it) is the temporary **Waterloo Bridge**, commanding the fine sweep of the Embankment, with its stately buildings and the majestic dome of St. Paul's. The view eastward from Blackfriars Bridge is marred by a

NOTABLE MODERN BUILDINGS.

Freemasons' Hall—Broadcasting House—London Transport Offices—South Africa House—Royal Institute of British Architects—Shell-Mex Building.

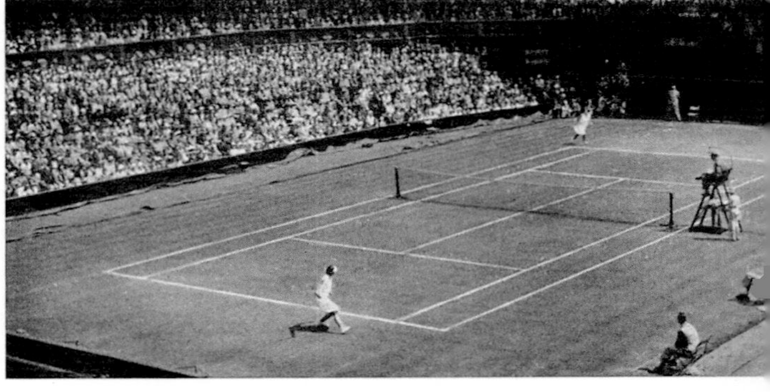

THREE FAMOU

Lord's Cricket Ground—Wembley S

ɔRTS ARENAS.

ım—The Centre Court, Wimbledon.

[*The Times.*

THE STRAND, LOOKING WESTWARD.

[*Fox.*

ALDWYCH AND THE STRAND,

Showing the Gaiety Theatre and Bush House.

railway bridge, but from a point a short distance along the Embankment the dome is well seen, and one is able to appreciate Wren's masterly grouping of spires in relation to it. The eastern side of **London Bridge** is nearly always lined by spectators, some of whom spend hours in watching the loading and unloading of vessels in the **Pool.**

Of street views, that from **Fleet Street** up Ludgate Hill to St. Paul's would be hard to beat, though the railway bridge is in the way. The view up Fleet Street itself, towards St. Dunstan's Church lantern and the Law Courts, is also worthy of note, particularly towards sundown. Another entrancing view is that from the end of **Parliament Street,** taking in the Abbey and its " baby," St. Margaret's, Westminster Hall and the Houses of Parliament. The little glimpse down **St. James's Street** from Piccadilly, with St. James's Palace at the foot of the slope, is worth noting. The new Regent Street—particularly at the Piccadilly Circus end—provides one of the best modern street views in London.

One of the finest Park views is that from a point in **Kensington Gardens** near the refreshment pavilion overlooking the Serpentine. The views from the **Serpentine Bridge** are also very fine. The same may be said of the view from the Buckingham Palace end of **St. James's Park.** The footbridge over the lake also provides a view eastward that of its kind is probably unsurpassed in any city.

Of lofty vantage-points, the most notable are the Monument (p. 242), the Stone and Golden Galleries of **St. Paul's Cathedral,** and the tower of the **Roman Catholic Cathedral** at Westminster (p. 115). All (except the last, where a lift is available) involve fatiguing climbs, and should not be attempted unless the day be quite clear. Even then, London's pall of smoke is apt to obscure the outlook. Good all-round views are to be obtained from the roof gardens that are a feature of several of the big stores and hotels and office blocks.

The view in clear weather from the summit of **Primrose Hill** is truly magnificent, especially near sunset. **Parliament Hill,** farther north, also gives a good idea of the " forest of houses " ; while from that famous vantage-point, the flagstaff on **Hampstead Heath,** a rural prospect is unfolded that will strike the stranger with amazement. The view from **Richmond Hill** needs no laudation here ; but it may be well to beg the visitor to **Windsor** not to skip, as many do, the ascent of the Round Tower, which affords a fine prospect of the winding Thames.

But no terrestrial point of view can be compared with that enjoyed by the passenger by aeroplane. Some of our views on other pages give an idea of the appearance of London from above. On clear days especially, it is doubtful if there is another prospect in the world to equal it in interest. Perhaps the most astonishing discovery the aerial passenger makes is that London, after all, is *small* !

WATER SUPPLY.—No fewer than 172 million gallons out of the daily total requirement of 281 million gallons are derived from the Thames in the neighbourhood of Laleham, Walton, Hampton and Staines. The huge reservoirs, of which the largest is the " Queen Mary " at Littleton with a capacity of 6,750 million gallons, hold 14,017 million gallons—sufficient for a seven weeks' supply for the whole of the Board's area.

The daily consumption per head in the area of 573 square miles under the care of the Metropolitan Water Board is 39.02 gallons.

SEEING LONDON.

Hints for the Hurried Visitor.

"fold on fold,
Grey to pearl, and pearl to gold,
Our London, like a land of old,
The land of Eldorado."

THE metropolis is so vast, its interests are so many and so intricate and so much of it is being transformed by the builder, that it may be doubted whether any man can truthfully say that he "knows London." Least of all will the life-long resident make that assertion, for if he be of an observant and reflective turn of mind every journey in an unaccustomed quarter will but add to his consciousness of abysmal ignorance. In a single suburb—even the most commonplace to outward seeming—there is matter for a library; while as to the central portion, with its crowded interests and constant changes, this closely-packed handbook, with its rigorous selections and equally rigorous exclusions, is about as good an illustration as could be offered of the impossibility of emptying the Atlantic with a limpet-shell.

Such being the frame of mind inevitably forced upon those who spend their working lives in and about London, it may well be asked despairingly: How can the casual visitor—the man or woman with one day, two days, three days, a week, or even a fortnight at disposal—hope in so short a time to gain an intelligent acquaintance with the sights and features of this so extensive metropolis, beyond all question the most bewildering that the world has ever known?

The answer is that the miracle is possible of accomplishment, is, in fact, accomplished every year by crowds of delighted strangers, who see more of the "Great Wen" in a few days, or even hours, than very many Londoners see in a lifetime. This is due partly to the apathy of Londoners, the majority of whom, it must be confessed, make but the feeblest response to the reflection that they are "citizens of no mean city"; partly to the fact that visitors from a distance have usually studied such books as this before arrival, and have formed definite ideas as to the things they wish to see and the things they are content to leave unseen. Of these considerations we should be disposed to attach the greater importance to the second. "System" and "selection"—especially, alas, "selection" with its inevitable corollary, "exclusion"—must be the watchwords of the hurried visitor.

The hustler who has demonstrated to admiring friends that London can be "done" in a day will smile at the leisurely nature of our daily programmes; others will find them far too full. We endeavour to indicate a middle course, allowing time for something more than a mental snapshot of each place, but little for lingering. And an overwhelming consciousness of the "much that lies beyond" prompts us to exhort even the most indefatigable sightseer not for one moment to imagine that "seeing London" and "knowing London" are phrases identical in meaning.

It is premised that the visitor will read these itineraries in conjunction with the notes as to days and hours of admission given in small type under the headings of our descriptions of the various places of interest. Some little care is necessary in this matter, for if economy of time be the governing consideration it is mortifying in the extreme to find on arrival that doors are closed, or will open only on the production of a previously procured order. It is useful to bear in mind also that certain Galleries and Museums (e.g. the National Gallery, the Victoria and Albert and the Science Museum) *remain open after dark on certain evenings*; but the Houses of Parliament can be seen *only on Saturdays and on Easter and Whitsun Monday and Tuesday*. It should be said, too, if economy of time be more important than economy of money, that *free days* are best avoided, especially in the height of the season. Apart from fares, sight-seeing in London is cheaper than anywhere, and an occasional sixpence or shilling is generally well spent in avoiding a crowd.

On pp. 47–61 will be found detailed notes on the various transport services. If expense be not so paramount a consideration as time, it is often advantageous to cover intermediate distances by taxi (for fares see p. 48), but on congested traffic routes the cab is often little quicker than the bus, and the tube may be quicker than either. In any case in the central parts it is rarely worth while to retain a taxi, as it can be discharged on entering a building, if a lengthy stay is likely, with a reasonable certainty of being able to secure another on leaving. But if a number of places are visited in succession, with only a short stay in each, it will often be found more convenient to direct the

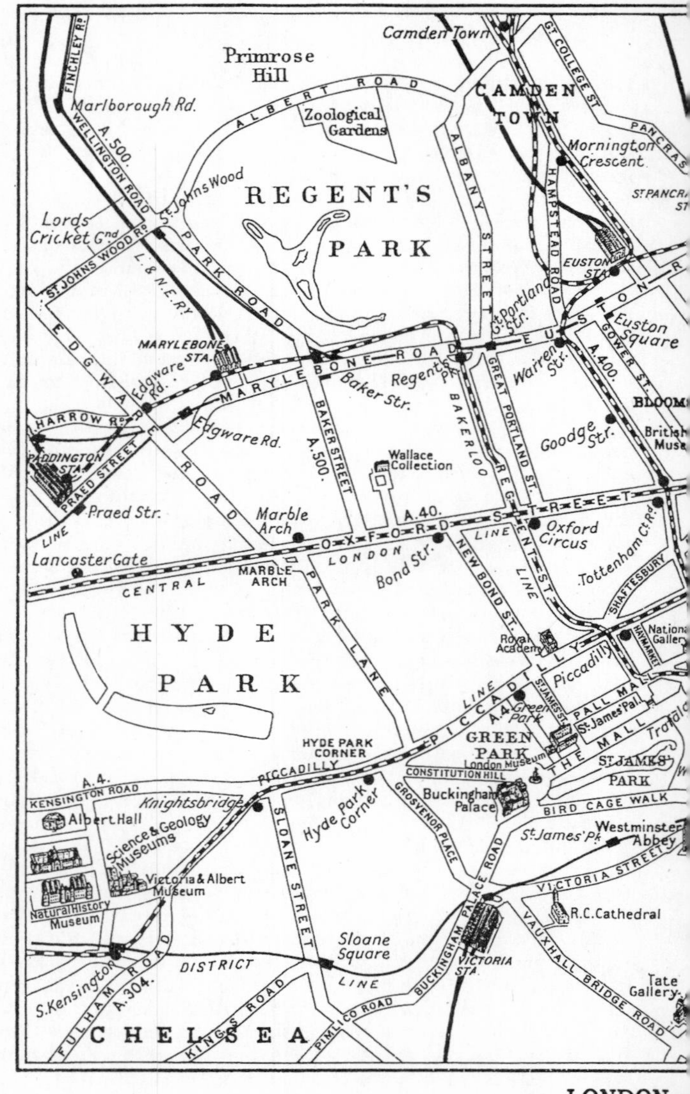

LONDON

Showing the Principal Buildings a

The Circles denote the intersections

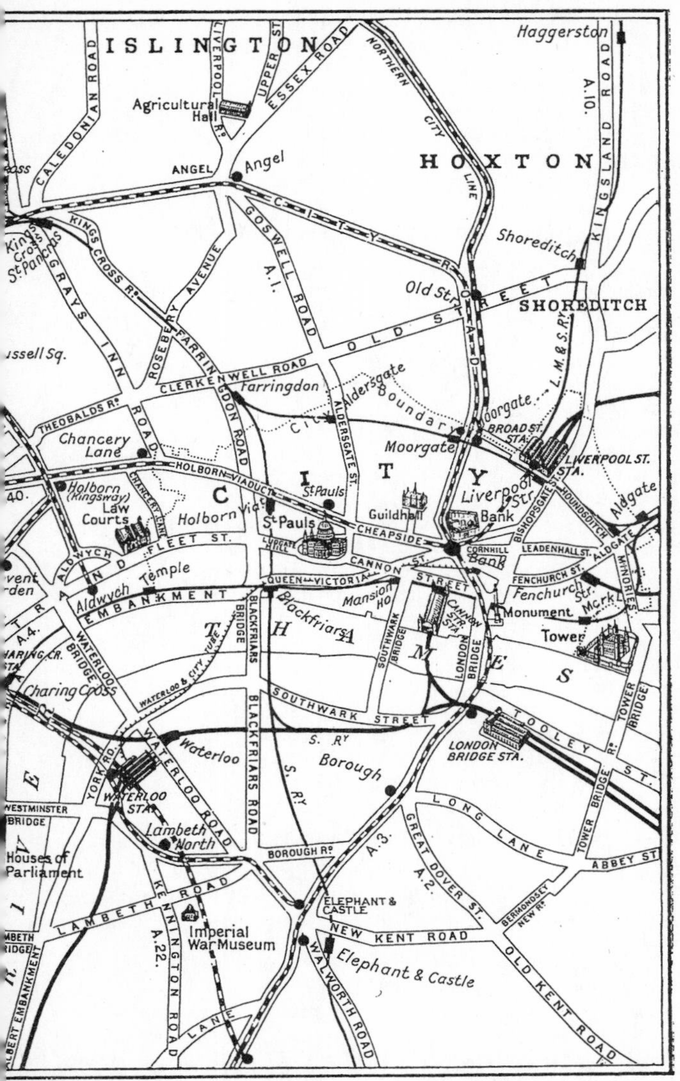

GLANCE.

oroughfares, Railway Termini, etc.

rincipal omnibus and traffic routes.

driver to wait. For distances of any length the Underground Railways are generally preferable, but given fine weather the motor-omnibuses afford a pleasurable mode of progression and give opportunities for noting objects of interest and the life of the streets that the railway passenger misses.

London at a Glance.

It will greatly assist the stranger to keep his bearings in the crowded streets of Central London if he forms at the outset a mental picture of the direction and intersections of the principal thoroughfares. To this end we have prepared a special map (*see* pp. 40–41), showing "London at a Glance," believing that this will be more helpful than pages of elaborate directions. Bear in mind that the river runs from west to east, with a siphon-like northward bend from Vauxhall Bridge to Waterloo; and that the two chief thoroughfares, Oxford Street with its continuations, and the Strand with its continuations, follow approximately the same course from west to east, eventually meeting at the Bank of England. Connection north and south between these two great thoroughfares is provided by Park Lane, Bond Street and Regent Street in the west; by Charing Cross Road and Kingsway and Aldwych, between Holborn and the Strand; and by Chancery Lane at the City boundary. Westminster and Victoria lie to the south of Charing Cross, off these main routes, and connected with the City by the Victoria Embankment and Queen Victoria Street, which converges to meet the two other through routes near the Bank.

In making any necessary modifications or adaptations of the following itineraries, one of the principal objects should be to avoid going over the same ground twice.

London in One Day.

Assuming that the reader is a "bird of passage," merely breaking his journey from or to the Continent or the provinces, how shall he employ the time at his disposal to the best advantage?

The following are a few alternative modes of spending what must perforce be a very hurried day, the proportion of time given to each place depending, of course, upon whether the pilgrim's "bent" is in the direction of art, architecture, historical association, or "shops" and the life of the streets. The routes start from Charing Cross (Plan III, K. 8), which for sight-seeing purposes may be regarded as the "hub" of London.

Morning.

National Gallery.
National Portrait Gallery.
Whitehall (passing Government Offices, Royal United Services Museum and the Cenotaph).
Houses of Parliament. (*Open on Saturdays and Easter and Whitsun Mondays and Tuesdays*).
Westminster Abbey.*
Westminster (R.C.) Cathedral.
Buckingham Palace (exterior).
St. James's Park.
London Museum, Lancaster House.
St. James's Palace (exterior).
Luncheon in neighbourhood of Piccadilly or Leicester Square.

Afternoon.

Regent Street.
Oxford Street.
Wallace Collection, Manchester Square.
Drive through Hyde Park and Kensington Gardens.
Piccadilly.
Royal Academy.
British Museum.
Lincoln's Inn (walk through).
Law Courts and Temple.
Fleet Street.
Ludgate Hill.
St. Paul's Cathedral.

If it is intended to stay in London overnight, and there be any hours of daylight left, they can be well employed in sauntering along the Embankment, with its pleasant riverside gardens, to the starting-point at Charing Cross. Dinner, and perhaps a visit to a theatre, will bring the traveller to the end of the day, and probably of his powers of endurance.

The route outlined has the disadvantage of almost excluding the City. An alternative might be :—

Morning.

Tower of London.
Monument.
Bank of England.
Royal Exchange (frescoes).
Guildhall, Museum & Art Gallery.
Cheapside.
St. Paul's Cathedral.
Luncheon at any of the neighbouring restaurants.

Afternoon.

Law Courts.
Temple Gardens.
Embankment.
London County Hall.
Houses of Parliament.
Westminster Abbey.*
National Gallery (open during evenings of certain days).

Any remaining hours of daylight could be employed in a stroll in St. James's Park, with a glance at Buckingham Palace and St. James's Palace, and at the many Government Offices.

London in Two Days.

The two-day visitor has a bewildering choice of possibilities. He might take the two one-day programmes already sketched, the fact that they overlap to some extent allowing him more

* Closed to the public for some time before and after the Coronation.

ample time for each. Or should he desire to extend the range of sight-seeing, he might proceed somewhat as follows:—

First Day.

Charing Cross.
National Gallery.
National Portrait Gallery.
Whitehall.
Houses of Parliament.
London County Hall.
Westminster Abbey (see footnote, p. 43).
(*Luncheon.*)
Imperial War Museum.
Lambeth Palace (exterior).
Tate Gallery.
Westminster (R.C.) Cathedral.
St. James's Park.
London Museum.
Green Park.
Hyde Park; Kensington Gardens.
Victoria and Albert Museum.
Natural History Museum.
Science and Geological Museums.

Second Day.

Tower of London.
Monument.
Royal Exchange.
Bank.
Guildhall.
Cheapside.
St. Paul's Cathedral.
(*Luncheon.*)
Holborn.
British Museum.
Oxford Street.
Wallace Collection.
Regent's Park.
Zoological Gardens (open until 11.30 p.m. on Wednesdays and Thursdays in summer).

London in Four Days.

All the really "first magnitude" sights in London proper have been included in the foregoing lists. It will depend upon the visitor's taste, and also, perhaps, upon the weather, if sights of second magnitude shall be included, or the time at disposal be devoted to a trip out of London, say to Windsor Castle or Hampton Court.

Of these "second magnitude" sights all the following are in or near the central part of London, and can be easily sandwiched into the programmes already given. The three-day visitor will have to exclude some of them, unless he be content with a very cursory glance:—

Chelsea Hospital, Carlyle's House, etc., at Chelsea (can be combined with South Kensington Museums).
Mint (order necessary). Can be combined with Tower.
Oratory, Brompton Road.
St. Bartholomew's Church, Smithfield (oldest in London, except Tower Chapel).
Charterhouse.
St. Margaret's, Westminster.
Record Office, Chancery Lane (historical deeds).
Soane Museum and Royal College of Surgeons (order necessary for latter), Lincoln's Inn Fields.
Temple Church and Gardens.
Royal United Services Museum, Whitehall.
St. Saviour's Cathedral.

London in from Four to Six Days.

The diligent visitor will be able to arrange programmes including all the first-rate and secondary sights already indicated,

Will F. Taylor,] [*London.*

STAPLE INN, HOLBORN.

[*Valentine, Alfieri, Scott.*

CHANGING GUARD.

At Buckingham Palace—St. James's Palace—The Horse Guards.

and to spare a morning or afternoon for a glimpse of South London, including not only St. Saviour's Cathedral, but Dickens's "Borough," the Library of Lambeth Palace, Battersea Park, the Dulwich Picture Gallery, the new National Maritime Museum at Greenwich, and the Horniman Museum. For a morning or afternoon trip from Town he will be able to select one or more of the following :—

Windsor Castle and Park.
Hampton Court
Virginia Water.
Kew Gardens.
Richmond.
Burnham Beeches, Stoke Poges, and possibly Penn.
Epping Forest.
Box Hill, Leith Hill, or other beauty spots in Surrey.
A Trip up the Thames, say from Kingston to Windsor, or from Windsor to Maidenhead or Henley.
Croydon Air Port.

Most of these trips can be made by public motor as well as by rail. The Tourist Agencies arrange many whole-day motor drives, one of the most popular of which is: Stoke Poges—Burnham Beeches—Maidenhead—Windsor—Hampton Court. Combined motor and launch trips are also arranged, such as car to Stoke Poges—launch Maidenhead to Windsor—car Windsor to Staines—launch Staines to Shepperton—car to Hampton Court and home (see also under "Motor Tours," p. 31).

London in a Week.

All the foregoing programmes have the advantage of elasticity and the corresponding disadvantage of vagueness. With a whole week at disposal it might be possible to draw up a more rigid programme, including practically everything of general interest. For such a programme the seven West End routes and the City and South London chapters into which this book is divided could be followed fairly closely. Any superfluous shoe-leather might well be devoted, if the weather be fine, to making closer acquaintance with London's parks and open spaces, of which, in our opinion, neither Londoners nor their visitors see half enough. One or two afternoons will probably be devoted to entertainments, but the sightseer will, of course, economize time by reserving these for the evenings or for days when the weather is unfavourable for distant journeys.

In selecting any of the following day tours due regard should be paid to opening and closing of show-places—the Houses of Parliament, for example, can be seen only on Saturdays and Easter and Whitsun Mondays and Tuesdays. Bear in mind, on the other hand, that the National Gallery and some of the Museums remain open in the evenings, and that the Zoological Gardens are open until 11.30 p.m. on Wednesdays and Thursdays.

First Day. Charing Cross—Northumberland Avenue—Victoria Embankment—Houses of Parliament—Westminster Abbey*—St. Margaret's Church—Cenotaph and Government Offices, Whitehall—Royal United Services Museum—Trafalgar Square—National Gallery—National Portrait Gallery.

Second Day. St. James's Park—Marlborough House—St. James's Palace—London Museum—Buckingham Palace—Green Park—Hyde Park—Kensington Gardens—Kensington Palace—Albert Hall and Memorial—Imperial Institute—Royal School of Art Needlework—Victoria and Albert Museum—Science Museum—Geological Museum—Natural History Museum—Brompton Oratory—Piccadilly—Royal Academy.

Third Day. Regent Street—Oxford Street—Wallace Collection—Regent's Park—Zoological Gardens—Hampstead Heath—Return by Tube to Tottenham Court Road—British Museum—Gray's Inn.

Fourth Day. Strand—Aldwych and Kingsway—Lincoln's Inn Fields (Soane Museum, etc.)—Lincoln's Inn—Law Courts—Chancery Lane—Record Office—Temple—Fleet Street—St. Paul's Cathedral—G.P.O.—St. Bartholomew's Church and the Charterhouse—St. Giles, Cripplegate—London Wall—Guildhall—Cheapside—Bank—Royal Exchange—Monument—Tower of London—Tower Bridge—Mint—Return to Charing Cross by boat or by District Railway or omnibus.

Fifth Day. Westminster Bridge—London County Hall—St. Thomas's Hospital—Imperial War Museum—Lambeth Palace and Church—Tate Gallery—Chelsea Hospital—Cheyne Walk (Carlyle's House, etc.)—Battersea Park—Victoria—Roman Catholic Cathedral—Westminster School—Church House.

Fifth Day (alternatives). Charing Cross to London Bridge by bus or train to Monument station—St. Saviour's Cathedral—The Borough—Tram or taxi to Dulwich Picture Gallery—Boat (from Tower Pier), tram or taxi to Greenwich for Park and National Maritime Museum—London Docks (Conducted tours organized on certain days by the Port of London Authority)—Bethnal Green Museum—Victoria Park—Epping Forest.

Sixth Day. By rail or road to Windsor (state apartments are not always open, but there is plenty otherwise to see). Afternoon steamer down River to Kingston—Hampton Court—Bushy Park.

Sixth Day (alternative). Kew Gardens—Richmond—Kingston—Hampton Court—Windsor Castle and Park—Slough—Burnham Beeches—Stoke Poges.

Seventh Day. Another excursion in the Environs (see "Trips from Town") or see places necessarily omitted in above rounds.

For **Sunday in London** see p. 36.

*See footnote, p. 43.

HOW TO GET ABOUT LONDON.

THE stranger to London may well be dismayed at the prospect of finding his way through its ten thousand streets and 700 miles of railway, but he may take comfort from the fact that most of the principal sights are in a comparatively small area. A few minutes' careful study of our maps, with the aid of these pages, should make clear the directions of the streets and railways most likely to be of service. At the head of our descriptions of the various show-places will be found notes on train and bus routes.

A NOTE FOR PEDESTRIANS.

Visitors unused to the traffic of great towns are prone to be either careless or needlessly apprehensive in crossing busy streets. The best advice is: Keep a sharp look-out in all directions, especially where there are converging thoroughfares or turnings at right angles. Wherever possible, use a pedestrian crossing, marked by orange-coloured globes known as "**Belisha Beacons,**" in reference to the Minister of Transport by whom they were introduced. At some of the most crowded crossings, as at the Bank, Mansion House station, Trafalgar Square, the foot of Whitehall, the northern end of Blackfriars Bridge and the Elephant and Castle, there are subways for pedestrians; at many points green lights signal when the pedestrian may safely cross; and at all important centres policemen are stationed to regulate the traffic. The general rule is for vehicles to keep to the left, pedestrians to the right; but this rule is suspended in the case of vehicles using "**one-way thoroughfares**" (open to vehicular traffic in one direction only) and at the busy crossings where the gyratory or "**roundabout**" **system** of traffic control is in force. On such routes pedestrians should be particularly vigilant against oncoming traffic from an unexpected quarter, and should cross the road at the points indicated by "Belisha Beacons." (See also p. 48.) In walking the streets, do not on any account step off the pavement into the roadway without a cautious glance behind as well as in front. In all the principal thoroughfares are ambulance stations, or ambulance "calls," and the police are trained to render first aid.

TAXIS.

Motor Taxi-Cabs are usually the speediest means of transport for short journeys, though in districts where traffic congestion is pronounced it is often quicker to use the Underground or

Tube (see p. 51). The taximeter automatically records the fare by a combination of time and distance as the journey proceeds. Four passengers can be accommodated. There are ranks in or adjoining all the principal thoroughfares. Some of the ranks can be communicated with by telephone. The following is the scale of charges :—

	s.	*d.*
Not exceeding two-thirds of a mile, or for time not exceeding 7½ minutes	0	9
Exceeding two-thirds of a mile or 7½ minutes—		
Each third of a mile, or time not exceeding 3¾ minutes, or for any less distance or time	0	3
Each additional person beyond two, the whole journey	0	6
Packages carried outside	0	3
Bicycles, mailcarts and perambulators	0	9

MOTORING.

Only drivers of nerve and experience should motor in the crowded thoroughfares of London. If it is necessary to cross London from north to south, or vice versâ, the existence of the river must not be forgotten, and the roads converging on bridges are almost invariably crowded. See also map facing p. 47.

It should be borne in mind that certain **one-way thoroughfares** are closed to all vehicular traffic except that proceeding in a prescribed direction ; and that at certain busy spots such as the Marble Arch, Trafalgar Square, Hyde Park Corner, etc., the gyratory or **" roundabout " system** of traffic control is observed : instead of cutting through crossing traffic one turns left and follows the " circus " until the desired turning is reached. By this means much annoying delay is obviated.

Visiting motorists, however, will be well advised to garage their cars on the outskirts during their stay ; the congested state of the streets robs motoring of any pleasure, while the Underground is generally much quicker. For trips from London, the car will be useful. In the notes dealing with suburban resorts we have given, wherever possible, the road route to each place of interest. Both to the south and north of London, the country a few miles out is very charming, particularly the leafy lanes and the stretches of open common. Bold as it may seem to make the assertion, there are beauty spots within sight of London smoke that will challenge comparison with any in Great Britain.

The headquarters of the **Automobile Association** are at Fanum House, on the west side of Leicester Square, W. The **Royal Automobile Club** is at 89, Pall Mall, S.W.1.

MOTOR PARKING.

Owing to traffic congestion the rules regarding car-parking have to be enforced strictly in the busier quarters of London, and before leaving a car standing it is well to consult a policeman concerning the period during which cars may be so left there, if indeed they may be left there at all; the police will also direct motorists to the nearest public motor park. In addition to parking places there are a number of large garages where cars may be left in safety.

THE LONDON PASSENGER TRANSPORT BOARD.

This remarkably comprehensive body, popularly known as "London Transport," was formed with the object of co-ordinating all the various transport services of London and its suburbs as a necessary step towards the solution of London's very serious traffic problem. The area controlled by the Board is nearly 2,000 square miles, and the undertakings which came under its management on July 1, 1933, include the Underground and Metropolitan Railways, the London General Omnibus Company and practically all the other omnibus concerns in and around London, the London County Council Tramways and all the outlying tramway and trolley-bus systems, Green Line Coaches and other coach companies, etc.

BUSES

were introduced into London in 1829 by George Shilibeer, from whom they were for some time known as "shilibeers": but this name was soon abandoned for that of omnibus, "a carry-all"—usually shortened to "bus." Until 1899 the vehicles were drawn by horses. In that year tentative experiments were made with motor-omnibuses, and from 1905 the use of this class of vehicle became so general that the last horsed bus of the London General Omnibus Company made its final trip on October 25, 1911. Some of the motor-buses now in use are the finest in the world. **Smoking** is permitted only on upper decks of buses, and at the rear of single-deck omnibuses.

In 1912 the Company came under the same management as the Underground Electric Railways and in 1933 both passed under the control of the London Passenger Transport Board. The omnibus fares are generally reckoned by penny stages (about a penny a mile is the average rate), and a shilling or so covers the cost of a ride from one end of London to the other. A slight idea of the magnitude of the traffic can be gained from the fact that during the year ended June 30, 1936, 6,298 buses and coaches carried 2,127 million passengers, with a total mileage of nearly 280 millions. Put in another way, it may be said that every person in the London Transport area makes more than two hundred bus journeys a year. Nearly eight million passengers have been carried in a single day.

The vehicles bear numbers indicative of the various routes, and boards in front and at the back display the names of the localities through which they run. Tables of fares are placed inside. The visitor should make himself acquainted with the relative positions of the chief localities by reference to the maps, in order to guard against the possibility of mistaking the direction in which the vehicle is travelling.

In entering trams, trolley-buses and motor-buses, especially the latter, hold firmly to the rail till you are either inside or safely on top. This is quite as important if the vehicle is stationary as if moving, for the jerk caused by a sudden start may send you headlong. Attempts to " board " buses in motion are attended with considerable risk. When desirous of alighting, ring the bell *once* for the driver to stop.

Certain thoroughfares are used by buses going in one direction only, those going the reverse way passing along a nearby and complementary " one-way street."

Visitors should endeavour to time their movements so as to avoid using the buses during the " rush " hours—say from 7.30 to 9.30 in the morning, and from 4.30 to 7 in the evening (Saturdays 12.30–2.30), according to district—for every vehicle is then loaded to full capacity, and even experienced travellers find it difficult to board a bus.

Do not attempt either to board or to leave a bus while it is moving.

Some of the journeys are of an astonishing length : for instance, Wood Green and Farningham (Route 21) 24 miles, Clapham Common and Dorking (Route 70) 21 miles. There are other such regular daily services to places as far afield as Watford, St. Albans, Epping Town, Brentwood, Windsor, etc., and practically every place of importance within a radius of 30 miles or so is linked by bus services with the heart of the metropolis, though one or two changes of vehicle may be necessary. On Sundays and Bank Holidays, and on the early closing days in certain districts, extended services are run.

TRAMS AND TROLLEY-BUSES.

On July 1, 1933, the entire tramway system of London and its suburbs was transferred to the London Passenger Transport Board. Recently the conversion of trams to trolley-buses has been begun. Visitors will probably find greatest use for the subway line (see p. 188) connecting Southampton Row, Bloomsbury, with the Victoria Embankment and Westminster (journey time 7 minutes), and the very quick and useful services along the Embankment itself, between Blackfriars and Westminster. The trams and trolley-buses are handy also when exploring South London—Battersea, Dulwich, etc.—and such places north of the river as Shoreditch, Islington, etc. Longer runs embrace such resorts as Hampstead Heath, Kew, Epping Forest and Greenwich.

Four hundred cars an hour serve Victoria Embankment ; 500 passengers a minute leave by tramcar during the rush hours. The Embankment gives easy access to the Horse Guards,

Trafalgar Square and the amusement area. It is only a minute's step from the crowded Strand, to which it is a speedy alternative.

The lowest fare is 1*d*. With a 1*s*. all-day ticket a passenger may on the day of issue board any car, change anywhere and travel at will on all tramways in the administrative County of London. The fare between suburban and central London is 2*d*. all-the-way during middle hours of the day, Monday to Friday, not public holidays. Return fares of 5*d*., 6*d*. and 8*d*. are issued for single fares of 3*d*., 4*d*. and 5*d*. respectively. Transfer tickets are issued where practicable between suburban and central London.

Maps and Time-tables (free) from Tramway inspectors and regulators or at the Offices of London Transport, 55, Broadway, S.W.1.

THE RAILWAYS OF LONDON.

See Railway Map facing p. 47.

There are in the area known as Greater London upwards of 600 passenger railway stations. The length of passenger lines in the same area is nearly 700 miles, more than the distance from London to Land's End and back again. Of "tube" and other underground railway stations alone there are about 200. It is of interest to note that 468 million passengers were booked in 1935 on the local railways in London, and even these stupendous figures are exclusive of the suburban traffic on main lines. The average number of journeys per head of the population of London in 1935 was 465 per annum.

The accompanying map shows all the Underground and other lines, and will repay careful study and constant consultation.

The railways of London are divisible into two groups—those which form the suburban sections of the great trunk lines, and the 140 miles of electrically driven and purely London railways which are run below street-level and are generally known as—

THE UNDERGROUND.

To the sightseer the Underground is chiefly of value for getting quickly to places at a distance; for short point-to-point journeys—unless on a direct line of route—and for seeing the streets themselves, a taxi or a bus is to be preferred. Although the journey times from station to station are short—Euston to Piccadilly Circus, for instance, in 10 minutes—allowance must be made for the time spent in lifts or on escalators and in traversing subways and stairs between them and station platforms, such time on short journeys often equalling or even exceeding that actually spent in the trains. But an Underground journey is often a speedier mode of transit than even a taxi, on account of the congestion of the streets.

From the traveller's point of view the various lines can now be considered a single huge system, though the connections are not so convenient as might have been the case had the principle of co-operation been adopted from the outset. Through bookings are in operation on all the lines, so that from almost any station one may, by changing at the proper point, or points, get to any other station, *whether on the same line or not.* Directions are usually given on the tickets as to the station, or stations, at which it is necessary to change, and the same information is conveyed by route outlines in the cars.

This vast network of electric railways comprises two systems—the District and the Metropolitan—which run only a short distance below ground, the station platforms being reached from the street by stairways—and five **"Tubes"** running at considerably greater depths and reached from the street by lifts or escalators (moving stairways). On all lines trains run at intervals of a few minutes, and there is only one class of carriage, except on the District and Metropolitan lines, where first and third class carriages are run.

To the stranger—and to many Londoners—the Underground Railways form a confusing network, and it will greatly aid the visitor if he can memorize the general directions of the various lines. To this end we have described each route in detail, adding notes on the more important stations. The description should be read in conjunction with our map of the London Roads and Railways.

The simplest route to memorize is that of—

The Central London Tube,

which runs in an almost straight line east and west. Starting from the Liverpool Street terminus of the L.N.E.R., it next has a station below the busy roadway at the *Bank of England.* Thence it passes below Cheapside, Newgate Street (*St. Paul's Station*), Holborn (*Chancery Lane* and *Holborn* (*Kingsway*) stations), and Oxford Street (stations at *Tottenham Court Road, Oxford Circus, Bond Street* and *Marble Arch*). Continuing below the Uxbridge road, on the northern edge of Hyde Park, it has stations at *Lancaster Gate, Queen's Road, Notting Hill Gate, Holland Park* and *Shepherd's Bush.*

At this point the route of the line leaves the Uxbridge road, goes northward past the White City (Wood Lane station), and by way of the G.W.R. to *East Acton, North Acton* and *West Acton* reaches *Ealing Broadway* station, on the G.W.R. main line. Visitors will find this line handy for reaching the neighbourhood of the Royal Exchange, Mansion House, Guildhall,

London Bridge, etc. (*Bank* station); St. Paul's Cathedral (*St. Paul's* station), Bloomsbury and the British Museum (*Holborn* (*Kingsway*) station), and the busy shopping district in and around Oxford Street.

At the *Bank* station, and again at *Tottenham Court Road*, connection is made with the Morden—Edgware Line (see p. 54). *Oxford Circus* station is shared with the Bakerloo Tube (see p. 56). At Holborn there is intercommunication with the Piccadilly Line.

The District Line

also runs from east to west, but less directly than the Central London Tube. The easternmost station likely to interest the visitor is *Mark Lane*, close to the Tower of London. Passing westward below Eastcheap (*Monument* station, for the Monument, London Bridge, etc., and escalator connection with Bank station) and *Cannon Street* (station of same name for Mansion House, Bank of England, etc.; *Mansion House* station for St. Paul's Cathedral, Cheapside, Guildhall, etc.), the line comes close to the river at *Blackfriars* station (for Fleet Street and Ludgate Circus, St. Paul's Cathedral, etc.). Then it runs below the Embankment to Westminster (*Temple* station for the Temple, Kingsway, the Strand; *Charing Cross* station for the Trafalgar Square neighbourhood; *Westminster* station for Houses of Parliament, Westminster Abbey, Whitehall, etc.). The line now turns westward to *St. James Park* station, on the south side of the Park, and *Victoria* (for the Southern Railway terminus, Westminster Cathedral, etc.). *Sloane Square* station is handy for Chelsea or Knightsbridge, and *South Kensington* serves "Museum Land."

Stations westward of this point likely to be of service to the visitor are *Gloucester Road* (for the Cromwell Road neighbourhood), and *Earls Court* (an important junction for lines to Putney and Wimbledon, Hammersmith, Richmond, Ealing, Hounslow, Uxbridge, etc.).

From *Gloucester Road* station—

The Metropolitan Line

runs first north and then east, finally rejoining the District line at Mark Lane station to form a loop known as the **Inner Circle.** This half of the circle passes close to the great railway termini on the north side of London and also serves the Kensington and Bayswater shopping centres, *Kensington High Street* station being well known to those frequenting Barker's and neighbouring stores. At *Notting Hill Gate* this line crosses the Central London Tube (stations adjoin). *Bayswater* is the station for Westbourne Grove and its shops, and *Paddington* (*Praed Street*) that for the G.W.R. terminus (subway connection). *Edgware Road* station adjoins the important thoroughfare of that name. The line now runs eastward below the Marylebone and Euston Roads. At *Baker Street* station it links up with the Metropolitan Extension Railway, with trains every few minutes to St. John's Wood (for Lord's Cricket Ground), Wembley, Stanmore and Harrow, Watford, Uxbridge and Rickmansworth, etc. (see p. 60). Baker Street station is also handy for Marylebone terminus of the L.N.E.R., Madame Tussaud's, Regent's Park, etc. ; *Great Portland Street* station, at the northern end of that thoroughfare, is close to Regent's Park and the Zoo. *Euston Square* is within a few minutes' walk of the Euston terminus of the L.M.S., and also serves Tottenham Court Road and Bloomsbury. *King's Cross* station adjoins the L.N.E.R. terminus of that name, and the St. Pancras terminus of the L.M.S. Railway. *Farringdon* station serves that important market and is handy for the eastern end of Holborn, Ludgate Circus, etc., and *Aldersgate* is within a few minutes' walk of St. Paul's Cathedral. At *Moorgate* station is the terminus of the **Northern City Line,** running northward to Highbury and Finsbury Park. Moorgate station lies close to the junction of Moorgate with London Wall (for the Bank, Royal Exchange, etc.), and *Liverpool Street* station is beneath the L.N.E.R. terminus of that name. At *Aldgate Station* the line passes beneath that busy highway, and at Mark Lane the District Line is rejoined and the Inner Circle is complete.

These two "east and west lines" are crossed by three deep Tubes running north and south and passing far below the Thames.

The Morden and Edgware Line.

This line, still familiarly **"The Hampstead Tube,"** serves the residential districts named, bringing them into close touch with the City and the West End. From Golders Green to Morden (via the Bank) is a distance of 17 miles—the longest tunnel journey it is possible to make on any railway in the world (the Simplon Tunnel, next longest, is 12¼ miles long). On this line (except for the section between Euston and Waterloo) it is necessary to see that one is in the right train, since the lines diverge at three points. The destination of each train is prominently indicated.

The southernmost station likely to be used by the casual visitor to London is *The Oval*, adjoining the Surrey Cricket Club's headquarters at Kennington. Southward from this point the line runs below the Clapham Road to *Clapham Common*, and following the course of the Balham Road continues through *Balham* to *Wimbledon* and *Morden*. Going in the other direction from the Oval (i.e. *towards* London), the line makes for *Kennington* and *Waterloo*, with a station below the great Southern Railway terminus at Waterloo, and interchange connections with the Bakerloo Tube (see p. 56). Leaving Waterloo the Tube passes far below the Thames to *Charing Cross* station (below Southern Railway terminus, and handy for the Embankment), with another station (*Strand*) below the main entrance to the S.R. terminus, and serving Trafalgar Square, the Strand, Whitehall, etc. The course of the line now follows the Charing Cross Road and Tottenham Court Road. *Leicester Square* station is close to the heart of Theatre-land, and *Tottenham Court Road* station serves the Oxford Street shopping quarter, Bloomsbury, the British Museum, etc. *Goodge Street* station is about midway along Tottenham Court Road, and *Warren Street* at its northern end, close to Maples' and other large stores. A sharp swing to the right brings the line beneath the *Euston* terminus of the L.M.S. Railway.

Camden Town station is an important junction. One line runs northward to *Highgate*; another north-westward via *Chalk Farm* station (for the Zoo), and *Hampstead* (for the Heath) to the Garden suburb at *Golders Green*, and thence as a surface railway to *Hendon Central* and *Edgware*. The line from Euston to the Bank first runs eastward to a station serving *King's Cross* and *St. Pancras* termini of the L.N.E.R. and the L.M.S. respectively (connection also with Piccadilly Tube); thence continues eastward to the *Angel* at Islington. Then it runs below the City Road and Moorgate, with stations at *Old Street* (for Bunhill Fields, Wesley's House, etc.) and *Moorgate* (for Finsbury Circus, Broad Street and Liverpool Street termini, etc.), to the *Bank*, where there is a very busy station serving also the Central London Tube and with escalator connection with Monument Station on the District line. The station, thronged at all hours with City workers, is between the Bank of England, the Mansion House and the Royal Exchange.

From this point the line runs beneath the Thames to *London Bridge* station, below the Southern Railway terminus of that name. Beneath Borough High Street (*Borough* station) and Newington Causeway it passes to the station below the *Elephant and Castle* (junction with Bakerloo line); and beneath Kennington Park Road (*Kennington* station) it rejoins the branch serving the West End already described.

The Bakerloo Tube

derives its name from the fact that in crossing from north-west London to the south-east it serves the termini of the Metropolitan and Southern Railway at Baker Street and Waterloo respectively. It extends beyond these stations, however—to *Elephant and Castle* in the south (where it links with the Morden-Edgware Line, for Clapham and Morden, etc.), and in the north-west to *Queen's Park* station, whence it runs over the London, Midland and Scottish suburban lines to Watford (see p. 57).

The section between Baker Street and Waterloo is very useful to those exploring the West End. *Baker Street* station (beneath the station of the Inner Circle (see p. 53) and the Metropolitan extension lines) is close to Regent's Park, Madame Tussaud's, etc. Westward are stations below the *Marylebone* terminus of the L.N.E.R. and the *Paddington* terminus of the G.W.R. ; thence the route closely follows the important highway known as Maida Vale to *Queen's Park* (see p. 57).

Cityward from Baker Street, the Marylebone Road is followed to *Regent's Park* station, for the Zoo, Regent's Park, Great Portland Street, etc. ; thence the Tube follows Regent Street to Trafalgar Square and passes under the Thames to Waterloo in close proximity to the Charing Cross Railway Bridge.

Oxford Circus station, at the junction of Regent Street and Oxford Street, serves that important shopping quarter, the Queen's Hall, Palladium, etc., and is also used by the Central London Tube. At the southern end of Regent Street is *Piccadilly Circus* station, recently reconstructed with immense engineering skill. It is in the centre of Theatreland and is near the Royal Academy, St. James's Park, etc. The *Piccadilly Tube* (see p. 57) runs north-east and south-west from this point. *Trafalgar Square* station faces the top of Whitehall, at the western end of the Strand, and is within a few yards of the National Gallery, etc. *Charing Cross* station is on the Embankment, and lies below the District line station, which in turn is below the Southern Railway terminus, so that here we have three stations superimposed. Here, too, the river is crossed by three railways—the Southern Railway using the ugly and unwanted bridge, and the Bakerloo and Morden and Edgware Tubes passing far below the Thames by tunnel. *Waterloo* is the busy terminus of the Southern Railway (South-Western section, see p. 58), and there are stations on the Bakerloo and Morden-Edgware Lines. For *Elephant and Castle,* the southernmost station on the Bakerloo Tube, see p. 55.

The Piccadilly Tube.

One other Tube Railway remains to be described. The Piccadilly Tube follows the course of Piccadilly from Piccadilly Circus westward to Hyde Park Corner, but it also extends as far westward as Hounslow West and Uxbridge, running on the surface from Baron's Court, and north-eastward to the populous suburbs of *Holloway* and *Finsbury Park* and on for another 7½ miles to Cockfosters. The section best known to visitors begins at *King's Cross* (below the L.N.E.R. terminus and close to St. Pancras terminus, L.M.S. Railway). The next station is at *Russell Square*, behind the Hotel Russell, in the heart of Bloomsbury, and thence the Tube follows the course of Southampton Row to *Holborn* (*Kingsway*) station (interchange station with Central London line), at the corner of Kingsway and Holborn, and close to the British Museum, Lincoln's Inn Fields, Holborn Restaurant, etc. A short line extends below Kingsway to *Aldwych* station, in the Strand, and close to Australia House, Somerset House, the Law Courts, etc., but the main route turns south-westward, and with a station at *Covent Garden* (for the Opera House and the Market), crosses the Morden-Edgware Line at Leicester Square station and the Bakerloo Tube at *Piccadilly Circus* station (see above). As already stated, the Tube then runs below Piccadilly, with stations at *Green Park* (for Bond Street, Royal Academy, London Museum, St. James's Palace, etc.), and *Hyde Park Corner*, for the Parks, Buckingham Palace, etc. From *Knightsbridge* station, at the top of Sloane Street, and close to Harrod's Stores, the course is below Brompton Road. At the next station, *South Kensington*, which serves Museum Land, the Piccadilly Tube runs close below the District Railway; and the two run side by side all the way to *Earls Court*, *Hammersmith*, *Acton Town* and *Northfields*.

OTHER ELECTRIC LINES.

All the foregoing lines are part of the great Underground system of the London Passenger Transport Board. There are, however, a number of important electric railways serving Greater London and forming the suburban sections of the Great Trunk lines. (For the Metropolitan Suburban Railway Line, see p. 54.)

From **Euston** (II. I. 5) electric trains run north-westward to South Hampstead, Kilburn and Maida Vale, Queen's Park (where the Bakerloo Tube is joined), Willesden Junction, Wembley, Harrow and Watford.

From **Broad Street Station** (II. O. 7) (London, Midland and

Scottish Railway) trains run through Shoreditch to Dalston, whence a branch runs eastward through Hackney to Bow and **Poplar.** Westward from Dalston this railway serves Highbury, Camden Town, Hampstead Heath, Kilburn, Brondesbury and Willesden Junction. From Willesden Junction branches run to Addison Road (for Olympia) and **Earls Court** (see above) and to Acton, Kew and **Richmond.**

The Southern Railway suburban system is so ramified as almost to defy description. Suffice it to say that from **Victoria** and **London Bridge** there is a loop through South London by way of Battersea Park, Clapham, Brixton, Denmark Hill, Peckham and Bermondsey. An extended loop connects London Bridge and Victoria with the **Crystal Palace** via West Norwood, passing through Brixton, Herne Hill, Sydenham, Forest Hill, Brockley and New Cross.

From **Waterloo** the electrified lines of the South-Western section of the Southern Railway comprise a large loop and four spurs. The loop runs from Waterloo via Clapham Junction, Wandsworth, Wimbledon (whence a connecting branch runs direct to Putney), Malden, Kingston, Teddington, Twickenham, Richmond, Mortlake and Putney, and so back to Clapham Junction. From Malden a branch runs via Surbiton to Hampton Court, and another by Surbiton and Claygate to Guildford; between Teddington and Strawberry Hill stations a line runs off to Fulwell, Hampton, Sunbury and Shepperton; while from Twickenham a loop runs to Hounslow and thence back to the main circle at Barnes by way of Isleworth, Brentford, Kew Bridge and Chiswick. Recently the lines to Windsor have been electrified.

The great trunk lines running out of London also maintain suburban services, but on some lines trains are infrequent during the day and in the morning and evening are thronged by thousands of busy workers getting to and from the City and West End.

TRUNK LINES NORTH OF RIVER.

London, Midland and Scottish Railway.

EUSTON (Plan II. I. 5) is the terminus of the **London and North-Western** section. This great line—a development of the earliest passenger railway in the world—provides the route to Ireland via Holyhead and the English portion of the West Coast Route to Edinburgh and Glasgow, serving either by its main line or its branches every place of importance in the northern and north-western counties, as well as many in the Midlands.

SUBURBAN TRAINS to Willesden Junction, Wembley, Harrow, Watford, Richmond, Kew, Acton, etc. (see above). The electric line for local passenger services is linked with the Bakerloo Line at Queen's Park. Also electric trains between Willesden and Earls Court, where connection is made with the District Railway.

Subway connection at Euston with the *Morden* and *Edgware Line* (see p. 54). For Central London Tube change at Tottenham Court Road or *Bank*. Euston Square (5 minutes' walk) is the nearest station on **Metropolitan Line.**

ST. PANCRAS (Plan II. K. 5) is the terminus of the **Midland** section of the L.M.S., serving the Midland Counties, and providing the Waverley Route to Scotland.

SUBURBAN TRAINS to Cricklewood, Hendon, Mill Hill, St. Albans, Luton, Bedford, etc. Branch line from Kentish Town to East Ham, also to Tilbury and Southend.

Subway connection with King's Cross station on *Morden* and *Edgware Line* **Piccadilly Tubes** and **Metropolitan Railway. Kentish Town,** on the Highgate branch of the **Morden and Edgware Line,** is also a convenient station for the Midland section, as the two stations adjoin.

BROAD STREET (Plan II. O. 7), the terminus of the former North London Railway, adjoins Liverpool Street (see below). For electric services from Broad Street see p. 57.

FENCHURCH STREET (Plan III. O. 8) is the terminus of the former London, Tilbury and Southend Railway. The line serves the east of London and continues to Tilbury (for Gravesend, Leigh, Westcliff, Southend and Shoeburyness). At East Ham connection is made with the District Railway.

Mark Lane is the nearest station on the **District Railway ;** Aldgate on the Metropolitan Railway. The Bank station of the **Central London** and **Morden and Edgware Lines** is about five minutes' walk.

London and North-Eastern Railway.

KING'S CROSS (Plan II. K. 5), the terminus of the **Great Northern** section, adjoins St. Pancras. The line runs to York, affording communication with the north and north-east of England, and forming the southern portion of the East Coast Route to Scotland.

SUBURBAN TRAINS to Finsbury Park, Highgate, Finchley, Alexandra Palace, Edgware, High Barnet, Enfield, etc.

Subway connection with King's Cross station on **Metropolitan Railway** and with **Piccadilly** and **Morden and Edgware Lines.**

MARYLEBONE (Plan II. G. 6) is the terminus of the **Great Central** section of the L.N.E.R. Trains to Rugby, Nottingham, Sheffield, Manchester, etc. ; and via Grimsby for the Continent. Also to Harrow, Northwood, Rickmansworth, etc., and to Wembley Hill (for the Wembley Stadium), South Harrow, Ruislip, Beaconsfield, High Wycombe, etc.

Subway connection with Marylebone station on **Bakerloo Tube.** Baker Street station on **Metropolitan Railway** is a quarter of a mile eastward.

LIVERPOOL STREET (Plan II. O. 7) is the terminus of the **Great Eastern** section of the L.N.E.R., which serves the Eastern Counties and provides the routes to the Continent via Harwich.

SUBURBAN SERVICES.—Almost a quarter of London's rail-borne workers use this part of the London and North-Eastern system. One of the most popular services is that to Southend-on-Sea. Among the suburbs served are Tottenham, Edmonton and Enfield ; Leyton,

Walthamstow and Chingford; Woodford, Forest Gate, Ilford, Romford, etc. About a thousand trains leave Liverpool Street daily. There is also a connection by electric trains with New Cross, in the South of London.

Subway connections with Liverpool Street stations on **Central London and Metropolitan Railways.** A few yards westward are the Moorgate stations of the **Morden and Edgware Line** and the **Northern City Line.**

Great Western Railway.

PADDINGTON (Plan II. F. 7) is the terminus of the **Great Western** Railway, which serves the Thames Valley, the West and South-West of England, and the greater part of Wales, having incorporated the Cambrian Railways. It also provides the routes to Ireland via Fishguard and Rosslare and to the Channel Islands via Weymouth.

SUBURBAN TRAINS to Acton, Ealing and riverside places such as Windsor, Maidenhead, Henley, etc. Also motor trains to Perivale, Greenford, etc.

Connected by escalators with station of same name on **Bakerloo Tube,** whence there is direct connection with the London, Midland and Scottish main line via Queen's Park and Willesden Junction. Connected also by Bakerloo with Baker Street, for Metropolitan Railway.

Nearest **Metropolitan Railway** stations, **Praed Street** and **Bishop's Road,** the former connected by subway, the latter by bridge.

Metropolitan Railway.

BAKER STREET (Plan II. G. 6) is the terminus of what must perforce be called the "country" lines of the Metropolitan Railway (now absorbed in the London Passenger Transport Board), familiarly "the Met.," and is also served by "Circle" trains (see p. 54). Between Baker Street and Wembley Park, Harrow and Uxbridge and Watford the trains are run by electricity, as also are the trains on the Aylesbury line as far as Rickmansworth, beyond which they are steam-hauled to Chesham, Aylesbury and Verney Junction. Many "through" trains (some with Pullman cars attached) are run from these places to and from the City, without change at Baker Street.

Subway connection with **Bakerloo Tube.** Change at Oxford Circus for Central London Tube, at Piccadilly Circus for Piccadilly Tube, and at Charing Cross for District Railway.

TRUNK LINES RUNNING SOUTH OF RIVER.

The great trunk lines have upwards of a dozen important termini in London, all linked with each other and with every part of the Metropolis by Underground Railways.

The three railways running southward from London were in 1923 "grouped" under the title of—

The Southern Railway.

WATERLOO (Plan III. L. 9), one of the largest railway termini in Europe, serves the *South-Western section*, running to Winchester, Portsmouth, Southampton, Bournemouth, Exeter, Plymouth, Ilfracombe, North Cornwall, etc. It also provides the services to the Isle of Wight and those via Southampton to the Channel Islands and Havre (for Paris).

Electrified SUBURBAN TRAINS to all parts of South-West London

Valentine & Sons, Ltd.,] *[Dundee.*

TRAFALGAR SQUARE.

Herbert Felton,] [*London.*

LONDON COUNTY HALL.

Valentine & Sons, Ltd.,] *[Dundee.*

THE CENOTAPH AND WHITEHALL.

THE HORSE GUARDS, WHITEHALL—THE ADMIRALTY ARCHWAY—CARLTON HOUSE TERRACE.

The **Waterloo and City Railway** provides a connection with the City (p. 55); the **Bakerloo Tube** with the Strand, Piccadilly Circus, Oxford Circus, Baker Street, Paddington, and Queen's Park, where the London, Midland and Scottish Railway is joined, and the Morden and Edgware Line connects Waterloo with Euston, King's Cross, and with West London, by changing at Tottenham Court Road. A direct connection is thus established between South London, the West End, and the suburban residential district bordering London on the north.

LONDON BRIDGE (Plan III. O. 9) is used by both the central and eastern sections of the Southern Railway. The former runs to Brighton, Hastings, Eastbourne, Portsmouth, etc., and provides the useful electric systems between London Bridge and Victoria and the Crystal Palace. The eastern section serves the popular towns and watering-places of Kent—Tunbridge Wells, Hastings, Folkestone, Margate, etc., and provides electric trains to the south-east suburbs, embracing Greenwich, Woolwich, Dartford, Gravesend, Lewisham, Chislehurst, Orpington, Catford, Beckenham, etc.

Subway connection with Morden and Edgware Line.

VICTORIA (Plan III. H. 10) is the West End terminus of the former Brighton and South Coast and South-Eastern and Chatham systems, and is a busy terminus of Continental traffic via the Dover-Calais, Folkestone-Boulogne, Newhaven-Dieppe routes. Victoria is among the largest and best-equipped stations in the world. Subway connection with District railway.

CHARING CROSS (Plan III. K. 8), **CANNON STREET** (Plan III. N. 8), **HOLBORN VIADUCT** (Plan II. M. 7) and **BLACKFRIARS** (Plan III. M. 8) are also termini of the Eastern section of the Southern Railway.

Charing Cross is connected by subway with the Strand station of the **Morden and Edgware** tube (to Euston, Hampstead and Highgate), and by subways and escalators with Charing Cross stations on the **District Railway** and **Bakerloo Tube** (change at Piccadilly Circus for Piccadilly Tube, or at Oxford Circus for Central London Tube). Trafalgar Square station on the **Bakerloo Tube** is only two minutes' walk.

For electrically equipped suburban lines see p. 58. Electric trains run all the way to Brighton and Worthing.

The facilities afforded by the main lines from London may be epitomized thus: For excursions to places of interest in Middlesex, Bucks and Herts, the visitor can avail himself of the London and North-Western and Midland sections of the London, Midland and Scottish Railway, the Great Northern, Great Eastern and Great Central sections of the London and North-Eastern Railway, and of the Metropolitan Suburban lines. For the riverside and western part of the country he will utilize the London and South-Western section of the Southern Railway, the Great Western and the Underground lines. Epping Forest and other parts of Essex are reached by the Great Eastern section of the London and North-Eastern Railway and the Tilbury section of the London, Midland and Scottish. Surrey, Sussex and Kent are served by the many ramifications of the Southern Railway.

AMUSEMENTS.

THEATRES, ETC.—CINEMAS—SPORTS AND GAMES.

LONDON is well provided with facilities for indoor entertainment, but, from a summer visitor's point of view, is sadly lacking in outdoor amusements.

THEATRES.

Evening performances usually begin at 8, 8.15 or 8.30, and terminate about 11 p.m. Matinées, beginning at 2, 2.15 or 2.30, are usual at most houses on at least three days a week. For details see daily newspapers. Seats for the better parts of the house should be booked in advance, either at one of the Agents or Libraries, or by wire or telephone. It frequently happens that Agents, owing to their advance bookings, have better seats for disposal than can be secured at the box offices. The price of seats usually includes the entertainments tax. For the cheaper (unreserved) seats it is generally necessary to wait in the *queues*, which, in the cases of popular performances, often begin to form hours before the doors are opened; but at certain theatres even the cheaper seats can be booked. The numbers immediately following the names of theatres in the following list refer to the sketch map on p. 63, showing the situation of most of the West End houses, and the nearest railway stations.

Certain theatres have an established reputation for a particular kind of play, but in others the nature of the performance varies from time to time, and in reading the third column in the following list due allowance should be made for changes of management, etc. In recent years there has been a tendency for theatres to run seasons of film shows.

	Situation.	Nature of Performance.
Adelphi (1)	410, Strand, W.C.2	Musical comedy, etc.
Aldwych (2)	Aldwych	Farce, drama, etc.
Ambassadors' (4) ..	West St., Shaftesbury Avenue .	Comedy, revue, etc.
Apollo (5)	Shaftesbury Avenue, W.C.1 ...	Comedy
Cambridge (49).....	Great Earl Street, W.C.2	Drama, etc.
Comedy (8)	Panton Street, Haymarket, S.W.1	Comedy
Covent Garden (see	Royal Opera House) (9)	

	Situation.	Nature of Performance.
Criterion (10)	Piccadilly Circus, W.1	Comedy, society plays, etc.
Daly's (11)	Leicester Square, W.C.2.......	Musical comedy
Duchess (46).......	Catherine Street, Aldwych	Comedy, drama, etc.
Drury Lane (12)....	Catherine Street, Strand, W.C.2	Spectacular plays, drama etc.
Duke of York's (13).	St. Martin's Lane, W.C.2	Comedy, drama, etc.
Fortune (14)	Covent Garden, W.C.2	Comedy
Gaiety (15)	Strand, W.C.2	Musical comedy, etc.
Garrick (16)	Charing Cross Road, W.C.2 ...	Comedy, society plays, etc.
Globe (17)	Shaftesbury Avenue, W.1	Drama, comedy, etc.
Haymarket (18) ...	Haymarket, S.W.1	Comedy, drama, etc.

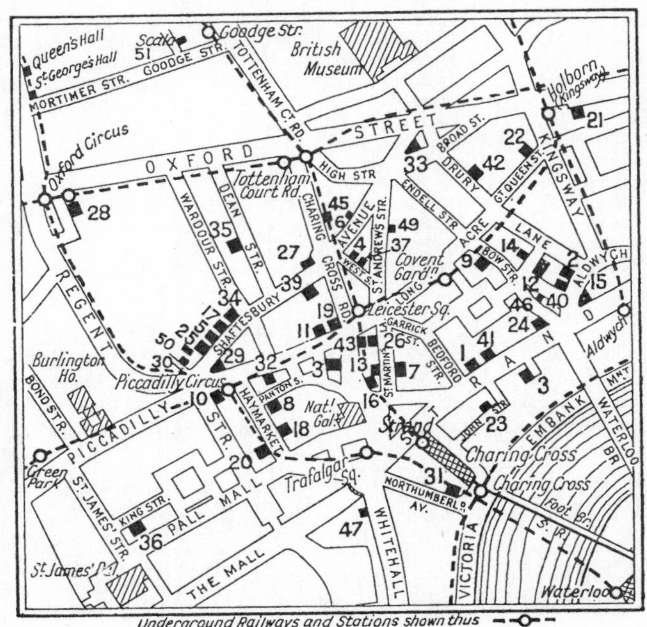

Underground Railways and Stations shown thus

	Situation.	Nature of Performance.
His Majesty's (20) .	Haymarket, S.W.1	Musical plays, drama, etc.
Kingsway (22)	8, Great Queen Street, W.C.2 .	Drama, comedy, etc.
Little (23)	17, John Street, Adelphi, W.C.2	Drama, revue, etc.
Lyceum (24)	Wellington St., Strand, W.C.2 .	Popular drama,pantomime
Lyric (25)	29, Shaftesbury Avenue, W.1 .	Musical comedy
New (26)	St. Martin's Lane, W.C.2	Musical comedy, etc.
"Old Vic"	Waterloo Road, S.E.1	Shakespeare; Opera in English.
Open Air Theatre...	Inner Circle,Regent's Park, N.W.	Shakespeare, etc.
Palace (27)	Shaftesbury Avenue, W.1	Musical comedy, etc.
Phœnix (45)	Charing Cross Road, W.C.2 ...	Comedy, drama, etc.
Playhouse (31)	Northumberland Avenue, W.C.2	Comedy, society plays, etc.
Prince's (33).......	Shaftesbury Avenue, W.C.2 ...	Drama, etc.
Queen's (34)	Shaftesbury Avenue, W.1	Society plays, drama, etc.
Royal Opera House(9)	Covent Garden, W.C.	Opera,fancy dress balls,etc.
Royalty (35)	73, Dean Street, W.1	Drama, comedy, etc.
St. James's (36) ...	King Street, St. James's	Society plays, drama, etc.
St. Martin's (37) ...	West Street, Cambridge Circus.	Drama, comedy, etc.
Saville	Shaftesbury Avenue, W.C.2 ...	Musical plays, comedy,etc.
Savoy (38).........	Strand, W.C.2	Comedy, society plays, etc.
Scala	Charlotte St., W.C...........	Various.
Shaftesbury (39)....	Shaftesbury Avenue, W.1	Musical comedy, etc.
Strand (40)	Aldwych	Drama, comedy, farce, etc.
Vaudeville (41)	404, Strand, W.C.2	Comedy, burlesque, etc.
Westminster	Palace St., Buckingham Gate,S.W.	Various
Whitehall (47)	Whitehall, S.W.1.............	Comedy, etc.
Winter Garden (42).	Drury Lane, W.C.2	Musical comedy, etc.
Wyndham's (43) ...	Charing Cross Road, W.C.2 ...	Comedy, society plays, etc

Suburban Theatres.

We have labelled as "suburban" all theatres not in the proximity of Charing Cross. Nearly every district of importance has one or more houses of entertainment. Some of these equal the West End theatres in comfort and class of performance, and the prices are considerably lower.

Britannia, 115–17, Hoxton Street, N.1.
Brixton, Brixton, S.W.
Broadway, New Cross Road, S.E.14.
Century, Archer Street, Notting Hill, W.
Embassy, 64, Eaton Avenue, N.W.3.
Everyman, Hampstead.
Golders Green, adjoining Tube station.
King's, Hammersmith, W.6.
Lewisham, High Road, Lewisham, S.E.
Lyric, Hammersmith, W.
Mercury, Notting Hill, W.
Q Theatre, near Kew Bridge.
Sadler's Wells, Rosebery Avenue, N.
Streatham Hill, Streatham, S.W.
Wimbledon, Merton Road, S.W.

Variety Theatres, etc.

Matinées generally at 2 or 2.30, evening performance at 7.45. In many houses two performances a night are given, beginning about 6.15 and 8.45 respectively. (One or two houses specialize in "non-stop" performances which usually begin about 1 p.m. and run continuously until about 11 p.m.) Smoking is permitted. Prices are generally lower than in theatres for the corresponding class of seat and are lowest for "non-stop" performances. The numbers immediately following the names in the following list refer to the sketch plan on p. 63.

	SITUATION.	NATURE OF PERFORMANCE.
Coliseum (7)	St. Martin's Lane, near Charing Cross, W.C.2	Cinema, varieties, musical plays, etc.
Hippodrome (19) ...	Cranborne Street, Leicester Square, W.C.2	Revue, etc.
Holborn Empire (21)	242, High Holborn, W.C.2.....	Varieties
Palladium (28)	Argyll Street, Regent Street, W.1	Varieties
Victoria Palace	Victoria Station, S.W.1	Varieties
Windmill..........	Piccadilly Circus, W.	Revues, etc.

Cinemas.

In and about the West End are numerous cinemas, large and small; and, as already stated, theatres are frequently used solely for film shows. Well-known cinemas are the *Tivoli*, Strand; *Gaumont* and *Carlton*, Haymarket; *Empire* and *Odeon*, Leicester Square; *Piccadilly*, Denman Street, W.; *Regal*, Marble Arch, W.; *Plaza*, Lower Regent Street; the *Stoll Picture Theatre*, Kingsway, W.C.; *New Gallery*, Regent Street; *Marble Arch Cinema*; *Rialto*; *Astoria*, Charing Cross Road; *New Victoria*, near Victoria Station, etc. Several cinemas specialize in the presentation of News Films.

SPORTS AND GAMES.

The Londoner not only works strenuously, but makes the most of his hours of leisure. The weekly half-holiday enacted by a beneficent legislature is generally devoted to games of one kind or another, and during week-ends the river is crowded with pleasure boats, and the roads with motors speeding to the Surrey Hills or the South Coast resorts, or northward to such delectable regions as the Chilterns. We can do no more than mention the headquarters of the various forms of sport, and the leading annual events :—

BADMINTON is played at the Horticultural Hall, S.W.—where the All-England finals are held—at the Alexandra Palace, and elsewhere.

BOATING.—The Serpentine in Hyde Park and the sheets of ornamental water in Regent's Park, Battersea Park, Finsbury Park, Victoria Park and Southwark Park are used for boating, the County Council charge per person being 6*d*. an hour. Parts of the River Lea are also available. But the most popular boating resort among Londoners is the Thames (see p. 274) from Hammersmith to Maidenhead and Henley. See our *Guide to the Thames*.

The **Oxford and Cambridge Boat Race,** invariably attended by huge crowds, is usually rowed on the Saturday before Holy Week, though in 1937 it was rowed on a Wednesday. The course is from Putney to Mortlake, a trifle over 4¼ miles. Oxford, dark blue ; Cambridge, light blue. The *Head of the River Race*, in which over 100 boats compete, is rowed at this time of year over the same course and is an excellent sight.

Of the **Regattas,** the most famous is that of Henley, usually held at the beginning of July. Other Regattas are held in July and August at Molesey, Staines, Kingston, Richmond, Marlow, Bourne End, etc.

Motor-boat racing is popular on the Welsh Harp, Hendon, and elsewhere.

BOWLS.—Provision is made for this popular game on a number of club grounds. There is a green near Alexandra Gate, in Hyde Park ; the L.C.C. maintain public greens in Battersea Park, Finsbury Park and Ravenscourt Park, and provision is also made in many of the suburban parks.

CRICKET.—Lord's, at St. John's Wood (p. 153), is the property of the Marylebone Cricket Club—the M.C.C. The principal annual fixtures are Eton *v*. Harrow and Oxford *v*. Cambridge, always attracting large crowds. The ground is also the headquarters of the Middlesex C.C. **Kennington Oval** (p. 258), on the south side, is the headquarters of the Surrey C.C. There are many private cricket grounds, and pitches are allotted to regular players in most of the local parks.

DANCING.—It need hardly be mentioned that the metropolis has plentiful provision for dances. From the great costume and other balls at the Royal Albert Hall, Covent Garden Opera House, etc., to the various suburban dance halls there are floors to suit all tastes and all pockets. Many of the larger hotels and restaurants make a feature of dance teas or dance dinners and suppers.

FISHING.—The fresh-water angler can do fairly well in the neighbourhood of London, but a short journey by rail or road is generally necessary. Fishing in the **Thames** is free up to the London Stone at Staines, and beyond that there is also plenty of free fishing, the only places on the main stream where riparian owners have succeeded in maintaining their "rights" being in the Maidenhead district and one or two other small reaches. All tributary streams are strictly preserved. To fish from the weirs it is necessary to obtain a permit from the Thames Conservancy (10s. per annum). For full details see the *Guide to the Thames* in this series. Coarse fish, such as roach, chub, dace, perch, barbel and pike, are fairly abundant. A good deal of restocking is done. The **Lea** is also frequented (especially at Rye House, Hoddesdon); and the rivers **Colne** and **Chess**, on the north-western confines of Middlesex, and the Essex **Blackwater** have many admirers. But enthusiasts will not look for detailed information in a book of this general character when they are so admirably served by special publications.

FLYING.—The Air Port of London is at Croydon (see p. 263), but Heston, Gatwick, Hanworth, Hatfield and other aerodromes are generally busy. "Joy Rides" can be taken on almost any day when the weather is favourable. Hendon Aerodrome is annually the scene of the Royal Air Force Pageant. For the regular Air Services see p. 17. And see p. 263.

FOOTBALL.—The principal London clubs playing the Association game are: Arsenal (Gillespie Road, Highbury, N.), Brentford (Griffin Park, Brentford, W.), Chelsea (Stamford Bridge, Fulham Road, S.W.), Clapton Orient (Millfields Road, Clapton, N.E.), Crystal Palace (Selhurst Park, Croydon), Fulham (Craven Cottage, Fulham, S.W.), Millwall (The Den, New Cross, S.E.), Queen's Park Rangers (Loftus Road, Shepherd's Bush, W.), Tottenham Hotspur (Tottenham, N.), West Ham United (Boleyn Castle, Upton Park, E.). The leading amateur teams are the "Corinthians" and the "Casuals." Cup Final matches are played in the great Stadium erected at Wembley Park in connection with the Empire Exhibition. At Leyton is the Army Sports Ground.

Rugby is also becoming increasingly popular, and there are several first-class teams in London. The Rugby Union International Matches and the Oxford *v.* Cambridge University Match are played at Twickenham. The headquarters of the London Rugby Football League are at Mitcham.

GOLF.—There are public 18-hole courses at Hainault Forest, at Mitcham (Prince's) and in Richmond Park, and practice is permitted in the early morning on public open spaces like Hampstead Heath and Clapham Common. In the various Golf Annuals will be found a complete list of the golf courses near London. In most cases visitors introduced by members are allowed to play for a day or two free, or on payment of a fee of about 2*s.* 6*d.* a day (generally more on Saturdays and Sundays). For weekly and monthly players the charges are reduced.

GREYHOUND RACING.—The meetings are announced in the London papers.

HORSE-RACING.—The race-meeting which most appeals to the Londoner is undoubtedly the famous **Derby,** run at Epsom on a Wednesday either a fortnight before or a fortnight after Whitsun, and succeeded two days later by the **Oaks.** On a Derby Day all the roads and railways leading south from London are packed with people, and the sight on the course is one never to be forgotten. **Ascot Week,** a great Society gathering generally attended by the King and members of the Royal Family, comes a fortnight after the Derby. **Goodwood** races begin on the last Tuesday in July. Other races are held at Alexandra Park, Sandown, Kempton Park, Windsor, Hurst Park, Gatwick, Newbury, etc. Pony-racing at Northolt.

ICE HOCKEY.—Popular matches are played at the Empire Pool at Wembley (and see under Skating), at Earls Court, Streatham, Richmond, etc.

LAWN TENNIS.—Hard and grass courts are provided in many of the public parks and squares, and can be used on payment of a small charge per hour. The Amateur Championship of the World is generally decided towards the end of June at the All England Lawn Tennis Club at Wimbledon. The Covered Court Championship and the Amateur Championships in tennis and racquets are usually held at the Queen's Club, West Kensington.

MOTOR RACING takes place on the famous track at Brooklands, easily reached by rail from Waterloo, and there is "speed track" racing at various centres nearer in. See current newspaper announcements.

MOTORING.—See pp. 48–9.

POLO is chiefly followed at Hurlingham and Ranelagh.

PUTTING GREENS in many of the parks and squares.

SKATING.—There are rinks at Westminster (Millbank), Streatham, Earls Court, Richmond, etc. and during the winter the Empire Pool at Wembley becomes a skating rink. Also at Wembley is an outdoor ice rink. Only at rare intervals are the waters around London frozen for a long enough period to give skaters satisfaction. The chief resorts are the Serpentine in Hyde Park, the lake in Regent's Park, the Hampstead Heath and Highgate ponds, the Welsh Harp water at Hendon, the Long Water at Hampton Court, the Pen Ponds in Richmond Park and Ruislip Reservoir.

SWIMMING.—See p. 18, under Baths.

HISTORICAL SKETCH.

AN exhaustive history of London would be that of the kingdom of which it is the capital; and it is, of course, impossible to find room for anything of the kind here. But there are points in the annals of the city which must be noticed in any Guide to London.

The **name** is probably derived—though there is much dispute on the subject—from the Celtic *Llyn* (pronounced *lun*), a pool or lake (the river at an earlier period expanded into a considerable lake—the part immediately below London Bridge is still "the Pool"), and *din* or *dun*, a hill, fort, or place of strength. The "hill" may have been that on which St. Paul's now stands, or Cornhill, or that crowned by the Tower; but recent research casts doubt on the theory that there was a large settlement here in pre-Roman days, and assigns the origin of London to the Roman Conquest in the first century A.D. Under the Romans *Londinium* arose, a splendid city, one of the nine *coloniæ* of Britain, but inferior in importance at first to Eboracum (York) and Verulamium (St. Albans). Great military roads radiated from the city to various parts of Britain and distances were measured from the *lapis milliaris* in the Forum of Agricola, in the heart of the Roman town (Leadenhall Market covers part of the site of the Forum). The stone, now known as the "London Stone," may still be seen in the wall of St. Swithin's Church, Cannon Street.

The direction taken by the old **London Wall,** dating from the first century A.D., is well known, and can be traced by the modern names of streets. Indeed, considerable sections, composed chiefly of Kentish ragstone and large Roman bricks, may be seen in the thoroughfare still known as London Wall, between Wood Street and Aldermanbury; in the churchyard of St. Giles's, Cripplegate; at the General Post Office, Newgate Street; in the offices of the Oxford University Press, Warwick Square; at the foot of Jewry Street, Aldgate; in America Square, off the Minories; in Trinity Square, and at the Tower itself. That the wall is a reality, and not a figment of the topographer's imagination, may be judged by the fact that contractors for sewers and other underground works find it necessary to stipulate that they shall be allowed to charge extra if they have to cut through or remove any portion of it. Outside the wall, a wide ditch, portions of which can still be traced, provided a further defence. At the eastern end of the wall, by the river side, was a strong fort, succeeded later by the White Tower. Thence the wall followed a line slightly westward of the Minories to Aldgate; then it curved to the north-west, between Bevis Marks and Houndsditch ("a ditch beyond the wall") to Bishopsgate, whence it followed the line still known as "London Wall" to Cripplegate. It next took a southern course to Aldersgate, and behind St. Botolph's Church, to Newgate; thence to Ludgate and along Pilgrim Street to the Fleet river (which then flowed in the valley now known as Farringdon Street). It skirted this stream to its junction with the Thames, where another strong fort was erected.[1] There were three **Gates,** Aldgate (Ale-gate or All-gate, i.e., open to all), Aldersgate and Ludgate (*Lydgeat*, a postern); and afterwards a postern (Postern Row marks the spot) on Tower Hill. The City Corporation have erected tablets marking the sites of the gates. On the northern side was an outwork or barbican (the modern street, Barbican, preserves its memory). Later, other gates were added, the names of which are still preserved in Billings-gate, Bishops-gate, Moor-gate, Cripple-gate (from the Anglo-Saxon *crepel-gate*, a covered way), New-gate and Dow-gate (Celtic *dwr*, water).

Under the **Saxons** London became the metropolis of the kingdom of Essex. Bede, writing in the early part of the eighth century, refers to London as the "mart of many nations resorting to it by sea and land." The city was constituted the capital of England by Alfred the Great, York and Winchester having previously enjoyed that dignity in succession—the former under the Romans, the latter under the Saxons. In 994, the first bridge across the Thames was built.

The White Tower, in the Tower of London, was erected by William I in 1078, on the site of the Roman fort already noticed. The same king granted a charter to the city (see p. 21) confirming the burghers in the rights enjoyed by them under Edward the Confessor. William Rufus in 1097 founded Westminster Hall. King John granted the citizens several charters, and in Magna Charta it was expressly stipulated that London should have all its ancient privileges and customs as well by land as by water.

Wat Tyler's Rebellion took place in 1381, and every schoolboy is familiar with the picturesque part played by the Lord Mayor

[1] This line corresponds almost exactly with the present boundaries of the City of London, with the exception of the "liberties," or wards, still known as "without," added at a later time.

of that time. Reference must also be made to Jack Cade's Rebellion (1450), immortalized in Shakespeare's *Henry VI.*: "Now is Mortimer lord of this city!" cried the insurgent leader, when he struck his sword on the London Stone.

In the sixteenth and seventeenth centuries, so rapid had become the increase of London that both Elizabeth and James I. issued proclamations against any further extension of the city. In the Strand, between London and Westminster, were many splendid residences of the nobility, with fine gardens reaching to the Thames. The names of most of the streets in the Strand—such as Essex, Norfolk, Burleigh, Buckingham and Northumberland—still preserve these aristocratic associations.

The reign of Mary witnessed the burning of heretics at Smithfield and that of Elizabeth the patriotic rally of the citizens in defence of the country against the Armada. During the Civil War, London sided with the Parliament, and the fateful January 30th, 1649, saw the execution of Charles I. at Whitehall. In 1665 London was desolated by the **Great Plague,** which carried off nearly a fifth of the inhabitants; and in the following year the **Great Fire** occurred, destroying more than 13,000 houses, St. Paul's Cathedral, the Royal Exchange, 86 churches and most of the guild halls. The damage was estimated at £10,730,500. Pepys forlornly wrote: "It has been computed that the rents of the houses lost by this Fire in the City comes to £600,000 per annum." According to popular legend the fire began at Pudding Lane and ended at Pye Corner. The lofty Monument near London Bridge marks the spot where the fire broke out. The Tower, Westminster Abbey and Hall, Guildhall, the Temple Church, portions of the Inns of Court, Whitehall, Charterhouse, and about a score of city churches, were almost the only buildings of importance spared by the conflagration. Sir Walter Besant well said:—

> "If, as some hold, the cause of the long-continued plague, which lasted, with intervals of rest, from the middle of the sixteenth century to 1665, was nothing but the accumulated filth of London, so that the ground on which it stood was saturated many feet in depth with poisonous filtrations, the fire of 1666 must be regarded in the light of a surgical operation, absolutely essential if life were to be preserved, and as an operation highly successful in its results. For it burned, more or less, every house and every building over an area of 436 acres out of those which made up London within the walls."

But it cannot be denied that the Fire was a great disaster.

In rebuilding the city many improvements were effected. Streets were widened and houses of more substantial materials constructed, but London has never ceased to regret that the masterly designs of Sir Christopher Wren and John Evelyn were not carried out in their entirety. St. Paul's Cathedral and fifty-three parish churches were rebuilt by Wren in such a way that, when viewed from such a standpoint as Waterloo Bridge, the lesser fanes, though differing from each other, all harmonize and serve to heighten the general effect of the stately Cathedral dome.

In 1716 it was ordained that every householder should hang a light before his door from six in the evening till eleven. Gas was first used as an illuminant in 1807. In 1767 numbers began to replace the old signs as distinguishing marks for houses.

Most of the City gates and barriers were removed before the end of the eighteenth century, but the most famous of them, Temple Bar, stood in its place until 1878, when, owing to the inconvenience caused to traffic, it was replaced by the present monument. The old "bar" now stands at the entrance to the park at Theobalds, about fourteen miles from London.

To the latter part of the eighteenth century belong some of the finest of the old buildings in London, such as Somerset House, the Mansion House, and the Horse Guards. But the metropolis, as we know it, is very largely a creation of the **Victorian Age,** most of the leading thoroughfares having been widened and improved—many of them actually constructed—and many of the chief public edifices remodelled, if not built, during that period. The formation of wide arteries—such as New Oxford Street and Regent Street, in the early years of the nineteenth century; of Farringdon Street and Queen Victoria Street, later on; of the Shaftesbury and Rosebery Avenues, and of Charing Cross Road; and during the present century the construction of Kingsway—cleared away many notoriously unsavoury localities. Healthful and outlying districts are now made accessible by cheap trains, "tubes," and motor-buses; while in the central areas are many large piles of flats for those who prefer town life to the suburbs.

London in fact is both one of the finest and one of the healthiest cities in the world. In spite of its huge size, the metropolis has almost the lowest death-rate among towns in England with a population of over 200,000, while it is incontestably far healthier than Paris, New York, or Rome. In recent years its death-rate has been lower than that of any capital in Europe.

By far the most noteworthy feature in London's modern history, however, is the rapid industrial development of Greater London. In 1934, 478 new factories were opened in Britain, and of these 209, employing 15,750 people, were in Greater London.

THE WEST END.

CHARING CROSS AND ITS NEIGHBOURHOOD.

HAVING endeavoured to give a general idea of London, and to supply visitors with all information needful to their stay, we will now conduct them through the principal thoroughfares, and do our best to "fairly streets and buildings trace, and all that gives distinction to the place."

There is so much to see in the great "Whirlpool," as George Gissing aptly called London, that the visitor may as well rid his mind at once of any intention of seeing *all*. None the less, by adopting a prearranged and methodical plan, he can greatly lighten his task and ensure that few places of real interest are overlooked. The visitor who has only a limited number of days at his disposal is recommended to refer to the suggested Itineraries on pp. 38–46, with a view to apportioning his time to the best advantage. The series of routes in this and the subsequent section, devoted to the City proper, have been so arranged that every part of Central London is covered, though we do not suppose for a moment that any large number of readers will literally follow in our footsteps. Where no lengthy stay is made in museums or galleries, the journeys can in most cases be accomplished in a morning or an afternoon.

Charing Cross, the centre of the fifteen-mile police radius, and a passing-point of a great number of omnibus routes, may fairly be considered the "hub" of London, and will make a convenient starting-place for our rambles. Before going farther, let us devote a morning to the neighbourhood.

ROUTE I.—CHARING CROSS—TRAFALGAR SQUARE—NORTHUMBERLAND AVENUE—VICTORIA EMBANKMENT—WHITEHALL—NATIONAL GALLERY.

Charing Cross.

Plan III. K. 8.

Nearest Stations.—Southern Railway terminus of the same name, Strand (Morden-Edgware line), Trafalgar Square (Bakerloo Tube), Charing Cross (District).

Buses connect, either directly or by one or two changes, with all parts of the metropolis.

Note.—West-bound buses stop almost outside the station yard, in the Strand; but *east-bound* buses (for the Bank, London Bridge, etc.) stop in Duncannon Street, in the shadow of St. Martin's-in-the-Fields Church.

"Why, sir," said Dr. Johnson, "Fleet Street has a very

animated appearance, but I think the full tide of human existence is at Charing Cross." The remark is hardly less true to-day.

Charing Cross derives its name from the last of the Gothic crosses erected by Edward I to mark the places where the coffin of Queen Eleanor was set down on its way to Westminster. At that time the little village of Charing, or Cheeringe, occupied a half-way position between London and Westminster. The cross was removed in 1647 by order of Parliament. In the forecourt of the railway station is a modern reproduction, but the original stood slightly to the west, on the site now occupied by the statue of Charles I (p. 75).

Trafalgar Square

(Plan III. K. 8),

so named in commemoration of Nelson's great victory, is a large open space, second only to Hyde Park in the estimation of those organizing political "demonstrations." It is a pity that a competent landscape gardener is not allowed to transform it by the introduction of a few small lawns and rockeries. The view down Whitehall is fine. The **Nelson Monument** is a granite Corinthian column, 184 feet 10 inches, surmounted by a statue of Nelson, 16 feet high. On the base are bronze bas-reliefs, cast with the metal of captured French cannon, representing scenes from the battles of St. Vincent, the Nile, Copenhagen and Trafalgar. Four colossal lions, modelled by Sir Edwin Landseer, crouch on pedestals at the base. Every year, on the anniversary of Trafalgar (October 21), the monument is decked with wreaths and festoons in commemoration of the victory.

A *subway* enables pedestrians to cross the traffic-crowded roadways in safety. Vehicular traffic passes through the Square on the "gyratory" system (see p. 48): a recent census revealed that this is the second busiest spot in London, over 66,000 vehicles passing through in twelve hours.

Below the parapet on the north side of the Square, and quite unknown to the majority of Londoners, are set out the *Standard British Lineal Measures*—inch, foot, yard, chain, etc. Of the statues the best is that of Charles I (see p. 75). **Trafalgar Square Station** (Bakerloo Line) is on the south side of the Square.

The northern side of the Square is occupied by the **National Gallery** (p. 84), behind which is the **National Portrait Gallery** (see p. 92). To the right is **St. Martin's-in-the-Fields,** sometimes known as the "Admiralty Church," erected 1721–6 by James Gibbs on the site of an earlier structure, and well known to wireless listeners.

The story goes that the church owes its foundation to Henry VIII's objection to seeing so many funerals go by his Whitehall windows, which was the way to the churchyard of St. Margaret's, Westminster. This feeling, unreasonable, perhaps, in a widower of such determination, yet not unnatural, induced him to set up a parish of St. Martin's-in-the-Fields, with church and churchyard complete.

One looks in vain now for the " fields." The Grecian portico is greatly admired, but its effect has been somewhat spoilt by the curtailment of the steps in front. The greater part of Buckingham Palace is included in the parish, and overlooking the sanctuary of the church is a commodious Royal box. The births of all Royal children born at the Palace are entered in the register. It will be noted that the vane is surmounted by a crown. George I was at one time churchwarden of St. Martin's, the only case of an English monarch who has held such a position. The register of the old church, still preserved, contains an entry of the baptism of Francis Bacon (1561). Nell Gwynne was buried here. So were Robert Boyle, the philosopher ; Farquhar, the comedy writer ; Lord Mohun, who was killed in a duel by the Duke of Hamilton, and who has achieved a dubious immortality in the pages of Thackeray's *Esmond* ; Roubillac, the sculptor ; John Hunter, the surgeon, whose remains were afterwards removed to Westminster Abbey ; and many others. The church is one of the most active in London, and its services are invariably well attended.

On the eastern side of the Square is **South Africa House,** the magnificent London headquarters of the Government of South Africa. The building was opened by King George V in 1933.

On the opposite (western) side of Trafalgar Square is the **Royal College of Physicians** (admission by member's order). The adjoining building was opened by King George V in 1925 as the London headquarters of the **Canadian Government. Norway House** is the semi-official centre of that country's interests in London.

From Nelson's Monument there is a fine vista down Whitehall and Parliament Street towards the Houses of Parliament, and through the triple **Archway** connected with the New Admiralty (p. 82) there is a fine view westward along the wide Mall to the Victoria Memorial and Buckingham Palace. The archway itself, however, is too hedged with buildings to be seen to advantage from this side.

The equestrian **Statue of Charles I** in the roadway (where once stood the original Charing Cross, see p. 74) is generally regarded as the finest piece of statuary in London. It was cast in 1633, but before it had been erected the Civil War broke out. By the Parliament the objectionable figure was sold as " scrap " to a brazier with the appropriate name of Rivet. An insatiable demand for "relics" of the unfortunate monarch arising, Rivet made a good thing by selling knives and forks with bronze handles, which he pretended were made from the effigy; but with a keen eye to the future he kept the statue intact. At the Restoration it was duly produced from his garden in Holborn, and in 1675 was set up on the site of the old Charing Cross.

The oblique thoroughfare connecting Charing Cross with the Embankment is **Northumberland Avenue,** which by its name commemorates Northumberland House, the town mansion of the Duke of Northumberland, demolished in 1874 to make way for the Avenue. Above the house used to stand the figure of a lion (now at Sion House, Isleworth: see p. 272), and it was a favourite joke with the wits of the period to inform credulous strangers that if they watched long enough the animal would be seen to wag its tail. Many of the public motors, to Brighton, Eastbourne, Windsor, etc., start in this locality. In the Avenue also are the **Constitutional Club** and the **Royal Empire Society** (formerly the Royal Colonial Institute), with a membership of over 16,000, and a library of 250,000 volumes (see p. 29), mostly on Empire subjects. Immediately below Charing Cross terminus is the **Playhouse Theatre.** In Craven Street, the thoroughfare between Northumberland Avenue and Charing Cross Station, *Benjamin Franklin,* "printer, philosopher and statesman," resided. At No. 32 *Heine* resided in 1827.

The Victoria Embankment

(See also pp. 191–2),

colloquially "the Embankment," extends from Westminster Bridge to Blackfriars Bridge, a magnificent curve of nearly a mile and a half. It is one of the finest and most air-swept thoroughfares in the metropolis, with attractive gardens, an always interesting outlook on the river, and the not inconsiderable advantage, when sunny days are few, of a south aspect. The broad roadway provides a favourite route for taxis and motors hastening to and from the City, and there is a constant chain of tramcars from all parts of London. (Buses do not ordinarily use the Embankment, though certain routes include it while Waterloo Bridge is closed to northbound traffic.) The neighbourhood of Charing Cross Bridge is a starting-place for many of the motor-coaches to such places as Brighton, Southend, etc. Formerly at high tide the river flowed right up to where the old York Water Gate (p. 191) still stands, and the area now covered by the Embankment and its gardens was an

Fox Photos, Ltd.,] [*London.*

THE HOUSES OF PARLIAMENT.

THE HOUSES OF PARLIAMENT.

unsightly expanse of mud. This great improvement, for which Londoners have never been sufficiently grateful to the old Metropolitan Board of Works, was effected in 1864–70, at a cost of a million and a half pounds. Owing to the sloppy nature of the subsoil the cost of maintenance is considerable. The granite protecting wall is 8 ft. thick. A mural monument at the foot of Northumberland Avenue worthily commemorates the engineer, *Sir Joseph W. Bazalgette.*

In connection with the Jubilee celebrations of King George V in 1935 it was decided to give the name of **The King's Reach** to the stretch of river between Westminster Bridge and London Bridge.

Throughout its length the Embankment is planted on both sides with plane trees, and seats face the river. Trams skirt the river-side from Westminster Bridge to Blackfriars Bridge, certain of them turning off at Waterloo Bridge to enter the tunnel beneath Aldwych and Kingsway that connects the southern tramway system with the northern. Beneath the Embankment runs the District Railway, with stations at Westminster, Charing Cross, the Temple, and Blackfriars. Close to Charing Cross Railway Bridge the Bakerloo Tube passes beneath the Thames, its Charing Cross Station being below that of the District Railway. On the Embankment, facing Charing Cross Station, is a bronze medallion, by Sir G. Frampton, R.A., of *Sir W. S. Gilbert,* the playwright, whose "foe was folly and his weapon wit."

The Embankment eastward from Charing Cross is described on pp. 191–2.

Turning in the direction of Westminster Bridge, we pass through pretty gardens with numerous statues. A few yards beyond **Montague House,** long the mansion of the Duke of Buccleuch, is a dignified turreted building, in the Scottish Baronial style, known as **New Scotland Yard,** the headquarters, since 1891, of the Metropolitan Police. It is of Dartmoor granite, hewn by convict labour. The name is popularly derived from the fact that on the site of Old Scotland Yard stood a palace belonging to the Kings of Scotland. In order that northern susceptibilities might not be offended, the spot was actually declared to be a part of Scotland and therefore not a possession of the English monarch—an interesting parallel to the modern holding with regard to foreign embassies, etc.

At one time it was proposed to erect a State opera-house on the site, and remains of foundations are still to be seen in the cellars of Scotland Yard.

On the river-side opposite Scotland Yard is a lofty monument forming the **Royal Air Force War Memorial.**

Continuing to Westminster Bridge, we have the *St. Stephen's Club* (Conservative) at the corner. Flanking the bridge is J. L. Thornycroft's fine group showing *Boadicea* in her chariot : those used to handling horses generally look—in vain—for the charioteer's reins.

Westminster Bridge

(**Plan** III. K. 9),

one of the widest and most graceful bridges in Europe, consists of seven low segmental iron arches, supported on granite piers. It is 1,160 ft. long and 85 ft. wide, and was opened in 1862. Wordsworth wrote of the view from the bridge of his day (the Charing Cross railway bridge had not then been built) : "Earth has not anything to show more fair" ; and dull indeed would he be who could fail to admire it now. Looking City-ward we have the noble sweep of the Embankment, lined by green foliage, beyond which rise attractive office and other buildings. Looking from the other side of the bridge (up river) we have to the right the Houses of Parliament, with the famous "Terrace" overlooking the river. Beyond are several huge blocks of offices, including those of the *Imperial Chemical Industries* and *Thames House*. Spanning the river is the new Lambeth Bridge, with Lambeth Palace (pp. 257–8) close at hand, and on the left are the detached buildings of **St. Thomas's Hospital.** The **Albert Embankment** borders the southern bank of the river from Westminster Bridge to Vauxhall Bridge.

On the Surrey side of Westminster Bridge is the—

London County Hall.

(**Admission.** Parts of the Hall are shown on Saturdays from 10.30 to 12, and 1.30 to 3.30. Also on Bank Holidays until 4.30 (except Boxing Day). The public are admitted to the Council meetings on Tuesday afternoons.)

This stately building was opened by King George V in 1922. It is in the English Renaissance style, from designs by *Ralph Knott*. The estimated cost when work was begun in 1909 was nearly a million pounds, but changed conditions brought about by the War raised the expenditure to more than three million pounds. The final section of the building, the northern wing, was completed in 1933, but already schemes are afoot for extensions. Some notes on the London County Council will be found on pp. 24–5.

The principal feature of the interior is the *Council Chamber*, a beautiful hall reached from the main entrance in Belvedere

Road by way of a marble Ceremonial Hall. Between the Chamber and the river are the Members' Library and the offices of important officials. The north and south blocks contain other offices, and on the ground floor is an education library much valued by teachers. An interesting collection of London prints and drawings is generally on view. Both externally and internally the County Hall is a very fine building, worthy of its site and of its functions. A light burns in the flèche whenever the Council is sitting after dark.

During excavations on the site in the summer of 1910 the workmen unearthed a Roman galley, of oak, 50 feet long by 16 feet wide. It is now carefully preserved in the London Museum (see p. 124). From the coins found within, the galley is believed to date from about the end of the third century A.D.

The Houses of Parliament, Westminster Abbey and other buildings hereabouts will require at least a morning to themselves (see p. 96), so we will turn along Bridge Street, past the **Westminster Station** of the District Railway, to the corner of **Parliament Street.** The **Government Offices** at the corner of Parliament Street and Great George Street extend right back to St. James's Park. The blocks fronting Parliament and Great George Streets are occupied by some departments of the **Board of Trade** and the **Ministry of Health.** The **Education Department** is housed in the portion facing King Charles Street.

Proceeding up Parliament Street on the west, or left-hand side, we next reach a fine quadrangle erected 1868–73 from the designs of Sir Gilbert Scott, including the **Home Office, the Colonial** and **Dominions Offices,** the **India Office,** and the **Foreign Office.** Only persons having business are, as a rule, admitted. Derby Street, on the other side of Whitehall, would take us to **New Scotland Yard,** the river front of which we have already seen (p. 77), a remark which applies also to Montague House. In the centre of Whitehall stands that fine symbol of an Empire's sorrow, **The Cenotaph,** inscribed with majestic simplicity, "The Glorious Dead."

The Cenotaph.

(**Plan** III. K. 9.)

This world-famous monument, designed by *Sir Edwin Lutyens, R.A.*, was intended at first merely as a temporary memorial in connection with the Peace Celebrations in July, 1919. Later, in deference to strongly expressed public feeling, it was re-erected in permanent form, "to represent an Imperial Grave of all those citizens of the Empire, of every creed and rank, who gave their lives in the War."

At 11 a.m. on Armistice Day (November 11) in each year the Cenotaph is the scene of a most impressive ceremony, when the King, or his representative, and many of the nation's leaders, together with a great concourse of ordinary folk, stand bareheaded at the shrine for two minutes, while throughout the Kingdom almost perfect silence is maintained, and all traffic is suspended. Large numbers of wreaths are deposited, not only on this occasion, but throughout the year. Every male passer-by will, of course, raise his hat.

We are now opposite historic **Downing Street** (Plan III. K. 9). No. 10, the official residence of the Prime Minister and the usual scene of Cabinet meetings, is a simple mansion of dull brown brick, bearing little outward indication of its importance. Traditionally, the Lord Privy Seal resides in the adjoining house (No. 11), but the rule is not hard and fast, and for some time at least Mr. Baldwin lived at No. 11 while Prime Minister. No. 12 is the Government Whip's Office. At the end of the street steps lead down to **St. James's Park** (see p. 120). A gateway and subway adjoining No. 10, Downing Street bring one out on the Parade Ground behind the Horse Guards. Across Whitehall from Downing Street is **Whitehall Gardens,** one of the old houses in which was from 1873–5 the residence of Benjamin Disraeli, another that of Sir Robert Peel, to which he was brought home to die after falling from his horse on Constitution Hill (1850). During his tenure of office he was accustomed to walk across to Downing Street to transact business, and the late Sir Algernon West related :

> " It is not so very long ago—indeed, I am told as lately as 1893–4—that a charge used to appear in the annual estimates presented to Parliament for a small annuity for the sweeper who kept the crossing clean, so that the Prime Minister should not dirty his boots on his passage from Whitehall to the Treasury."

With reference to what has been said as to the former limits of the river, it is interesting to recall Sir Robert's statement that his " house was built in 1824, and there were formerly steps leading to the river. He remembered that on one occasion, when a boy, preparations were made to remove the family and valuables by boats on the occasion of a threatened attack by a mob on his father's house."

Plans have been prepared for a great new block of buildings on this side of Whitehall, to house the many Government departments now scattered in various houses here and elsewhere in the neighbourhood.

Between Downing Street and the Horse Guards is the long

range of buildings housing the **Treasury,** the **Privy Council,** and other more or less important bodies and functionaries. Dover House is the **Scottish Office.** By a paradox typically British, these buildings, from which the affairs of a mighty Empire are actually administered, display none of the pomp of power, while the **Horse Guards,** now little more than a guard-house for the Household Cavalry, is always in day-time sentinelled by gigantic Life Guards, whose appearance is calculated to excite awe and admiration in all beholders. The two mounted sentries at the gate are relieved every hour. The ceremony is not uninteresting, but a far more imposing spectacle is provided at a little before 11 every morning (Sundays, 10), when the operation of **Changing the Guard** takes place, and at 4 p.m. when the Guard is inspected. Readers of W. E. Henley will recall the lines on *The Lifeguardsman* :

> " He wears his inches weightily, as he wears
> His old-world armour ; and with his port and pride,
> His sturdy graces and enormous airs,
> He towers, in speech his Colonel countrified,
> A triumph, waxing statelier year by year,
> Of British blood and bone and beef and beer."

The old stone building, dating from 1758, stands on the site of the tiltyard of Westminster, so renowned in the courtly annals of Tudor times. A passage under the picturesque clock tower gives access to **St. James's Park,** and is much frequented by foot-passengers, but only royalty and a few privileged persons on the Lord Chamberlain's list are allowed to drive through.

The **Parade Ground** behind, the largest " clear " space in London, is the scene of the **Trooping of the Colour** on the King's birthday. Here are *Statues of Field-Marshal Earl Kitchener of Khartoum* (John Tweed), *Field-Marshal Viscount Wolseley* (Goscombe John, R.A.), and *Field-Marshal Lord Roberts*. On the western side is the **Guards Division Memorial,** unveiled by H.R.H. the Duke of Connaught in memory of the 14,000 Guardsmen who laid down their lives during the Great War. " Never have soldiers more nobly done their duty."

The quadrangular pile, with cupolas, to the north of the Parade Ground, is the **Admiralty.** The wireless aerials above may almost be described as a " nerve centre " of the British Empire, for they provide direct communication with warships, even in far-distant seas. At the corner of this building is a graceful memorial, designed by *Sir Edwin Lutyens, R.A.*, to the officers and other ranks of the *Royal Naval Division* who fell in the Great War. Another Admiralty block is at the eastern end of the

Mall, with residences for the First Lord and the First Sea Lord. Here is the fine triple **Archway** (see p. 75) through which State processions pass between Buckingham Palace and Westminster. The handsome wrought-iron and bronze gates were designed by Sir Aston Webb, P.R.A. The rooms over the Arch house the valuable *Admiralty Library*, containing many rare naval books of all periods and an interesting collection of old signal books.

Facing Whitehall, and separated from the Horse Guards only by the dingy building which serves as the **Paymaster-General's Office,** is the **Old Admiralty**—not so very old after all, but few people ever think that almost down to Nelson's time the business of our great Navy was conducted in the City, in Mark Lane and Crutched Friars to be precise (see Pepys' immortal *Diary*). The earliest letter of Nelson's which has been preserved is dated from the Navy Office, Crutched Friars, April 14, 1777 (see p. 241).

Emerging from the Horse Guards, we cross Whitehall to the **Royal United Service Institution.** It might be described as an annexe of the Whitehall Banqueting Hall, were it not the fact that the Hall is rather, in its present uses, an annexe of the Institution. The Royal United was founded in 1830, and has a membership of about 5,500, comprising both services.

The **Whitehall Banqueting Hall** is the only completed portion of the palace intended by successive monarchs to replace York House, the famous residence of Wolsey, which was appropriated by Henry VIII on the downfall of his former favourite.

The outbreak of the Civil War prevented the completion of the grand design of Inigo Jones, who projected a palace which should occupy a site of twenty-four acres, extending from the river to St. James's Park. The Court was held at Whitehall from the reign of Henry VIII, who died here, to that of William III. From an opening made in the wall Charles I stepped to the scaffold on the memorable 30th of January, 1649. A tablet below the lower central window records the fact. On the inner side of the window are displayed the gloves handed by Charles to Bishop Juxon as he stood on the scaffold. Afterwards Cromwell kept Court in the old palace, with John Milton as his secretary, and here he died. Here, too, Charles II died, and his brother, James II, lived, till one night he stole quietly away and England had a new king in William of Orange. The Palace was burned down in 1698, the fire sparing only the portion reared by Inigo Jones, and from that time "our Palace of St. James's" has been the official royal residence. The Hall was long used as a Chapel Royal, though apparently never consecrated, but in 1893 it was given by Queen Victoria to the Royal United Service Institution, in order to house the—

Royal United Service Museum.

(**Plan** III. K. 9.)

Admission, 1*s*. Open daily, Sundays excepted, from 10 a.m. to 5 p.m. Wednesdays and Saturdays after noon, 6*d*. Soldiers, sailors and Royal Air Force in uniform free.

Nearest Stations.—Trafalgar Square (Bakerloo Tube); Strand (Morden Edgware Line); Westminster (District).

The Museum, which no one should miss seeing, contains a large number of national trophies and mementoes, ranging from the earliest times of an Empire which, in the words of the soldier's poet, has been " Built with the sword and the flame, and salted down with our bones "—from a Saxon shield to trophies of the Great War.

Entering, we pass at once up a short flight of stairs, lined with weapons and curios, to the **Banqueting Hall,** a superb specimen of the Later Renaissance, with a ceiling, painted on canvas by Rubens and restored in 1907, representing the apotheosis of James I.

There are models of the Battle of Waterloo and of the Battle of Trafalgar, the latter standing on a table made of oak from the *Victory*; and Chantrey's bust of Nelson is perched on part of the mainmast of the same famous vessel. Glass cases contain relics of such national heroes as Drake, Raleigh, Nelson and Wellington.

In the *Basement*, or Crypt, are placed the heavy exhibits, ancient and modern cannon, shells, torpedoes, Zeppelin and submarine relics, and some German arms and equipment. Very beautiful, too, are the models of warships. Recently there have been added a number of models and dioramas illustrating famous battles, aircraft, etc.

The **War Office** occupies the whole of the irregular quadrangle between Whitehall Place and Horse Guards Avenue, and extends back to Whitehall Court. It is built of Portland stone, with groups of Ionic pillars and four circular flanking towers, 156 feet high, which mask the architectural difficulty arising from the fact that not one of the corners is a right angle. The block contains 1,000 rooms, and there are 2½ miles of corridors. In the centre of the Whitehall roadway, opposite the War Office, is appropriately placed a lofty equestrian *Statue of the Duke of Cambridge*, for nearly fifty years Commander-in-Chief of the British Army.

Then we pass Great Scotland Yard, the former headquarters of the Metropolitan Police. Here are the **Central London Recruit-**

ing Depôt and the **Admiralty Recruiting Depôt.** Across Whitehall is the **Whitehall Theatre.**

We have now reached again the starting-point of our ramble at Trafalgar Square, and shall perhaps be disposed to utilize a spare hour in gaining a superficial acquaintance with the pictures in our great national collection. A whole morning or afternoon will hardly suffice to see them properly.

The National Gallery.

Plan III. K. 8.

Admission.—Free on Mondays, Tuesdays, Wednesdays, 10 to 8, Saturdays, 10 to 5 and on Sundays from 2 to 5.

Sixpence on Thursdays and Fridays (10 till 5). Closed on Christmas Eve, Christmas Day and Good Friday.

Catalogues, arranged in alphabetical order of painters' names, and with biographical notices, 1*s*. 6*d*. Copies may be hired, 3*d*. (deposit, 1*s*. 6*d*.).

Lectures (free) Mondays, Wednesdays, Thursdays and Fridays 11 a.m. to 1 p.m.; Tuesdays 12 to 2 p.m.; Saturdays 2 to 4 p.m.; Wednesday evenings, 6.30 to 7.30. Other lectures may be arranged by written application to the Lecturer, the Secretary's Office, National Gallery, W.C.2.

Nearest Stations.—Trafalgar Square (Bakerloo Tube), Strand (Morden–Edgware line), Charing Cross (Southern and District Railways).

Buses.—With the exception of services using the Holborn and Oxford Street route, nearly all the principal bus routes pass through Trafalgar Square.

The National Gallery had its origin in the purchase, in 1824, by Lord Liverpool's Government, of the Angerstein collection of thirty-eight pictures. The building, erected 1832–8, has a length of 460 ft., but is spoilt architecturally by the low elevation and the insignificant dome and "pepper-box" turrets. At first both the national collection and the pictures of the Royal Academy were housed here, but the collection had grown so by 1869 that the Academy had to migrate to Burlington House, and in 1896 the Tate Gallery (p. 117) was built to house the National Collections of British Art, though there is a representative display in Rooms XXII–XXV of the building we are about to enter. Various additions have since been made, the latest being the Duveen Room and a room to contain the splendid Mond Bequest. Hardly less important in the public estimation was the introduction, in 1935, of artificial lighting, enabling the gallery to be kept open during the evening.

The most important presentations, bequests and purchases have been the Vernon Collection (1847), the Turner Collection (1856), the Peel Collection (1871), the Wynn Ellis Collection (1876), the Vaughan Collection (1900), the Cohen Collection (1906), the Salting Collection (1910), the Carlisle Collection (1913), the Wertheimer Bequest of nine portraits by J. S. Sargent (1923), and the Mond and Phillips bequests (1924). Notable acquisitions have been the "Rokeby" Velazquez, 2057. "Venus and Cupid," presented by the National Art-Collections Fund; 2285. The large Family Group by Frans Hals, bought for £25,000; 2457. "The Duchess of Milan," by Holbein, bought by the National Art-Collections Fund, aided by a grant from the Treasury, for £72,000; 2790. "The Adoration of the Kings," by

Gossaert of Mabuse, known as "The Castle Howard Mabuse," bought for £40,000. In 1918 several fine examples of nineteenth-century French art were acquired. In 1922 Van Dyck's "George Villiers, 2nd Duke of Buckingham, and his brother" was acquired. In 1929 the Titian family group known as the "Cornaro Titian" was bought for £122,000, and the world-renowned Wilton Diptych secured for £90,000. With the aid of the National Art-Collections Fund Rubens's "Watering Place" was acquired in 1936.

The National Collection now includes over 3,300 works, of which about one-third, being pictures by modern British artists (from the eighteenth century onwards), must be sought at the Tate Gallery, at Millbank (see p. 117). At the Tate Gallery also are displayed nearly all the Turner pictures, except those mentioned on p. 91, and the Wertheimer Sargents. Though still, as regards the number of its masterpieces, inferior to some of the great Continental collections, the National Gallery is quite unequalled as a representative collection of the various schools of painting. It is especially rich in examples of the Italian and Dutch schools. "The particular and special value of the National Gallery among European galleries depends largely upon the unique collection and comprehensive sequence of finished and unfinished works and studies by Turner, England's greatest artist, who is also the greatest landscape painter of the world."

Catalogues, with biographical notes, are on sale at the entrance, but the inscriptions on the pictures themselves, giving name and school of painter, dates of birth and death, and title, sufficiently serve the purpose of the general visitor.

In the vestibules are a series of mosaics illustrating various aspects of modern life and including portraits of film stars, footballers and other figures.

The centre of the Gallery is occupied by the Italian Schools, but these have already overflowed into neighbouring rooms, necessitating some retracing of steps if one desires to follow, room by room, the development of Italian art. The West Wing (to the *left* of the entrance) is chiefly devoted to the French and British Schools. The corresponding rooms in the East Wing (to the *right* of the entrance) are occupied by the Spanish, Flemish, and Dutch Schools.

Rooms I–IX, XI, XVI, XXVI–XXIX and the Duveen Room. Italian Schools.

Rooms X, XII, XIII, XIV, XV. Dutch and Flemish School.

Rooms XVII, XVIII. Spanish School.

Room XIX. German School.

Rooms XX and XXI. French School.

Rooms XXII, XXIII, XXIV, XXV. British School.

Space will not permit the enumeration of every picture in this wonderful collection—the note of which, it should be remembered, is the consecutive history of painting. We indicate some of the more important works; the attendants will readily furnish information regarding the positions of other pictures.

Early Italian Schools.—The visitor who has not been initiated into the history of pictorial art will probably be at first not a little puzzled to discover what interest attaches to many of the paintings of the earlier Italian schools. Some of the pictures—stiff, angular, devoid of proportion and perspective—appear grotesque and even ludicrous; but they enable the student to trace the development of mediæval art from its crude beginnings to the wonderful perfection attained in the palmy days of Italian artistic supremacy, when "the canvas glowed beyond e'en nature warm," and the works of such painters as Raphael, Michelangelo, Titian, and their compeers were looked upon as holding a place among the wonders of the world. After the fall of Rome, Constantinople became the centre of civilization and culture. The Byzantine school of painting was hard and stiff. There was no attempt at a faithful rendering of nature in form or colour, of the representation of rounded surfaces nor of distance by the use of perspective. After the conquest of Constantinople by the Latins in 1204, Byzantine artists were transplanted to Italy, and painting slowly emancipated itself from the trammels of the Byzantine school. Gradually the range of subjects embraced widened and increased, and classical, mythological and historical scenes employed the pencils of the Italian painters.

On the walls of **Room I** notice 583. "Rout of San Romano," *Uccello* (1397–1475); 292. "Martyrdom of St. Sebastian, *A. Pollaiulo* (1432–1498). 665. "The Baptism," and 908. "The Nativity," *P. della Francesca* (1416–1492).

Room III, to the right, has an interesting series by *Lorenzo Monaco* (1370–1425).

Return to Room I and so to **Room V.** Note altar-piece by *Sassetta* (1392–1450) representing the life of St. Francis.

Room VI is devoted to the Venetian School XV–XVI century. Note several splendid *Bellinis,* including (189) the famous "Portrait of the Doge Leonardo Loredano, in his State Robes," 280, "Madonna and Child," etc. This latter picture is generally called the "Madonna of the Pomegranate," from the fruit in the hand of the Virgin. 902. "Triumph of Scipio," *Andrea Mantegna* (1431–1506).

At the west end of Room VI is the new **Duveen Room,** containing earlier pictures of the Italian school. It cannot be said that the lighting experiment is entirely successful. 629. "Madonna and Child Enthroned," *L. Costa* (1460–1535); 739. "The Annunciation," *Crivelli* (1430–93), and 788. The Demidoff Altarpiece; 1093. "The Virgin of the Rocks," *Leonardo da Vinci* (1452–1519); 274. "Virgin and Child and St. John the Baptist," *Andrea Mantegna* (1431–1506).

In a new room opening out of Room VI on the north is displayed the splendid collection forming the greater part of the **Mond Bequest.** Particularly notable are 3943. "The Cruci-

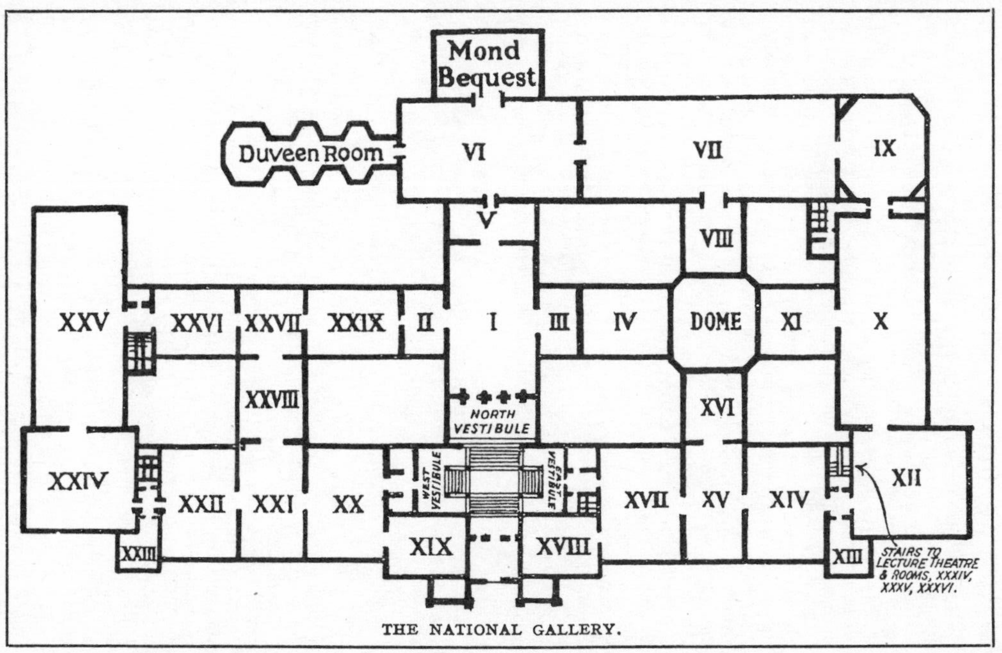

THE NATIONAL GALLERY.

fixion," *Raphael*; 3914. "Adoration of the Child," *Fra Bartollomeo*; 3918, 3919. "Life and Miracles of St. Zenobius," *Botticelli* (1444–1510); 3947. "St. Jerome," *Sodoma* (1477–1594); 3948. "Mother and Child," *Titian*.

Room VII. Later Venetian School.—The characteristic of the Venetian painters is their predilection for gorgeous and magnificent scenes; nature adorned with the highest brilliancy of colour. "They are especially fond of saints who have been cardinals, because of their red hats, and they sunburn all their hermits into splendid russet-brown." Then, also, it has been rightly observed that they had before them the colour of Venice, "that melodrama of flame, and gold, and rose, and orange, and azure, which the skies and lagoons of Venice yield almost daily to the eye." Among the gems of this school is: 35. "Bacchus and Ariadne," *Titian* (1477–1576). Living to the great age of ninety-nine years, Titian is distinguished alike for the greatness of his achievements and the length of his career. He was one of those fortunate painters whose merits were fully recognized in their own time. He was the friend and companion of princes and kings; and it is recorded that Francis I., visiting his studio, did not disdain to stoop to pick up the pencil the aged master had let fall. Note 4452. "The Cornaro Family," acquired in 1929 for the sum of £122,000. Another of his works, the famous 1944. "Portrait of Ariosto," was acquired in 1904 for £30,000. Note 4. "The Holy Family Adoring," and 34. "Venus and Adonis," both by *Titian*, also *Titian* 4222. "The Trinity Receiving Charles V." "The Origin of the Milky Way," *Il Tintoretto* (1518–1594). 1041. "The Vision of St. Helena," and 268. "Adoration of the Magi," both by *Paolo Veronese* (1528–1588). 294. "The Family of Darius," *P. Veronese*, and other large works by the same artist. "Raising of Lazarus," *Sebastiano del Piombo* (1485–1547). Here also are (697) *Moroni's* famous "Portrait of a Tailor" and other portraits from the same brush.

Room IX—18th-century Venetian artists—is notable for examples of *Canaletto* (1697–1768).

Rooms X, XII, XIII, XIV and XV. Dutch and Flemish.—The distinguishing features of this school are the strict fidelity to nature, wonderfully accurate delineations of real life, and marvellous preservation and freshness of the works after centuries. Notice especially the works of Rembrandt, Rubens, Ruisdael, Jan Vermeer, Peter de Hooch, Cuyp, P. Potter, and Van Dyck.

In Room X are 3679. *Honthorst's* "Christ before Pilate," and 289. *Lundens's* copy [1] of *Rembrandt's* famous "Night Watch."

[1] This copy was painted in 1660 for Captain Frans Banning Cocq, the central figure in the original picture. The original of "The Night Watch" was ruthlessly cut down in the eighteenth century that it might the better fit a room to which it had been removed. The small copy by Lundens is therefore of considerable interest as showing the picture as it was originally painted.

From Room X we enter **Room XI,** with (179–180) *Francia's* altar-piece, "Virgin and Child."

Two self-portraits and other famous works by *Rembrandt* (1606–1669) will be found in Room XII—775. "Portrait of an Old Lady"; 45. "Woman taken in Adultery"; 54. "Woman Bathing"; 1674. "Portrait of a Burgomaster." Here, too, are 4042. "Man in Fur Cap," *Carel Fabritius*; 830. the world-famous "Avenue," *Hobbema* (1638–1700); 835. "Court of a Dutch House," and other works by *P. de Hooch*; 2528. "Man with a Glove," *Franz Hals* (1580–1666). In Room XII is an interesting "peepshow" of a Dutch Interior by *S. van Hoogstraten* (1626–78).

The small Room XIII contains some interesting religious works of the Flemish school.

From this point a staircase (lined with water-colours by *J. M. W. Turner*) leads to the **Lecture Theatre** and **Rooms XXXIV–XXXVI,** with further examples of the Dutch School.

Among the wonderful Rubens pictures in Room XIV note 852. "Chapeau de Poil"; 59. "The Brazen Serpent"; 853. "Triumph of Silenus"; 194. "Judgment of Paris"; 38. "Abduction of the Sabine Women"; 46. "Blessings of Peace." *Van Dyck* (1599–1641) is represented by 49. "Portrait of an Artist"; 50. "The Emperor Theodosius," and 3011. "Lady and Child."

Room XV contains: 186. "Portraits of John Arnolfini and his Wife," *Jan van Eyck* (1390–1441); 1045. wing of an altar-piece: "A Canon and his Patron Saints," *Gheeraert David* (1461–1523); 2790. "The Adoration of the Kings," *Mabuse* (1470–1541), known as "The Castle Howard Mabuse." 3556. "Adoration of the Kings," *Pieter Brueghel* (1525–69), and 3664. "Virgin and Child with SS. Catherine and Barbara," *Q. Massys*. 944. "Two Usurers," *M. van Reymerswael*. Here too is "The Crowning with Thorns," *Jerome Bosch* (1613–1660).

In **Room XVI** the place of honour is occupied by 1847. *Signorelli's* "Madonna and Child, with Saints."

Rooms XVII and XVIII. Spanish School. The National Gallery possesses many of the greatest works of Velazquez and Murillo, and has lately acquired some characteristic examples of El Greco. 1129. "Philip IV of Spain," 1148. "Christ at the Column," and 2057. "Venus and Cupid" (The Rokeby Venus), all by *Velazquez* (1599–1660). 1457. "Christ driving the Traders from the Temple"; 3476. "The Agony in the Garden," *El Greco*, 1473. "Dona Isabel Cobos," by *Goya*. In the smaller Room XVIII, 13. *Murillo's* "Holy Family" (1617–1682).

From Room XVII we pass to the Vestibules and may spend a few moments endeavouring to identify the various well-known sportsmen, artists, film-stars, etc., who figure in the mosaics. At the top of the steps is *Van Dyck's* great portrait of Charles I, painted for Charles at his Court. " One remembers only, in looking upon this picture of him, Charles's graces, not his faults." Here, too, is 3605. *Van Dyck's* " George and Frederick Villiers." In the west vestibule are such well-known works as 1030. *Morland's* " Interior of a Stable " ; 78A. *Reynolds's* " Holy Family " ; 498. " Dido Building Carthage," *Turner*, and several landscapes by *Claude*.

From the West Vestibule enter Room XX, in which at once turn left to **Room XIX,** where we encounter interesting examples of the German School. The principal are : 1938. *Durer's* " Portrait of his Father " and *Holbein's* " Ambassadors " (1314) and his " Duchess of Milan " [1] (2475).

Rooms XX and XXI are devoted to works of the **French School.**

In Room XX are canvases by *Claude* (Gellée, 1600–1682), and the *Poussins* (Nicholas, 1594–1665, and Gaspard (Dughet), 1613–1675). 30. " Seaport : the Embarkation of St. Ursula," and other pictures by *Claude*. 1449. " Cardinal Richelieu," *Philippe de Champaigne* (1602–1674), is a replica of that in the Louvre.

In recent years a number of valuable pictures by modern French artists have been added to the national collection. The greater number are shown at the Tate Gallery (p. 117), but here, in Room XXI, Manet (1832–1883) is worthily represented by the " Bar aux Folies Bergères " and 3294. " A Soldier " ; *Cezanne* perhaps less worthily by " Montagne Sainte Victoire." Well known are 1952. " Mr. and Mrs. Edwards " *Fantin-Latour* (1836–1904) and 1653. " Self Portrait," *Madame Vigée le Brun*. A recent acquisition is 4821. " Madame Moitessier," *Ingres*. The much reproduced heads of *Greuze* (1725–1805) will call for notice, but connoisseurs will be more interested in the precious " Four Ages of Man " (101–104), by *Nicholas Lancret* (1690–1743).

Room XXVIII is devoted to the small but valuable collection of pictures loaned by Mr. C. S. Gulbenkian.

Rooms XXII–XXV contain representative examples of the **British School,** but the greater number of British works in the national collection are at the Tate Gallery (see p. 117).

In Room XXII note 3420. " Nocturne," *J. M. Whistler* ; 615. *Frith's* " Derby Day " ; 1394. " Christ Washing Peter's Feet," *Ford Madox Brown* ; 1272. " The Cenotaph " ; 1207. " The Hay Wain " ; 130. " The Cornfield " ; 1273. " Flatford Mill "—all by *Constable*.

Room XXIV is notable for its landscapes, including several fine Turners. At his death *J. M. W. Turner* (1775–1851) left all his pictures to the National Gallery, " provided that a room

[1] Holbein's " Duchess of Milan," after being on loan to the National Gallery for thirty years, was suddenly offered for sale by the late Duke of Norfolk. It was saved for the nation at the last moment by an English lady abroad, who gave £40,000 on condition that her name should never be revealed to the public. It was found that the sum amounted to a third of her fortune.

or rooms be added to the present National Gallery, to be, when erected, called Turner's Gallery." By far the greater number of the master's works, numbering in all over five hundred, will be found at the Tate Gallery (see p. 118), but here he is worthily represented by some of his most gorgeous and characteristic canvases. 481. "Spithead, Boat's Crew recovering an Anchor"; 472. "Calais Pier"; 508. "Ulysses and Polyphemus"; 538. "Rain, Steam and Speed"; 1988. "Petworth Interior"; 535. "The *Sun of Venice* going to Sea"; 524. "The Fighting *Téméraire.*"

Note 926. "Windmill on Mousehold Heath"; 2694. "The Poringland Oak" and other examples of *Crome*; also 5247. "Queen Charlotte"; 129. "J. J. Angerstein" (whose art collection formed the nucleus of the National Gallery); 785. "Mrs. Siddons," all by Sir T. Lawrence.

The large Room XXV is principally devoted to portraits. *Gainsborough:* 3812 and 1811. "The Painter's Daughters"; 683. the famous portrait of Mrs. Siddons; 1283. "View of Dedham," 2284. "The Bridge," 80. "The Market Cart," and other landscapes. The many *Romneys* speak for themselves. Note also *Reynolds's* (111) "Lord Heathfield," (79) "The Three Graces"; (307) "The Age of Innocence," and (182) "Heads of Angels." See also 4756. "The Graham Children," 1962. "The Shrimp Girl," and 1374. "Hogarth's Servants," *Hogarth* (1697–1764).

From Room XXV we pass by Rooms XXVI, XXVII, XXIX, devoted to the Italian School.

Room XXVI. 1171. "The Virgin and Child, attended by St. John the Baptist and St. Nicholas of Bari," *Raphael* (1483–1520). This picture is commonly known as the **Ansidei Madonna,** from the Ansidei family of Perugia, for whom it was painted. It was purchased from the Duke of Marlborough in 1885 for £70,000, and is one of the greatest pictures in the world. Raphael Sanzio, of Urbino, was remarkable alike for his prodigious genius and his wonderful activity. Dying at the early age of thirty-seven, he yet lived long enough to enrich the world with many masterpieces and to win for himself the foremost place in Italian art. Here, too, are Raphael's 744. "Madonna, Child and St. John," 2919. his "Procession to Calvary" and the small 213. "Vision of a Knight"; 690. "Portrait of a Sculptor," by *A. del Sarto,* the artist himself; *Correggio's* 10. "Mercury instructing Cupid," and 15. "Ecce Homo"; 790. the unfinished "Entombment," by *Michelangelo*; 651. "Venus, Cupid, Folly and Time," *Bronzino.*

In **Room XXVII** are 2923. "The Three Maries," *A. Carracci* (1560–1609); 193. "Lot and his Daughters," *G. Reni* (1575–1642); 172. "Christ at Emmaus," *Caravaggio* (1569–1609).

Room XXIX. 698. "Death of Procris," *Piero di Cosimo* (1461–1521); 592. "Adoration of the Magi," *Botticelli* (1444–

1510); 666. "The Annunciation," *Filippo Lippi* (1406–69); 727, 3162, 3230, 4428. altar-piece by F. Pesellino (1422–57). For many years the component parts of this great work were scattered in various countries; skilful and painstaking research led to the reassembly in 1929.

Occupying pride of place in **Room II,** to which we now pass, is the glass case containing the Wilton Diptych, acquired in 1929 at a cost of £90,000. The main subject shows King Richard II, introduced by St. John the Baptist, in adoration before the Mother and Child. In this room, too, are 663. *Fra Angelico* (1387–1455), "Christ Surrounded by Angels, Patriarchs, etc."; 591. "The Rape of Helen," *Gozzoli* (1420–1498).

Leaving the National Gallery (note the fig-trees flourishing in the gardens), we turn to the left, passing the copy of Houdon's statue of *Washington*, presented by the State of Virginia. It is dwarfed by its surroundings, and a more suitable site should be found. We turn to the left at the corner opposite the Church of **St. Martin's-in-the-Fields** (see pp. 74–5), and make our way to the National Portrait Gallery. Facing the entrance to the Gallery is a much-discussed statue of Nurse Cavell (see p. 130).

The National Portrait Gallery.

Plan III. K. 8.
Access.—See National Gallery, p. 84.
Admission.—The days and hours are exactly the same as for the National Gallery (see p. 84).
Lectures daily at 3 p.m.
Lift to all floors.

The building, in the Italian style, was opened in 1896, and cost £96,000, of which £80,000 was a gift to the nation for the purpose from W. H. Alexander. Thanks to a handsome offer from Lord Duveen, a much-needed extension was made in 1933. The collection comprises about 1,900 portraits of eminent men and women of all ranks and ages. Royal personages, statesmen, poets, judges, writers, scientists, warriors, actors, all who have played a part in national history are represented. The word "portrait" is read in its widest sense, for not only does the collection include paintings, drawings and photographs, but numerous presentments in bronze and marble as well. There are also many cases containing medals, specimens of handwriting, autographs and other personal relics. The Gallery comprises three floors and a basement. Generally speaking, the works downstairs are shown in groups, while those on the upper floors are arranged in chronological order. From the artistic point of view, the works in the earlier rooms, by Van Dyck, Kneller, Zuchero, Gainsborough, Romney, etc., are of most interest. Apart from the fine series by G. F. Watts, the portraits of the Victorian era are commonplace in comparison.

It is best to take the lift to the top floor at once, and commence with No. 1, opening out of Room 7. The contents of the rooms may be summarized as follows :—

Top Floor.

Room 1. **Tudor and Stuart Room.**—Henry VII., Henry VIII., Wolsey, Anne Boleyn, Queen Elizabeth, Essex, Leicester, Raleigh, etc.

Room 2 **Literary.**—The Chandos Shakespeare, Ben Jonson, etc.

Room 3. **Early Stuarts.**—James I., George Villiers, Duke of Buckingham, Francis Bacon, etc.

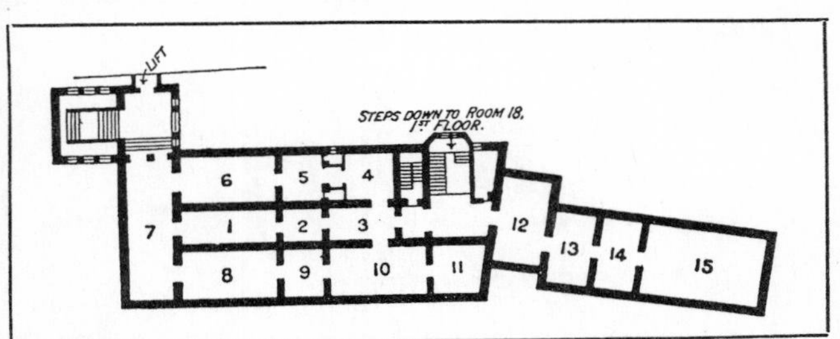

TOP FLOOR.

Room 4. **James I. and Charles I.**—Children of Charles I., Inigo Jones, Interior of Old Somerset House, London, etc.

Room 5. **The Civil War.** Oliver Cromwell, Sir Thomas Fairfax, John Hampden, John Milton, Izaak Walton, etc.

Room 6. **Charles II.**—Catherine of Braganza, Monmouth, Nell Gwynne, Bunyan, Pepys, etc.

Room 7. **James II and William III.**—Isaac Newton, Wren, William Russell, etc.

Room 8. **18th Century.**—Thornhill, Marlborough, Addison, Swift, Robert Walpole, etc.

Room 9. **George I. and George II.**—Wesley, Hans Sloane, Handel, Pope, etc.

Room 10. **18th Century.**—Warren Hastings, Pitt, Washington, Fox, Wellington, Nelson, Clive, etc.

Room 11. **Art and Literature, Science, etc.**—Reynolds, Mrs. Siddons, Romney, Sheridan, Goldsmith, Burns, Dr. Johnson, David Garrick, Capt. Cook, James Watt.

Room 12 (in new wing). George IV, the old House of Commons in 1793, House of Lords in 1829, etc.

Room 13. 18th Century Generals.—Wellington, Moore, Napier, etc.

Rooms 14 and 15. Mid-18th Century leaders of political and religious life.

Steps near the entrance to Room 12 lead down to the First Floor, at the long gallery known as Rooms 17–18. Turn left to **Rooms 24–8**, in the new wing; with busts and paintings of "the leading figures in arts, letters and science in the 18th century."

Return to the staircase and then inspect the long gallery already referred to, its walls covered with 17th–19th century drawings.

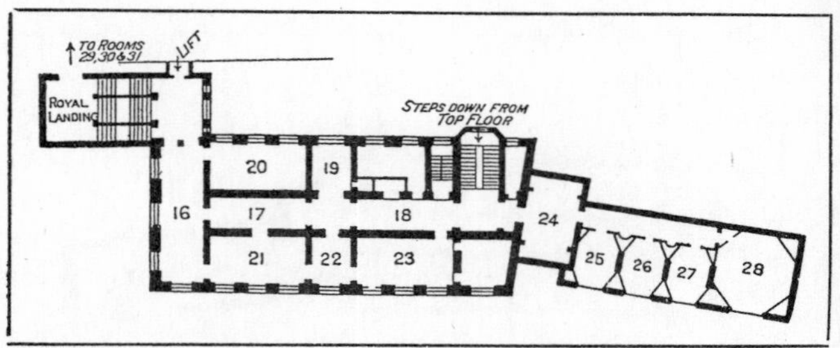

FIRST FLOOR.

Room 20. British Artists, 1800–1860.

From **Room 16**, used for the display of recent acquisitions, pass to the main staircase and descend a short flight of steps to the **Royal Landing,** with portraits of members of the Royal Family.

Rooms 29, 30 and 31, opening from this landing, illustrate respectively the Literature, Science and Art of the 19th Century.

Regain the landing and descend to the **Ground Floor,** where on the right is Room 32, with a good view of the two large groups of War-time generals and admirals displayed in Room 38. At the end of the room opposite is Sir James Cathcart's large canvas, "Some Statesmen of the Great War."

The walls of Rooms 32 and 33 are hung with portraits of writers, artists and leaders of the 19th century.

WESTMINSTER.

ROUTE II.—WESTMINSTER—THE HOUSES OF PARLIAMENT—ST. MARGARET'S CHURCH—WESTMINSTER ABBEY—THE ROMAN CATHOLIC CATHEDRAL—THE TATE GALLERY.

THE present **City of Westminster**—constituted a municipality in 1900, though it has been a city by royal charter for centuries—extends from the river to Oxford Street, and from Temple Bar to Kensington. In this excursion we shall only traverse a small part of it. Westminster, the reader should remember, was a busy spot long before London had being. Hemmed in to the east and west, the river here spread in a wide and shallow stream, near the north brink of which was a small eyot, overgrown with briars and brushwood, known as Thorney Island, or the Isle of Brambles. As it was impossible to cross the river with safety for miles on either side, the Britons established a ford at this point, and built houses for the accommodation of travellers, and marts at which they might obtain necessaries. The Romans, following their example, brought the main roads, Watling and Dover Streets, into connection with the ford, a reminder of which we still have in the adjacent Horseferry Road.

We will assume that the round, which will occupy a full day, is begun at **Westminster Bridge** (p. 78), in the shadow of "Big Ben." Across the river is the long façade of the **London County Hall** (p. 78). Walking a few yards westward, to the corner of Parliament Street, we have on our left one of the most striking and picturesque scenes in the Metropolis, or, indeed, in any capital. On the left are Westminster Hall and the stately Houses of Parliament, with their fretted pinnacles; to the south is the venerable Abbey, partly hidden by St. Margaret's Church, the greyness of the stone set off by the smooth green lawns of **Parliament Square.** Beyond the trees on the far side of the Square is the Middlesex Guildhall. Wheeled traffic passes through this busy Square on the gyratory or "roundabout" system.

Here are statues of *Lord Palmerston* (1865), the *Earl of Derby* (1869), *Sir Robert Peel* (1850), *George Canning* (1827), and *Lord Beaconsfield* (1881), the last-named always fondly decked with flowers and wreaths on Primrose Day (19th April). Here also is a statue of *President Lincoln*, by Gaudens. Against Westminster Hall is a fine statue of *Oliver Cromwell* (1658), by Thornycroft.

In the shadow of the tall Clock Tower is **New Palace Yard,** the quadrangle from which Members enter the Houses of Parliament. It was one of the two courtyards of the old Palace of Westminster built by Edward the Confessor and occupied by the sovereign of England until Henry VIII. took possession of Whitehall. **Old Palace Yard,** between the Abbey and the Houses of Parliament, to which we must make our way to secure admission to the present legislative chambers, was another courtyard of the Palace, though its identity has almost been lost in the roadway.

The Houses of Parliament.

Plan III. K. 9 and 10.

Admission.—The Palace of Westminster is open to the general public on Saturdays, Easter Monday and Tuesday, Whit Monday and Tuesday and August Bank Holiday, providing the Houses of Parliament are not sitting on these days. Entrance by the Norman Porch adjoining Victoria Tower from 10 a.m. to 3.30 p.m.

Strangers' Galleries.—When Parliament is sitting, persons of either sex desirous of listening to the debates in the House of Commons can gain admission to the Members' Gallery (should there be any vacant seats), after 4.15 p.m. (11.15 a.m. on Fridays), by applying at the Admission Order Office in St. Stephen's Hall. To ensure admission on any important occasion, it is advisable to apply to a Member for an *Order in Advance.* These are balloted for six days beforehand, and must be signed by a Member and bear the name and address of the holder.

Admission to the *Special Gallery* and *Under the Gallery* is only granted on the personal application of a Member to the Serjeant at Arms.

Foreigners desirous of listening to a debate should apply to their Embassy or Legation.

Ladies' Gallery.—The seats are balloted for, two orders being sent to each successful Member. The orders must be signed by the Member, and the names and addresses of the ladies must be filled in before admission. Supplemental orders for the Ladies' Gallery, if there is room, are issued by the Serjeant at Arms after 4.15 p.m. or 8.5 p.m., and after 11.15 p.m. on Fridays. The famous *Grille* was removed in 1917. Ladies can now also gain admission to the Members' Gallery (see above).

The House usually meets at 2.45 p.m. and rises at 11 p.m. (Friday 11 a.m. to 4 p.m.). Under the present rules of procedure, "all-night sittings" are much rarer than in the past. When the House of Lords is sitting as a Court of Appeal no order for admission is necessary.

Nearest Station.—Westminster (District).

Buses on Victoria–Trafalgar Square routes, or running over Westminster Bridge, pass through Parliament Square.

Tramways.—Trams to Westminster Bridge.

St. Stephen's Chapel, built by Edward III., was for centuries the meeting-place of the House of Commons—a fact which explains the still frequent allusions to "St. Stephen's." The old building having been destroyed by fire in 1834, designs were invited for a new structure, and of the ninety-seven sent in that of *Barry* was selected, the first stone being laid in 1840, and the building completed in 1857. The House of Lords was used for the first time on the 15th April, 1847, the House of Commons at the commencement of the 1852 Session. The building is in the richest Gothic style (Tudor or Perpendicular), and occupies an area of 8 acres. It contains 11 courts or quadrangles, and cost £3,000,000. The principal façade, overlooking the river, is 940 ft. in length. Unfortunately, the external stone (magnesian limestone) is too soft for the climate, and extensive repairs have become necessary.

The **Clock Tower,** overlooking Westminster Bridge, is 316 ft. high and 40 ft. square. When the House is sitting a light is shown from the Clock Tower by night, and a Union Jack flies from the Victoria Tower by day.

The **Clock,** which has four dials, each 22½ ft. in diameter, was constructed by Dents, under the direction of the late Lord Grimthorpe. It is one of the finest timekeepers in the world. The minute hands are 14 ft. long, the hour hands 9 ft.; the figures are 2 ft. long, and the minute spaces one foot square. The hours are struck on the famous **Big Ben,** so named in compliment to Sir Benjamin Hall, First Commissioner of Works at the time the bell was cast. It weighs 13½ tons, and in calm weather its resonant note may be heard over the greater part of London. Wireless broadcast has made its notes familiar throughout the world. The quarters are struck upon four smaller bells.

The **Central Tower,** 300 ft. high, is used as a ventilating shaft. The great **Victoria Tower,** at the south-west angle of this great block, is 336 ft. high and 75 ft. square. The archway beneath, 50 ft. high, forms the **Royal Entrance,** and is used by the King when opening Parliament. Note in old Palace Yard, Marochetti's fine *Statue of Richard Cœur de Lion.*

Beyond, the **Victoria Tower Gardens** extend to Lambeth Bridge. A notable feature is *Rodin's* fine sculpture, *The Burghers of Calais.* It is unfortunate that the pedestal is 17 feet high. Here, too, is a statue of *Mrs. Pankhurst,* one of the pioneers of the "Votes for Women" movement.

The **Public Entrance** is by the door adjoining the Victoria Tower, whence we ascend the Royal Staircase to the **Norman Porch,** a small square room with groined roof supported by a beautiful central pillar. A door on the right leads to the **King's Robing Room,** decorated with frescoes and panels representing the Legend of King Arthur. Having robed, His Majesty and his attendants, on the occasion of opening Parliament, proceed in procession to the House of Lords by way of the **Royal Gallery,** a handsome hall, 110 ft. long, paved with beautiful mosaics, and having a richly-gilded panelled roof. On the walls are two large frescoes by Maclise—"The Death of Nelson" and "The Meeting of Wellington and Blucher after Waterloo." Two bronze figures on the right, by John Tweed, form the Peers' War Memorial. The title of J. S. Copley's "Death of the Earl of Chatham" is a misnomer, for Pitt did not die until some time after the seizure depicted.

We next enter the **Prince's Chamber,** panelled with dark wood.

The **House of Lords,** sumptuously decorated, is a "gilded chamber" indeed. It is 90 ft. long, 45 ft. broad, and 45 ft. high, and is lighted by twelve stained-glass windows containing portraits of the kings and queens of England. In the niches between the windows are statues of the barons who compelled King John to sign Magna Charta. The red morocco benches of the 550 noble lords entitled to sit in the House are ranged right and left of the Thrones. The cross-benches are occupied by princes of the blood. The seats on either side of the **Thrones,** at the south end, are reserved for Ambassadors and distinguished visitors. The cushioned ottoman immediately in front is the famous **Woolsack,** on which the Lord Chancellor sits. At the other end of the House is the **Bar,** at which the faithful Commons attend to hear the speech from the Throne, and to hear the Royal Assent to the Bills they have passed. Above are galleries for strangers and reporters. The frescoes over the Thrones represent " Edward III. conferring the Order of the Garter on the Black Prince," " The Baptism of Ethelbert," and " Judge Gascoigne committing Prince Henry to the Tower."

Beyond the **Peers' Lobby** is the **Peers' Corridor,** leading to the Central Hall, and containing frescoes relating to the Stuart period by *C. W. Cope*—

Funeral of Charles I. (*first on left*).

Parting of Lady Russell from her husband, Lord William Russell, before his execution (*first on right*).

Expulsion of Fellows of a College at Oxford for refusing to sign the Covenant (*on left*).

Departure of the *Mayflower* for New England (*on right*).

Defence of Basing House by Cavaliers (*on left*).

Departure of London Trained Bands to relieve the garrison of Gloucester (*on right*).

Charles I. raising his Standard at Nottingham (*last on left*).

Speaker Lenthall defending the Rights of the House of Commons against Charles I., when he attempted to arrest the five members (*last on right*).

The octagonal **Central Hall,** 60 ft. in diameter and 75 ft. high, has a vaulted stone roof, inlaid with Venetian mosaics. Above the doors leading to the Lords and the Commons respectively are mosaics by Sir E. Poynter representing St. George and St. David. Other mosaics represent St. Andrew of Scotland and St. Patrick of Ireland. The niches contain statues of English sovereigns, while ranged around are statues of statesmen.

On the right is a corridor leading to the Waiting Hall and panelled with six frescoes representing the Tudor Age:

Henry VIII. and Katherine of Aragon, by *Frank O. Salisbury.*

Latimer preaching before Edward VI. at St. Paul's Cross, by *E. Board.*

Queen Mary I. and the Princess Elizabeth entering London, by *Byam Shaw.*

The War of the Roses: Dispute in Temple Gardens, by *Payn.*

Henry VII. grants a charter to the Cabots, by *P. Eden.*

More and Erasmus visiting the children of Henry VII., by *F. C. Cowper.*

Immediately opposite the door by which we entered the Central Hall is the door leading to the **Commons' Corridor,** lined, like the Peers' Corridor, with eight large frescoes :—

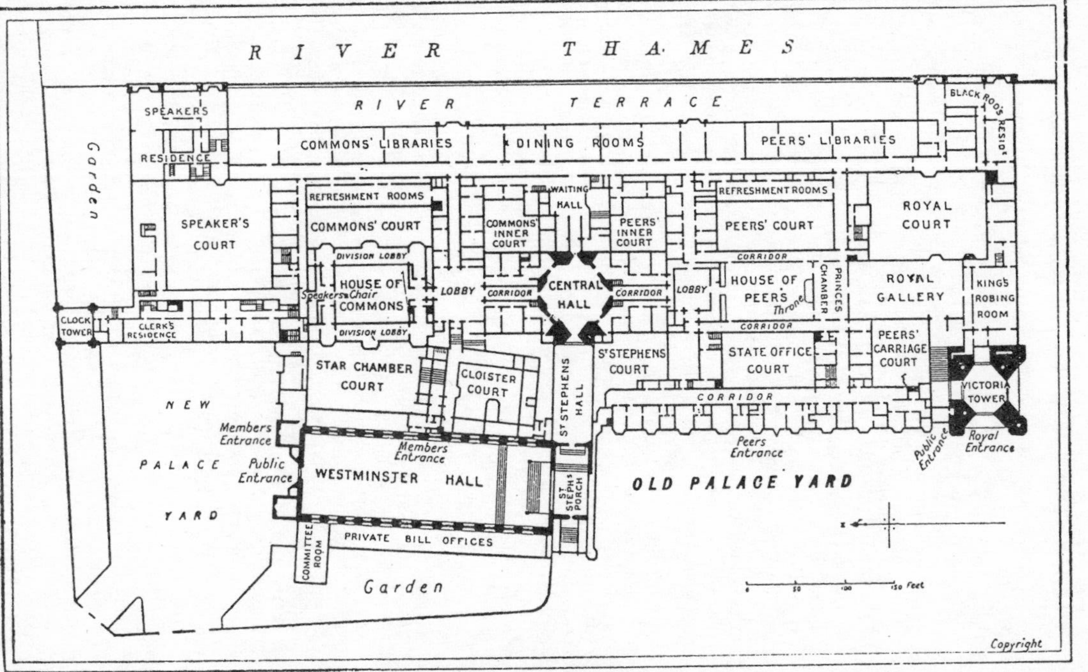

THE HOUSES OF PARLIAMENT.

Alice Lisle concealing fugitives after the battle of Sedgemoor (*first on left*).

Jane Lane assisting the flight of Charles II. (*first on right*).

The Last Sleep of Argyll (*on left*).

The Execution of Montrose (*on right*).

The Lords and Commons presenting the Crown to William and Mary (*on left*).

The Landing of Charles II. at Dover (*on right*).

The Acquittal of the Seven Bishops (*last on left*).

General Monk declaring for a free Parliament (*last on right*).

We then pass into the **Lobby**—on occasions of political excitement often more interesting than the House itself. Here is John Tweed's striking statue of the *Rt. Hon. Joseph Chamberlain*. So past the boxes where the door-keepers sit, to—

The **House of Commons.** After the magnificence of the Lords the Lower House strikes the visitor as severely plain and businesslike. The first impression is generally one of surprise at the apparent smallness of this historic chamber. It is 75 feet long, 45 feet wide, and 41 feet high. Though the House, by the establishment in 1922 of the Irish Free State, reduced the number of its members to 615, there is only room for 450, and an important debate still gives rise to keen competition for seats. Cards are used for the purpose of keeping places. Members receive a salary of £400 a year. The **Speaker's Chair** is at the north end. On the Speaker's right are the **Government Benches,** to the left the **Opposition Benches.** The front benches on either side are occupied only by Cabinet Ministers, or ex-Cabinet Ministers. When a division is taken members supporting the motion file into the "Aye" lobby, to the right of the Speaker, the "Noes" to the other side. A bell rings beforehand to warn members who may be in other parts of the House, the doors are then locked, and the voters are counted by "tellers" as they return to their seats. Below the Speaker sits the Clerk of the House, and at the other end of the table reposes the **Mace,** the symbol of the House's dignity and privileges. Over the Speaker's Chair is the **Press Gallery,** and above that the **Ladies' Gallery.** The **Members' Gallery** (for admission see p. 96) is at the other end, above the **Peers'** and **Distinguished Strangers' Galleries.**

Returning to the Central Hall, a door on the right side leads to **St. Stephen's Hall,** occupying the site of the old St. Stephen's Chapel (p. 96), where the Commons met for centuries. Brass studs in the floor mark the position of the Speaker's chair and table ; and in appropriate reference to the great struggles in our Parliamentary history which were here fought, the walls of the hall have been decorated with a series of paintings relating to "the Building of Britain," while at the ends are mosaics by *R. Anning Bell, R.A.*, representing "St. Stephen, King Stephen and Edward the Confessor" (a group having reference to the founding of St. Stephen's Chapel), and "Edward III. giving instructions for the rebuilding of St. Stephen's Chapel."

[W. & K.

THE HOUSE OF LORDS.

[Fox.

THE HOUSE OF COMMONS.

[*Alfieri.*

WESTMINSTER HALL.

ST. STEPHEN'S CRYPT.

Walter Scott,] *[Bradford.*

WEST FRONT, WESTMINSTER ABBEY.

Walter Scott,] [*Bradford.*

THE NAVE, WESTMINSTER ABBEY.

[*Grave of Unknown Warrior in foreground.*]

In order that the mural paintings may be viewed in historical sequence, it is best to proceed at once to the far end of the Hall and to begin with the fourth picture on the right :—

King Alfred's Ships attack Danish invaders, 877 (*Colin Gill*).
Richard I. leaves England to join the Crusade (*Glyn Philpot, R.A.*).
King John gives consent to Magna Charta, 1215 (*Charles Sims, R.A.*).
The English people gather secretly to read aloud Wycliffe's English Bible (*George Clausen, R.A.*).

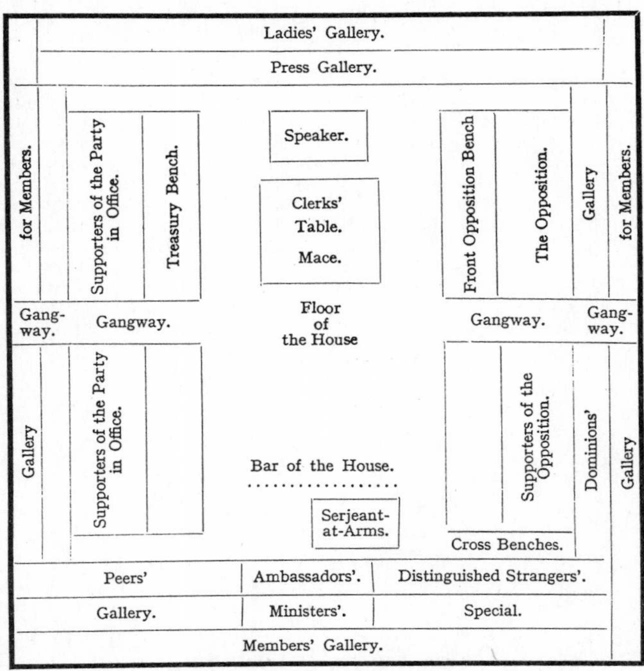

PLAN OF THE HOUSE OF COMMONS.

Now crossing to the north side of the Hall we have—

Sir Thomas More refuses to grant Henry VIII. a subsidy, 1523 (*Vivian Forbes*).

Queen Elizabeth commissions Sir Walter Raleigh to sail for America and discover new countries, 1584 (*A. K. Lawrence*).

Sir Thomas Roe, envoy to the Moghul Emperor, lays the foundation of British influence in India, 1614 (*W. Rothenstein*).

The English and Scottish Commissioners present to Queen Anne the Articles of Union, 1707 (*W. T. Monnington*).

Steps at the east end of the hall lead down to **St. Stephen's Porch,** with a fine stained-glass window and the stone screen forming the Members' War Memorial. On the right is—

Westminster Hall.

Admission.—When Parliament is not in session the Hall is open from 10 a.m. to 4 p.m. When Parliament is in session the Hall is open only from 10 to 2.45 p.m. Monday to Thursday. Not open on Fridays during the sittings of either House. On Saturdays the Hall may be seen from 10 a.m. to 4.30 p.m.

Westminster Hall, next to the Tower and Westminster Abbey, is the most historic building in London. It was begun by William Rufus in 1097 and enlarged by his successors. Richard II., in 1397, caused it to be rebuilt, and added the grand **Oak Roof,** rightly described as "one of the finest feats of carpentry extant." Only British oak grown in the Sussex Weald was used, and the trees must have been planted not later than the sixth century. The wood, having in the course of centuries become seriously decayed, has been judiciously patched and reinforced with steel. Much of the Norman masonry was cut away to provide for the fourteenth-century windows still visible, and in 1644 the Norman walls were still further mutilated and relined with stone. Small doors have been cut in the newer stone lining, so that antiquaries may examine the older work at will. Westminster Hall is probably the largest hall in the world with a roof unsupported by pillars, excepting, of course, modern steel structures. Its length is 238 ft.; breadth, 67½ ft.; height, 90 ft.

The historical associations of the Hall are full of interest. From 1224 until 1882 the Law Courts were held within and around. The hall was the scene of the trial and condemnation of Charles I. and of the proclamation of Cromwell as Lord Protector. Here, a few years later, Cromwell's head was brought from Westminster Abbey, with those of Bradshaw and Ireton, and impaled on an iron-tipped pike on the southern gable for something like a quarter of a century. The Protector's head was blown down during a heavy storm in 1686 and secreted, it is said, by a sentry. It is still preserved in this country and was exhibited to one of the learned societies in 1911. In Westminster Hall were tried and condemned William Wallace, Lord Cobham, Sir Thomas More, the Protector Somerset, the Earl of Essex, Sir Thomas Wyatt, Guy Fawkes, and the Earl of Strafford. It was the scene, too, of the acquittal of the Seven Bishops (1688), and of the long trial of Warren Hastings.

Tablets on the stairs and in the middle of the Hall mark the spots where Wallace, Charles I. and Strafford stood during their trials, and record the lying-in-state of King Edward VII. and King George V.

From the east side of the staircase landing a flight of steps leads down to **St. Stephen's Crypt** (or the **Chapel of St. Mary**), a remnant of old St. Stephen's which escaped the fire of 1834 and after a long period of neglect has in recent years been restored and is again used for services and marriages. It is a richly decorated, vaulted apartment, 90 ft. in length, 28 ft. wide, and 20 ft. high.

Emerging in Old Palace Yard, we cross the road to—

St. Margaret's Church.

Plan III. K. 9.
Access.—See Houses of Parliament, p. 96.
Admission daily between 11 a.m. and 4 p.m., except Saturdays. Entrance by east door, opposite Westminster Hall. Visitors are expected to contribute to the maintenance of public worship. (For services, see p. 20.)

In this church the Speaker and members of the House of Commons attend service on special occasions, the Speaker's pew being immediately in front of the lectern. The church is of special interest to Americans—more so perhaps than any other London church—and it is also the scene of many society weddings. The building was erected in the reign of Edward I., on the site of an earlier structure founded by Edward the Confessor, but has undergone many restorations. The Perpendicular arches separating nave and aisles, and the tracery of the window over the entrance to the vestry in the south aisle, date from the end of the fifteenth century.

The large *East Window*, representing the Crucifixion, is generally considered one of the most beautiful in England, and has a curious history.

It was painted in Holland, and was intended as a gift from King Ferdinand of Spain to Henry VII., to commemorate the intended marriage of Prince Arthur to Katherine of Aragon. Arthur died before the window was completed ; so instead of being erected in Henry VII.'s Chapel at Westminster, as intended, it was presented by Henry VIII. to the Abbot of Waltham. At the Dissolution it was transferred from the Abbey Church to New Hall, Essex. During the Civil War it was taken to pieces by General Monk's order and buried in chests. A few years later the window was bought by John Conyers for 50 guineas, and by his son sold in 1759 to St. Margaret's for 400 guineas, which sum formed part of a parliamentary grant asked for the repair of the parish church of the House of Commons. A strong Protestant wave was at that time passing over the country, and the erection of this "superstitious picture" excited no little outcry, and gave rise to a lengthy lawsuit.

The *West Window* is a memorial, presented by American citizens in 1882, of *Sir Walter Raleigh*, who was beheaded in Old Palace Yard and buried in the chancel, as a tablet—modern, but copied from an old one—quaintly records :—

"Within ye chancel of this church was interred ye body of ye great Sir Walter Raleigh, Kt., on the day he was beheaded in Old Palace Yard, Westminster. Oct. 29, anno domini 1618. Reader: Should you reflect on his errors, remember his many virtues and that he was mortal."

At the east end of the south aisle is the *Caxton Window*, with a verse by Tennyson. Caxton's press was set up in 1476 in the old Almonry, where Victoria Street and Tothill Street now meet.

The *Milton Window*, at the west end of the north aisle, has beneath it a fine tribute by Whittier. Milton's second wife and little daughter were buried here—the child within six weeks of her mother (1657). The marriage had only taken place in the previous October, so that the poet's happiness was short-lived. Pepys, the famous diarist, and Campbell, the poet, were married in this church, and windows and tablets commemorate many other famous persons.

WESTMINSTER ABBEY.

Note.—*Except for the daily services in the Chapel of St. Faith (weekdays, 7.45, Sundays, 8 a.m.), and the Museum in the Norman Undercroft, no public admission to the Abbey from January, 1937, until some time after the Coronation (May 12th), during the erection and dismantling of the special seating and other accommodation.*

Plan III. K. 9 and 10.

Access.—All buses on routes serving both Victoria and Charing Cross pass the Abbey. Trams to Westminster Bridge.

Nearest "Underground" Station—*Westminster* (District Rly.).

Admission (*but see note above regarding special Coronation arrangements*).—In summer the usual hour of opening is 9 a.m., or as soon as the Westminster School service is over. During the rest of the year the opening is at 9.30. In November, December and January the Abbey is closed at 3 p.m. In March and October it remains open till 5 p.m.; in April and September, till 5.30 p.m.; and in May, June, July and August, till 6 p.m.

On Sundays the Nave and Transepts are open to visitors between the services.

The nave and transepts are open to the public free. The charge for admission to the Ambulatory and Chapels is *6d.* each person, except on Mondays, when they are open free. *They are not open to the public on Sundays.* On paying days parties are conducted round the Chapels containing the Royal tombs at intervals of 15 minutes, starting from the south gate of the Ambulatory. Tickets must first be obtained at the little table close by. There is also a charge of *6d.* (*3d.* on Mondays) for viewing the wax figures in the chamber over the Islip Chapel, and a charge of *3d.* for viewing the Museum in the Norman Undercroft in the Cloisters. The Cloisters can be seen at any time. The Crypt below the Chapter House can be seen only on Mondays between 11 and 5. The public are not admitted to view the monuments on Sundays, Good Friday, Christmas Day, or during the hours of divine service.

Services.—*Week-days:* Holy Communion (generally in the Chapel of St. Faith) at 8; Morning Prayer, 10; Evening Prayer, with Sermon or Lecture on Saints' Days, Holy Days, Mondays or Saturdays in Advent, and Fridays in Lent, at 3. The boys attending Westminster School have a service daily at 9.30 a.m. (9 on Saints' Days).

Sundays: Holy Communion at 8; Morning Prayer, with Sermon, at 10.30; Holy Communion, 11.30; Evening Prayer, with Sermon, at 3; Special Service with Sermon, at 6.30.

Dimensions.—Total length, including Henry VII.'s Chapel, 513 feet; breadth across transepts, 200 feet; internal height of nave, 102 feet; height of western towers, 225 feet.

According to tradition, the first church on the site was built between the years 605 and 610 by Sebert, King of the East Saxons, and was consecrated by St. Peter himself, who suddenly appeared for the purpose, rewarding the ferryman who carried him across the river with a miraculous draught of salmon. Being built on the west side of the City of London, it was called the "West Minster." In the time of St. Dunstan (960) we find a Benedictine Monastery established. Edward the Confessor is, however, usually regarded as the founder of the church. He was crowned in the Abbey, as has been every monarch since, with the exception of Edward V., who died uncrowned. Here, too, a few days after the consecration of the building he had done so much to rear, the Confessor was buried, and henceforth, for hundreds of years, until the time of George III., the Abbey was the last resting-place of kings and queens. In later generations it has become much more than that, for room has been found for England's leading statesmen and warriors, poets, artists and men of letters—all, in fact, whom the nation delights to honour. In addition are numerous monuments, but it by no means follows from the existence of a monument that the person commemorated was actually interred in the Abbey.

Like all our great churches, the Abbey has been the growth of centuries. In the main, the present building is the work of Henry III., who pulled down all the eastern part of the Confessor's church in order more worthily to enshrine the body of the saint. The western portions were added at various periods between 1340 and 1483. The north and west cloisters, and the Jerusalem Chamber, near the south-west tower, were built by Abbot Litlington in the reign of Edward III. The magnificent chapel at the eastern end was added by Henry VII., between 1502 and 1512. The towers at the western end were added in 1738–9, it is believed from designs by Hawksmoor, one of Wren's pupils. The central tower designed by Wren is still wanting. Since the seventeenth century masons have been at work replacing, stone by stone, the decayed exterior, with the result that externally, in the words of Mr. L. E. Tanner, "the church is a copy, not by any means faithful, of the original." The intensely "new" appearance of certain parts of the exterior is mainly due, however, to the limewash with which the building is being protected against the smoke-laden atmosphere.

The form of the Abbey is that of a Latin cross, but the choir extends beyond the transepts almost to the middle of the nave. Behind the high altar is the Chapel of the Confessor, the "burial-place of kings," and beyond that again the noble Henry VII.'s Chapel. Round the Confessor's Chapel runs a spacious Ambulatory, from which open numerous other chapels.

The Abbey is usually entered by the door in the North Transept, close to St. Margaret's Church. The entrance bears the name of **Solomon's Porch,** though the original porch, erected in the reign of Richard II., was entirely transformed by Wren, and Sir G. Scott was responsible for the present triple portico.

The **North Transept,** which we first enter, is generally known as the **Statesmen's Aisle.** To the right, though sadly obscured by monuments, on entering is the *Bunyan Memorial Window*, representing scenes from the *Pilgrim's Progress.* Note the beautiful window in the South Transept.

We now turn rightward to the **North Aisle of the Choir,** frequently called the **Musicians' Aisle,** on account of the number of organists and composers buried or commemorated in it. Hereabout also are graves of eminent scientists, *Sir J. F. Herschell* (1871), *Charles Darwin* (1882) and *Lord Kelvin* (1907). In 1936–7 a new **Organ**—one of the finest in the world—was installed. This, like its predecessor, stands on each side of the choir.

One of the most characteristic views of the interior of the Abbey is gained from the west end of the nave. Here is that touching symbol of a nation's grief and remembrance—

The Grave of the Unknown Warrior.

All that is necessary is said by the inscription:

BENEATH THIS STONE RESTS THE BODY
OF A BRITISH WARRIOR
UNKNOWN BY NAME OR RANK
BROUGHT FROM FRANCE TO LIE AMONG
THE MOST ILLUSTRIOUS OF THE LAND
AND BURIED HERE ON ARMISTICE DAY
11 NOV: 1920, IN THE PRESENCE OF
HIS MAJESTY KING GEORGE V
HIS MINISTERS OF STATE
THE CHIEFS OF HIS FORCES
AND A VAST CONCOURSE OF THE NATION

THUS ARE COMMEMORATED THE MANY
MULTITUDES WHO DURING THE GREAT
WAR OF 1914–1918 GAVE THE MOST THAT
MAN CAN GIVE LIFE ITSELF
FOR GOD
FOR KING AND COUNTRY
FOR LOVED ONES HOME AND EMPIRE
FOR THE SACRED CAUSE OF JUSTICE AND
THE FREEDOM OF THE WORLD

THEY BURIED HIM AMONG THE KINGS BECAUSE HE
HAD DONE GOOD TOWARD GOD AND TOWARD
HIS HOUSE.

The slab is of black marble, quarried from one of the Belgian battlefields. On a pillar close by is suspended the *Ypres Flag,* which was carried in France during the War and for the first twelve months rested on the grave. Below is the *Congressional Medal,* bestowed on the Unknown Warrior by the United States Government in 1921.

The **North Aisle of Nave** contains windows commemorating famous engineers. About half-way down the aisle a small stone in the centre of the walk marks the grave of "*Rare Ben Jonson*" (it is thought by some that the inscription was intended to be

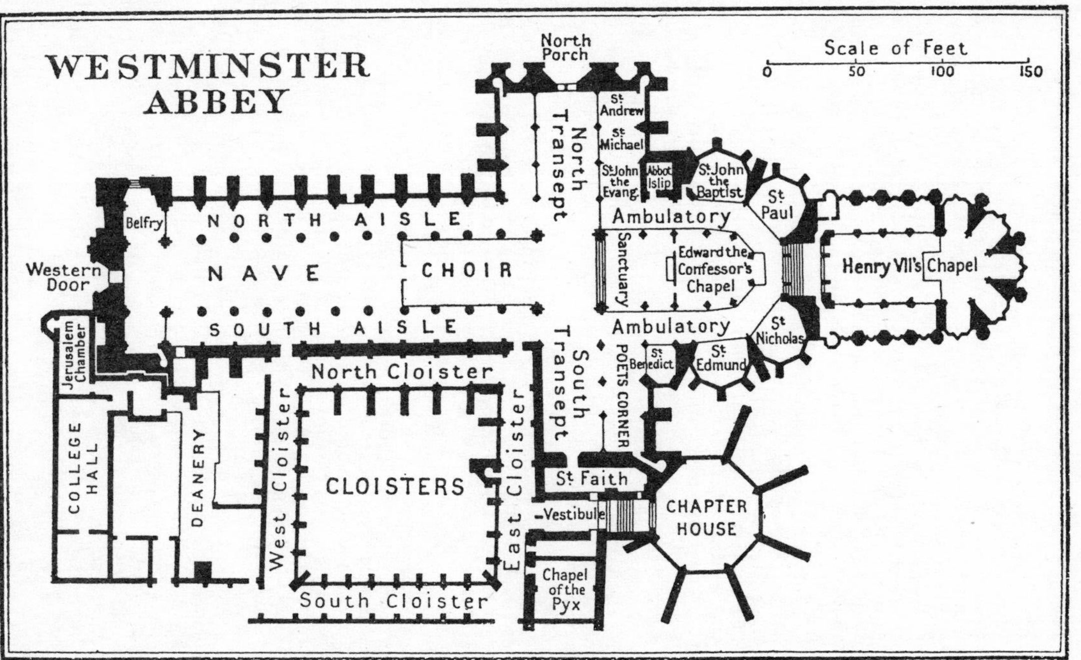
WESTMINSTER
ABBEY
Scale of Feet
0
50
100
150
North Porch
St. Andrew
St. Michael
St. John the Evang.
Abbot Islip
St. John the Baptist
North Transept
St. Paul
Henry VII's Chapel
Belfry
NORTH AISLE
Ambulatory
Western Door
NAVE
CHOIR
Sanctuary
Edward the Confessor's Chapel
SOUTH AISLE
Ambulatory
St. Nicholas
Jerusalem Chamber
St. Benedict
St. Edmund
South Transept
POETS CORNER
North Cloister
COLLEGE HALL
DEANERY
West Cloister
CLOISTERS
East Cloister
St. Faith
Vestibule
CHAPTER HOUSE
Chapel of the Pyx
South Cloister

ORARE Ben Jonson) (1637), and near by are the *R.A.M.C.* War Memorial and window. Another window, the gift of the Hon. J. W. Gerard, is "In memory of British prisoners who died in Germany, 1914–18, a tribute from the American Ambassador in Berlin, 1909–1917."

Towards the east end of the Nave are the graves of Peabody, the philanthropist (1869), David Livingstone (1873), Sir C. Barry (1860), Sir G. Scott (1878), G. E. Street (1881), and J. L. Pearson (1897), all architects; and Lawrence (1879), Clyde (1863), and Outram (1863), of Indian Mutiny fame; Bonar Law, statesman (1923).

The south-west corner of the nave—the **Warrior's Chapel**—has been set apart in memory of those who fell in the Great War. Here is the memorial erected by the Imperial War Graves Commission to the One Million Dead of the British Empire. Here, too, lie the ashes of Field-Marshal Viscount Plumer.

Above the neighbouring door in the **South Aisle of Nave** is the **Abbot's Pew,** a small oak gallery erected by Abbot Islip early in the sixteenth century.

The stained-glass window west of the doorway giving access to the **Cloisters** (p. 113) is a memorial of Y.M.C.A. War work.

In the **South Aisle of Choir** the most notable monuments are those to *Isaac Watts*, the hymn-writer (1748), and *Charles* and *John Wesley* (1788 and 1791).

We have now reached the **South Transept,** or **Poets' Corner,** to many visitors the most interesting part of the Abbey. The transept is famous throughout the English-speaking world, for here are memorials of all our greatest bards and writers, from Chaucer to Tennyson and Kipling. Only a few are actually buried here, but this is the spot chosen for such commemoration as art can give. The tomb of *Chaucer* (1400), from which the Corner "derives the origin of its peculiar glory," stands beneath a stained-glass window representing scenes from the immortal "Pilgrimage." Ironically, he was buried here not as a poet, but because he happened to be Clerk of the Works at Westminster. Immediately in front are the graves of *Browning* (1889) and *Tennyson* (1892). Near at hand is a bust of *Longfellow* (1882). *Ben Jonson* (1637), *Milton* (1674), *Edmund Spenser* (1599) and *Gray* (1771) are close together. The monument of *Shakespeare* (1616) adjoins that of *Burns* (1796), while *Dickens* (1870), *Thackeray* (1863), and *Macaulay* (1859) are near each other. Here too lies *Rudyard Kipling* (1936), and below the aisle rest the ashes of *Thomas Hardy* (d. 1928; his heart is buried at Stinsford, "Mellstock" in Wessex). At the foot of the Shakespeare monument is the tomb of *Sir Henry Irving* (1905). Above the memorial to *Scott* (1832) is a bronze medallion of *John Ruskin* (1900). In the middle of the transept a white slab marks the grave of *Old Parr*, who died in 1635, at the reputed age of 152. Australians are interested in the memorial to *Adam*

Lindsay Gordon (d. 1870). The beautiful **Rose Window** is best seen from the North Transept.

The **Chapel of St. Faith** is used for early communion services and private devotion.

Next to the monument to *Dryden* is the gate of the **South Ambulatory,** *from which parties are conducted round the Chapels and Royal Tombs at intervals of a quarter of an hour, at a charge of 6d. each person. On Mondays there is no charge and the vergers do not accompany visitors.*

Should there be an interval of waiting, the time may well be occupied in glancing round the central portion of the church.

The Stalls of the **Choir** are noteworthy, in their newly acquired coats of gilt and colour. In 1935 the 17th-century Pulpit was restored to use.

The **Sanctuary**—the space within the altar rails—is of extraordinary interest, for here all the sovereigns of England since the Conquest have been crowned. The Altar and Reredos were designed by Sir G. Scott, the sculptured figures being by Armstead, the mosaics by Salviati. The seats for the officiating clergy rest on a part of the tomb of *King Sebert*, the Saxon founder of the church. On the same side (south) is the tomb of *Anne of Cleves* (1557), the fourth wife of Henry VIII. The *Portrait of Richard II.* is interesting as being probably the earliest painting of an English sovereign made during his lifetime. On the north side are the three fine tombs, similar in design, of *Aveline, Countess of Lancaster* (1273), *Aymer de Valence, Earl of Pembroke* (1324), and *Edmund Crouchback, Earl of Lancaster* (1296).

Returning to the South Ambulatory, we begin the round of—

The Royal Tombs.

A glance at the plan will show that the central portion of the eastern end of the church is occupied by Edward the Confessor's Chapel, round which run the South and North Ambulatories, or walking-places, and from these open out a number of minor Chapels, three on the south and three on the north. King Henry VII.'s Chapel is at the extreme eastern end. Many of these tombs were long thought to be covered merely with the grime of centuries, but recent investigations have proved the "grime" to be a heavy varnish intended to protect the colouring of the tomb and canopy, now again revealed.

Entering the South Ambulatory, then, we see first on the left the traditional tomb of *King Sebert* (p. 104). Note above it the old paintings—fine examples of the brilliant restoration work carried out here recently.

Passing a small altar-tomb over the graves of four children of Henry III. and four of Edward I., we reach the **Chapel of St. Edmund,** King of the East Anglians, which has been principally used as a burial-place for relatives of sovereigns. The tomb of *William de Valence, Earl of Pembroke,* half-brother of Henry III.

(1296), still retains portions of the beautiful Limoges enamel with which it was originally decorated. In the Chapter House can be seen a representation of the figure when the decorations were complete.

The **Chapel of St. Nicholas** is dedicated to the young Bishop of Myra, the patron saint of children. It contains the private vault of the Percy family of Northumberland, members of which still have a right (not always claimed) to be interred in the Abbey—the only persons in England possessing such a privilege. Note the tombs of the *Widow of the Protector Somerset* (1587) and of *Sir George Villiers and his Wife* (1605 and 1632). Across the aisle is a 13th-century painted altarpiece—" the most remarkable example of mediæval painting known."

We now ascend a flight of twelve black marble steps, at the foot of which is the vault of the *Earls of Clarendon,* to—

The Chapel of King Henry VII.

the most magnificent portion of the Abbey and doubly magnificent since its restoration. The first stone was laid on the 24th January, 1502–3, but the chapel was not completed until ten years after the king's death. The entrance gates are of bronze, mounted on oak and embellished with the " roses " united by the marriage of Henry with the Princess Elizabeth of York, the portcullis, fleur-de-lis and other Tudor badges. The vaulted roof, with its airy network and luxuriant ornamentation, fantastic and fairy-like, is almost unrivalled for beauty. Washington Irving has well said : " On entering, the eye is astonished by the pomp of architecture, and the elaborate beauty of sculptured detail. Stone seems, by the cunning labour of the chisel, to have been robbed of its weight and density, suspended aloft, as if by magic, and the fretted roof achieved with the wonderful minuteness and airy security of a cobweb." The beautiful stalls appertain to the *Knights of the Bath* ; the lower seats are for their esquires (three to each knight). No installation had been held from 1812 until the ceremony was revived by King George V. on July 22, 1913. Above the stalls are suspended the gorgeous banners, swords, helmets and scarves of the Knights, all newly made for the ceremony. Some of the carvings on the stalls are very grotesque. Nearly a hundred richly-carved niches, each containing a small statue, run round the Chapel below the clerestory windows. At the eastern end is the beautiful **Tomb of Henry VII.** (1509) and his wife, Elizabeth of York. The tomb was the work of a Florentine sculptor, Pietro Torrigiano, but the screen is of English workmanship. *James I.* (1625) also lies in the vault below, and a little in front, beneath the altar, is the grave of the founder's grandson, the youthful *Edward VI.* The graves of George II. (1760) and his queen, Caroline of Anspach (1737), are in the western part of the nave, but without monuments.

The magnificent High Altar—a reproduction of Torrigiano's original altar—was the Jubilee Gift (1935) of the Order of the Bath.

The apse consists of five small Chapels, in which are several monuments. In the middle chapel were buried in 1658 *Oliver Cromwell*, his mother and sister, and other Puritan leaders; but their bodies were exhumed and dishonoured after the Restoration. Here is generally kept the chair made for the coronation of William and Mary. Here, too, are some of the old banners of the Knights of the Bath, removed from King Henry VII.'s Chapel when it was restored in 1913.

The South Aisle contains, amongst others, a monument to *Mary Queen of Scots* (beheaded 1587, and first buried in Peterborough Cathedral; reinterred here in 1612). In the vaults of this aisle lie Charles II., William III., Mary II., Queen Anne, and various other royal personages. Wall tablets near the door commemorate Lord Cromer (1841–1916), the "Regenerator of Egypt," Lord Milner (1854–1925), "Servant of the State," and Lord Curzon.

In the North Aisle are buried in the same tomb *Queen Mary* (1558) and *Queen Elizabeth* (1603). Let into a glass-covered recess in Elizabeth's tomb is the Essex Ring, given by the Queen to the favourite as a pledge of clemency should he at any time need it. It was his endeavour to return the ring which led to his execution. Nearby rest the Princes murdered in the Tower; *Addison* (1719), and others.

From Henry VII.'s Chapel we pass into the **North Ambulatory.**

A short flight of steps leads up to the **Chapel of Edward the Confessor,** where lie the bodies of no fewer than six kings and six queens. In the middle is the large *Shrine of the Confessor* (1066), erected by command of Henry III. in 1269, and for centuries an object of veneration to the devout. Few traces are left of its former magnificence. On the north side lies his Queen, *Editha* (1075). Observe that all the kings here are placed not below, but *above* the ground. The other monarchs, starting from the north side, are *Edward I.* (1307), inscribed *Malleus Scotorum*, "hammer of the Scots" (when the tomb was opened in 1774 the body was found to be 6 ft. 2 in. in length); *Henry III.* (1272); *Queen Eleanor*, first wife of Edward I. (1290); *Henry V.* (1422), the hero of Agincourt, "too famous to live long"; *Queen Philippa*, wife of Edward III. (1369); *Edward III.* (1377); and *Richard II.* (1399), and his Queen, *Anne of Bohemia*. The **Chantry of Henry V.** demands special notice. By a curious coincidence, apparently undesigned, it is in the shape of the modern letter H. The tomb, surmounted by a headless wooden effigy, is beneath the arch and close to the top of the stairs by which we entered the Chapel. Overhead hang the king's shield, saddle and helmet.

Against the **Stone Screen** at the other end of the Chapel, representing scenes in the life of the Confessor, is usually placed the **Coronation Chair,** one of the most famous pieces of furniture in the world. It was made for Edward I., and has beneath it the **Stone of Scone,** which was brought from Scotland in 1297, and led later, on the accession of James I., to the fulfilment of the ancient prophecy :—

"If Fates go right, where'er this stone is found,
The Scots shall monarchs of that realm be crowned."

Tradition declares it to be the identical stone upon which Jacob pillowed his head at Bethel. Upon it the kings of Scotland were crowned for many centuries, and it has served the same purpose for every English monarch from the time of Edward I. to King George V. The stone is 26 inches long, 16 inches wide, and 11 inches thick, and is attached to the chair by clamps of iron. At the Coronation the chair, then covered with cloth of gold, is moved to the other side of the screen, before the high altar. Near the chair are the sword (7 ft. long) and wooden shield of Edward III.

Passing again to the North Ambulatory, we cross to the small **Chapel** or **Shrine of St. Erasmus,** with its beautiful fifteenth-century clustered columns. This forms the entry to the **Chapel of St. John the Baptist,** where the most interesting tomb is that of *Thomas Cecil, Earl of Exeter* (1622), and his first wife. Space was reserved on the left for his second wife, but with proper spirit she declined to be buried here, as the place of honour was already occupied!

Abbot Islip's Chapel is distinguished by the frequent repetition of his name and rebus, "I slip"—an eye with a bough clasped by a hand and a man slipping from a tree. Above the Chapel is a chamber in which is placed a remarkable collection of **Wax Figures** of eminent persons interred in the Abbey. *These are shown to visitors at a charge of sixpence per head, or threepence on Mondays. Tickets must be obtained at the table near Poets' Corner.* It was a mediæval custom to carry wax effigies of the deceased in funeral processions, and some of these we now inspect. Among them are William and Mary in their coronation robes (the king standing on a cushion, as was his wont, to increase his height); Queen Anne; Queen Elizabeth; Charles II.; Lord Nelson (the effigy was made *after* his burial in St. Paul's, to lure sightseers back to the Abbey); Pitt, Earl of Chatham (also made after the funeral); Frances Theresa, Duchess of Richmond, "La Belle Stuart," in the robes worn by her at Queen Anne's coronation (she it was who sat for the figure of Britannia on our coins); the Duchess of Buckingham, in robes worn by her at the coronation of George II., with her infant son, and also her third son, the last Duke of Buckingham. Some similar effigies, of wood, are exhibited in the Norman Undercroft (p. 113).

Passing the huge cenotaph of *General Wolfe* (1759), the hero of Quebec, we enter—

The **Chapels of St. John the Evangelist, St. Michael** and **St.**

Andrew, on the east side of the north transept. Here are many interesting monuments and tablets, that to *Lady E. Nightingale*, by *Roubillac*, attracting most attention. Note also the fine monument to *Sir Francis Vere* (1608), with its kneeling knights, and the tablet to *Lord Rayleigh* (1842–1919), the eminent scientist. Near the exit is the memorial to *Sir John Franklin* (1847), with Tennyson's fine epitaph.

We have now accomplished the round of the Church, but several features of the great Abbey of which it merely formed a part remain to be seen.

The **Cloisters,** consisting of four "walks," and dating from the thirteenth to the fifteenth century, though portions are even older. Here are tombs of many abbots, with nearly obliterated inscriptions, and about a hundred other tablets and memorials.

From the east walk a pointed archway, with mutilated figures (note on left the Roman sarcophagus), admits to—

The **Chapter House,** an octagonal chamber, 58 ft. in diameter, with stone seats all round and a single central pillar. In order to protect the fine floor, visitors don overshoes before entering the Chapter House. The Chapter House was begun in 1250, and from 1377 to 1547 was the meeting-place of the House of Commons. The glass cases contain ancient documents, royal and ecclesiastical seals, etc. J. Russell Lowell (1819–1891) is commemorated by a window and tablet above the entrance stairway, and another tablet commemorates the noble-minded Walter Hines Page (d. 1918), United States Ambassador to Great Britain during the War.

In the **Crypt** (the Ancient Treasury) below the Chapter House are displayed the Coronation Copes, altar fronts and other beautiful "ornaments" of the Abbey. (*Admission Mondays only*, 11–5.30.)

Adjoining is the **Chapel of the Pyx,** so named because here was kept the pyx, or box, containing the standard gold and silver coins. Access is gained from the East Cloister by a door secured by six locks. The Chapel, part of the original building of Edward the Confessor, is shown to the public on *Tuesdays and Saturdays* only.

Beyond is the **Museum** in the Norman Undercroft (*admission* 3*d*.), a range of five vaulted bays also containing much of the original stonework of Edward the Confessor's building. Here are placed cases containing a quaint and interesting assortment of royal effigies similar to those in the Islip chamber (p. 112), but earlier in date and all of wood. There are also various relics of earlier buildings, coins, etc.

A passage on the left, just beyond the Undercroft entrance, leads to the **Little Cloisters,** surrounded by residences of the clergy,

At the south-west end of the Abbey, and forming part of the Deanery, is the **Jerusalem Chamber,** taking its name from the tapestries with which it was decorated. Here Henry IV. died in 1413, on the eve of starting for the Holy Land, thus fulfilling the prophecy that he would die in Jerusalem (*vide* Shakespeare's *King Henry IV., Part II.*). The Chamber can only be viewed by order from the Dean.

The Abbey's fine peal of **Bells** are the heaviest in London.

Turning to the left on leaving the Abbey by the door in the North Transept, we pass along the Green to the western end. The open space here is the **Broad Sanctuary,** a great resort in former days of people who sought the protection of the Church against the civil power. Edward V. was born in the Sanctuary in 1470. An archway on the south leads to **Dean's Yard,** where is **Westminster School,** refounded by Queen Elizabeth in 1560.

A portion of the old Abbey dormitory is used for entertainments, etc., and the large College Hall is the dining-room (the tables are said to be made from timber of the Spanish Armada). There are 60 foundationers or king's scholars, of whom 20 are non-resident, and about 200 Oppidans or Town Boys. The *Westminster Play,* given annually just before Christmas, has usually a witty epilogue alluding to current events. The time-honoured custom of *Tossing the Pancake* takes place annually on Shrove Tuesday, the boy who succeeds in getting the largest piece being rewarded with a guinea by the Dean.

On the south side of Dean's Yard is the **Church House,** "the central business house of the Church of England," now in process of rebuilding.

On the north side of the Broad Sanctuary is **Westminster Hospital,** founded in 1720, the first of the voluntary hospitals. It will shortly move to new buildings. The beautiful Renaissance edifice adjoining is the **Middlesex Guildhall,** rebuilt in 1913. Note the friezes representing Magna Charta, Henry III. granting a charter to Westminster, and Lady Jane Grey accepting the Crown from the Duke of Northumberland. The **Methodist Central Hall,** an imposing square block in the Renaissance style, is frequently used for concerts, exhibitions, etc. The dome is the third largest in London, being exceeded only by those of St. Paul's Cathedral and the British Museum Reading Room. It has a diameter of 90 feet, and the height to the lantern is 220 feet.

Tothill Street leads to **St. James Park Station** and the huge block housing the offices of the **London Passenger Transport Board.** The sculptures by *Jacob Epstein* have provoked more than a little comment.

In **Victoria Street** are the offices of many famous engineering firms. In the building at the corner (since reconstructed) was framed the Act of Union by which the Dominion of Canada was constituted in 1866–7. This building occupies the site of

Caxton's house in the Almonry, where he showed the first printing press to Edward IV. in 1477. On the left of Victoria Street, farther down, are the *Army and Navy Stores*.

Towards the western end of Victoria Street, Ashley Gardens (left) bring one in a few yards to—

Westminster Cathedral.

Plan III. I. 10.

Admission.—The Nave and Chapels may be inspected freely, but visitors will, of course, refrain from walking about during services. Organised parties of visitors may only be conducted by a member of the Cathedral staff.

Tickets of admission to the tower (*Lift* 1/–) or to the Cathedral roof, may be obtained from the Cathedral Porter. 6*d*. is charged for viewing the Crypt, containing the tombs of Cardinals Wiseman and Manning.

Services.—Low Masses: 7, 7.30, 8, 8.30, 9; Prime and Terce, 10.10 a.m.; 10.30, Capitular High Mass, followed by Sext and None; 3.15, Sung Vespers, Compline and Benediction; 6, Matins and Lauds (of following day); 8.15, Sermon and Benediction.

Sundays: Masses at 6, 6.30, 7, 7.30, 8, 8.30, 9; Prime and Terce, 10.10; 10.30 (High Mass at High Altar, followed by Sext and None); 12 (Low Mass with Sermon), 3.15 (Vespers and Solemn Benediction), and 7 (Compline, Sermon, Benediction, at High Altar), 8.30 p.m. (Matins and Lauds).

Dimensions.—Exterior: Length, 360 ft.; width, 156 ft.; height of nave, 117 ft.; height of campanile, 284 ft. Interior: Length, 342 ft.; width across nave, aisles, and side chapels, 148 ft. (nave only, 60 ft.); height of domes, 112 ft.; diameter of domes, 60 ft. The building covers an area of 54,000 square feet.

This vast and imposing, yet simple, structure of brick and stone, in the Early Byzantine style, was designed by J. F. Bentley, whose early death in 1902 robbed him of the satisfaction of seeing his work complete. The foundation stone was laid by Cardinal Vaughan on the 29th June, 1895. The structure was opened for use in 1903, but as under the laws of the Roman Catholic Church no place of worship may be consecrated unless completed as to fabric and free from all debt, the actual consecration ceremony did not take place until June 28, 1910. Much remains to be done to the interior, and many years will elapse before the decorations are complete. In the opinion of Norman Shaw, the Cathedral is "beyond all doubt the finest church that has been built for centuries. Superb in its scale and character, and full of the most devouring interest, it is impossible to overrate the magnificence of the design."

The dominating external features are the great **Campanile** (or St. Edward's Tower), 273 ft. high (top of cross, 284 ft.), and the dignified **West Front,** with its finely balanced pillars and arches. The mosaic Tympanum over the main doors was designed by *R. Anning Bell, R.A.* At present the interior, though awe-inspiring in its vastness and in the majestic simplicity of its design, strikes one as bare and sombre; but when the work of incrustation is complete, and the lower surfaces are covered with coloured marbles and the vast domes and vaulting with mosaics, the effect will be indescribably rich and grand. The **Nave** is the widest of any church in England, and owing to the fact that the sanctuary is 4½ ft. above the level of the nave, every part commands an uninterrupted view of the High Altar, with its imposing marble and mosaic baldachino, on which the light is cleverly concentrated. In 1937 the great Crucifix, weighing 2 tons, was restored to its original position at the entrance to the Sanctuary. If the Cathedral had no other feature of interest, the beautiful marble pillars (nearly all the gifts of various benefactors) would well repay a visit. All the pillars have elaborately carved caps of white Carrara marble, no two alike. The side-chapels are elaborately decorated. Adjoining the *Chapel of the Blessed Sacrament* (to the left of the High Altar) is a white marble monument to Cardinal Vaughan (d. 19th June, 1903). The screen and gates in this chapel, surmounted by a gold pelican, are very beautiful. In a corresponding position on the other side of the Sanctuary is the *Lady Chapel*. On the right as one enters the nave are the *Chapel of St. Gregory and Augustine*, the *Chapels of St. Patrick and the Irish Saints* and of *St. Andrew and the Saints of Scotland*, and the *Chapel of St. Paul* ; on the left are the *Chapel of the Holy Souls* and the *Chapel of St. George and the English Martyrs*, known as the Soldiers' and Sailors' Chapel and containing memorial panels, and the *Chapel of St. Joseph*. The finely sculptured *Stations of the Cross* are by *Eric Gill*. The *Great Organ*, with beautiful marble screen, is in the West Gallery.

Below the choir is the Crypt, or St. Peter's Chapel (admission 6*d*.), also with fine columns. Here are monuments covering the remains of *Cardinals Wiseman* and *Manning*, transferred from their original place of interment at Kensal Green. Those who make the ascent of the Tower (*lift*) will be rewarded in clear weather with a magnificent view over London. The tower is about 60 ft. higher than the western towers of Westminster Abbey, but is 30 ft. lower than the Clock Tower of the Houses of Parliament. *Archbishop's House* adjoins the Cathedral, in Ambrosden Avenue.

Slightly to the east, at the top of Rochester Row, is the **Greycoat School,** founded 1698. The neighbouring **Burdett-Coutts and Townshend School** is of interest, especially to Australian visitors, as the *Alma Mater* of Mr. W. M. Hughes, the distinguished Commonwealth statesman. He also acted as a pupil teacher here before emigrating to Australia. **Vincent Square** forms a playground for the boys of Westminster School. On the west side is the **Horticultural Hall,** used for exhibitions, Badminton, etc. The Horticultural Society's new hall is in Greycoat Place. In Horseferry Road is the Home Office **Industrial Museum** of safety appliances, etc. (*week-days*, 10–1, 2–4 *free*).

For the **Victoria Stations** of the Southern Railway see p. 61.

In Grosvenor Gardens is an excellent statue of **Marshal Foch,** by *Georges Malissard*.

In Buckingham Palace Road are the *National School of Cookery* ; the **St. George's Baths** and **Free Library ;** one of London's largest Motor Coach Stations, and the **Royal Sanitary Institute.** The Institute is

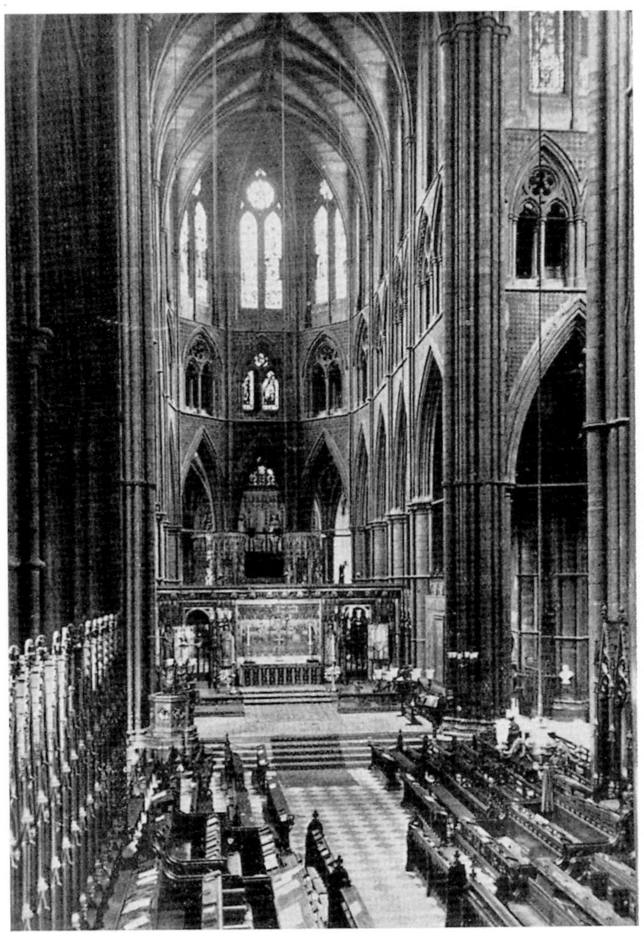

Sport & General,] [*London.*

THE CHOIR, WESTMINSTER ABBEY.

Walter Scott,] [*Bradford.*

THE CORONATION CHAIR, WESTMINSTER ABBEY.

H. Felton,] [*London.*

HENRY VII'S CHAPEL.

HENRY VII'S CHAPEL, WESTMINSTER ABBEY

Valentine & Sons, Ltd.,] [*Dundee.*

WESTMINSTER CATHEDRAL.

specially concerned with questions of public health. The **Parkes Museum** of sanitary appliances, etc., is *open free daily*, 10–5 ; *Sats.* 10–1.

Vauxhall Bridge Road, to the east of Victoria Station, leads to **Vauxhall Bridge.** Turning to the left from Vauxhall Bridge along Millbank, we reach—

The Tate Gallery.

Plan III. K. 11.

Access.—By 88 or 32 bus from Oxford Circus, Piccadilly, Trafalgar Square or Whitehall to the side of the Gallery. The nearest station is Victoria. Thence take motor-bus or tram along Vauxhall Bridge Road, alighting at the Bridge and turning left along Millbank. Or bus, tram or train (District Railway) to Westminster, and walk past Houses of Parliament and along Millbank, skirting the river.

Admission.—Free on Mondays, Thursdays, Fridays and Saturdays, April to September, 10 to 6 ; February, March, October, November and December, 10 to dusk; January, 10 to 4. Also on Sundays, 2 to 6 ; winter, 2 to dusk.

Sixpence on Tuesdays and Wednesdays (Students' Days), 10 to 6 summer, 10 to 4 or 5 winter.

Guide Lecturers conduct parties daily at 11 a.m. and noon.

Refreshments (luncheons, teas, etc.). There is a lavishly decorated Restaurant.

This fine gallery is an offspring of the National Gallery in Trafalgar Square, the object being to gather in one great national collection the finest examples of British art—a purpose which has recently been extended to include contemporary foreign art, including sculpture. The original building, designed by *Sidney R. J. Smith,* was presented to the nation, together with sixty-five pictures, by the late Sir Henry Tate (d. 1899). It was enlarged in 1899, and again in 1910 by the addition of the Turner Wing. In 1926 Sir Joseph Duveen placed the nation further in his debt by extensions of the Turner Galleries, and more recently he has presented a **Sculpture Gallery** and wings to house Modern Foreign Art.

In addition to the pictures presented by Sir Henry Tate, and some 200 paintings of the older British School transferred from the National Gallery (Trafalgar Square), the collection includes the works (now approaching 300 in number) purchased from year to year under the terms of the Chantrey Bequest ; the Vernon Collection, removed from the National Gallery ; twenty-three pictures by G. F. Watts, R.A. ; a number of sculptures ; upwards of 500 oils and water-colours forming the Turner collection ; the magnificent series of portraits by Sargent forming the Wertheimer Bequest ; a large and valuable collection representative of nineteenth-century French and Dutch art, and a number of examples of contemporary art, both British and continental. The examples of foreign art have for the most part been acquired through the generosity of Mr. Samuel Courtauld, who in 1923 presented a sum of £50,000 for the purpose.

We need give no more than a general indication of the contents of each room. All the pictures are plainly labelled, and catalogues containing biographical and historical notes are on sale in the hall, as also are post card and other reproductions of the most popular works. A large proportion of the pictures at the Tate are well known owing to their frequent reproduction.

Room I. Eighteenth-century artists. Note *Hogarth's* " Marriage á la Mode " series and well-known works by *Gainsborough* and *Reynolds*.

Room II. Water colours by *William Blake*. The mosaic pavement, after Blake's design, illustrates the Proverbs.

Room III. Early 19th century. *Landseer's* " Shoeing the Bay Mare " ; several examples of *Wilkie* ; *Constable's* " Valley Farm " and other works ; *E. M. Ward's* " South Sea Bubble."

Room IV. The Pre-Raphaelites. Note *Millais'* " Christ in His Parents' House " ; 1561, *G. F. Watts'* portrait of himself ; Burne-Jones's " King Cophetua."

Room V. Sporting Pictures.

Rooms VI, VII, VIII, IX are given up to the large and important Turner Collection (see pp. 90–91).

Rooms X and XI. Modern French Art: Degas, Manet, Monet, Millet, etc.

Room XII. The Modernists : Van Gogh, Cezanne, etc.

Room XIV contains the magnificent Wertheimer Bequest of portraits by *J. Sargent*. From this Room steps lead to the Ground Floor (water colour paintings, etc.).

Room XIII is notable as a successful experiment in lighting. Flemish and French Schools : *J. Israel's* " Philosopher " and his " Shipwrecked Fisherman " ; " Amsterdam," *James Maris* ; " The Horse Fair," *Rosa Bonheur*.

Room XV. Later nineteenth-century artists : *Dicksee* (" Harmony ") ; *Millais* (" The North-West Passage " ; " Raleigh's Boyhood," etc.) ; *Fildes* (" The Doctor "), etc.

Room XVII. The *Watts Collection*, presented by the artist.

Room XVIII. The Stevens Collection of cartoons, etc.

Room XIX. Chantrey Bequest and other pictures : Walker, Orchardson, Shannon, etc.

Rooms XX. Recent acquisitions.

Rooms XXI and XXII. Contemporary painters. *Augustus John* well represented.

Room XXIII. Sculpture.

Room XXIV. Chantrey Bequest pictures.

Room XXV. Contemporary Art.

Eastward from the Tate Gallery the Victoria Embankment extends to Westminster Abbey and the Houses of Parliament, passing the new **Lambeth Bridge,** and the fine headquarters of the Imperial Chemical Industries (note the fine nickel doorways and the busts of Alfred and Ludwig Mond, and others). In Thames House will be found the **Warburg Library** and **Institute,** appealing especially to art lovers and students of European civilization.

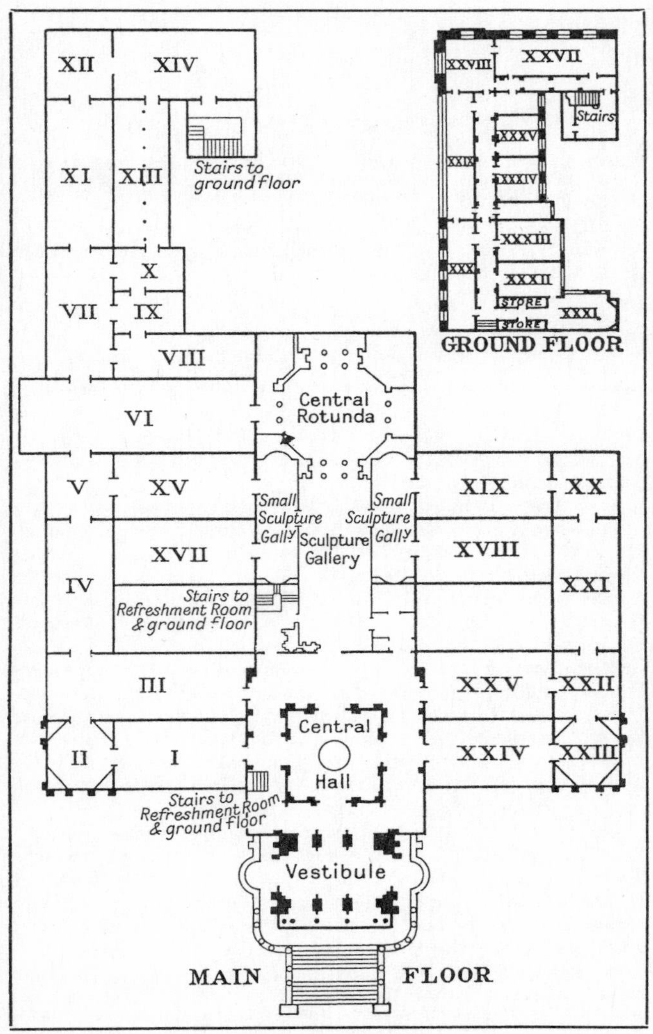

THE TATE GALLERY

THE PALACES AND CLUBLAND.

ROUTE III.—ST. JAMES'S PARK—BUCKINGHAM PALACE—THE LONDON MUSEUM—ST. JAMES'S PALACE—MARLBOROUGH HOUSE—PALL MALL—THE HAYMARKET—LEICESTER SQUARE—SHAFTESBURY AVENUE.

STARTING again from Charing Cross, let us cross the top of Whitehall and pass through the handsome **Admiralty Arch,** with its triple gateway (see p. 82), to—

St. James's Park.

Plan III. I. & K. 9.
Nearest Stations.—Trafalgar Square (Bakerloo Tube), Strand (Morden-Edgware Line). St. James Park (District). Green Park (Piccadilly Line).
Buses connect Trafalgar Square and Charing Cross with all parts of London.

The **Mall,** leading from the Admiralty Arch to Buckingham Palace, flanked on either side by an alley, with double rows of plane trees, forms a splendid processional road on occasions of State pageantry.

St. James's Park (93 acres) is one of the oldest and in the opinion of many the most beautiful of London's pleasure grounds. Up to the reign of Henry VIII. it was a marshy expanse, with a hospital for lepers, dedicated to St. James the Less, on its northern boundary. That sagacious monarch built a palace for himself (St. James's) on the site of the hospital, and converted the marsh into a deer-park. Charles II. played *paille-maille* on the broad roadway known as the Mall, and employed the French landscape gardener, Le Notre, to convert the deer-park into a garden. It was still, however, far from being a pleasant place until George IV. commissioned Nash, the architect, to improve it. A lake extends nearly the entire length, and is the haunt of many varieties of wild-fowl. The bridge commands one of the most exquisite views in London.

On the eastern side of the Park are the **Foreign Office** and other Government buildings, the **Horse Guards Parade** and the **New Admiralty** (see p. 81). On the south the Park is bordered by **Birdcage Walk,** probably deriving its name from an aviary maintained by Charles II. The flower beds on this side of the Park are among the best in London.

The **Bird Life** of London is remarkably varied—thanks in great degree to the sanctuary provided by the many Parks. Willow warblers, whitethroats, spotted flycatchers, kingfishers, chaffinches, sandpipers, wrynecks, and other more or less uncommon birds—uncommon certainly in cities—have all made their homes or been seen within half a mile of Hyde Park Corner during recent years. A few years ago a pair of kestrels built a nest in the tower of St. Michael's, Cornhill, in the heart of the city, and recently a pair of kestrels made their home in the Victoria Tower of the Houses of Parliament (see also p. 140).

At Storey's Gate is housed His Majesty's Office of Works, which has the charge, among other things, of the birds in the Royal parks. Here, too, is the **Institution of Mechanical Engineers,** while close at hand, in **Great George Street,** is the **Institute of Civil Engineers.**

Outside No. 13, **Queen Anne's Gate,** is a quaint little *Statue of Queen Anne,* and in many ways this thoroughfare wears an air that is in marked contrast to the great modern buildings on every hand. At No. 1 are the London headquarters of **"Toc H."** Towering high above the Park is the huge ugly block of residential chambers known as *Queen Anne's Mansions,* among the loftiest in London. Students of architecture are more interested in the neighbouring pile (see p. 114) built for the "Underground" and now housing the London Passenger Transport Board.

To the west are the **Wellington Barracks,** the headquarters of the Brigade of Guards, comprising the Grenadier and Coldstream Guards and the Scots, Irish, and Welsh Guards.

When not in khaki, all the Guards regiments wear scarlet uniforms with blue facings, but the various units may be distinguished by their cap-bands, or when guard-mounting, by the plumes in their bearskins, that of the Grenadiers being white, that of the Coldstreamers red, the Irish blue, while the Scots have none. The Welsh Guards wear a white plume with a horizontal strip of green. The Brigade of Guards furnishes the King's Guard, i.e., the Palace sentries. The protection of the person of the Sovereign is the function of the Household Cavalry, who (stationed at Knightsbridge Barracks) may be distinguished by their blue tunics and red helmet plumes.

The chancel of the **Royal Military Chapel** is enriched with mosaics in memory of King Edward VII., the late Duke of Cambridge, and a number of distinguished soldiers. At the west end is the impressive memorial to the 652 officers, 2,548 warrant and non-commissioned officers, and 11,650 men of the Brigade of Guards who fell in the War, 1914–19. The public are admitted without orders of admission to the evening service (6 p.m.), and to the parade service (11 a.m.) if a ticket has previously been obtained (write to the Chaplain).

At its western end St. James's Park is overlooked by—

Buckingham Palace,

(**Plan** III. I. 9)

the front of which was in 1913 reconstructed in Portland stone from designs by *Sir Aston Webb, P.R.A.* The Palace derives its name from a mansion erected by John Sheffield, Duke of Buckingham, in 1703, when keeper of the Mulberry Garden planted in connection with James I.'s scheme for founding a British silk industry. The house was purchased by George III. some sixty years afterwards, when his family had outgrown St. James's. His son and successor, George IV., commissioned his favourite architect, Nash, to remodel it, but the Palace was little used until 1837, when Queen Victoria chose it as her town residence. King Edward VII. made constant use of it, an example which was followed by King George V. and Queen Mary, and our present King and Queen took up residence there early in 1937. King Edward VII. was born in the Palace on the 9th November, 1841, and died here on the 6th May, 1910. With the wing added in 1847, the Palace forms an extensive quadrangle, the east front, facing the Park, being 360 ft. long. When the King is in residence the ceremony of Changing the Guard (which otherwise takes place at St. James's Palace) invariably attracts here a crowd of interested spectators.

The gardens and lake at the back of the Palace occupy the whole of the triangle, about 40 acres, between Constitution Hill and Grosvenor Place. The *Royal Mews* may be seen on Wednesday and Saturday afternoons by those who have written, beforehand, to the Master of the Horse, enclosing an addressed envelope for the reply.

In front of the Palace stands the **Queen Victoria Memorial,** designed by the late *Sir Thomas Brock, R.A.* The central figure of the Queen (13 ft. high) is carved from one solid block of marble, and has to the left and right groups representing *Justice* and *Truth,* while facing the Palace is a group symbolic of *Motherhood.* The whole is surmounted by a winged figure of *Victory,* poised on a sphere supported by the figures of *Courage* and *Constancy.*

A semicircular colonnaded screen, having a radius of about 100 ft., encloses the **Queen's Garden,** in which the statue stands, and around which traffic circulates on the gyratory system. The wrought-iron gateways bear the names and heraldic emblems of the principal countries of the Empire, by whom they were given.

From Buckingham Palace the tree-bordered **Constitution Hill,** 95 feet wide, runs obliquely to Hyde Park Corner (p. 138), where is the **Wellington Arch** crowned by a large bronze quadriga, representing Peace, by *Adrian Jones, M.V.O.* This group is unique among the London statues because the silhouette is practically the same from both sides of the arch, a *tour de force* which is seldom accomplished in monumental sculpture.

The **Green Park** (Plan III. H. and I. 9) is a triangular space of 53 acres, between Constitution Hill and Piccadilly. Its eastern side is formed by the Queen's Walk, overlooked by the massive Devonshire House and *Ritz Hotel,* and, to the south, by **Lancaster House** (formerly Stafford House), acquired in 1913 by the late Lord Leverhulme and presented to the nation for the purpose of housing—

The London Museum.

(Plan III. I. 9.)

Admission.—Free Mondays, Fridays and Saturdays; Tuesdays, Wednesdays and Thursdays, *6d.* Children under 14, free. Open every week-day, April 1 to October 31, 10–6; November 1 to March 31, 10–4. Open on Sundays after 2 p.m. Closed on Good Friday, Christmas Eve and Christmas Day.

Guides to Collections and to individual sections, as well as postcards, etc., are on sale at the entrance.

Nearest Station.—Green Park (Piccadilly Tube). Thence walk down St. James's Street, turning to right at foot into Cleveland Row, and past the north front of St. James's Palace to Lancaster House; or walk down the side of Green Park to the small gateway leading to the house.

Bus.—Any bus along Piccadilly will serve. Alight at top of St. James's Street, thence as above.

No lover of London should miss this most interesting collection, which strikes a note of homeliness and intimacy that is not generally a characteristic of our great Museums. The collection is designed especially to illustrate the history and the social and domestic life of London in all periods, the exhibits ranging from unpolished flint weapons of the Stone Age to modern dolls and toys.

The house was originally built for that Duke of York whose column looks down on St. James's Park from Waterloo Place (see p. 126). He did not live to see its completion, and the property passed in 1841 to the Duke of Sutherland. It was long regarded as the finest private residence in London, though the top storey (a later addition) is hardly worthy of the lower portion.

As the collections (apart from the heavy exhibits in the basement) are arranged generally in chronological order, beginning on the ground floor, it is best *not* to proceed at once up the staircase, but to turn left on entering. The objects all bear descriptive labels, so we need give no more than the barest summary of the general contents.

The Ground Floor.

Stone, Bronze and Iron Ages. Flint and other weapons discovered in the London district.

Roman Period (roughly 40 A.D. to 383 A.D.). We are reminded that *Londinium*, the Colonia Augusta of the Romans, underwent many changes in that period, the London destroyed by Boadicea being an undefended commercial town, the walls coming considerably later, and not reaching their final stage until the time of Constantine. Lamps, writing materials, brooches, articles of toilet, domestic utensils, grave-furniture, etc., help us to realize the life of the Roman Londoner. In relics of this period, however, the Guildhall Museum (p. 209) is richer.

Saxon, Danish, and Norman Periods. Pottery, knives, battle-axes, etc. Articles from a pagan Saxon cemetery.

Gold and Silver Room. This corner room, with its strongly protected windows, is out of chronological order, its contents being too valuable for general dispersal. Gold and silver ornaments, cups, enamels, badges, etc.

It is best now to descend to—

The Basement,

where is shown what is perhaps the most important exhibit, the remains of a *Roman Ship*, discovered in 1910 in the course of excavations for the foundations of the London County Hall, at the eastern end of Westminster Bridge. It was probably a cargo vessel, and dates to the 4th century A.D. Beside it is a dug-out canoe of the pre-Roman period.

The *Models of Old London*, by Thorpe, are fascinating, especially that of the Great Fire. The model of the Tower in the 17th century should also be seen and there is a series depicting life in Early Britain. Here are many charming doorways and other features from old London houses ; and a section is devoted to prison relics, with two reconstructed London cells, and a grim display of " execution " bills.

Return to the entrance hall and pass up the Great Staircase to—

The First Floor.

Mediæval Period. (13th to 16th centuries inclusive.) Here London is almost lost sight of in a multiplicity of articles few of which were peculiar to the capital, though of the greatest interest to students of those times.

In the Rooms devoted to the **Tudor, Commonwealth** and **Restoration Periods,** items of special interest are the pedlar's pack, the reproduction of Sir Thomas Gresham's steel-yard (1572), the fine Tangye collection of Cromwellian relics and documents, the Chelsea and Bow china, and the *Costume Gallery*, containing the Joicey, Abbey and Seymour Lucas collections of costumes, showing that fashion is indeed a fickle goddess. In the *Royal Room* are garments and personal relics of Queen Victoria and King Edward VII. and the coronation robes of King George V. and Queen Mary.

The Top Floor

has a number of small rooms principally devoted to prints and paintings and models of old London buildings. There are also collections of nineteenth-century pottery and of theatrical relics. The small apartment known as the **Children's Room** contains toys, dolls and dolls' houses of all ages.

Walter Scott,] [*Bradford.*

GATEWAY, ST. JAMES'S PALACE.

[*Daily Herald.*

TRAFALGAR SQUARE.

On the left is the Admiralty Archway, from which the Mall skirts St. James's Park. To the right is the Duke of York's column.

Adjoining the Museum on the east is—

St. James's Palace.

(**Plan** III. I. 9.)

"Our Court of St. James's," to which foreign ambassadors and ministers are still accredited, stands on the site of the leper hospital referred to on p. 120. It has long ceased to be the sovereign's official residence, but the western portion, known as **York House,** was adopted as his London residence by King Edward VIII. when Prince of Wales, and so used for some time after his accession. More recently York House has become the home of T.R.H. the Duke and Duchess of Gloucester. Henry VIII.'s palace, begun in 1532, is said to have been designed by Holbein, but was forsaken for Whitehall on the downfall of Wolsey, and did not become the official residence of the sovereigns of England until the reign of William III. Little of the old palace now remains. In 1809 a fire destroyed the eastern wing; and all that is now left of Henry VIII.'s edifice are the picturesque Gateway facing St. James's Street, the Presence Chamber and the Chapel Royal.

Here lived not only Henry VIII., but Edward VI., Elizabeth and Mary. On the morning of his execution Charles I. attended divine service in its Chapel, walking thence through the Park, guarded by a regiment of foot, to the scaffold at Whitehall. George III. was married and George IV. born here; William IV. and Queen Adelaide made it their principal residence. The building was less distinguished during the reign of Queen Victoria, being used only for courts, levees, and other ceremonies. Here the oath was administered to King Edward VII. on his accession, to King George V. in 1910, to King Edward VIII. in January, 1936, and to King George VI in December of the same year.

Overlooking Friary Court is the balcony from which, on the death of a sovereign, the proclamation is made. "The King is dead! Long live the King!"

As already stated, when the King is not in residence at Buckingham Palace the Mounting of the Guard takes place here.

The **Chapel Royal** is entered from the Colour Court. The services on Sunday mornings (see p. 20) are open to the public.

Clarence House, the London residence of the Duke of Connaught, adjoins the Palace.

Marlborough House

is on the other side, separated from St. James's Palace only by the roadway. It was the London home of King Edward VII. from his marriage in 1863 to 1902; from that date until 1910 was the residence of King George V., then Prince of Wales; from 1911 until her death the London residence of Queen Alexandra. It is now the home of Queen Mary. It was built by Wren in 1709 for the great Duke of Marlborough and "Sarah," but alterations have deprived it of its original character. The memorial of Queen Alexandra facing St. James's Palace was the work of the late *Sir Alfred Gilbert.*

Vernon House, Park Place, is the headquarters of the **Overseas Club and Patriotic League.**

By the roadway between Marlborough House and St. James's Palace we return to the Mall, where we turn to the left and along the Mall we pass below **Carlton House Terrace**: at No. 13 and subsequently at No. 11 Mr. W. E. Gladstone resided for many years; at No. 10 is the **Union Club** (social and non-political), founded in 1822, and here is the new home of the **Savage Club. Waterloo Place** occupies the site of Carlton House, so famous in Regency annals and scandals. At the house next the steps on the western side is the *German Embassy and Consulate.* The **Duke of York Column,** a granite pillar, 112 ft. high, commemorates the second son of George III., he of the "marching" proclivities. It is a curious fact that the monument bears no inscription. Although a "national" memorial, the greater part of the bill was paid by the simple expedient of stopping one day's pay from every officer and man in the British Army. Unkind comment of the time explained the height of the monument by the Duke's habit of keeping away from his creditors! Among other monuments in and around the square note that of *Captain Scott* (1912), the Antarctic explorer: it was the work of Lady Scott, and was erected by officers of the Fleet. The equestrian bronze figure of *King Edward VII.* was sculptured by *Sir Bertram Mackennal,* with *Sir Edwin Lutyens* as architect.

Waterloo Place being close to the headquarters of London's motoring world, a curious interest attaches to the stones erected there by desire of the Iron Duke to assist clubmen of his day to mount their horses.

The corner on the right is occupied by the **United Service Club** ("The Senior"). On the other side of Pall Mall, at the foot of Regent Street, are the **Crimean Monument** and *Statues of Florence Nightingale,* the "Lady of the Lamp" (d. 1910), and of *Sidney Herbert,* who was Secretary for War at the time of her devoted labours. On the corner are the headquarters of Cox's, the Army bankers, now amalgamated with Lloyds Bank.

Pall Mall,

(**Plan** III. I. and K. 8 and 9.)

the heart of Clubland, is generally believed to derive its name from the ball game of *paille-maille,* played by Charles II. and his merry associates in St. James's Park. Strangers may care to be informed that the pronunciation should be *pal mal*, not *pawl mawl*. We can do little more than enumerate the great clubs which are its distinguishing feature (see also pp. 22–4). The **Athenæum** celebrated its centenary in 1924. The frieze adorning the building is a replica of that of the Parthenon. The wits of the day hailed with delight Decimus Burton's refusal to carry out the wishes of members: "Instead of an ice-house he gave them a frieze." At No. 106 is the **Travellers' Club,** and at No. 104 the **Reform Club,** the premier club of Liberalism, with the **Carlton Club,** the headquarters of the Tory party, adjoining (No. 94). Next (No. 89) are the luxurious premises of the **Royal Automobile Club.** Then we have the **Oxford and Cambridge Club** (No. 71). **Marlborough House,** already mentioned (see p. 125), has an entrance in Pall Mall.

On the other (north) side we have at No. 52 the **Marlborough Club**; at No. 36 the **Army and Navy,** familiarly known as the "Rag," and at the opposite corner (No. 30) the **Junior Carlton,** occupying the greater part of the south side of—

St. James's Square (Plan III. I. 8). This fine square, to the north of Pall Mall, was laid out early in the eighteenth century, and retained the favour of the aristocracy until a quite recent period. Now, however, many of the fine Georgian houses are tenanted by business firms.

In an old building, just behind No. 31, at the south-east corner, George III. was born in 1738. No. 10 is noteworthy as having been the residence of three Prime Ministers, namely, William Pitt, Lord Derby and W. E. Gladstone. In 1923 the house was anonymously presented by two Canadians as headquarters of the **Royal British Institute of National Affairs,** formed to encourage and facilitate the study of foreign affairs. Outside are link extinguishers, reminders of the London that existed before lamp-posts and electric light standards. In the Square, too, are the **Windham** (No. 13), the **East India United Service** (No. 16), the **Portland** (No. 9), and other clubs, and a number of Government and Royal Commission offices. At No. 14 is that invaluable institution to literary workers and lovers of books, the **London Library,** founded in 1841. There are at present about 400,000 volumes on the shelves. Town members are entitled to take ten volumes at a time: country members are entitled to fifteen volumes. Entrance fee, £3 3*s.*; annual subscription, £4 4*s.*

In **King Street,** west of the Square, are the **Orleans Club** and the **St. James's Theatre,** where the late Sir George Alexander achieved so many triumphs. The street is the headquarters of some of the most famous dealers in works of art and antique furniture. At No. 8 are the well-known auction rooms of *Christie, Manson and Woods.*

St. James's Street leads upwards from the fine gateway of St. James's Palace to Piccadilly. Here are some of the oldest clubs, though in most cases their quarters have been rebuilt. On the left, ascending, we have, at the corner of Cleveland Row, the **Thatched House Club,** and at the next corner (No. 74) the **Conservative Club.** Also on the left are **Arthur's, Brooks's,** the **New University** and the **Devonshire.** On the right from the Palace are **Boodles'** and **White's.**

No. 22 St. James's Place (tablet), a *cul-de-sac* on the east, was the residence of Samuel Rogers, the banker-poet.

Jermyn Street runs parallel to Piccadilly on the south. It is a busy little thoroughfare and affords an interesting route to Lower Regent Street, where we turn down to the right at the *Plaza Cinema* and so regain Waterloo Place.

As we descend the hill, there is a nice view of the Duke of York's Column, pleasantly backed by the greenery of St. James's Park and the venerable towers and spires of Westminster. Beyond the Crimean Monument (see p. 126) we turn (left) into **Pall Mall East,** and follow it past the foot of Haymarket. On the north side are the headquarters of the **Royal Society of Painters in Water Colours,** whose spring and winter exhibitions are always largely attended, and also of the **Royal Society of Painters and Etchers.** Behind, in Suffolk Street, is the gallery of the **Royal Society of British Artists,** where spring and autumn exhibitions are held. In the open space formed by the junction of Pall Mall East and Cockspur Street is an equestrian *Statue of George III.* The artist has perpetuated the costume of the period (the uniform of an officer of the Royal Horse Guards, Blue), and while the likeness of the king is excellently preserved, equal justice is done to the wig and pigtail. It is strangely ironical that the chief American shipping offices should have grown up around this memorial of the obstinate monarch who was so largely responsible for the severance of the United States from England.

The **Haymarket** (Plan III. K. 8) (available only for vehicles proceeding *southward*), hardly so rural in aspect as its name would imply, has at its lower corner the *Carlton Hotel,* one of the most sumptuous establishments in London. It stands on the site of the old Her Majesty's Theatre, demolished in 1893, and replaced by **His Majesty's Theatre,** with which the late Sir Herbert Tree was so long associated. On the eastern side is the **Haymarket Theatre ;** on the left are the *Carlton* and *Gaumont Cinemas.* In Panton Street is the **Comedy Theatre.**

Almost facing the top of Haymarket is the *Corner House Restaurant* (Messrs. J. Lyons & Co., Ltd.), an enormous establishment capable of dealing with 4,500 customers at a time.

At the corner of Whitcomb Street and Leicester Square, to the right, is *Fanum House,* the headquarters of the **Automobile Association.**

Leicester Square (Plan III. K. 8) is best known to-day as a theatrical centre (with a pronounced leaning towards cinemas), and comparatively few will care to know that it derives its name from Leicester House, "the pouting-place of princes," where George II., when Prince of Wales, having quarrelled with his father, set up an opposition Court, an example dutifully followed by his son Frederick, father of George III. The open space, then known as Leicester Fields, was long a favourite resort of duellists. The Square is now laid out as an ornamental garden, with a statue of *Shakespeare* in the centre, and busts of *Reynolds, Hunter, Hogarth* and *Newton,* all of whom lived hereabouts, at the corners. The **Empire,** on the north side of the Square, has been rebuilt as a cinema, and a similar fate has overtaken the old Alhambra, whose site is occupied by the *Odeon Cinema.* On the south of the Square are the **Royal Dental Hospital** and the *Leicester Square Cinema.*

In the south-east corner of the Square Hogarth had his studio. At No. 47 (west side: house demolished 1937), Sir Joshua Reynolds lived from 1761 until his death. So numerous were his callers and sitters that, as Cunningham records, "Sir Joshua gave his servant six pounds annually of wages, and offered him a hundred pounds for the door"—i.e. the gratuities. At No. 28 lived John Hunter, the famous surgeon, whose anatomical collection, bought by the Government for £12,000, is now at the Royal College of Surgeons (p. 194). In St. Martin's Street, south of the Square, Sir Isaac Newton lived for many years. An unauthenticated anecdote records that a hungry friend, being shown into the dining-room, where Sir Isaac's dinner was laid, grew tired of waiting, and consumed the chicken, leaving the bones under the cover. When at last the great man entered, he removed the cover, and, seeing the bones, exclaimed : "How absent we philosophers are ! I really forgot that I had dined." The house was afterwards occupied by Dr. Burney, father of the lively Fanny, subsequently Madame D'Arblay. It was demolished in 1913, and on the site is the new home of the **Westminster Public Library.**

Leicester Square and the district known as **Soho** (p. 157) have long been famous as the home of a colony of French, Italians and Swiss. Hereabouts are many excellent restaurants, frequented not only by foreigners but by Londoners themselves.

Leaving the Square at its north-east corner by way of Cranbourn Street, we pass **Daly's Theatre,** famous for musical comedies, and the **Hippodrome,** at the corner of Charing Cross Road, another popular house of entertainment.

Charing Cross Road (Plans II. K. 7 and III. K. 8) runs between Charing Cross and Tottenham Court Road. It is intersected about a quarter of a mile from Oxford Street by **Shaftesbury Avenue,** leading from Piccadilly Circus to Broad Street and High Street, and so into New Oxford Street and Holborn. At the point of intersection, known as *Cambridge Circus*, is the **Palace Theatre ;** and close at hand are the **Cambridge Theatre,** the **Phœnix** and (in Old Compton Street) the **London Casino.**

In High Street, near the northern end of Shaftesbury Avenue, is the Church of **St. Giles-in-the-Fields,** originally built as the chapel of a leper hospital by Matilda, Queen of Henry I., and reconstructed for the third time in 1734. As in the case of St. Martin's (p. 74), the "fields" are now far to seek. Here are the tombs of Andrew Marvell, Shirley the dramatist, and George Chapman, the first translator of Homer; also of "Unparalleled Pendrell," who helped Charles II. to escape after Worcester. Hogarth's "Idle Apprentice" recalls the old churchyard. Until the construction of New Oxford Street, the main highway to the West went round by the present Broad Street and High Street, and malefactors on their way to Tyburn were given their last cup of ale from the steps of St. Giles's Church. It was in St. Giles's parish that the Great Plague originated in 1665.

Both Shaftesbury Avenue and Charing Cross Road contain a number of modern playhouses. Near the southern end of the latter (at No. 22) are the headquarters of the *Royal National Lifeboat Institution* ; close by is **Wyndham's Theatre,** and, nearer to Trafalgar Square, the **Garrick.** Adjoining is the **Westminster City Hall,** the municipal headquarters of the City of Westminster.

In the centre of the roadway, at the foot of St. Martin's Lane, is the **Nurse Cavell Memorial,** the work of the late *Sir George Frampton, R.A.* It bears Nurse Cavell's memorable words shortly before her execution : "Patriotism is not enough ; I must have no hatred or bitterness for anyone." In **St. Martin's Lane** is the **Coliseum,** a huge house of entertainment, with a revolving stage. Higher up, on the west side, are the **New Theatre** and the **Duke of York's Theatre.**

PICCADILLY TO KENSINGTON.

ROUTE IV.—PICCADILLY—THE ROYAL ACADEMY—PARK LANE—HYDE PARK—KENSINGTON GARDENS—KENSINGTON PALACE.

WE will assume this time that the start is made from **Piccadilly Circus** (Plan III. I. 8). This famous spot has been to a great extent transformed during recent years, very striking modern buildings having replaced the more humble shop premises dating from Nash's time (see also p. 144). Change of another kind has overtaken the famous old *London Pavilion*—now a cinema. Great as the alteration is above ground, the reconstruction below the Circus has been even more remarkable, although in the new Tube station serving the Piccadilly and Bakerloo lines there is little hint of the extraordinary engineering feats entailed by its construction. Piccadilly Circus is a very important traffic "hub," both above and below ground, main thoroughfares and "tube" railways radiating hence to north, south, east and west. *Piccadilly Circus Station* is used by more than 25,000,000 passengers yearly. Upwards of 48,000 road vehicles alone pass through the Circus in the course of a day; the "roundabout" system is in use here, the central point being occupied by the late Sir Alfred Gilbert's graceful statue of *Eros*.

On the south side of the Circus is the **Criterion Theatre**; a few yards eastward of the Circus is the enormous *Corner House Restaurant* (see p. 129). To the west, with entrance in Glasshouse Street, is the *Regent Palace Hotel*.

Resisting for a while the blandishments of rebuilt Regent Street, which sweeps magnificently northward (see p. 144), we turn along—

Piccadilly,

(Plan III. H. 9 and I. 8.)

one of London's most attractive thoroughfares, though it, too, has to a great extent been rebuilt. It is said to derive its name from the pickadils, or ruffs, worn in the early Stuart period. Commencing at Piccadilly Circus, it extends westward for nearly a mile to Hyde Park Corner, and is continued as Knightsbridge, Kensington High Street and Kensington Road to Hammersmith, after which it forms the great Bath Road to the West of England. It is thronged at nearly all hours of the day. The eastern portion is occupied by shops, but the western portion, skirting the Green Park, is overlooked by fine mansions and clubs. Evidence of its commercial value is the fact that the ground rent alone of the site of the Geological Museum and Library (now moved to South Kensington—see p. 176) is no less than £11,000 a year. At the junction of Piccadilly with Piccadilly Circus we have the striking modern building of *Messrs. Swan & Edgar*. The imposing *Piccadilly Hotel* occupies the site of St. James's Hall, or " Jimmy's," long famous among music-lovers. Opposite the hotel is the *Popular Restaurant* and a few yards westward is **St. James's Church,** lying a little back from the road. It was built by Wren in 1684, and, though plain and unadorned without, has a very fine interior, with font and altar carvings by Grinling Gibbons. It is also notable as possessing an open-air pulpit. The charming little bank building beside the church was the work of Sir Edwin Lutyens. At No. 191 are the galleries in which are held the spring and autumn exhibitions of the **Royal Institute of Painters in Water Colours** and the **Royal Institute of Oil Painters.** Occupying the ground floor of the same block is *Prince's Restaurant*. Another well-known restaurant is *Hatchett's*, on the opposite side of Piccadilly, where used to stand the old "White Horse Cellars," the starting-place of West of England coaches.

On the north side of Piccadilly, between Sackville Street and Burlington House, is the quaint, old-fashioned **Albany,** so frequently figuring in novels of the last century. These bachelor chambers—" a bachelor village " someone has called them—have had many distinguished tenants, including Byron, George Canning, Bulwer Lytton and Lord Macaulay (the famous *History* was written here).

At No. 20, **Savile Row,** to the north, Sidney Smith resided from 1827 to 1832 ; No. 14 was the last home of Sheridan ; and at No. 12 Grote lived and wrote his *History*. The Row is famous for its tailoring establishments.

The Royal Academy of Arts.

Plan III. I. 8.

Admission.—The Summer Exhibition (1*s.* 6*d.*) is held from the first week in May to the middle of August (9 a.m. to 7 p.m.). Winter exhibitions, January and February, 9 till 5. The Gibson and Diploma Galleries are reached by a staircase to right of main entrance (free daily from 11 to 4).

Catalogues.—Official Catalogue, 1*s.*

Nearest Stations.—Green Park (Piccadilly Tube), Piccadilly Circus (Piccadilly and Bakerloo Tubes).

Buses.—A large proportion of the bus services pass through Piccadilly Circus, a few minutes distant, and many run along Piccadilly, past the doors of Burlington House.

Burlington House was erected early in the eighteenth century by Richard Boyle, Earl of Burlington, and purchased by the Government in 1854 at a cost of £140,000. A number of extensions have since been made, and a storey added. The Royal Academy occupies the inner or northern portion, while various learned societies are accommodated in the blocks on either side. The best known of these societies is the **Royal Society,** incorporated by Royal Charter in 1662. Its roll of Fellows and Presidents includes such illustrious names as those of Newton, Halley, Davy, Darwin, Kelvin, and many others. Members append the letters F.R.S. to their names. The Society's Library contains about 50,000 volumes, some fine portraits and busts, Newton's telescope, the original model of Davy's safety lamp, and other objects of interest. Admission by order of a Fellow. Other bodies include the **Geological, Chemical, Royal Astronomical** and **Linnean Societies,** the **Society of Antiquaries of London,** and the **British Association for the Advancement of Science.** The libraries and museums of these Societies can generally be seen on application.

Crossing the inner court, we reach the part best known to the public. The **Royal Academy of Arts** was founded by George III. in 1768, its first President being Sir Joshua Reynolds. From 1838 to 1869 the annual exhibitions were held in the National Gallery. There are forty Royal Academicians (who add R.A. to their names) and about thirty associates (A.R.A.), as well as a number of retired and foreign Academicians and Associates. The **Annual Exhibition** (familiarly "The Academy") usually opens on the first Monday in May, and is preceded by the "Private View"—a Society function in which dress plays at least as important a part as Art—and the "Academy Dinner," generally presided over by royalty, and attended by leading politicians of all parties. The pictures to be shown are selected by a "Hanging Committee," whose judgments by no means always commend themselves to the general body of artists. The works must have been finished during the previous year and not exhibited elsewhere. In the upper part of the building occupied by the Academy and open (free) throughout the year, are the **Gibson and Diploma Galleries,** with a very interesting collection of pictures presented by Academicians on their election, the Gibson Collection of Sculptures, and some valuable old masters. A study by *Leonardo da Vinci* is a special attraction and there are palettes and other mementoes of many famous artists.

On the west side of Burlington House is the **Burlington Arcade,** for the most part sacred to hosiers, bootmakers and jewellers. The **Royal Arcade** is a similar structure connecting Old Bond Street and Albemarle Street. The **Piccadilly Arcade,** on the south side of Piccadilly, provides a shop-lined covered way between that thoroughfare and Jermyn Street.

Continuing westward, we pass the foot of **Old Bond Street,** where are many famous shops—notably jewellers—and the galleries of a number of well-known art dealers. In recent years Bond Street has been invaded by motor-car dealers. It runs northward to Oxford Street, the upper and wider portion being known as **New Bond Street.** On No. 147, New Bond Street is a tablet recording that Nelson lived there, but the house has been entirely rebuilt. The famous thoroughfare—

> "Where each who wills may suit his wish,
> Here choose a Guido—there his fish,"

takes its name from Sir Thomas Bond, by whom it was built in 1686.

Albemarle Street is so named from the second Duke of Albemarle, son of General Monk. Near the top is the **Royal Institution,** founded in 1799 for the promotion and teaching of science. The lectures given to juvenile audiences in the weeks succeeding Christmas always attract wide attention. Next door, at No. 20, is the **Davy-Faraday Laboratory,** presented by the late Dr. Ludwig Mond. At No. 7 is the **Aeronautical Society of Great Britain,** which has done so much for aviation.

St. James's Street, running south from Piccadilly to Holbein's fine gateway at St. James's Palace, we have described on p. 128. No. 20, **Arlington Street** was long the town mansion of the Marquess of Salisbury. No. 5, now an annexe of the Devonshire Club, was for years the residence of Sir Robert Walpole, and later of his son, Horace Walpole. The *Ritz* is one of the most sumptuous of London's hotels. The restaurant overlooks the **Green Park** (p. 122), which borders the south side of Piccadilly all the rest of the way to Hyde Park Corner, affording the favoured occupants of houses on the other side a magnificent view across to Westminster. *Green Park Station,* on the Piccadilly Tube, has replaced Dover Street Station. Across the way is the enormous block of *Devonshire House,* perpetuating the name of the town residence of the Duke of Devonshire, which long occupied the site. A beautiful memento of old Devonshire House is the fine iron gateway on the other side of the road, in the railings of Green Park.

Berkeley Street (Pope lived for a time at No. 9) leads to **Berkeley Square** (Plan III. H. 8), noted for its plane trees, and reminding one of Thackeray's "Jeames of Barkley Square." Although the builders are busy here, as elsewhere, many houses in the Square have associations of interest, the past being especially recalled by the quaint ironwork and the torch extinguishers in front of the doors. The southern side of the Square has been filled with another of the huge blocks which have become so characteristic of this quarter—one can but hope (though the hope seems vain) that neighbouring old buildings of interest and character will be spared for many years yet.

West of Berkeley Square, in Farm Street, is the **Church of the Jesuit Fathers,** where Cardinal Manning was received into the Church of Rome. In Charles Street, Berkeley Square, is Dartmouth House, the home of the **English-Speaking Union.**

Continuing along the north side of Piccadilly, we pass the foot of **Clarges Street,** taking its name from Nan Clarges, the needlewoman, whose father was a blacksmith, and who married General Monk and became Duchess of Albemarle. No. 85, Piccadilly is the **Turf Club.**

Beyond **Half Moon Street,** deriving its peculiar name from a long lost tavern, at one time of considerable repute, are the **Naval and Military Club** (No. 94, formerly occupied by Lord Palmerston) and the **American Club** (No. 95).

White Horse Street leads to **Shepherd's Market,** which has been described as " a modest little country town . . . small but busy . . . a strange survival set in this most aristocratic quarter." Though in great part rebuilt, it still retains a pleasantly rural flavour, and is characteristic of many oases in London which unexpectedly greet the explorer who forsakes the main thoroughfares.

Opposite the American Club, at No. 96, is the **Junior Naval and Military Club.** Continuing along Piccadilly, we pass the **Badminton** (No. 100), **Junior Constitutional** (101), **St. James's** (106), **Cavalry** (127) and other clubs. At No. 128 is the **Royal Air Force Club.** In the stately mansions between Hamilton Place and Apsley House several members of the Rothschild family reside. No. 145 was the residence of the King and Queen at the time of their accession.

Apsley House (Plan III. H. 9), the residence of the Duke of Wellington, was presented to the Great Duke by the nation in 1820, as part of the reward for his services.

It was originally built in 1785 as a red-brick mansion for Lord Chancellor Bathurst, who, it is said, in order to secure the land, had to buy out the proprietor of an apple-stall, an old soldier to whom George II., in an excess of generosity, had given the site as a reward for bravery at the battle of Dettingen. During the Reform Bill agitation the mob smashed the windows, so the Duke had them encased in iron shutters. Later, when the changeable crowd followed him with cheers from Constitution Hill, he took no notice until the shutters were in sight, when he bowed sarcastically and passed into the court without a word.

In the roadway island opposite is a fine equestrian **Statue of the Duke of Wellington,** by Boehm.

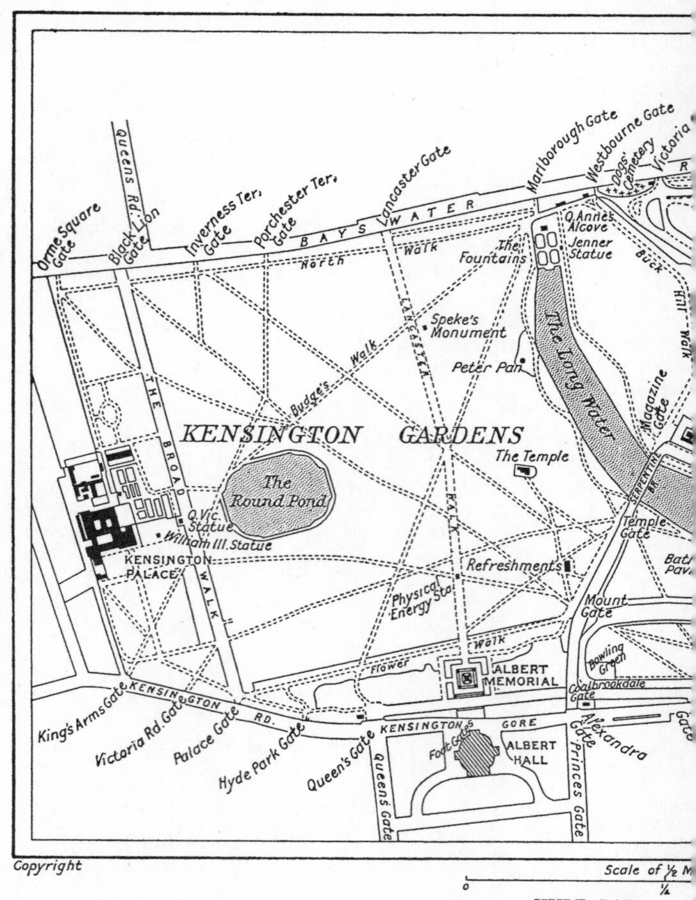

Copyright

Scale of ½ M

0 ¼

HYDE PARK AN

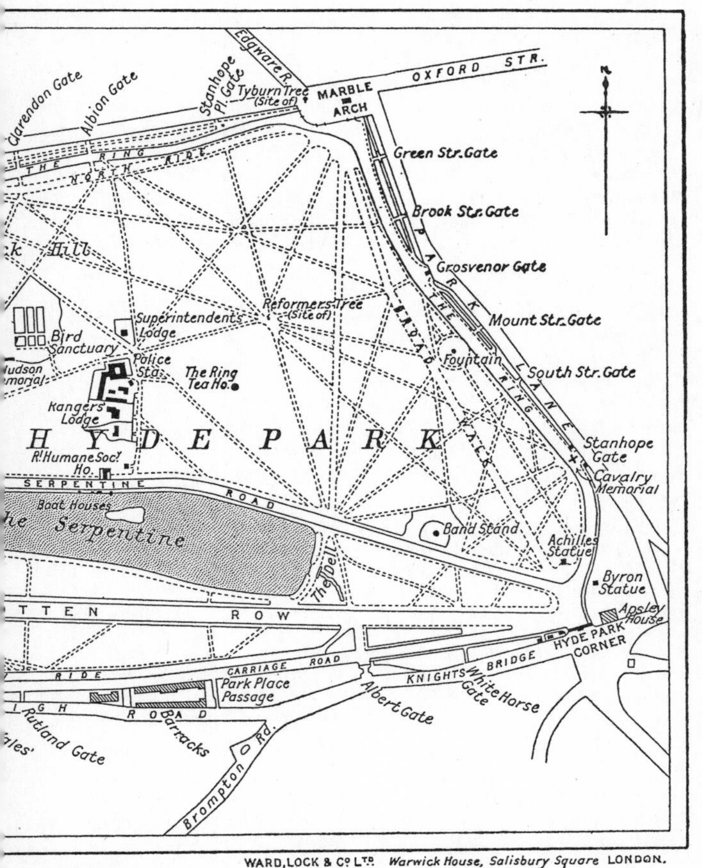

WARD, LOCK & Co. Ltd. Warwick House, Salisbury Square LONDON.

½

INGTON GARDENS.

Park Lane (Plan III. G. and H. 8 and 9), overlooking the eastern side of Hyde Park, was long famous for its splendid mansions, many of them filled with some of the world's most celebrated pictures and statuary, but its character has changed in recent years and it is now notable on account of the huge buildings in modern style which have replaced such famous residences as Grosvenor House (long the London home of the Dukes of Westminster), and Dorchester House, wherein Mr. Whitelaw Reid resided when American Ambassador. Although these huge piles, such as *Grosvenor House* and the *Dorchester Hotel,* have been much criticized, they have architectural distinction, a fact which is forcibly brought home to those who trouble to compare them with other large buildings in the vicinity.

Just within the Stanhope Gate of Hyde Park is the **Cavalry War Memorial,** with a striking sculpture of St. George and the Dragon by *Adrian Jones, M.V.O.*

Between Park Lane and Bond Street lies the "blue-blooded" and reverently regarded district of **Mayfair,** for which the visitor may look in vain in the Directory, for it has no parochial or other official recognition. The name is the only survival of the old May Fair, an annual scene of debauchery suppressed at the end of the eighteenth century.

In **Curzon Street** (Plan III. H. 8), on the site of Sunderland House, stood a Chapel long famous for marriages at a minute's notice. Hasty beauties and eager swains were here tied together with the utmost celerity; and it is said that no fewer than 6,000 pairs were thus united in one year. The beautiful Miss Chudleigh was wedded in this fashion to the Duke of Kingston; and the still more beautiful Miss Gunning, the youngest of the lovely sisterhood who turned the heads of young Englishmen at that period, came hither with the Duke of Hamilton, half an hour after midnight, and was married with a bed-curtain ring.

At the corner of this street and South Audley Street a block of flats occupies the site of Chesterfield House, where the famous letters were penned, and in a room of which E. M. Ward's well-known picture represents Dr. Johnson impatiently awaiting an audience. At 25, **Brook Street,** Handel lived for over thirty years. In this street is *Claridge's Hotel.* **Grosvenor Square** (Plan III. H. 8) is one of the finest in London. No. 4 is the **Italian Embassy.** Lord Lytton, the novelist, lived at No. 12; *Rienzi* and *The Last Days of Pompeii* were written at 36, Hertford Street.

We now return to **Hyde Park Corner** (Plan III. H. 9—station on Piccadilly Tube), another of London's landmarks, and one of the world's busiest traffic centres. Vehicular traffic passes the "Corner" on the gyratory system. A recent census showed that some 83,000 vehicles pass this point between 8 a.m. and 8 p.m. —or nearly 100 a minute. The large building at the corner of Grosvenor Place is **St. George's Hospital.** At the entrance to the Green Park (p. 122) is the **Wellington Arch,** surmounted by Adrian Jones's imposing quadriga. The arch is matched in grace by the screen entrance to Hyde Park, a triple gateway erected in 1826 from the designs of Decimus Burton. The reliefs are copied from the Elgin Marbles. On the road "islands" are memorials to fallen members of the **Machine Gun Corps** and of the **Royal Regiment of Artillery.**

Hyde Park

(**Plan** III. F., G. and H. 8 and 9)

has an area of 361 acres, and is joined on the west by **Kensington Gardens** (Plan III. E. and F. 8 and 9), with 275 acres, the two together forming London's finest lung. From Park Lane to Kensington Palace is about a mile and a half, while from Marble Arch to Hyde Park Corner is the best part of a mile. What London owes to this delightful stretch of greenery can never be told. Prior to the Dissolution the park formed part of the Manor of Hyde, and was the property of the Abbey of Westminster. By Henry VIII. it was converted into a deer-park and under the Stuarts it was used for horse-racing. King William and Queen Anne caused a number of improvements to be made; but it is to Queen Caroline, the consort of George II., that we owe its most attractive feature, the **Serpentine,** an artificial sheet of water, stretching from Lancaster Gate in a south-easterly direction to the **Dell,** opposite Albert Gate, and having with the Long Water an area of 41 acres. Notice boards point the way to the various gates (see plan, pp. 136–7).

Motors may use the avenues through the Park, but carts and wagons are not permitted to enter. Cyclists may use all roads open to wheeled traffic. The speed of motor vehicles is limited to twenty miles an hour, and they are not allowed to use the road between the Achilles statue and the Powder Magazine.

Chairs.—A *2d.* ticket entitles one to the use during the day of a chair in Hyde Park, Kensington Gardens, St. James's, or the Green Park.

Bathing (Mixed) is allowed in the Serpentine all day from May to September on weekdays and from 6 a.m. to 10 a.m. on Sundays; in the winter months the hours are from 7 a.m. to 8.30 a.m. on weekdays and from 7 a.m. to 9 a.m. on Sundays. A charge of *3d.* is made for use of dressing accommodation in the Pavilion or the marquees; free dressing enclosures are also provided. A few hardy enthusiasts have achieved a well-earned notoriety by taking their morning dip all the year round.

Boating can be enjoyed for 1*s.* to 1*s.* 6*d.* per hour (boathouse on north side, close to the Humane Society's Receiving House).

Teas, light luncheons, etc., can be obtained at the Ring Tea House, between the Marble Arch and the Serpentine, and also at the Tea House in Kensington Gardens, near the Serpentine Bridge.

Entering from Hyde Park Corner, we have on the left the well-known **Rotten Row,** a corruption of *route du roi,* a course of a mile and a half reserved for riders. The drive adjoining is thronged on fine afternoons in the season with the motors of the fashionable. On the north side of the Serpentine is the **Ladies' Mile.** The **Bandstand** is occupied in summer by a first-class band. The **Ring Tea House,** a little north of the Serpentine, is popular in summer. The "Ring" was a great resort of rank and fashion in Stuart and Commonwealth times.

As already mentioned (p. 120) the bird-life of London is remarkably rich, and in 1925 an "official" **Bird Sanctuary** was opened a few hundred yards west of the Superintendent's House in Hyde Park. The Sanctuary forms a **Memorial of W. H. Hudson,** "writer and field naturalist"; but the pretty bird bath is, in the opinion of many, marred by *Epstein's* panel of Rima (see Hudson's *Green Mansions*).

The Flower Beds are in spring and summer a blaze of colour, the displays of flowers attracting thousands of admirers.

Their leafy glades and vistas give to Kensington Gardens a charm denied to Hyde Park, the northern part of which is for the most part bare and flat. Advantage is taken of this fact by the promoters of political meetings and demonstrations, which often attain to huge proportions. At week-ends and on summer evenings the corner nearest the Marble Arch is generally the venue of a number of earnest orators, each with his knot of more or less appreciative listeners. It is a side of London life of which little is seen at other times, and the visitor in search of mild amusement may be recommended to take a stroll in this direction.

The Marble Arch,

(**Plan** III. G. 8)

at the north-east corner of the Park, was intended by George IV. to form the portal of Buckingham Palace, but by a miscalculation it was made too narrow to admit the State coach. It cost £80,000, and the gates another £3,000. The arch was placed in its present position in 1851. This is another of the busy corners of London, a recent census showing that between 8 a.m. and 8 p.m. no fewer than 60,000 vehicles passed. With a view to relieving this congestion, the park boundary was a few years ago set back, leaving the Marble Arch in the centre

Herbert Felton,] *[London.*

ST. JAMES'S PARK.

[*Topical.*

PARK SCENES.

(1) ST. JAMES'S PARK; (2 & 3) IN HYDE PARK.

[*Fox.*

PICCADILLY CIRCUS.

[*Felton.*

REGENT STREET.

F. Frith & Co., Ltd.,] [Reigate.

ROTTEN ROW, HYDE PARK.

of a spacious "circulating area." Traffic passes on the "roundabout" or gyratory system.

(For a note concerning **Tyburn** see p. 154.)

To the west of Hyde Park are—

Kensington Gardens,

which with their broad avenues and charming water scenery give sudden surprises of landscape scarcely surpassed for beauty in any part of England. The gardens, first laid out in the reign of William III., were considerably enlarged in that of George II. At this period Queen Caroline appropriated about 300 acres of the old Hyde Park and separated them from the park by a fosse and sunken wall.

The Serpentine is crossed at the entrance to Kensington Gardens by a five-arched stone **Bridge,** the view from which on either side, with its combination of water and woodland, is exquisite. On the Kensington Gardens side of the bridge is a popular *Refreshment Pavilion*; and on the other side is the **Powder Magazine.** The **Round Pond,** with an area of 7 acres, is beloved by juvenile yachtsmen. At the end of the **Broad Walk,** 50 ft. wide, between the Round Pond and Kensington Palace, is a white marble *Statue of Queen Victoria* by Princess Louise. The huge equestrian statue by G. F. Watts, 12 ft. high, representing *Physical Energy*, is a replica of the central portion of the Rhodes Memorial on the slope of Table Mountain, Cape Town. Youthful visitors especially will seek out with eagerness the *Statue of Peter Pan*, by *Sir George Frampton, R.A.* In the Children's Playground is an "Elfin Tree," with gnomes, fairies, etc.

Kensington Palace.

Plan III. E. 9.
Nearest Stations.—High Street, Kensington (District); Queen's Road (Central London).
Buses serving Kensington High Street or Notting Hill Gate pass the ends of the Broad Walk.
Admission.—The State Apartments are open to the public from March to October (inclusive) on *Saturday and Sunday afternoons only*, from 2 until 6 (October till 5 only). Admission 6*d*.

Here Queen Victoria was born (May 24, 1819) and spent her childhood; and here on the morning of June 21, 1837, she received the news of her accession to the throne. Here, too, was born on the 26th May, 1867, the Princess May, now Queen Mary. William III. purchased the mansion, then known as Nottingham House, from Lord Chancellor Finch; and Sir Christopher Wren was employed to extend and adapt it as a royal residence. King William, Queen Mary, Queen Anne, her husband (Prince George of Denmark), and George II. all died here. Under George I. an additional suite of state rooms was constructed by Wm. Kent. Several suites of rooms in the Palace are still occupied by relatives of the Royal Family.

In that mellow part of Kensington which lies between the Gardens and Holland Park are many delightful residences favoured by successful lawyers, literary men and artists. At No. 2, Palace Gardens (Plan III. D. 9), close to the west boundary of the gardens, Thackeray died in 1863. At No. 16 (formerly 13), Young Street, on the other side of High Street, *Vanity Fair*, *Pendennis*, and other works were written. Lord Macaulay died at Holly Lodge, Campden Hill, in 1859.

Slightly farther west, in extensive grounds bordering the Kensington Road, is **Holland House,** built by Sir Walter Cope in 1607.

At the Commonwealth it passed to General Fairfax, and Cromwell and Ireton were often here. On his marriage to the Countess of Warwick (a daughter of Sir W. Cope) in 1716, Addison became the nominal master of the house. Here, in 1719, he died, and the house passed from the Warwick family to Henry Fox, the father of the famous statesman, Charles James Fox. For a long period it was the recognized rallying-place of the Whigs, and the most brilliant social and literary centre in London. It is the residence of Lord Ilchester.

A turning just beyond the grounds of Holland House leads to Holland Park Road, where at No. 12 (north side) is **Leighton House** (Plan III. C. 10), designed and used as a residence by Lord Leighton, P.R.A. (d. 1896). In 1925 the house and its contents were generously presented by Mrs. Russell Barrington to the Kensington Borough Council, who have also acquired the freehold of the property. (*Admission free* ; Mondays, Tuesdays, and Thursdays, 11–3 ; Wednesdays and Fridays, 11–1 ; Saturdays, 11–5. *Closed on Sundays.*)

The house contains several oil paintings by Lord Leighton, a large collection of his original drawings and sketches, and proof engravings and photographic reproductions of his principal pictures. The chief feature is the beautiful Arab Hall. The tiles were collected by Lord Leighton and his friends during visits to the East, and most of them are three hundred years old, while two are of the fourteenth century. The Damascene windows, with their gorgeous colouring, are very fine.

We can make our way back to Charing Cross either by train from Kensington High Street, or by bus along Kensington Gore and Knightsbridge. The latter route affords an opportunity for noting a few features of interest omitted on our outward ramble through the parks. **Kensington High Street** is a favourite shopping quarter, with many large stores, including *Barkers.*

Kensington Gore takes its name from *Gore House,* almost as famous as Holland House in the early part of the last century as a literary and political centre. The word Gore, by the way, has no sanguinary significance. It is used in the sense, known to dressmakers, of "a wedge-shaped piece"—in this case a plot of ground.

The **Royal Albert Hall** (Plan III. F. 9) was built 1867–1871 as a memorial of the Prince Consort, at a cost of £200,000.

It is one of the largest halls in the world, and will comfortably seat 8,000 people, with another 1,100 in the orchestra. Though frequently used for political demonstrations, boxing contests, and other great gatherings, it is principally famous for musical performances on a large scale. Not every singer or speaker emerges successfully from the ordeal of facing that vast audience. In the arena alone there is space for 1,000 persons, while the amphitheatre holds nearly 1,400. Above are three rows of boxes, many of them private property, and still higher are the balcony and a picture gallery and promenade. The magnificent **Organ,** built by Willis and recently enlarged, has over 1,000 pipes and is probably the largest organ in the world.

On the west side of the Hall is **Alexandra House,** a hostel for women students. In the district immediately south of the Albert Hall are several important colleges, as well as the South Kensington Museums (see pp. 171–180).

Opposite the Albert Hall, just within Kensington Gardens, is the **Albert Memorial** (Plan III. F. 9), erected to the memory of the Prince Consort.

The memorial cost £120,000, and was designed by Sir Gilbert Scott, on the model of an Eleanor cross. The pedestal is adorned with 178 marble relievos of musicians, poets, painters, architects and sculptors of all times. Among the public undertakings with which the Prince identified himself was the Great Exhibition of 1851, held in the neighbouring Hyde Park. Hence the statue holds a copy of the exhibition catalogue.

Lowther Lodge is the home of the **Royal Geographical Society.** The Museum contains mementoes of Captain Scott's Antarctic expedition and many other objects of geographical interest. There is an excellent reference library. Note the statue of Sir Ernest Shackleton, facing Exhibition Road.

No. 13, Prince's Gate, was for some time the home of the late J. Pierpont Morgan; on his death he presented the mansion to the United States Government for the use of the Ambassador to the Court of St. James's.

Passing **Knightsbridge Barracks,** we reach the *Hyde Park Hotel*, opposite which the **Brompton Road** runs off in a south-westerly direction to Cromwell Road and the South Kensington Museums (p. 170); while **Sloane Street** leads due south to Chelsea. No. 60, Knightsbridge (with pillared portico) is the home of the **Royal Thames Yacht Club.** The fine mansion on the eastern side of **Albert Gate** is the **French Embassy,** built originally for George Hudson, the "railway king."

REGENT STREET AND REGENT'S PARK.

ROUTE V.—REGENT STREET—OXFORD CIRCUS—THE WALLACE COLLECTION—MARYLEBONE ROAD—REGENT'S PARK—THE ZOOLOGICAL GARDENS—EDGWARE ROAD—BAYSWATER ROAD.

AGAIN starting from Piccadilly Circus, let us turn up Regent Street and further explore "Shopland."

Regent Street.

Plans II. and III. I. 7 and 8.
Nearest Stations.—North end: Oxford Circus (Central London and Bakerloo Tubes). South end: Piccadilly Circus (Bakerloo and Piccadilly Tubes).
Buses from all quarters pass through the street or touch Piccadilly Circus (at the southern end) or Oxford Circus (to the north).

Both Regent Street and Regent's Park owe their existence to a magnificent whim of George IV., who, as Prince Regent, lived in Carlton House, which stood on the spot now occupied by the southern half of Waterloo Place. He conceived the idea of building a villa on or near Primrose Hill (then a rural spot), and projected a fine new road, three miles long, to connect it with Carlton House. The villa never became a reality; but Regent Street did, and the New or Regent's Park followed. The street was laid out in 1813–20 by the architect Nash, of whom it was said:—

"Augustus at Rome was for building renown'd,
For of marble he left what of brick he had found;
But is not our Nash, too, a very great master,
He finds us all brick and he leaves us all plaster?"

After a century of service, Nash's buildings have in recent times been razed, their place being taken by marble and ferro-concrete "palaces" that make Regent Street without question the finest shopping thoroughfare in the world. The architect mainly responsible was Sir Reginald Blomfield. It would be difficult to beat the fine view from Piccadilly Circus into Regent Street, with the splendid sweep of the Quadrant and the fine building of the County Fire Office, and the observant loiterer will find many interesting details in doorways, balconies, etc.

Overlooking Piccadilly Circus are the blocks housing Swan & Edgar's. Next comes the *Piccadilly Hotel*, with frontages both to Regent Street and Piccadilly. Glasshouse Street on the right leads to the *Regent Palace Hotel* (Messrs. J. Lyons & Co.), and to **Golden Square,** familiar, in name at least, to readers of *Nicholas Nickleby*. Farther north is **Great Marlborough Street,** with a noted police court where the seamy side of West End life is focused. A notably beautiful Tudor building in Great Marlborough Street forms part of *Liberty's* premises. Children love to watch the clock, St. George engaging the Dragon at each quarter hour and slaying him at the hour. Note the fine frieze on the Regent Street front of Liberty's premises. Near at hand is the **Palladium.**

Hanover Street, on the west side of Regent Street, brings one to **Hanover Square,** where are the headquarters of several learned societies, and a striking modern building forming the headquarters of the Celanese Corporation. In George Street, south of the Square, is the church of **St. George's, Hanover Square,** the scene of so many fashionable marriages. It dates from 1725, and contains several stained-glass windows made in Mechlin at least two centuries earlier.

Among the marriages recorded in the registers are those of Sir William Hamilton to Nelson's "Emma" in 1791; Benjamin Disraeli to Mary Ann Lewis in 1839; George Eliot in 1880; "Theodore Roosevelt, twenty-eight, widower, ranchman," and "Edith Kermit Carow" (Dec. 2, 1886); and Lord Oxford and Asquith (1894).

Oxford Circus,

(Plan II. I. 7)

one of the busiest bus and tube centres, has, like Regent Street itself, been transformed by the rebuilding of business premises. Above and below ground, it is a busy spot: 36 million passengers used the tube station during a recent year; important improvements have made it capable of handling 50 million passengers per annum. Here Regent Street crosses **Oxford Street** (p. 157), and then continues northward, as Langham Place and Portland Place, to the Marylebone Road. At the head of Regent Street is **All Souls' Church,** with its peculiar "extinguisher" spire, designed by Nash. On the western side is the **Polytechnic,** founded by Quintin Hogg in 1882 and rebuilt at a cost of £90,000 in 1911 as a memorial of King Edward VII. This institution has something like 11,000 students attending its numerous classes. The large hall is frequently used as a cinema. On the other side of Regent Street is **Queen's Hall,** seating 3,000. Here many of the principal London concerts are held, including the famous "Proms" and the broadcast symphony concerts: indeed, Queen's Hall, with the adjacent St. George's Hall, so long associated with "Maskelyne's

Magic," are now to be regarded as studios attached to **Broadcasting House,** the magnificent home of the **British Broadcasting Corporation,** at the foot of Portland Place. The transmitting aerial is at Brookman's Park, on the northern outskirts of London. Even this huge building and the adjacent halls are insufficient for the purpose, however, and there are large and important "studios" in Maida Vale and elsewhere. Television is transmitted from Alexandra Palace (p. 228). In Ridinghouse Street, opposite the Queen's Hall, is the **Radium Institute.** The **Philharmonic Hall,** in Great Portland Street, is used for concerts, cinema displays and lectures.

Portland Place is one of the most spacious of London's thoroughfares, having a width of 120 ft. The severely plain mansions on either side contain some beautiful Adam ceilings, doors and fireplaces and in contrast are some striking modern buildings, one of the best being at No. 66—the new home of the **Royal Institute of British Architects,** founded in 1837, with a valuable library of architectural works and now incorporating the Society of Architects. In the roadway is a statue of *Quintin Hogg* (see p. 145). Opposite No. 47 (residence of the late Field-Marshal Earl Roberts: d. 1914) stands an equestrian statue by John Tweed of *Field-Marshal Sir George White* (d. 1912). Opposite No. 92 is a statue of *Lord Lister,* and close by (at No. 28), appropriately, is the **Institute of Hygiene.** At No. 26 is the *Royal Society of Tropical Medicine and Hygiene.* At No. 39 is the *British College of Nurses.* Portland Place terminates in **Park Crescent,** with the *Regent's Park Station* of the Bakerloo Tube beneath the garden in front of it. Near the eastern horn of the Crescent is *Great Portland Street Station,* on the Metropolitan (Circle) Railway, and across the road is Regent's Park (p. 151). In **Great Portland Street,** a leading centre of the motor-car and accessories industries, are the **Royal National Orthopædic Hospital** and the **National Institute for the Blind,** and in Hallam Street (44–46) is housed the **General Medical Council.**

In **Margaret Street,** which crosses Regent Street immediately to the north of Oxford Street, is **All Saints' Church.** Mortimer Street leads through a somewhat frowsy locality to the busy **Middlesex Hospital,** recently rebuilt. At No. 76 (tablet), Charlotte Street, Constable, the great landscape painter, lived from 1822 until his death in 1837. Here, too, is the **Scala Theatre.** In **Fitzroy Square** are the headquarters of the **British Drama League,** with a valuable library, and **St. Luke's Hostel,** providing treatment and a nursing home for the clergy, their wives and children.

On the other (western) side of the upper part of Regent Street we have **Cavendish Square,** an important feature of which is the **Cowdray Club,** for nurses and professional women. **Harley Street, Wimpole Street,** and other thoroughfares in the neighbourhood are noted for the large number of consulting physicians and specialists residing in them. The imposing Grecian building at the corner of Wimpole Street and Henrietta Street is the headquarters of the **Royal Society of Medicine.** The parent Society was founded in 1805; the present organization is a fusion of fifteen former societies. The library contains over 100,000 volumes.

The streets hereabouts have interesting associations:

Holles Street, connecting Cavendish Square with Oxford Street, was the birthplace of Lord Byron in 1788. The site of the house (formerly No. 24) forms part of the premises of Messrs. John Lewis and Co., who have erected a bronze bust to the poet's memory.

No. 50, Wimpole Street (tablet) was the home, before her marriage, of Elizabeth Barrett Browning; Henry Hallam's *Constitutional History of England* and *The Literature of Europe in the 15th, 16th and 17th Centuries* were written at No. 67 (tablet), where he resided from 1819 to 1840; and at No. 82 Wilkie Collins died in 1889. At No. 73, Harley Street, lived Sir Charles Lyell, the great geologist, and later, W. E. Gladstone; No. 38 (formerly 13) was the home of Barry Cornwall and Adelaide Anne Proctor; William Beckford, the eccentric author of *Vathek*, lived at No. 100. Anthony Trollope died at 34, Welbeck Street; No. 48 (tablet) was the residence of Dr. Thomas Young, the Egyptologist. No. 23, Queen Anne Street (tablet) was the home of J. M. W. Turner. In Devonshire Street, farther north, lived Sir John Herschel, the great astronomer (No. 56—tablet); while No. 1, Devonshire Terrace, at the corner of High Street and Marylebone Road (tablet), was the home from 1839 to 1851 of Charles Dickens. Here he wrote, among other works, *The Old Curiosity Shop*, *Martin Chuzzlewit* and portions of *Dombey & Son* and *David Copperfield*.

In Wigmore Street are **Wigmore Hall** and **Grotrian Hall,** well-known to music-lovers.

Bentinck Street leads into **Manchester Square,** on the north side of which is **Hertford House,** the stately mansion containing—

The Wallace Collection.

Plan II. H. 7.
Nearest Stations.—Bond Street (Central London Tube), Baker Street (Metropolitan Railway and Bakerloo Tube).
Buses passing along Oxford Street or Baker Street bring one within a minute's walk of the Collection. Alight at Selfridge's or at George Street.
Admission.—Free except on Tuesdays and Fridays, when *6d.* is charged. Open daily from 10 a.m. to 5 p.m.; Sundays, 2 to 5. Closed on Good Friday, Christmas Eve and Christmas Day.
Catalogues of Paintings, Furniture and Objects of Art, European Arms and Armour, and a General Guide can be obtained at entrance.
Lectures are given each afternoon except Wednesday and on Saturday morning on subjects of interest in the Collection. Particulars on application to the Director.

This superb, and in some respects unrivalled, collection of

pictures, furniture, porcelain, miniatures, enamels and European and Oriental arms and armour was bequeathed to the nation by Lady Wallace, on condition that the Government should give a site in a central part of London, and build thereon a special museum to contain it. Eventually the conclusion was come to that no temple could more fittingly enshrine these priceless treasures than their old home. Hertford House was accordingly purchased and reconstructed for the purpose, at a cost of £100,000, the public opening taking place in 1900. The collection was formed in the main by Francis Charles, third Marquis, and Richard, fourth Marquis of Hertford, and supplemented by Sir Richard Wallace, to whom it passed by bequest. The first-named nobleman enjoys a dubious fame as the Marquis of Steyne of Thackeray's *Vanity Fair*. Judged merely as a picture gallery, the collection is one of the finest in Europe, being notably strong in masters of the French School of the eighteenth century. The English, Dutch, Italian and Spanish schools are also worthily represented. The collection of artistic furniture of the periods of Louis XIV., XV. and XVI. is unique; while the Sèvres porcelain can only be rivalled by the collections at Windsor Castle and Buckingham Palace. The collection of arms and armour includes the choicest pieces of the Debruge, Meyrick and Nieuwekerke collections.

Passing the turnstile, we at once go through the door on our right to—

Room I–II.—In the centre is a case containing medals and relics of the French royal house.

Room III.—The chief attraction here is the collection of Limoges enamels and Palissy and Nuremberg wares.

Room IV. is interesting on account of the coloured tiles with which floor, walls and ceiling are covered. Cases in the centre of the room contain beautiful metal-work and some curious reliefs and portraits in coloured wax—sixteenth and seventeenth century work. In the wall cases is the fine display of Oriental armour, which constitutes one of the chief attractions of the collection. Note the case, beside the stairs at the farther end of room, containing exquisitely jewelled swords and daggers.

Room V.—The first room in the famous collection of European armour. Early firearms, many of them beautifully decorated. In centre of room is 851, "Equestrian Suit in Black and Gold," said to have belonged to Joseph of Bavaria.

Room VI.—In the centre of the room is a large mounted suit of complete war harness for man and horse, of French manufacture and fashion, 1460–80. Probably the most perfect sets in existence of this class. The walls and cases are taken up with helmets, shields, swords, etc.

Room VII. contains swords, helmets, shields, armour, etc.,

[*Daily Herald.*

MARBLE ARCH AND HYDE PARK.

[*Dixon Scott.*

STATUE OF PETER PAN, KENSINGTON GARDENS.

THE UNIVERSITY OF LONDON.

The first section of this magnificent pile, facing Montague Place, was completed in 1936.

Herbert Felton,] *[London.*

THE BRITISH MUSEUM.

all beautifully decorated, and a notable carved walnut dressoir of the fifteenth or sixteenth century.

Room VIII.—Pictures, sculptures and furniture.

Founder's Room (old Board Room).

Room IX.—Portraits of royalty. 564, *Sully's* Queen Victoria; 563, George IV, *Hoppner*. Also 37, *Romney's* "Perdita"; 45, "Perdita," by *Reynolds*; 39, "Miss Siddons," *Lawrence*.

Room X.—In the centre of this room is a case of lovely miniatures. Around the room are *Armoires* and caskets beautifully decorated with marqueterie work.

Room XI.—Here again miniatures are the principal attraction.

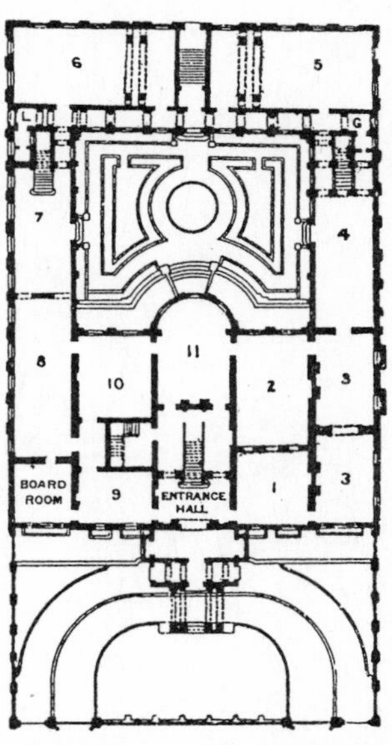

WALLACE COLLECTION: THE GROUND FLOOR.

We now return to the Entrance Hall and ascend the handsome staircase of marble, surmounted by a Louis XIV. balustrade and decorated with large paintings by *Boucher*.

At the top of the stairs we turn to the left.

Room XII.—In this room stands a magnificent armoire of the period of Louis XVI., inlaid with tortoise-shell. Observe also a series of paintings of Venice by Guardi. In the middle of the room are cases containing Sèvres porcelain.

Room XIII. Dutch Pictures.

Room XIV. contains pictures of the Dutch School of the seventeenth century. Note 99, "Landscape with Water-Mill," by *Hobbema* (1638–1709), and Rembrandt's "Portrait of the Artist in a Cap" (52).

Room XV.—Here note especially 41, "A Lady Unknown"; 558, "Countess of Blessington," both by *Sir T. Lawrence*; 281, *Corot's* "Macbeth," paintings by Bonington, and a charming series of small pictures by *Meissonier* (1815–1891) in his best style.

Room XVI.—This room contains many of the gems of the picture collection. Those who find pleasure in comparing the styles of various portrait painters have here an almost unique opportunity, for there are characteristic examples by some of the world's masters. 84, "The Laughing Cavalier," *Frans Hals* (1580 or 81–1666); 6 and 12, "Don Baltasar Carlos," and 88, "Lady with Fan," by *Velazquez* (1599–1660); 94, *Van Dyck's* "Philip le Roy"; 38, "Nelly O'Brien," and 35, "Mrs. Carnac," by *Reynolds*; 42, *Gainsborough's* "Perdita" (Mrs. Robinson), of whom portraits by Romney (37) and Reynolds (45) are also in the Wallace Collection (Room IX.). There are also examples of Rubens: 63, the "Rainbow Landscape," and 93, "Christ's charge to Peter."

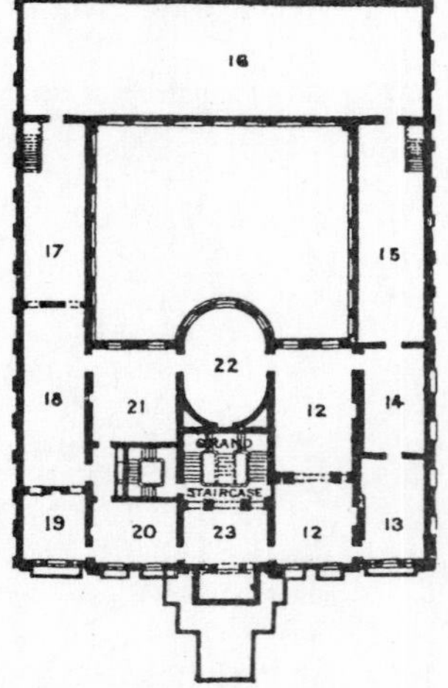

WALLACE COLLECTION: THE FIRST FLOOR.

Room XVII.—Sixteenth and seventeenth century schools. Note especially 8, "Virgin and Child," by *Luini*; 9, "Virgin and Child, with St. John and the two Angels," by *Andrea del Sarto* (1486–1531).

Room XVIII.—Pictures by *Watteau, Lancret, Fragonard, Boucher,* etc. Note also 449, "Boy in Red," *Madame Le Brun.*

Room XIX.—Decorative pieces by *Boucher.*

Room XX.—Pictures by Greuze, Pater, Lancret, etc.

Room XXI.—Pictures by Greuze, Pater, etc.

Room XXII.—Pictures by Greuze and Pater.

Vestibule.—French schools of eighteenth century.

Facing Spanish Place, a few yards north of the Wallace Collection, is **St. James's Roman Catholic Church,** built in 1890 to replace the old Spanish Embassy Chapel.

In Portman Square is Home House, generously presented by Mr. Samuel Courtauld to the trustees of the **Courtauld Institute of Art,** to serve as a temporary headquarters pending the construction of the Institute which is to form part of the new London University Building (see p. 159).

West of Hertford House is **Baker Street,** a busy thoroughfare connecting Oxford Street with the Marylebone Road and Regent's Park, and containing the studios of some of the leading photographers. On the west side are the **Portman Rooms,** a resort of Beau Brummell and other famous men of his period, and much used for dances, etc. In King Street is the **London Club,** with a large ballroom and restaurant. Close at hand is the **French Chapel,** in King Street.

No. 31, Baker Street (tablet) was the birthplace of Lord Lytton, the novelist. No. 12, Seymour Street (tablet) was the residence (1861–4) of M. W. Balfe, the composer. No. 14, York Place (tablet) was the residence of William Pitt and Lady Hester Stanhope during 1803 and 1804.

Baker Street Station (Plan II. G. 6), as well as being an important station on the Underground Railway, is the starting-point of the Metropolitan Extension Railway to Wembley Park, Harrow, etc. (see p. 60). Note the fine premises of the *Abbey Road Building Society.*

The **Marylebone Road** (Plan II. G. and H. 6), with its continuation **Euston Road** (Plan II. I. and K. 5 and 6), runs from Edgware Road to King's Cross. Though a thoroughfare of little attractiveness, it is important, for here are no fewer than four of the principal railway termini. A quarter of a mile to the west of Baker Street is **Marylebone Station,** the terminus of the Great Central Section of the London and North-Eastern Railway and the administrative headquarters of the Group. Almost facing the station entry is the **Marylebone Town Hall,** a classical building, of Portland stone. **Marylebone** (Mary-le-bourne) derives its name from the old Tyburn stream, which flowed from Kilburn to the Thames. A small obelisk in the churchyard of **Marylebone Parish Church,** a short distance east of Baker Street, marks the grave of *Charles Wesley* (1788). Almost opposite is **Madame Tussaud's,** the famous waxwork exhibition. At York Gate is the **Royal Academy of Music,** granting the coveted degrees of A.R.A.M. and L.R.A.M. The Academy was founded in 1822 and incorporated by Royal Charter in 1830.

Upper Baker Street leads directly to the Clarence Gate of—

Regent's Park.

Plan II. G. and H. 4, 5 and 6.
Nearest Stations.—Baker Street, Great Portland Street and St. John's Wood (Metropolitan); Baker Street and Regent's Park (Bakerloo Tube); Chalk Farm or Camden Town on the Morden–Edgware line.

This is one of the largest of the London parks, having, with Primrose Hill to the north, an area of 473 acres. It was laid out by Nash for the Prince Regent, after whom it is named, in accordance with the same royal plan which led to the construction of Regent Street (see p. 144). Around the Park runs a pretty road, two miles in circuit, known as the **Outer Circle.** The much smaller **Inner Circle** encloses the gardens formerly maintained by the Royal Botanic Society, but now open to the public and known as **Queen Mary's Gardens.** A very successful modern innovation is the **Open-Air Theatre.** On the western side of the Park is a large, many-armed **Lake,** with islands and bridges. Between this and Queen Mary's Gardens is **Bedford College,** affiliated to London University, the most important college for women in London. *St. John's Lodge* is now occupied by the *Institute of Archæology.* An attractive feature of the Park is the **Broad Walk,** from near the Marylebone Road entrance to the Zoological Gardens. Its flower-beds present at nearly all seasons a display of great beauty, and the chestnut avenue in spring rivals the more famous avenue in Bushy Park. Additional interest is lent to the park by the presence of large numbers of squirrels and wood-pigeons.

The recently razed St. Dunstan's Lodge, on the western side of the Park, gave its name to the famous **St. Dunstan's** institution for men blinded in the Great War.

The Zoological Gardens.

Admission.—The Gardens are open daily from 9 a.m. until sunset or 7 p.m. when sunset is later. (Wednesdays and Thursdays, June 2 to Sept. 9, until 11.30 p.m.) Admission, 1*s.* except on Mondays (other than Bank Holidays), when only 6*d.* is charged. Children, 6*d.* at all times. Admission to Aquarium, 1*s.*; children, 6*d.* Admission on Sundays only by order from a Fellow of the Society.

Bath Chairs, with attendants, can be obtained at Main Entrance.

Entrances.—The *Main Entrance* is in the Outer Circle of Regent's Park. The *North Entrance* is in Albert Road, on the northern side of the Regent's Canal. The *South Entrance* is near the head of the Broad Walk.

Motor Parking Place opposite main entrance (Plan II. H. 5).

Nearest Stations.—Camden Town, on the Morden–Edgware Line, is the nearest station.
St. John's Wood (Met.) is about ½ mile west of Main Entrance. Great Portland Street (Met.) and Regent's Park station, on the Bakerloo Tube, are about half a mile south of South Entrance. Enter Regent's Park opposite Park Square, and follow Broad Walk northward.
Chalk Farm Station (North London—L.M.S.) is about half a mile north of North Entrance.

Refreshments.—There are large Refreshment Pavilions towards the eastern side of the Gardens, where luncheons, teas, etc., can be obtained at moderate prices. There is another near the Mappin Terraces and smaller buffets are scattered in various parts.

Feeding Times.—With many visitors, particularly juveniles, the question of personal refreshment is here for once eclipsed in interest in the feeding of other creatures. The usual times are as follows: Pelicans, 2.30; polar bears and others, 3; eagles, 3.30 (except Wednesdays); lions, tigers and other beasts of prey, 4 (winter 3); seals and sea-lions, 4.30 (winter, 3.30); diving-birds, 3.15 p.m.; reptiles, Fridays, 3; Aquarium, Tuesdays and Fridays, noon. Carrots, raisins, bananas, oranges and pea-nuts are among the most popular dainties for distribution by the visitors.

The Zoological Gardens, familiarly known to Londoners as "the Zoo," occupy an area of about 34 acres in the northern part of Regent's Park. The grounds are intersected by the Outer Circle and by the Grand Union Canal, three divisions being thus formed, known respectively as the North Garden, the Middle Garden, and the South Garden. The three portions are connected by tunnels under the Outer Circle and by two bridges over the Canal. The houses of the larger animals: elephants, rhinoceroses, hippopotamuses, giraffes, etc., are in the middle portion; while the bears, lions, monkeys, reptiles, etc., are in the southern part of the Gardens. The northern strip bordering the Grand Union Canal accommodates the cranes, owls, pheasants, etc. The western part of this section is connected by a footway (forming part of the Primrose Hill bridge over the Canal) with the zebra and giraffe houses. The **Mappin Terraces** have tiers of enclosures for the animals, rising one above the other, with walks in between for the public, the animals being retained by deep ditches and walls, without the aid of the usual prison-like bars. By means of a glass window the Polar bears may be watched as they dive through the water for their food. The **Aquarium,** beneath the Mappin Terraces, is the largest of its kind in the world, and its 3,000 inhabitants provide one of the greatest attractions of the Zoo. Behind the Mappin Terraces is **"Monkey Hill,"** a rocky prominence that is less natural than it looks, for the caves are heated on cold days, while in dull weather they are bathed in ultra-violet "artificial sunlight" by means of electric lamps. The Reptile House is in its way equally well-equipped.

We give a plan showing the various houses, but limits of space forbid any attempt at description. Parents and friends taking children are advised to coach themselves up beforehand as to the habits and degrees of ferocity of the various animals. To betray ignorance here is to forfeit all claim to respect. The most popular section with juveniles is probably **Pets' Corner,** where various animals may be fondled, and a photographer is in attendance.

The number of visitors exceeds two millions annually, for the Zoo is now London's almost sole place of outdoor entertainment. The number of vertebrate animals exhibited is usually over 3,000, the total number of inmates is about 10,000, and the annual food bill some £15,000. To attend to the wants of the varied family at the Zoo a staff of about a hundred men is required. (For the Society's "country Zoo" at **Whipsnade** see p. 275.) The **Zoological Society** was incorporated by Royal Charter in 1829.

Close to the South Entrance to the Zoo is the interesting **Royal Chapel of St. Katherine,** containing some splendid woodwork. From Stephen's reign the Queens of England have been patrons of St. Katherine's, which forms part of the dowry of the Queen Consort.

To the north of Regent's Park rises the grassy slope of **Primrose Hill** (see p. 37). Close to the north-west confines of the Park, and reached by the St. John's Wood Road, is **Lord's Cricket Ground** (Plan II. F. 5), the headquarters of English cricket (nearest station, St. John's Wood). The ground took its name from an early owner; it is now the property of the Marylebone Cricket Club—the M.C.C. The gateway forms a memorial of *W. G. Grace.* Here are played in June and July the Eton and Harrow, Oxford and Cambridge, and other great matches.

St. John's Wood Road drops down to the **Edgware Road,** a great trunk road—part of the old Watling Street—running in a north-westerly direction from the Marble Arch to Kilburn and Cricklewood, thence on to Hendon and St. Albans, and eventually through the Midlands to Holyhead. **Edgware Road Station** (Metropolitan and District Lines; Plan II. F. 7) may be entered either from Chapel Street or the Marylebone Road (p. 151). A few yards to the north is the station of the same name on the Bakerloo Tube.

Another important thoroughfare in this direction is the **Harrow Road,** which branches off from the Edgware Road beyond Chapel Street, and leads north-westward through Paddington to Willesden, and thence on to Harrow, passing **Wembley Stadium,** erected in connection with the British Empire Exhibition and now used for Greyhound and speedway racing and Football Association Cup Ties. The Stadium is most directly reached by rail from Baker Street or Marylebone stations. Adjoining it is the Empire Swimming Pool (skating and ice hockey in winter) and Sports Centre. **Kensal Green Cemetery** (Plan II. A. and B. 5), about 2 miles from Edgware Road, covers about 70 acres, and contains over 40,000 graves. Among the host of notabilities here interred may be mentioned Leigh Hunt, Thackeray, Tom Hood, Anthony Trollope, John Leech, and the Duke of Cambridge.

Turning southward along the Edgware Road, in the direction of the Marble Arch, we have on the right **Praed Street,** leading to **Paddington Station** (Plan II. F. 7), the terminus of the Great Western Railway, connected with the Bakerloo Tube and with the Paddington (Praed Street) and Paddington stations of the Metropolitan Line. Close at hand is the large **St. Mary's Hospital.** Set into the wall of *Lloyds Bank,* 195, Edgware Road, at the corner of Star Street, is an old stone marking "half a mile from Tyburn Gate" (see below).

At the **Marble Arch** (p. 140), the Edgware Road joins Oxford Street, which here changes its name to the Bayswater or **Uxbridge Road,** forming the northern boundary of Hyde Park and Kensington Gardens. At the intersection of the roadways stood the famous, or infamous, **Tyburn** gallows, the scene of countless executions.

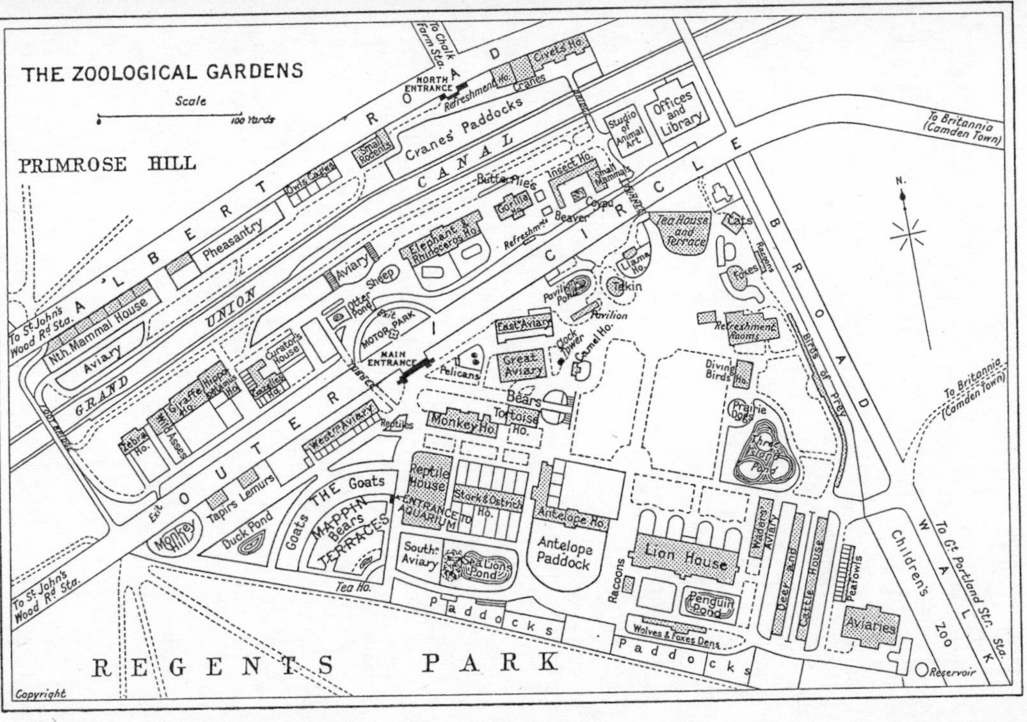
THE ZOOLOGICAL GARDENS
Scale
100 Yards
PRIMROSE HILL
REGENTS PARK
ALBERT ROAD
OUTER CIRCLE
GRAND UNION CANAL
BROAD WALK
To Chalk Farm Sta.
To St. John's Wood Rd. Sta.
To Britannia (Camden Town)
To Gt. Portland Str. Sta.
NORTH ENTRANCE
MAIN ENTRANCE
Civets Ho.
Refreshment Ho.
Cranes
Cranes' Paddocks
Studio of Animal Art
Offices and Library
Small Rodents
Owls Cages
Pheasantry
Nth. Mammal House
Aviary
Butterflies
Insect Ho.
Small Mammals
Gorilla Ho.
Coypu
Beaver
Refreshments
Elephant & Rhinoceros Ho.
Aviary
Sheep
Otter Pond
Exit
MOTOR PARK
Curator's House
Gazelles Ho.
Giraffe Ho.
Hippopotamus Ho.
Wild Asses
Zebra Ho.
FOOT BRIDGE
TUNNEL
Tea House and Terrace
Cats
Racoons
Foxes
Llama Ho.
Takin
Pavilion Pond
Pavilion
East Aviary
Clock Tower
Camel Ho.
Great Aviary
Pelicans
Refreshment Rooms
Diving Birds Ho.
Birds of Prey
Bears
Tortoise Ho.
Monkey Ho.
Reptiles
Western Aviary
Prairie Dogs
Three Island Pond
Reptile House
ENTRANCE TO AQUARIUM
Stork & Ostrich Ho.
Antelope Ho.
Antelope Paddock
THE Goats
Goats
MAPPIN TERRACES
Bears
Tapirs
Lemurs
Exit
Monkey Hill
Duck Pond
Tea Ho.
South Aviary
Sea Lions Pond
Paddocks
Racoons
Lion House
Penguin Pond
Wolves & Foxes Dens
Waders Aviary
Deer and Cattle House
Peafowls
Aviaries
Children's Zoo
Reservoir
Copyright

The exact site is indicated by a tablet on Hyde Park railings. The first recorded execution was that of William FitzOsbert, or "longbeard" (1196). Here also, to name only a few, William Wallace, the Scottish patriot (1305); Perkin Warbeck, the pretender (1499); Elizabeth Barton, the "Holy Maid of Kent" (1534); the notorious highwayman, Jack Sheppard (1724), were done to death. Two notable Roman Catholic martyrs were Dr. John Story (1571) and Oliver Plunket, Archbishop of Armagh (1681). A movable gallows was about 1760 substituted for the old fixed structure. After 1783 all executions took place at Newgate.

Close to the Marble Arch are the *Regal* and the *Marble Arch Cinemas, Maison Lyons Restaurant,* and the huge *Cumberland Hotel.*

Westward the busy roadway is overlooked by the stuccoed frontages of Hyde Park Gardens and Lancaster Gate. At No. 10 Hyde Park Place is the **Smallest House in London.** A short distance from the Marble Arch is the secluded old *Burial Ground of St. George's, Hanover Square.* The tombstones and monuments have been removed and ranged round the walls, which latter, by the way, were long patrolled at night by "Charlies" (watchmen) on account of the depredations of "body snatchers." At the entrance to the burial-ground is the *Chapel of the Ascension,* founded by the late Mrs. Russell Gurney, not for services, but expressly for "rest, meditation and prayer." The building (*open 2 to 4 or 5*) is elaborately decorated with Scriptural paintings by Frederic Shields (d. 1911).

Close to the Victoria Gate is the curious **Dogs' Cemetery.**

The cathedral-like fane of **Christ Church, Lancaster Gate,** is opposite the gate of the same name. A notable feature of **Queen's Road** is *Whiteley's* great store (now owned by Selfridge's).

By continuing westward along the Uxbridge Road, or taking the Central London Tube from Lancaster Gate or Queen's Road stations, we should reach **Shepherd's Bush** (Plan III. A. 8), by no means so rural as its name suggests. It is the site of the "White City," erected for the Franco-British Exhibition of 1908. The Stadium, in Wood Lane, is used for athletic meetings, baseball, etc.

From the **Marble Arch** an omnibus will take us back along the western part of **Oxford Street** to Regent Street, passing *Selfridge's* (on the left) and several other well-known establishments of the kind (see p. 157).

In Duke Street is the **King's Weigh House Chapel,** built to replace the famous chapel of that name in the City.

Herbert Felton,] [*London.*

THE VICTORIA AND ALBERT MUSEUM.

[*Felton.*

THE BROMPTON ORATORY.

[*Fox.*

THE GEOLOGICAL AND SCIENCE MUSEUMS.

OXFORD STREET AND HOLBORN.

ROUTE VI.—OXFORD STREET—SOHO—TOTTENHAM COURT ROAD—UNIVERSITY OF LONDON—BLOOMSBURY—THE BRITISH MUSEUM—HOLBORN.

WE will assume this time that the start is made from **Oxford Circus** (see p. 145), at the junction of Oxford Street with Regent Street.

Oxford Street.

Plan II. H. and I. 7.
Stations, commencing at west end, Marble Arch, Bond Street, Oxford Circus, Tottenham Court Road and Holborn (Kingsway). All these are on the Central London Tube, which runs below Oxford Street throughout its length. At Oxford Circus connection is made with the Bakerloo Tube, at Tottenham Court Road with the Morden–Edgware Line, and at Holborn with the Piccadilly Tube.
Buses.—A constant stream of buses from all parts of London passes through Oxford Street.

This has always been the principal traffic artery between the west and north-west of London and the City. Beneath it runs the Central London Railway. Although Oxford Street proper, from the Marble Arch to Tottenham Court Road, has only a length of a mile, it forms part of a great highway extending from the Bank to Shepherd's Bush, and thence viâ Acton and Ealing to Uxbridge and so to Oxford. In Oxford Street are some of the best-known shops in London, including *Peter Robinson's, Jay's, Marshall and Snelgrove's, Bourne and Hollingsworth's, D. H. Evans's, Waring's, Selfridge's,* and many others. Some idea of the value of sites in this favourite shopping quarter may be gathered from the statement that £30 a square foot is a not unusual price. Recent rebuilding has transformed the appearance of Oxford Street, and the process is being continued.

Eastward from Oxford Circus is **Wardour Street,** once noted for its old furniture and curiosity shops, but now the headquarters of the cinema trade. It lies near the heart of the **Soho** quarter, almost entirely occupied by foreigners of various nationalities, and famous for its restaurants. It is also becoming noted for the number of its motor garages. In recent years the foreign quarter seems to have overflowed to the other side of Oxford Street, about Charlotte Street. At the north-west angle of **Soho Square** is the **French Protestant Church ;** on the east side is the Roman Catholic **Church of St. Patrick.** The Duke of Monmouth's house—it will be recalled that " Soho " was his battle-cry at Sedgemoor—stood on the site of the present Hospital for Women.

At No. 51, **Frith Street,** south of the Square, Mozart lived as a boy. Hazlitt died at No. 6, in 1830. In **Dean Street,** to the west, are the **Royalty Theatre** and **St. Anne's Church,** the latter notable as the burial-place of William Hazlitt (d. 1830), and of the unfortunate Theodore, King of Corsica, who died at Soho in 1756, as a tablet on the west wall of the tower records—

"Immediately after leaving the King's Bench Prison by the benefit of the Act of Insolvency, in consequence of which he registered his kingdom of Corsica for the use of his creditors."

> "The Grave, great Teacher, to a level brings
> Heroes and Beggars, Galley slaves and Kings,
> But Theodore this Moral learn'd ere dead.
> Fate pour'd its lessons on his living Head:
> Bestow'd a Kingdom, and denied him Bread."

Close to the junction of Oxford Street with Tottenham Court Road are the *Frascati Restaurant* and the *Oxford Corner House,* one of Lyons's great restaurants. At the opposite corner is the **Dominion Theatre,** used principally as a cinema.

Tottenham Court Road (Plan II. I. and K. 6 and 7), with a number of important furnishing establishments—such as *Maple's* and *Heal's*—runs northward for rather more than half a mile to the Euston Road, and is thence continued as the Hampstead Road, leading, viâ Camden Town, to Hampstead Heath. At the corner of Great Russell Street is the **Central Young Men's Christian Association,** with halls for meetings, restaurants, a splendidly equipped gymnasium, swimming baths, social rooms, a boys' department, and bedrooms with 240 beds for young men. Many classes are held for business training, and in various ways the Association renders excellent service to the young men of London. In 1929 Queen Mary laid the foundation stone of the neighbouring **Y.W.C.A. Central Club** for London's business girls. The building was designed by Sir Edwin Lutyens. About half-way down Tottenham Court Road is the **Whitefield Tabernacle,** an important "institutional" church of the Congregational body.

Any street to the right will lead into **Gower Street,** many of the houses in which have been formed into hostels for university students and for business people employed in neighbouring stores. At No. 110 Charles Darwin lived when first married (1839–42), and a memorial on the wall of University College reminds us that near the spot Richard Trevithick ran in 1808 the first steam locomotive to draw passengers. (The actual spot was in Euston Grove.)

University College, near the north end of Gower Street, is affiliated to London University, and has accommodation for upwards of twelve hundred students. Attached to it are important Chemical Laboratories, second to none in Europe.

The cost of the **Institute of Anatomy** was defrayed out of a munificent gift from the Rockefeller Foundation.

University College School is now housed in a fine building at Frognal, Hampstead. Its former site is occupied by the **Institute of Physiology,** in connection with the University of London.

The University of London.

At first merely an examining and degree-conferring body, it is now a teaching University, with numerous affiliated schools, and with residential halls at Bloomsbury, Ealing and elsewhere. The full University degree can be taken even by students only able to attend evening classes. Those attached to certain recognized institutes can obtain their degree as "internal students" of the University, while others who do not comply with the necessary conditions can take the degree as "external students." The "internal" degree may be taken not only at those institutions which are known as "schools of the University," such as University College, King's College, Bedford College, the Queen Mary College, the London School of Economics, or the Medical Schools, but also at the polytechnics in different parts of London. Women are admitted to all degrees. The number of "internal students" exceeds 13,000; all told, the University teaches over 20,000 students. In addition to the University courses a large number of extension lectures are organized on subjects of general interest (see also p. 178).

In 1927 an area of eleven acres was acquired—thanks in great part to the munificence of the Rockefeller Trustees—for the erection of a home worthy of the University. The site lies between the British Museum and Torrington Place and Gordon Square, and extends from Malet Street to Woburn Square. On June 26, 1933, the foundation stone of the vast block was laid by King George V. The first section reached completion in 1936, when it was occupied by the administrative staff. In addition to this building others in the neighbourhood house a number of University institutions and departments. Chaucer House, in Malet Street, is the **National Central Library;** in the same street are the **University Union Hall,** the **Royal Academy of Dramatic Art** and the temporary home of the **Institute of Historical Research.**

Facing University College in Gower Street is **University College Hospital,** rebuilt in the form of a diagonal cross, at the cost of the late Sir J. Blundell Maple. At the junction of Gower Street with the Euston Road is **Euston Square Station** (Plan II. I. 6), on the Underground Railway. **Euston Station** (Plan II. I. 5; see pp. 57–8), the terminus of the London and North-Western section of the London, Midland and Scottish Railway, is a short distance eastward. Across the road are the **Friends' House** and the

Wellcome Research Institute. Close at hand, in **Gordon Square** (Plan II. K. 6), is the **Catholic Apostolic Church,** of cathedral-like proportions. Adjoining is **Dr. Williams's Library,** containing about 40,000 volumes, chiefly theological and historical, which may be borrowed freely by ticket-holders. On the east side of Woburn Square is **Christ Church,** with a reredos in memory of Christina Rossetti, the poetess (d. 1894).

We are now in the well-known quarter of—

Bloomsbury,

more favoured by visitors than any other part of London. Many houses provide " apartments," and there are a large number of hotels and boarding houses. The popularity of the district is accounted for partly by the fact that it is within easy reach of the City and West End and of the great railway termini ; and partly by the attractiveness of the numerous **Squares,** each with its lovely lawns, flower beds and luxuriant trees.

The largest, **Russell Square,** has figured in several well-known novels, notably *Vanity Fair*. The east side of the Square is occupied by the *Russell* and *Imperial Hotels* ; elsewhere are the headquarters of a number of well-known societies. In Queen Square, with entrance from Guilford Street, is the **Royal Institute of Public Health ;** further down Guilford Street are the new buildings of the **Royal Children's Hospital.**

In Tavistock Square, north of Russell Square, are the headquarters of the **British Medical Association.** Note the beautiful memorial gates in the courtyard. Across the road, at Woburn House, is the **Jews' College.** Close at hand are the new headquarters of the **National Free Church Council.**

Southampton Row (Plan II. K. 7), leading from Russell Square to Kingsway, is one of the most important arteries of traffic between North and South London. Here are the *Bedford*, the *Imperial* (with Turkish Baths), and a number of other hotels, much resorted to by provincial visitors. At the junction of Southampton Row with Theobald's Road the tramway emerges from below Kingsway (see p. 188). Here are the imposing offices of the *Liverpool Victoria Friendly Society*. The **London Day Training College for Teachers** and the **Central School of Arts and Crafts** are both under the London County Council. Adjoining is the **Baptist Church House,** with a statue of John Bunyan at the corner. Here Dr. John Clifford, the redoubtable Nonconformist leader, died in 1923. Between Southampton Row and Bedford Row is **Red Lion Square,** where the bodies of Cromwell, Ireton, and Bradshaw are said, on doubtful authority, to have been exposed after their exhumation from Westminster Abbey, and where lived the heroic Hanway, the first man to use an umbrella in London.

On the other side of Southampton Row **Great Russell Street** leads past **Bloomsbury Square,** in which is the **College of Preceptors.** No. 6, Bloomsbury Square (tablet) was the residence of Isaac D'Israeli ; and No. 31 that of Sir Anthony Panizzi, the famous chief librarian of the British Museum.

The British Museum.

Plan II. K. 7.

Admission.—The Exhibition Galleries are open free on week-days during summer from 10 a.m. to 6 p.m. In January, February, November and December after 4 p.m., and in March and October after 5 p.m., some only of the galleries remain open, viz., on Mondays, Wednesdays and Fridays, the MSS. and Printed Books, Prehistoric, Coins and Medals, Roman—British, Anglo-Saxon, Oriental, Religious and Ethnographical Collections, Babylonian Room (including Ur), and China and Mediæval Collections ; and on Tuesdays, Thursdays and Saturdays the Egyptian, Assyrian, Greek and Roman Sculpture, Gold Ornament Room, the Prehistoric, Terra-cotta, Greek and Roman Life, Bronze, Vase and 1st–3rd Egyptian Rooms, Babylonian Room, and Print Exhibition Gallery.

The Museum is closed on Christmas Day and Good Friday.

On **Sunday** afternoons the Museum is open from 2 till 6 throughout the year.

The Reading Room (see p. 162) is only available to ticket-holders, but visitors may obtain permission to go as far as the doorway and see the room, on application to the officials in the Entrance Hall. It is open daily from 9 a.m. to 6 p.m., except during the week beginning with the first Monday of May.

Catalogues, Handbooks, Pictorial Postcards, other Reproductions and Photographs are on sale in the Entrance Hall. The general Guide, with plans, is quite sufficient for the ordinary visitor. Handbooks to Sculptures, Coins, Antiquities and other departments, can be bought. Some of these are excellent, and double the interest of a visit. Casts of sculptures, etc., can be obtained.

Guide-Lectures.—Experts conduct parties round the Galleries every week-day at 12 noon and 3 p.m., starting from the Entrance Hall. No charge is made. Particulars of each day's lectures can be gleaned from the notice-boards. A programme may be had on application. Private parties are conducted if application has been made four days in advance. Authorized guides supplement the official Guide-Lectures, making a small regulated charge.

Nearest Stations.—Holborn (Central London and Piccadilly Tube), Tottenham Court Road (Central London and Edgware Tubes), Euston Square (Metropolitan), Euston (London Midland and Scottish).

Buses.—All buses running along New Oxford Street, Tottenham Court Road or Southampton Row pass within a few yards of the Museum. Alight at Museum Street or Great Russell Street.

Trams.—From North and South London to Southampton Row.

The Museum originated in 1753 with the purchase of the library and collection of Sir Hans Sloane and of the Harleian manuscripts, a public lottery having been set on foot for the purpose of raising the necessary funds. Added to by the Cottonian collection of manuscripts, which had long been public property, the Museum, arranged in Montague House, was opened to the public in 1759. Many libraries and collections of natural objects, coins and antiquities were added—especially the magnificent library collected by George III. (1823), and the renowned Elgin Marbles (1816)—and the Museum became one of the most extensive and valuable in Europe. A new building being imperatively required, the erection was entrusted to the brothers Smirke, with the result that, between the years 1823 and 1847, Montague House disappeared, and the present structure took its place. The great Reading Room was built in 1857; the White Wing, on the east, in 1884. A further extension, the King Edward the Seventh Galleries, on the north, was opened in 1914; and a new gallery, to house the marbles from the Parthenon, is being erected as the gift of Lord Duveen.

It would require months to become acquainted with all the contents of this vast national storehouse, and we can do little more than give such clues as will enable the hurried visitor to make the best of the single morning or afternoon he is likely to be able to devote to the purpose. The excellent *Summary Guide* will be found of great assistance, and the various *Guides* to Departments, sold in the Entrance Hall, are veritable mines of information. Special students' rooms are attached to most of the departments, and the officials are always willing to give all the assistance in their power to genuine inquirers. Most of the objects are plainly labelled, and in many cases explanatory notes are added.

Entering from Great Russell Street, we cross the courtyard, to the Ionic portico. The figures on the pediment are by *Westmacott*, and represent the progress of the human race and the development of Art, Science, etc. The entire front is 370 ft. in length, and has an Ionic colonnade of 44 columns.

In the **Entrance Hall** (2) are bookstalls and the **Lift** to the upper floor, and here also sticks and umbrellas must be left.

Lynx-eyed officials guard a doorway inscribed "Ticket-Holders only." This leads to the famous **Reading Room,** a huge circular hall, accommodating between 450 and 500 readers, who sit at desks radiating like the spokes of a wheel from two concentric circles, in the inner of which sit the officials, while the printed *Catalogue*, mounted in about 1,400 sheaf-volumes, is ranged round the outer circle and overflows into the inner. The dome is 106 ft. high, and has a diameter of 140 ft., only 2 ft. less than the dome of the Pantheon, Rome. The window panels bear twenty of the most illustrious names in English literature. About 25,000 of the volumes most in request, such as dictionaries, encyclopædias, bibliographies, etc., are ranged round the Room itself and may be consulted without filling up a form. For other works it is necessary to look under the names of authors in the Catalogue. When the name of an author is not known, the excellent *Subject Index* will frequently give the needful clues for books acquired subsequently to 1880. A copy of every book published in the United Kingdom has to be sent here. There are already over four million volumes, occupying 80 miles of shelving, and the number is increasing at the rate of 50,000 per annum. There is a Newspaper Repository at Colindale. "Readers" average

760 daily. Thackeray's opinion has probably been echoed by many a literary worker:—

"It seems to me one cannot sit down in that place without a heart full of grateful reverence. I own to have said my grace at the table, and to have thanked Heaven for this my English birthright, freely to partake of these bountiful books, and to speak the truth I find there."

Persons desirous of becoming "Readers" must apply to the Director, specifying the purpose for which they wish to use the Room, which is confined to research not possible elsewhere, and enclosing a recommendation from a person of recognized position. Tickets are renewable every six months, and are not granted to persons reading for examinations or competitions, or under 21 years of age. The hours are from 9 a.m. to 6 p.m.

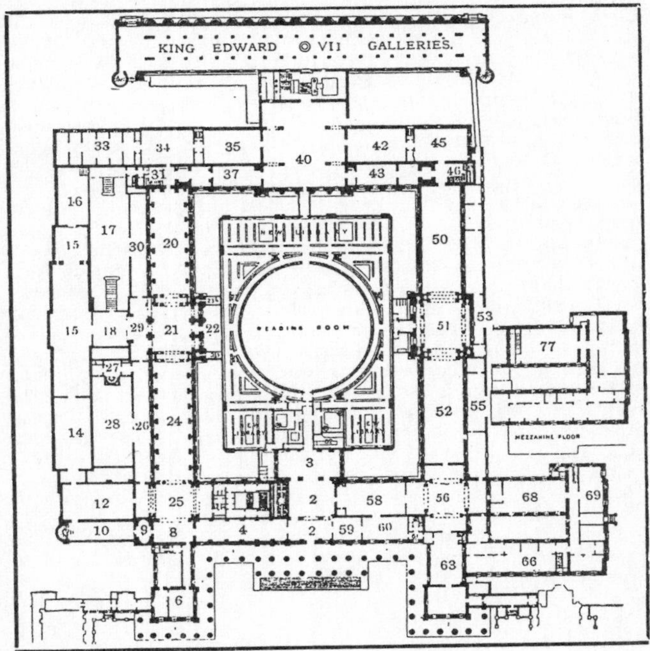

BRITISH MUSEUM: GROUND FLOOR.

From the main doorway of the Museum it is but a step into—

The Sculpture Galleries. The first is (4) the **Roman Gallery,**

with a number of inscribed stones found in England, and portrait busts of Augustus, Nero, and other worthies and unworthies familiar to us by name from childhood. In (8, 9, 10) the three **Græco-Roman Rooms** beyond are some of the most beautiful sculptures in the world. The **Archaic Room** (12) contains early Greek sculpture, principally from the colonies in Asia Minor. The **Ephesus Room** (14) named after fragments of the great Temple of Diana at Ephesus (see Acts xix.), which ranked as one of the wonders of the world, now contains 4th century B.C. sculptures generally. We next enter the **Elgin Room** (15), containing the Elgin Marbles, which formerly adorned the Parthenon at Athens, and were brought to this country in 1801–3 by Lord Elgin. Many of the figures were executed by Pheidias, the greatest sculptor the world has ever known, and even in their mutilated condition excite the wonder and admiration of all who see them. At the north end of the Elgin Room is (16) the **Phigaleian Room,** with marbles from the Temple of Apollo Epicurios, near the ancient Phigaleia in Arcadia. Steps lead down into the (17) **Mausoleum Room,** named after the magnificent Mausoleum at Halicarnassus, erected to the memory of Mausolos, Prince of Caria, about 354 B.C., by his widow, Artemisia. This was accounted one of the seven wonders of the world, and gave rise to our modern term mausoleum, applied to all such monuments. Ascend the steps at farther end to (18) the **Nereid Room,** where are exhibited the sculptures of the Nereid monument, from Xanthos in Lycia, probably erected about 370 B.C. The monument takes its name from the Nereids, or sea-nymphs, with which it was adorned. From (28) the **Assyrian Saloon,** containing slabs and figures discovered by Layard, we pass to the **Egyptian Galleries,** in which is an immense and most interesting collection of Egyptian statues, sarcophagi and inscriptions, including the famous Rosetta Stone, a slab of black basalt with three inscriptions, which gave the key to the decipherment of the Egyptian hieroglyphics. By their side are the **Nineveh Gallery** and other rooms in which are stored the deeply interesting collection of Assyrian reliefs, discovered by Rassam, George Smith and others. Here too are results of more recent expeditions.

During the reconstruction of certain rooms it is necessary to return from the Egyptian Galleries to the main Hall and to ascend by the lift or main staircase to the—

Upper Floor.

Immediately at the top of the main stairway, with its Buddhist carvings, is the collection illustrating **Prehistoric Britain.** Facing us on the right are the two small rooms of **Plaquettes and Coins and Medals.** Turning to the right we pass through the **Terracotta Room** to that filled with objects connected with **Greek** and **Roman Life.** (Here is the entrance to the *Students' Coin Room.*) On the left as we enter this room is a narrow passage leading to the **Room of Gold Ornaments and Gems,** including specimens of ancient jewellery, cameos, etc.—probably the finest collection in the world. Beyond the Greek and Roman Life room is the **Bronze Room** with numerous Greek and Roman statuettes and implements, and then we enter the four **Vase Rooms** with the magnificent collections of Greek pottery from the seventh to the third centuries B.C.

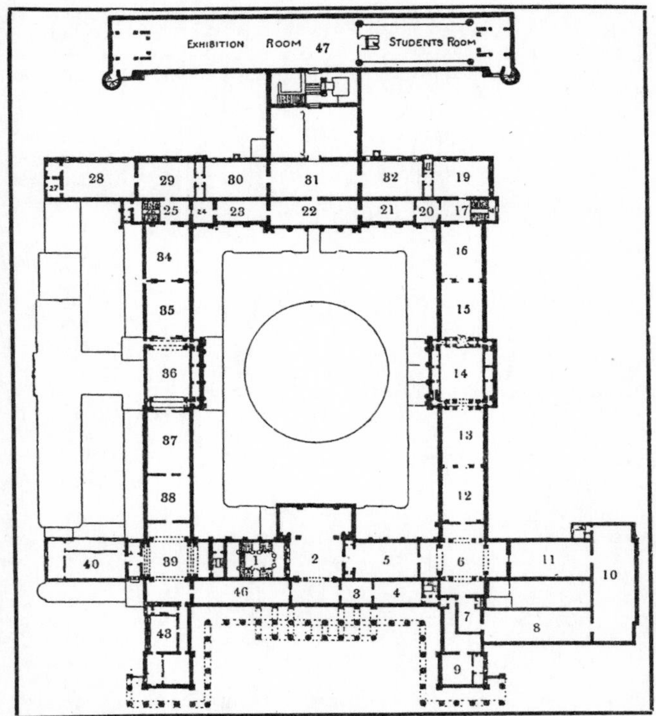

BRITISH MUSEUM: FIRST FLOOR.

From the Vase Rooms we pass to that part of the Egyptian collection which is normally and preferably seen immediately after the collections of Egyptian antiquities on the ground floor. These upper rooms are known as the **First to Fifth Egyptian**

Rooms. Interest is chiefly excited here by the mummies, both of men and animals, of which there is a very large collection, dating from about 3600 B.C. to 500 A.D. Recently commendable arrangements have been made for the exhibition of inscriptions and paintings from ancient tombs.

From the Egyptian Rooms we may reach the **King Edward VII. Galleries,** the upper floor devoted to the Museum's collection of prints and drawings. Do not descend to the lower floor after inspecting the prints, but return to the Egyptian Rooms and continue to the **Babylonian Room** and the extensive **Ethnographical Collections.**

These end at the **Asiatic Saloon,** with collections from Tibet and Central Asia, Indian and Persian arms and metal work. The room on the left contains Indian antiquities; beyond is the **Chinese and Japanese Room** (including the famed Eumorpopoulos Chinese Collection), and at the end is a small collection illustrating **Early Christianity.** From this we pass into the **Iron Age Gallery,** and so to the *Maudslay Collection* of Maya sculptures from Central America.

The King Edward VII. Galleries.

The memorial stone of this extension was laid by King Edward VII. in 1907, and King George V. formally opened the building in May, 1914. The Galleries may be entered by way of the Egyptian rooms (see above): but for the ground floor turn to the *right* in the entrance hall of the Museum and then to the left through the King's Library (see below). A lift connects the two floors. As already stated, the upper floor is devoted to the collection of prints and drawings.

In the lower gallery are **Pottery, Glass and Mediæval Antiquities,** including the *Waddesdon Bequest.* Hence we pass to the **King's Library,** so named from the collection of over 60,000 volumes, acquired by George III. and "presented"—for a valuable consideration—by George IV. in 1823. Here are exhibited many famous English books, such as first editions of *Paradise Lost* and *Pilgrim's Progress*, and Shakespeare First Folios. In cases in the middle of the room is the *Tapling Collection of Postage Stamps.*

We next pass into the **Manuscript Saloon,** where are exhibited letters and autographs of famous authors and historical personages, the log-book of the *Victory*, Nelson's Trafalgar memorandum and other MSS. of great interest. In the adjoining lobby are shown the Codex Sinaiticus and an original copy of Magna Charta. Turning to the right, we pass into the **Grenville Library,** with cases containing illuminated MSS. of great beauty, and so back to the Entrance Hall.

In Bedford Square is the recently-enlarged home of the **Architectural Association,** including a School of Architecture with accommodation for 200 students.

Museum Street leads from the British Museum to New Oxford Street near its junction with the oblique Hart Street. **St. George's Church,** designed by Hawksmoor, has an extraordinary steeple, surmounted by a figure of George I. in Roman toga. This incongruity gave rise to the following rhyme:—

"When Harry the Eighth left the Pope in the lurch,
He ruled over England as head of the Church;
But George's good subjects, the Bloomsbury people,
Instead of the Church, made him head of the steeple."

Further eastward, at the corner of High Holborn and New Oxford Street, is the **Holborn Town Hall,** with a public library adjoining. Eastward, beyond the *Holborn Restaurant* and Kingsway, are the **Holborn Empire** (varieties) and the **Holborn Stadium** (boxing, etc.).

Hart Street would bring us back to the southern end of **Southampton Row** (p. 160), from which electric trams, on emerging from the subway, run along an important line of thoroughfare which starts at **Theobald's Road,** and is continued as Clerkenwell Road and Old Street to Shoreditch. Lord Beaconsfield was born at No. 22, Theobald's Road (tablet), in 1804. At the junction of Theobald's Road with the Gray's Inn Road is **Holborn Hall,** belonging to the Methodists.

Rosebery Avenue runs thence in a north-easterly direction to the *Angel* at Islington. **Lamb's Conduit Street** (the name recalls the conduit by which a Mr. Lamb in the sixteenth century carried water to Snow Hill) leads to **Guilford Street,** in which long stood the **Foundling Hospital,** founded in 1739 by Thomas Coram, a retired sea captain, for "exposed and deserted children."

The original establishment was in Hatton Gardens, but "fresh air being as necessary for children as for plants," the Governors decided to erect a new hospital "in the balmy meads of Lamb's Conduit Fields, then far away out in the green pastures." Once more have the Governors gone in search of "balmy meads," and the Hospital is now established at Berkhamsted, in Hertfordshire. The Royal Academy had its origin in the Guilford Street building. The chapel organ was a gift from Handel, and the institution is fortunate enough to possess the full score of *The Messiah*, bequeathed by the composer. Appropriately, the Bloomsbury site of the Hospital is now a children's playground.

In Great Ormond Street are the **Royal Children's Hospital** and the **Homœopathic Hospital.**

The streets hereabouts have many interesting literary and artistic associations. At No. 32, Brunswick Square, lived John

Leech, the caricaturist. Ruskin lived at 54, Hunter Street. At 13, Great Coram Street, Thackeray lived before going to Kensington. In 1925 the Dickens Fellowship acquired No. 48, Doughty Street (Plan II. L. 6) as the **Dickens House and Library** (*open weekdays* (*Bank Holidays excepted*) 10–5. *Admission* 6*d.*) Here Dickens lived from 1837–9, writing the final portions of the *Pickwick Papers*, the whole of *Nicholas Nickleby* and *Oliver Twist*, and the commencement of *Barnaby Rudge*. The Museum contains a most interesting and valuable collection of Dickens relics and a very complete Dickens library. *Bleak House* and *Little Dorrit* were written while Dickens was living in Tavistock Square. The British Medical Association headquarters mark the site.

From Doughty Street, John Street leads us back to Theobald's Road, which we cross to **Bedford Row,** a short but wide road, tenanted almost entirely by solicitors. At the top turn left into—

Gray's Inn (Plan II. L. 7), one of the four great Inns of Court originally founded for the education and lodging of law students, to one or other of which all barristers are "admitted." Gray's Inn occupies an extensive area, from Holborn to Theobald's Road. Most of the offices line the western side of Gray's Inn Road and overlook the pleasant gardens, with their fine plane trees and well-kept lawns, laid out by Francis Bacon, who was admitted a member of the Inn in 1576, at the age of fifteen, and held the high office of Treasurer for nine years. The contorted catalpa trees near the centre are said to have been planted by him. A statue of the Inn's greatest son, by *F. W. Pomeroy, A.R.A.*, in South Square, marks the tercentenary of his election as Treasurer (1608). In the Elizabethan **Hall** (there is a contemporary portrait of the Virgin Queen over the Benchers' dais) Shakespeare's *Comedy of Errors* is believed to have been acted in 1594. The timbers of the roof and of the gallery at the lower end are very fine ; and there is a splendid collection of heraldic stained glass. The Archbishops' Window in the **Chapel** has figures of Becket, Whitgift, Juxon, Laud and Wake, the last four all members of the "Ancient and Honourable Society." The new Library building is noteworthy.

Gray's Inn Road is a dingy and unattractive thoroughfare running northward to King's Cross, passing the **Royal Free Hospital** and the **Eastman Dental Clinic,** a valuable institution due to the generosity of Mr. George Eastman of Rochester, U.S.A.

Turning to the right on emerging from the Inn into the Gray's Inn Road we come, in a few yards, to where stone pillars—**Holborn Bars**—mark the City Boundary. A striking bronze statue, by *Albert Toft*, forms the **War Memorial of the London Fusiliers.**

Holborn,

(Plan II. L. and M. 7)

the eastward continuation of New Oxford Street, takes its name from the *Old Bourne*, or burn, a tributary of the Fleet River, which formerly flowed through the hollow now spanned by the Viaduct. Here are some good shops and stores, including *Gamage's* and *Wallis's*. The large red-brick block occupied by the *Prudential Assurance Company* marks the site of Furnival's Inn, where Dickens was living when he began the *Pickwick Papers*.

Chatterton, the boy poet, committed suicide in a garret in **Brooke Street,** immediately west of the Prudential offices. At the north end of this street is **St. Alban's Church** (*open daily*), superbly decorated and noted for its ritualistic services.

Opposite Gray's Inn Road are some of the **Oldest Houses in London,** dating from the Elizabethan period, their projecting timbered fronts forming the street side of **Staple Inn.** An archway beneath gives access to the quaint little Inn, with its old-world courtyard. Though long an inn connected with the law, it owes its name to an earlier use, when it served as a kind of custom house where wool was weighed and the dues upon it collected. No. 10 is of special interest, for here lived "Mr. Grewgious" of *Edwin Drood*. Recently the old buildings have been very skilfully restored.

"Staple Inn," wrote Dickens, "is one of those nooks the turning into which from the dashing street imparts to the relieved pedestrian the sensation of having put cotton wool in his ears, and velvet soles on his boots." The old Hall is occupied by the *Institute of Actuaries*.

The visitor who proceeds through the courtyard and under the second archway will be rewarded by one of the most unexpected sights in London—a charming **Old-World Garden,** with flagged pathways, a trickling fountain, a pond with goldfish, and neat little rows of dwarf cypresses, backed by a mellow mid-eighteenth-century hall and timepiece.

Farther east, close to Fetter Lane, stood Barnard's Inn. The site is occupied by the **Mercers' School,** the 14th century hall of the inn being utilized as a dining-room. The school has a history extending over four centuries and a half. Dean Colet, of St. Paul's, and Sir Thomas Gresham, founder of the Royal Exchange, were scholars.

An omnibus, or the Central London Tube (from Chancery Lane Station, a short distance westward), will take us back, in a few minutes, to our starting-point at Oxford Circus.

THE SOUTH KENSINGTON MUSEUMS AND CHELSEA.

ROUTE VII.—BROMPTON ROAD—THE ORATORY—VICTORIA AND ALBERT MUSEUM—SCIENCE MUSEUM—NATURAL HISTORY MUSEUM—IMPERIAL INSTITUTE AND LONDON UNIVERSITY—CHELSEA.

ONE more excursion will complete our sight-seeing in the West of London, and leave us free to devote some attention to the City and South London. This trip to South Kensington, or "Museum Land," must perforce be omitted by the hurried visitor, but no one with time to spare should fail to make himself acquainted with our great national collections.

From Charing Cross we may go by Underground to South Kensington Station, or from Piccadilly Circus by the Piccadilly Tube to the same destination. The bus ride viâ Piccadilly, Knightsbridge and the Brompton Road is one of the most interesting and enjoyable in the Metropolis. **Piccadilly** has already been described (p. 131). At **Albert Gate** (p. 143) we turn in a south-westerly direction along the **Brompton Road,** passing on the left *Harrod's Stores*. In about half a mile from Albert Gate we reach—

The Church of the Oratory.

Plan III. F. 10.
Admission free at all times when the Church is open, and to all the services. Open daily from 6 a.m. to 10 p.m. On Saturdays and during the services visitors are not allowed to walk about the Church for the purpose of seeing it.
Services.—Sundays: Masses at 6.30, 7, 7.30, 8, 8.30, 9 and 10 a.m.; High Mass, 10.45; Low Mass and Sermon, 12; Vespers and Benediction, 3.30; Sermon and Benediction, 7 p.m.
Weekdays: Mass, 6.30, 7, 7.30, 8, 8.30 and 10 a.m.; Benediction, Thursdays and Saturdays, 4.30 p.m.; Evening Service and Sermon, 8 p.m. (except Saturdays).
Nearest Station, South Kensington (District and Piccadilly Lines).

The Oratory of St. Philip Neri is largely attended, even by non-Catholics, on account of its musical services. It was opened by Cardinal Manning in 1884, and is a fine specimen of the Italian Renaissance, from the designs of H. Gribble. The nave is the widest in England, except those of Westminster Cathedral and York Cathedral. There are nine side chapels, all elaborately decorated with mosaics and carvings. Behind the high altar is a picture of St. Philip Neri, the sixteenth-century founder of the community. In the eastern transept is the Lady Altar, originally erected at Brescia in 1693, and brought to this country in 1886. The organ contains upwards of 4,000 pipes. On the west side of the Oratory grounds, overlooking the Brompton Road, is a *Statue of Cardinal Newman* (1801–90), who seceded to the Catholic Church in 1845, and introduced the Institute of the Oratory to England.

Beyond is the long façade of—

The Victoria and Albert Museum.

Plan III. F. 10.

Admission.—The Museum is open free daily, except on Good Friday and Christmas Day, from 10 a.m. to 6 p.m. On Sundays from 2.30 to 6 p.m.

Bath Chairs and lifts are available.

Catalogues.—Brief Guide, 3*d*. Guides to collections at various prices. These, as well as photographs and pictorial postcards, are on sale at Main Entrance.

Nearest Station.—South Kensington (District Railway and Piccadilly Tube). Subway connection with Exhibition Road entrance.

Bus.—Any bus passing along Cromwell Road (to South Kensington, Earls Court, Putney, etc.) will serve.

Guide-Lecturers.—Experts conduct parties daily at 12 noon and 3 p.m. (also at 7 p.m. Thursdays and Saturdays), starting from the main entrance hall. The tours last about an hour, and are so designed as to cover, broadly, the whole of the collections in a fortnight.

Restaurant on north side of the central quadrangle of the older part of the main building, adjoining the Galleries numbered 12 to 16. The suite includes Central Room, artistically decorated, Green Dining Room, and Grill Room or Dutch Kitchen. Excellent luncheons, teas and dinners are served at moderate prices.

The New Buildings, with a frontage to the Cromwell Road of 720 ft. and to Exhibition Road of 275 ft., were opened by King Edward VII. and Queen Alexandra in state in 1909, the foundation-stone having been laid by Queen Victoria ten years previously (May 17, 1899). The older portions of the main building, dating from 1860 onwards, lie to the north. In the new buildings alone there are over a mile of galleries, and the entire Museum covers an area of 12 acres, so that even the sightseer who devotes a whole day to the purpose can hardly hope to take more than a superficial glance at these vast collections. For parallel reasons we cannot possibly describe the contents of this treasure-house in detail. The most we can do is to guide the visitor through the maze of courts and galleries, noting briefly the contents of each, so that he may at least form an idea of the collections and may also know where to find those sections in which he is particularly interested.

Generally speaking, it may be said that this Museum is not concerned with antiquities as such—these being represented at the British Museum—but with such objects as illustrate the arts and crafts of various countries and periods. The collections are classified under eight general Departments, with numerous technical, historical and local subdivisions.

This method of classification necessitates the scattering of many miscellaneous objects associated with particular countries, periods or individuals. Some of the loan collections, however, remain intact, the Octagon Court (40) having been reserved for that purpose. The Salting Collection is also, under the terms of the donor's will, kept intact (Rooms 128–131, 144 and 145).

Before entering by the main portal in Cromwell Road, it is well to take a glance at the exterior of the fine building designed by *Sir Aston Webb, P.R.A.* It is in the Renaissance style, with domes and towers. The lofty central lantern has the outline of an Imperial Crown and is surmounted by a figure of Fame. The niches between the first-floor windows are occupied by figures of thirty-two famous British painters, craftsmen, sculptors and architects. Over the great archway are also various emblematic and royal statues.

The square **Central Hall,** with its lofty dome and quarter domes, and double rows of beautifully veined marble columns, is the most imposing feature of the interior. On the left is Alfred Stevens's original plaster model for Wellington's monument in St. Paul's Cathedral (see p. 219). The East and West Halls extend on either hand, each spanned at the commencement by a balustraded stone bridge, or gallery, connecting the rooms on the upper floor. Beyond the East and West Halls extend a series of lofty Courts, all marble paved and top-lighted, the principal being the **Loan Court,** at the west end. North of these courts, again, is the grassy Quadrangle, round which are ranged the older portions of the building with their fine terra-cotta embellishments.

All the rooms, courts and galleries, both in the old and new buildings, are numbered consecutively from 1 to 145, beginning with the Woodwork section on the lower ground floor of the new building, close to the Exhibition Road entrance, and ending in the Ceramic section on the second floor.

Rooms 11 to 39, devoted to Metal Work, are all in the old part of the building. The visitor who has entered from Cromwell Road, however, cannot be expected to proceed at a bound from the basement of the new building to the extreme north-west corner of the old building. Hence numerical continuity of description is impossible.

The **Lower Ground Floor** (descend staircases on either side of the Cromwell Road entrance). **Rooms 1 to 7,** on the left, are principally devoted to Woodwork ; **Rooms 8 to 10,** on the right, to Mediæval Sculpture.

Ground Floor.

The **East Hall** is given up to Italian, Flemish, Spanish and French architecture (mostly stone and marble), including some fine chimney-pieces and altar-pieces. Particularly noteworthy is the marble rood-loft dividing the Hall into two.

Between the East Hall and the Cromwell Road, but on a higher level, are **Rooms 62 to 64,** illustrating the development of Italian sculpture from the thirteenth to the seventeenth century, including reliefs in marble by Donatello and enamelled terra-cottas by the famous Della Robbia family (Room 63).

Around the **West Hall** (No. 48) are examples of English, French, Italian and Eastern architecture (wood shop-fronts, staircases, etc.). There are also a state barge, some coaches, etc., and at the far end a display of Near Eastern art.

In the **Octagon Court** is displayed fine English furniture, including reconstructions of a number of famous rooms. Hence a corridor leads to the **Central Courts** (Nos. 41 to 45), containing a variety of articles in metal and glass. The walls are framed with beautiful tapestries and carpets that are among the greatest treasures of the Museum. The Persian carpets in the arcaded West Central Court (No. 42) are especially fine.

The Central Court (43) is reserved for the display of recent acquisitions.

In the East Central Court (No. 44) are sculptures given by *Rodin* himself in honour of British soldiers who fought beside his countrymen in the Great War. Note the sculptor's portrait, by *Sir John Lavery.*

The adjoining **East Court** (No. 45) contains an interesting collection of old musical instruments.

No. 46, the **Square Court,** or Architectural Court of the old building, is devoted to reproductions of famous architectural works, many of them of huge dimensions. As the Court is very crowded, some of its contents can be better seen from the gallery above (No. 111 of the first floor), especially the fine plaster cast, in two parts, of Trajan's Column, erected in Rome A.D. 114. In the corridor bisecting the Square Court are old carriages and coaches.

From the Square Court pass to the **South Court,** which, with the rooms and corridors around the **Quadrangle,** are devoted to Metal Work. Here may be seen some of the most superb specimens of the goldsmiths' art that the world contains, with clocks, watches, jewellery, arms, armour, and Eastern and other metal work. Particularly fine is the wrought iron. The collection is continued to Room 21, at the far end of which pass through turnstile and then to left and up the stairs.

Rooms 52 to 54, between the Exhibition Road entrance and the Cromwell Road angle of the building, are devoted to English woodwork of the sixteenth and seventeenth centuries; and **Rooms 55 to 58,** south of the West Hall, to late seventeenth and eighteenth-century furniture and woodwork (English, German and French). In this section are oak-panelled rooms of various periods, and elaborately carved bedsteads. An interesting exhibit is a chair said to have belonged to Nell Gwynne.

In **Room 57** is the furniture from David Garrick's villa at Hampton.

Opening out of the rooms forming the northern corridor of the Quadrangle (12 to 16) is the **Restaurant.** The pillared Central Room is cased with elaborate ceramic decorations by J. Gamble; the small Green Dining-Room was decorated by no less a hand than that of William Morris; and the Grill Room, or Dutch Kitchen, has tiled panels designed by Sir E. J. Poynter, P.R.A.

A staircase close to the Restaurant, and another from Room 16c, lead up to the—

First Floor.

In **Rooms 65–69** is the Jones Collection of paintings, porcelain, bronzes, etc. In **Rooms 73 to 75** and the adjacent **Book Production Gallery** are displayed illuminated manuscripts, book illustrations, and etchings, as well as many elaborate and tasteful bindings, and other exhibits illustrating type founding, printing, binding, and other processes in book production. The exhibits in Rooms 70 and 71 relate more particularly to the art of the theatre. On the south side of the Quadrangle is the **Library** (76 to 78), containing about 160,000 volumes, especially rich in older books and works of art. There are also about 250,000 photographs. Entrance at east end (from Room 25). *Open weekdays,* 10 *a.m. to* 4.50; *Thursdays and Saturdays until* 8.50 *p.m. Students or regular readers require tickets* (*issued free*).

Extending all round the walls of **Room 79,** the gallery above the East Court, are reproductions of the famous Bayeux tapestry, representing William of Normandy's conquest of England.

Nos. 81 to 108 are all on the east side of the Quadrangle, being mostly galleries above or adjoining the North and South Courts. Here are displayed the many fine paintings belonging to the Museum, including a large number of water-colours, and the Sheepshanks, Dyce and Forster (with MSS. by Dickens), Ionides, Constable and Jones Collections, the last-named comprising also examples of French furniture, porcelain, sculpture, bronzes, etc. By visiting Rooms 82, 81, 87, 88 and 90 in the order named one obtains a chronological survey of water-colour painting between 1800 and the present time. In No. 94 are hung the famous **Raphael Cartoons,** designed in 1515 for Pope Leo X. as copies for tapestry for the decoration of the Sistine Chapel at Rome. Originally there were ten, but three having been lost are here represented by copies. The designs were bought by Charles I. on the advice of Rubens, and removed from Brussels in 1630. By William III. they were fixed at Hampton Court, where they remained (with brief excursions to Windsor and Buckingham Palace) until 1865. They are the property of the King. Rooms 96–99 contain the main collection of oil paintings.

No. 110 and No. 111 are bridge-like galleries running over the South Court and the Square Court. They are devoted to the display of coloured window glass and other glass work. In the

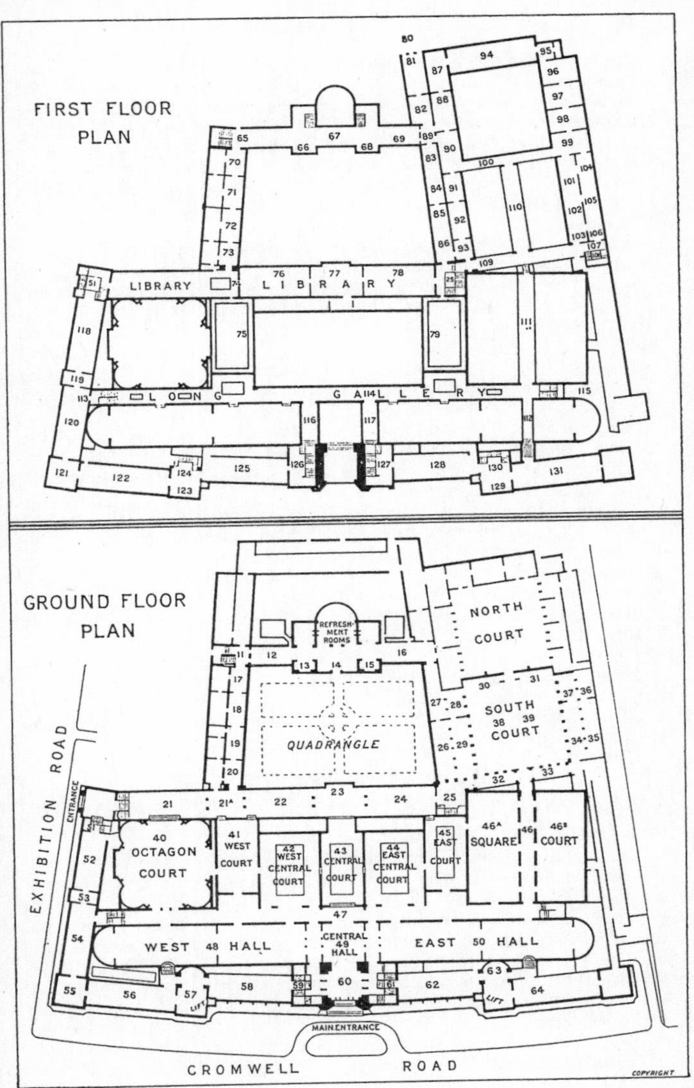

THE VICTORIA AND ALBERT MUSEUM.

galleries at the southern end of the courts is a display of medals, orders, etc.

The **Long Gallery** (114), running the entire length of the new frontage, above the East and West Halls and the Central Hall, is devoted to costumes, arranged chronologically, starting at the west end. The Textile section is continued in **Nos. 116 and 117,** the bridges spanning the great Halls, and looking down on the Central Hall, and in **Rooms 118 to 125,** all above the West Hall.

Nos. 128 to 131 are similar rooms above the East Hall, and looking down on the Cromwell Road. They are almost entirely occupied by the **Salting Collection,** bequeathed by the late Mr. George Salting on the express condition that it should not be distributed over the various sections, but kept all together. The collection includes faïence, enamels, bronzes, marbles, wood carvings, furniture, Chinese porcelain, miniatures, etc. The pictures included in the bequest are in the National Gallery, and the prints and drawings in the British Museum.

The Ceramic Department is continued on the **Second Floor,** these rooms (**133 to 145**) being, indeed, entirely devoted to it. Here may be seen earthenware and porcelain in every known style, ancient and modern.

Room 142 contains French and German ware. **Room 141** contains Dutch tiles of the sixteenth–eighteenth centuries presented by Mr. Henry van den Bergh. In **Room 140** is the English Porcelain Collection, and in **Room 139** is the **Schreiber Collection** of English earthenware and stoneware.

Rooms 134 to 136 are devoted to Near Eastern earthenware and Italian majolica, and in **Room 133** is Egyptian and Persian pottery.

Room 132 opens on to the **Students' Room,** where may be seen books and prints, etc., not to be found in the galleries.

Almost facing the doorway by which we step from the Museum into the Exhibition Road is the new home of the—

Geological Museum.

Open free, daily, 10–6; Sundays, 2.30–6 p.m. Closed Christmas Day and Good Friday.
Guide Lectures daily.

The building, which forms the headquarters of the Geological Survey, is light and airy and the contents of the Museum are admirably displayed. The centre of the ground floor is occupied by cases of precious and semi-precious stones—note the model of the Cullinan Diamond. Round these are some excellent models and dioramas of British scenery, and beyond these and on the first floor are maps, photographs and specimens illustrating the geology of various parts of Britain, the collections being arranged territorially. The exhibits in the upper galleries are designed to illustrate Economic Geology and Mineralogy.

Behind the exhibition galleries are the offices of the Geological

Survey and a large Reference Library (open to public on weekdays free, 10–5).

A few yards northward, and almost opposite the **Royal School of Art,** is the entrance to—

The Science Museum.

Open free, daily, 10–6; Sundays, 2.30–6 p.m.
Entrances in Exhibition Road and Imperial Institute Road (see footnote, p. 179).
Lectures (free) daily at 12 and 3. (Saturdays and Bank Holidays, 2.15 and 4.15.)
Demonstrations daily at advertised times.

Much-needed new buildings worthily house this fine collection, but pending the rebuilding of the older portion many groups of exhibits are not on view, and it is useless for us to do more than indicate the general departments.

To the right on entering is Gallery 1, reserved for special exhibitions, usually of topical interest. On the left, beyond the Foucault Pendulum, steps lead down to the **Children's Gallery,** with fascinating dioramas and working models.

Directly in front of the entrance is a wonderful collection of steam and other engines of all kinds. The Railway section, on the right, includes locomotives, from Stephenson's *Rocket* onwards, that are an irresistible attraction to boys, especially as many of the engines can be made to " go." Here is a model of James Watt's workshop.

Lifts and stairways take us to the—

First Floor : Sailing ships, steam warships, mining and metallurgy, textile machinery, tools, electrical engineering, telegraphy and telephones.

Second Floor : Merchant steamers, mathematical instruments, magnetism and electricity, acoustics, meteorology, geophysics, clocks and watches, civil engineering, etc.

Third Floor : Yachts and fishing boats, photography, geodesy and surveying, astronomy, optical instruments, chemistry, etc.

On the ground floor, beyond the East Hall, is the *Aeronautical* section, with a fine range of exhibits headed by the original aeroplane in which the Wright brothers, in 1903, made the historic " first flight." Other notable machines of later date are here ; notably the plane with which the first trans-Atlantic flight was made, and that with which the Schneider Trophy was won, at a speed of 407·5 miles per hour, in 1931. The aeronautical section extends into the old building, and is continued (ground floor) by collections illustrating docks and marine engines, and road transport (from the steam carriage to the latest examples of mass-production motor-cars) ; upstairs are printing and ore-dressing, radio communication, glass and pottery.

The **Science Library** contains about 70,000 volumes and the transactions of nearly all learned societies, as well as a complete collection of British Patent Specifications.

The **Imperial War Museum** was in 1936 moved to Lambeth (Plan III. M. 10) (see p. 257). The quickest way of reaching it from South Kensington is by Underground to Westminster station, whence walk, tram or bus over Westminster Bridge to St. George's Road.

North of the Science Museum is—

The Imperial Institute.

Plan III. F. 10.
Admission.—The Colonial and other collections are open free daily (except Good Friday and Christmas Day) from 10 to 5 in summer and from 10 to 4 in winter. Sundays, 2.30 to 6. Guide lecturers conduct parties round on certain afternoons.
Nearest Station.—South Kensington (District Railway and Piccadilly Tube). (See footnote, p. 179.)

The Imperial Institute was erected as a national memorial of the Jubilee of Queen Victoria, by whom it was opened in 1893.

Its principal object is to promote the utilization of the commercial and industrial resources of the Empire.

In 1916 the Institute was by Act of Parliament placed under the general control of the Secretary of State for the Colonies and an executive council on which the Dominions, Colonies and India are represented. The staff includes officers with special qualifications in chemistry, botany, geology, mineralogy, and certain branches of technology in their relation to agriculture and to the commercial utilization of economic products.

Collections illustrative of the general and commercial resources of India and the Dominions are arranged in the public galleries.

On the second floor are research laboratories for the investigation of new or little-known natural products and of known products from new sources, with a view to their utilization in commerce. Here, also, is provided trustworthy scientific and technical advice on matters connected with the agriculture, trade and industries of India and the Dominions.

A comparatively new feature of the Institute is the **Imperial Gallery of Art,** containing scholarship work of the British School at Rome, and work of contemporary artists from every part of the Empire, at home and overseas.

There is also a Cinema (*admission free*) in which films are shown illustrating scenes and activities throughout the Empire.

The **Library and Reading Rooms** (*open* 10–5.30, *Saturdays* 10–1, *to persons introduced*) contain a large collection of Dominion works of reference, and are supplied with the more important official publications, and with the principal newspapers and periodicals of the United Kingdom, India and the Dominions. The *Bulletin of the Imperial Institute* (quarterly) deals with progress in tropical agriculture and the industrial utilization of raw materials.

From 1900 until 1936, when the first section of the new buildings in Bloomsbury was completed, the central block and the east wing of the Institute housed the administrative section of the **University of London** (see p. 159).

At the eastern end of the Imperial Institute is the entrance to the **Indian Museum** (*admission as to Victoria and Albert Museum* (see p. 171); *Guide Lectures, Wednesdays and Saturdays,* 3–4 *p.m.*). A branch of the Victoria and Albert Museum. There is a large collection illustrating the architecture, art, religion and daily life of the peoples of the Indian Empire.

On the other (south) side of the road is the main block of the **Imperial College of Science and Technology,** founded under Royal Charter in 1907 and incorporating several older institutions. The courses of instruction are intended to prepare students for industrial careers in which scientific knowledge is essential. The College is affiliated to the University of London.

At the corner of Imperial Institute Road and Exhibition Road is the **Royal School of Art Needlework** (Plan III. F. 10): *open free daily,* 10 to 6; *Saturdays,* 10 *to* 1. Ladies, and indeed all art lovers, will be interested in the showrooms, where are displayed ancient and modern furniture, embroideries, tapestries, *objets d'art,* etc. Lessons are given in needlework and every kind of embroidery, and also in design.

To the north, in Exhibition Road, is the **City and Guilds of London Central Technical College,** now incorporated with the Imperial College. In Prince Consort Road, immediately south of the Albert Hall, is another imposing block occupied by the Imperial College of Science and Technology. Here, too, is the **Royal College of Music,** opened in 1894, and providing a thorough musical training to some 500 pupils. On the ground floor is shown the Donaldson Collection of Musical Instruments (*open free daily in term-time except Saturday,* 11–2 *and* 3–5). The **Albert Hall** has already been described (p. 143).

The most inveterate sightseer will probably be by this time in a state of collapse, but there still remains to be seen what many people regard as the most fascinating of the treasures of South Kensington.

We turn south down **Exhibition Road,**[1] a broad, straight thoroughfare leading from Kensington Gardens and deriving its name from the Great Exhibitions for which the site was long used. Beyond the new home of the Geological Survey and Museum we have on our right the sunk garden surrounding—

[1] A subway runs from South Kensington station, passing below Exhibition Road and serving the Museums, etc.

The Natural History Museum.

Plan III. F. 10.
Admission.—The Museum is open free daily from 10 to 6 throughout the year. Also on Sundays from 2.30 to 6 p.m. Closed on Christmas Day and Good Friday.

Students' Tickets, giving special facilities, are issued on application to the Director, subject to certain conditions.
Catalogues.—Summary Guide, 3*d.* Guides to various Departments, 4*d.*, 6*d.*, 1*s.* and 2*s.*
Official Guides conduct visitors round certain departments at 11.30 a.m. and 3 p.m. each week-day and on Sunday afternoons at 3 and 4.30.
Refreshment Room on first floor at head of staircase.
Nearest Station.—South Kensington (District Railway and Piccadilly Tube). (See footnote, p. 179.)

Intended as a branch of the British Museum, the Natural History Collection—the finest in the world—occupies a striking building of terra-cotta, designed by Alfred Waterhouse, and erected in 1873–80. The length of the front is 675 ft., and the towers are each 192 ft. high.

The lofty central hall contains a most interesting epitome of the whole Museum. Behind the staircase on the ground floor is a large room containing cases of animals under domestication including the skeletons of three famous racehorses—Persimmon, Eclipse and St. Simon. At the top of the first flight of stairs is a *Statue of Charles Darwin*, by Boehm. Birds, corals, shells, star-fish, reptiles, insects and fish occupy the ground floor of the west wing, and mammals are exhibited on the first and second floors. The ground floor of the east wing contains the fossil mammalia, fossil reptiles and fishes, cephalopoda, mollusca, corals, sponges and plants; on its first floor are minerals and meteorites; on the second floor are the botanical and osteological collections. The mammalian section was enriched in 1919 by the collection of the late F. C. Selous, the big-game hunter, who is commemorated by a bust at the head of the grand staircase. In 1934 a new *Whale Hall* was added.

A detailed description of the objects in this collection is unnecessary, as every specimen is labelled, and special care is taken to render these labels intelligible to the general visitor. Indeed, it is a pleasure to testify to the pains taken by the authorities to render the priceless collections under their care at once interesting and instructive.

Having thus dutifully " done " the Museums, we could make our way past South Kensington station to Chelsea (see below). Or from the Albert Hall we may take bus westward through **Kensington High Street**—a popular shopping quarter. Slightly farther west (see p. 142) are **Holland House** and **Leighton House.** Still farther west is **Olympia,** the scene of the Royal Tournament and of other important shows and exhibitions. Nearer to Museum-land is **Earls Court,** where preparations are being made for a revival of the fame of the Exhibition which Imre Kiralfy made such a feature of London life in pre-War days. The new Earls Court will boast large exhibition halls suitable for motor shows and similar exhibitions, in addition to facilities of the most modern kind for swimming, skating and other forms of amusement. The *Empress Hall* (skating and ice hockey in winter) is used for pageants, etc.

By continuing westward along the Hammersmith Road we should pass, opposite Brook Green, **St. Paul's School,** for boys, founded by Dean Colet in 1509, and removed from behind St. Paul's Cathedral to this site in 1884. **Nazareth House,** adjoining, is the headquarters of a busy Catholic community known as the Sisters of Nazareth, devoting themselves to the care of the poor.

Hammersmith, chiefly known to-day as a busy railway, tram and bus centre, has many interesting associations. The **Lyric Theatre** has become associated with many successful revivals of old plays such as *The Beggar's Opera*. Near at hand is the **King's Theatre.** At Hammersmith the Thames is spanned by a fine Suspension Bridge, and on the Middlesex bank are the boat-houses of several well-known rowing clubs. Moored off the Middlesex bank is the training ship *Stork* (450 tons), under the auspices of the Navy League. Beyond the boat-houses is the Upper Mall, with many delightful riverside residences of an earlier period. No. 26 bears a tablet recording that it was the residence of William Morris, "poet, craftsman and socialist" (1878–1896). Another house records that "the first electric telegraph, 8 miles long, was constructed here in 1816 by Sir Francis Ronald, F.R.S."

To the south of Kensington lies old-world—

CHELSEA,

with its many literary and artistic associations. It is best reached by way of Sloane Square station. Whole volumes have been written about this fascinating quarter, and we can do no more than indicate a few of its leading features. At Chelsea, then a country village, lived Sir Thomas More, among his frequent visitors being Henry VIII., Holbein and Erasmus. Beaufort Street, to the north of the present Battersea Bridge, occupies part of the site of his house. Other distinguished residents at various periods were Dean Swift, Sir Richard Steele, Addison, John Locke, Sir Robert Walpole, Gay, Newton, Smollett, Sir Hans Sloane, whose collection originated the British Museum, J. M. W. Turner, Leigh Hunt, Thomas Carlyle, D. G. Rossetti, George Eliot, General Gordon, J. McNeil Whistler, and scores of others.

From Sloane Square station turn to the left along **King's Road,** named after King Charles II. In a few yards will be seen the former Duke of York's School (now the headquarters of several Territorial regiments), founded in 1801 for the support and education of the sons of soldiers, and removed in 1909 to Dover.

Taking the next left-hand turning we reach the Royal Hospital Road, in which is the principal entrance to the world-famous—

Chelsea Royal Hospital.

Admission on week-days from 10 to 12, and from 2 to 4 or later if the public gate be open. No charge, but the country's defenders have never been known to show any marked aversion to a trifling addition to their " tobacco money." The Great Hall and the Chapel are open to view by visitors between 10 a.m. and noon, and 2 and 4 p.m. Visitors are also admitted, so far as room permits, to the Sunday services in the Chapel at 11 and 6.30.
Nearest Station.—Sloane Square (District Railway).

In 1682 Charles II., at the instigation of Sir Stephen Fox and possibly also, as is traditionally asserted, of Nell Gwynne, converted a theological college into an asylum for old and invalid soldiers, employing Sir Christopher Wren as architect. The frontage to the Thames consists of a centre and two wings of red brick, with stone dressings. The buildings form three courts, two of which are spacious quadrangles ; the other is open to the river. In the centre of the front quadrangle is a statue of Charles II. in Roman toga by Grinling Gibbons. Accommodation is provided for about 550 inmates, and there are a great number of " out-pensioners." In winter the aged warriors are clothed in dark blue coats : in summer the colour is scarlet.

The show parts are the large Hall and the Chapel, though the courtyards where the picturesque old warriors sun themselves, and fight their battles o'er again, should also be seen. The **Hall** contains a collection of tattered flags, captured in battle, portraits of Charles II. and other Royalty, and of past Governors, cases of unclaimed medals, and some old leather " black Jacks." The **Chapel,** the scene of Herkomer's picture, " The Last Muster," contains a fine altar-piece, carvings by Grinling Gibbons, an altar-cloth presented by Charles II., and a further collection of flags, among which are several British Regimental colours, and Eagles captured from the French during the Napoleonic Wars. The Communion service was a gift from James II.

Between the Hospital and the river are some attractive **Gardens** with shady avenues, admission to which is free. They occupy part of the site of the old Ranelagh Gardens, the scene of so many merry junketings in the eighteenth century. The **Chelsea Flower Show** is held here in May. To the east is the **Chelsea Suspension** (or Victoria) **Bridge,** rebuilt in 1935–7. In Chelsea Bridge Road are the **Chelsea Barracks,** occupied by the Guards, and the **Lister Institute of Preventive Medicine.**

Turning westward along the pleasant **Chelsea Embankment,** with **Battersea Park** (p. 258) on the opposite bank, we shortly reach the **Chelsea Physic Garden,** given by Sir Hans Sloane in 1722 to the Apothecaries' Company as "a physic garden, so that apprentices and others may better distinguish good and useful plants from those that bear resemblance to them and yet are hurtful."

Since 1899 the Garden has been maintained by the Trustees of the London Parochial Charities. It is used for important research work in connection with the Imperial College of Science. Specimen plants of great botanical value are grown here for distribution to various colleges and institutes. The Garden is accessible to teachers and students on week-days from 9.30 to 5 or sunset. Orders for a single visit can generally be obtained on application to the Curator.

Cheyne Walk (pronounced "Chainey"), a terrace of red-brick Queen Anne mansions overlooking the river, has many interesting associations. At No. 4 lived and died Maclise the painter; here, too, George Eliot died in 1880, after a residence of three weeks only. In the Embankment Gardens a fountain, surmounted by a bust by Ford Madox Brown, recalls the fact that Dante Gabriel Rossetti (1828–1882), lived at No. 16, known as the "Queen's House," from an erroneous tradition that it was the residence of Catherine of Braganza, Charles II.'s neglected wife. A *Statue of Thomas Carlyle* by Boehm marks the foot of **Cheyne Row,** a spot which no literary pilgrim omits to visit. **Carlyle's House** (No. 24—formerly 5—Cheyne Row) was purchased by public subscription in 1895, and is *open daily, 10 till sunset, at a charge* of 1s. (*Saturdays*, 6*d*.), *or* 6*d*. *each for parties of ten or more.* The house contains a number of interesting personal relics, furniture, etc.

In Danvers Street, near the foot of Beaufort Street, linking **Battersea Bridge** and the King's Road, has been re-erected **Crosby Hall,** an interesting relic of mediæval London removed from Bishopsgate Street in 1908. The hall was built in 1466 by Alderman Sir John Crosby, and occupied by Richard of Gloucester when he plotted the murder of the two princes and his own accession. Later it was bought (but not occupied) by Sir Thomas More, and it is on the site of his last home that the Hall now stands. It forms part of an international hall of residence and clubhouse for women graduates studying in London under the British Federation of University Women.

West of Cheyne Row is Lawrence Street, where the manufacture of the famous old *Chelsea China*, which fetches almost fabulous prices, was carried on. Monmouth House, Lawrence Street, was the residence of Fielding and of Smollett, and here Gay wrote *The Beggar's Opera.* At the corner of Church Street is **Chelsea Old Church,** built early in the fourteenth century. (*Open daily* 10 *to* 1, *and* 2 *to* 4. *At other times on application to the verger*, 35, *Danvers Street*.) There are many ancient monuments, and some chained books, including a "Vinegar Bible." The headless remains of Sir Thomas More may possibly be in the tomb he himself erected here, in blissful ignorance of the impending tragedy, but it is very doubtful. His head, we know, was interred at St. Dunstan's, Canterbury, after being exposed for fourteen days on London Bridge. The Church was partly restored in 1910, and the 13th-century chancel roof, formerly covered with plaster, now displays its timber beams. In Church Street is the *Rectory*, where the brothers Charles, George and Henry Kingsley passed their boyhood.

Cheyne Walk extends beyond Battersea Bridge, and here, at the extreme western end (No. 118—tablet by Walter Crane), Turner, the great landscape painter, spent his last years and died. Up to his last illness, it is said, he would always endeavour to get on to the balustraded roof to see the sun rise over London and at the close of the day to watch it set in splendour beyond Putney. J. M. Whistler lived at No. 96.

By following any northward turning from the river we should strike the King's Road again. In Manresa Road is the **Chelsea Public Library,** containing interesting prints of bygone Chelsea.

South-westward, King's Road leads through **Parsons Green** to **Putney Bridge,** close to which are the starting-point of the Oxford and Cambridge Boat-races and the London quarters of several famous rowing clubs. On the Middlesex bank, close to the bridge, is **Fulham Palace,** for upwards of seven centuries the official residence of the Bishops of London. Nearly opposite, on the Surrey side, are the grounds of the **Ranelagh Club** (polo, etc.). The house, known as Barn Elms, was a gift from Queen Elizabeth to Sir Francis Walsingham.

CHARING CROSS TO THE CITY.

ROUTE VIII.—THE STRAND—COVENT GARDEN—ALDWYCH AND KINGSWAY —THE VICTORIA EMBANKMENT—TEMPLE BAR—LINCOLN'S INN FIELDS —THE TEMPLE—FLEET STREET—LUDGATE CIRCUS.

TURNING this time City-wards, let us follow the Strand and Fleet Street, a line of thoroughfare surpassing even Oxford Street in the volume of traffic constantly passing between west and east. The latter part of the route, after passing Temple Bar, is within the City of London, and therefore outside the strict limits of this section of the Guide, but it will be better for purposes of continuity to regard Ludgate Circus as marking the boundary.

The Strand.

Plan III. K. and L. 8.
Nearest Stations.—Western end, Trafalgar Square (Bakerloo Tube); Strand (Morden-Edgware Line); Charing Cross (Southern Railway—terminus); Charing Cross (District). Eastern end, Aldwych (Piccadilly Tube); Temple (District Railway).

With its medley of hotels, playhouses and shops, the Strand is one of the most famous thoroughfares in Europe, but sadly lacking in architectural dignity. With the falling-in of leases, a certain amount of rebuilding is taking place, and opportunity is being taken to widen so important an artery, while several of the new buildings are of good design. But the interest of the Strand is far indeed from being confined to buildings. The intelligent visitor has only to pause in any doorway and watch the crowds of all ranks, ages, conditions and nationalities that surge by, to have an epitome not merely of metropolitan life but of the life of the world.

In Elizabethan times, and long afterwards, the Strand was bordered by aristocratic mansions, with gardens extending down to the river-side. The names still survive in such streets as Burleigh Street, Villiers Street, Bedford Street, Southampton Street, etc. Indeed, there is hardly a street in the neighbourhood of the Strand the name of which would be sought unsuccessfully in the British peerage. From Charing Cross to Temple Bar, where the famous griffin marks at once the commencement of the City and of Fleet Street, the Strand is almost exactly seven-eighths of a mile long.

Northumberland Avenue we have already dealt with (p. 76). **Charing Cross Station** (Southern Railway) has in its courtyard a copy of the old Charing Cross (p. 74). Though still a busy terminus, the station is no longer the starting-point of the Continental boat trains with their far-reaching connections—traffic which made the name Charing Cross almost a synonym for important railway junctions. In the forecourt is an entrance to the Strand station of the Morden-Edgware Line.

In King William Street is the **Charing Cross Hospital.** Rhodesia House, at the corner of Agar Street, is the London headquarters of the **Government of Southern Rhodesia.** The building was erected as the home of the British Medical Association (see p. 160), for whom Epstein sculptured the statues which still remain. A little farther along the Strand are the headquarters of the High Commissioner for **New Zealand** (on the left). The *Tivoli Cinema* is among the most important in London.

To the south, between the Strand and the river, lies the quarter known as **The Adelphi,** built by the brothers Adam in 1768–70, and long one of the architectural glories of London. Unfortunately the hand of Progress has been laid on the Adelphi and housebreakers set about the demolition of the famous Terrace in 1936. In John Street is the **Royal Society of Arts,** established in 1754 for the encouragement of arts, manufactures and commerce. Next door is the **Little Theatre.** No. 6 is the headquarters of the **British Science Guild.**

On the north side of the Strand, opposite Adam Street, is the **Adelphi Theatre,** reconstructed in modern style. Just beyond is the **Vaudeville.** On the opposite side of the Strand stood the Hotel Cecil; but the hotel is no more and its place has been taken by a huge block of offices for Messrs. Shell-Mex, Ltd.—best seen from the Embankment, however. Next door is the **Savoy Hotel,** extending from the Strand to the Embankment. In the east block is *Simpson's Restaurant,* making a speciality of English food cooked in the English style. The **Savoy Theatre** was long identified with the burlesque operas of Sir W. S. Gilbert and Sir Arthur Sullivan. Recent reconstruction has made this one of the most charming of London's theatres. The huge *Strand Palace Hotel* (Messrs. Lyons) occupies the site of the old Exeter Hall, famed for its religious meetings. The **Savoy Chapel,** reached by Savoy Hill, on the right, stands on part of the site of the ancient Palace of the Savoy, given by Henry III. to his uncle Peter, Earl of Savoy. It afterwards passed to John of Gaunt. King John of France, the captive of Poitiers, died here in 1364, and the Palace is believed to have been the scene of Chaucer's marriage. The palace was burnt down in the reign of Richard II. by Wat Tyler. Henry VII. in the year 1505 built a hospital on the site, and the church we see to-day was the chapel. It was made a Chapel Royal by George III., a title it retained until 1925. Savoy Hill became known far and wide as the home of the British Broadcasting Corporation, with the famous "studios" of the London Station (2LO); but in 1933 the Corporation moved to larger and more magnificent premises in the vicinity of Queen's Hall (see p. 146).

Either of the thoroughfares running northward from the Strand would bring us in a few minutes to **Covent Garden Market** (Plan III. K. 8), the chief market in London for fruit, vegetables and flowers. It takes its name from the fact that it was of old the Convent Garden of St. Peter's, Westminster (the Abbey). After that Convent was, with so many others, disestablished and disendowed, the site remained vacant, and in course of time stalls were erected for the sale of vegetables against the wall of the garden of Bedford House, in the Strand. In 1631 the Earl of Bedford built around it the quadrangle (about three acres in extent); and the Piazza, designed by Inigo Jones, was long the favourite lounging place of fashionable men about town. The market buildings were erected in 1831, but have been extended and improved in recent years. The central avenue is lined with shops, in a few of which fruits and flowers are displayed for retail sale. About 6 a.m. on Tuesdays, Thursdays and Saturdays, when the wholesale market is in full swing, a very animated scene may be witnessed. The Piazza and the taverns connected with it were conspicuous in the social, literary and dramatic history of the eighteenth century. On the western side of the market is **St. Paul's Church,** built by Inigo Jones in 1633. In the churchyard were buried Samuel Butler, the author of *Hudibras*; Sir Peter Lely, who painted the portraits of so many frail beauties of the Stuart Court; Wycherley, the dramatist; Dr. Arne, the composer of "Rule, Britannia"; Grinling Gibbons, the wood-carver; Charles Macklin, the actor; and John Wolcot ("Peter Pindar"). Here, too, are the ashes of Dame Ellen Terry (d. July, 1928).

Running parallel with the Strand, between Bedford Street and Southampton Street, is **Maiden Lane,** a narrow street in which Voltaire lodged, and where Andrew Marvell was living when he refused Charles II.'s bribe of £1,000 to support the then Government. J. M. W. Turner, the great landscape painter, was born at No. 20, his father being a hairdresser. *Rule's Oyster House*, on the north side, is a favourite haunt of theatrical and literary people, and has many interesting old play-bills, portraits, caricatures, etc. At 27, Southampton Street (tablet),

David Garrick lived from 1750–1772, prior to his removal to Adelphi Terrace. In Garrick Street, on the north-west side of the market, is the **Garrick Club,** possessing a valuable collection of portraits of famous actors. This street leads into **Long Acre,** long a centre of horse and harness dealers and coach-builders, but now a haunt of motor agents. The labyrinth of streets hereabouts is rather confusing to strangers; we are in the neighbourhood of the notorious **Seven Dials,** at one time the haunt of the most disreputable of London's residuum, and even now none too savoury. Long Acre runs in a north-easterly direction, and after crossing Drury Lane is continued as **Great Queen Street** to **Kingsway.** In Great Queen Street is the magnificent new **Freemasons' Hall,** erected at a cost of about a million pounds as a Peace Memorial and dedicated by H.R.H. the Duke of Connaught in July, 1933. Near the Kingsway end of Great Queen Street is the **Kingsway Theatre.** In **Drury Lane** we have the famous and historic **Drury Lane Theatre** (Plan III. L. 8—main entrance in Catherine Street), the painted pillars of its colonnade well calculated to put waiting "pittites" in a mood to appreciate the spectacular glories within. This, the fourth theatre on the site, can seat 2,500 persons. Across the road is the **Fortune Playhouse.** One of the doorways in its frontage leads to the adjoining **Church of Scotland,** and it has been remarked that so well has the architect done his work that only notice boards distinguish the entrance to the church from the way into the pit. Towards the northern end of Drury Lane is the **Winter Garden Theatre.** In Bow Street is the **Royal Opera House,** used also for balls, etc. **Bow Street** will always be associated with the famous "Bow Street runners"; and with Fielding, the novelist, and his brother, Sir John Fielding, the blind magistrate. In **Wellington Street,** by which we can return to the Strand, is the **Lyceum Theatre,** so long associated with Sir Henry Irving and the late Dame Ellen Terry, and in more recent times noted for real drama.

Kingsway and Aldwych.

Plan II. L. 7 and III. L. 8.

Stations.—North end, *Holborn* (*Kingsway*) (Piccadilly Tube and Central London Tube); south end, *Aldwych* (Piccadilly Tube), Temple (District Railway).

Tramway.—Beneath the whole length of Kingsway runs the **Tramway Subway,** a link between the tramways of North and South London (see p. 50). The northern end of the subway emerges at Southampton Row; the southern on the Embankment below Waterloo Bridge. There are intermediate stations opposite Bush House and near Holborn.

These thoroughfares were constructed by the London County Council in 1905 to provide direct communication between North and South London. **Kingsway,** lined almost throughout with tall and stately blocks of offices, starts from the junction of High Holborn with Southampton Row. It extends southward in

[*Taylor.*

THE LAW COURTS.

[*Sport & General.*

AUSTRALIA HOUSE, STRAND.

[*Topical.*

THE ROYAL EXCHANGE.

a straight line for a third of a mile and then forms a crescent, known as **Aldwych,** the western horn of which debouches into the Strand almost opposite Waterloo Bridge, while the eastern horn enters the Strand at St. Clement Danes Church.

The **Church of St. Anselm and St. Cecilia,** a Roman Catholic fane at the northern end of Kingsway, was opened in 1909 to replace the historic Sardinian Chapel, which stood near by. Another rebuilt edifice, on the opposite side of the road, is **Holy Trinity Church,** the successor of a building dating from 1831, which was undermined by the Tube railways and had to be condemned as unsafe. On the west side of Kingsway is **Kingsway Hall,** used for concerts and lectures. Almost opposite are the headquarters of **Mudie's Library** (see p. 29), and a little lower down is the **Stoll Picture Theatre,** erected by Oscar Hammerstein of New York, at a cost of £200,000, and opened in 1911 as the London Opera House. At the opposite corner of Sardinia Street is a huge ten-storied block serving as the **Offices of the Public Trustee.** In a large block at the south end of Kingsway are the headquarters of the **Royal Air Force.** Meteorological charts are displayed giving indications of coming weather. Across the road is the huge portal of Bush House. For **Lincoln's Inn Fields,** see p. 193.

Marking the western end of Aldwych is the **Gaiety Theatre,** famed for its musical plays. Its very imposing neighbour is **India House,** a fine building forming the London headquarters of the Indian Government. The architect was Sir Herbert Baker, A.R.A., and the manner in which the design conforms to that of Bush House and yet includes much distinctive detail is admirable. In Aldwych are the *Waldorf Hotel* and two playhouses, the **Aldwych Theatre** (noted for farce), and the **Strand Theatre,** and in Catherine Street is the charming **Duchess Theatre.** Aldwych owes its name to the fact that the district was in Saxon times the site of a Danish settlement. The lofty and massive **Bush House** is among the largest single buildings in London. It is mainly occupied as offices, including those of the *Commercial Attaché to the United States Embassy.* The principal portico faces up Kingsway and is undeniably impressive. It bears the inscription, " To the friendship of English-speaking people," and is surmounted by symbolic figures by *Malvina Hoffman.* The roof of Bush House commands magnificent all-round views of London. At the eastern end of Aldwych is **Australia House,** an imposing building in Doric classical style erected by the Commonwealth to serve as offices for the various States. The foundation-stone was laid in 1913, and the formal opening took place in 1918, both ceremonies being performed by King George V. The colonnaded building is so well proportioned that at a first glance its hugeness is scarcely apparent.

There are ten floors. Much of the stone and woodwork is Australian, as are also the beautiful marble pillars. The site cost nearly £400,000 and the total cost amounted to nearly £1,000,000.

St. Mary-le-Strand Church was built by Gibbs in 1717, and is an edifice worthy of its prominent island site, though it is overshadowed by the great bulk of Bush House. Thomas à Becket was for a time rector. For **St. Clement Danes,** see p. 192.

Across the Strand from the Gaiety Theatre is the dignified façade of **Somerset House,** occupying the site of the palace begun in 1547 by the Protector Somerset, who, however, did not live to see its completion, the headsman of Tower Hill abruptly closing his career.

The proud and unscrupulous Duke provided some of the materials by pulling down the cloisters of St. Paul's, with the charnel-house and chapel, flinging the bones to rot in what is now the Bunhill (Bonehill) Fields Cemetery (p. 224). After Somerset's death the palace became royal property. Inigo Jones, the great architect, died here in 1652. In 1775 it was rebuilt at a cost of £360,000 as a home for the Royal Academy, the Royal Society, and other learned bodies, and into the interior decorations of this fine example of English classical architecture such men as Reynolds, Gainsborough, and Cipriani put some of their finest work. The south and principal front, 780 ft. long, presents a noble façade in the Palladian style, with a terrace which, before the construction of the Embankment, was lapped by the waters of the Thames. The eastern wing was added in 1828, and the western wing, with frontage to Wellington Street, in 1854–6. The *Audit Office*, the *Inland Revenue Office* (west wing), whence stamps are issued and where taxes are paid, the *Probate Registry*, where wills are kept and may be inspected for a small fee, and the *Office of the Registrar-General of Births, Deaths and Marriages*, are located in the building.

The east wing of Somerset House is occupied by **King's College,** founded in 1828, and now affiliated to London University (see p. 159). There are several large halls and a number of laboratories and class-rooms. Close at hand is the *Aldwych Station* of the Piccadilly Tube Railway. The line between the Aldwych and Holborn stations is a spur from the main line, and it is always necessary to change at Holborn.

The southern part of Wellington Street leads or led to **Waterloo Bridge** (Plan III. L. 8), considered by Canova the finest bridge in Europe. In 1924 it was found that a dangerous settlement had taken place in the foundations of the pier arches, and the bridge has been taken down. A modern structure is to replace it ; meanwhile a temporary bridge alongside carries traffic across the Thames at this busy point. The view down the river is fine, though apt to be obscured by fences, gantries and other adjuncts of the great undertaking.

By descending the steps at the end of Waterloo Place we can reach—

The Victoria Embankment

and make acquaintance with one or two features of necessity overlooked in our journey eastward by way of the Strand. Across the road is the end of the Kingsway tramway (see p. 188). Next to Savoy Hill is the **Institute of Electrical Engineers.** The fine situation of the Savoy Hotel and the neighbouring Shell-Mex building are better appreciated from this side. They overlook the **Embankment Gardens,** one of the sunniest and most delightful spots in London. The Gardens contain numerous statues.

Indisputable evidence of the fact that all this " good dry land " has been filched from the river is afforded by the presence at the far end of the Gardens of the beautiful **York Water Gate,** designed by Inigo Jones for York House, the seat of the first Duke of Buckingham and the birthplace of Bacon (1561).

The river is here spanned by the unsightly **Charing Cross Railway Bridge,** which has a separate footway for pedestrians. Near here stood the blacking factory at which Dickens worked in boyhood. The bridge superseded the Hungerford Suspension Bridge, the ironwork of which was utilized for the lofty Suspension Bridge now spanning the Avon at Clifton. Important changes have been proposed, involving the transfer of Charing Cross station to the south bank of the Thames and the replacement of the present bridge by a great new viaduct to carry road traffic. The work has been deferred, but compared with Paris, London is poorly provided with bridges, and for many years " the question of the bridges " will form an integral part of the even greater Traffic Problem.

We can return to Waterloo Bridge along the Embankment, noting as we go that famous Egyptian obelisk known as **Cleopatra's Needle,** brought to this country in 1878.

This and the companion monolith now in New York originally stood before the great temple of Heliopolis many centuries before the time of Cleopatra. The " Needle," of red granite, is 68½ ft. high, and weighs 180 tons. The inscriptions relate its history. While the obelisk was being towed to England the steamer had to abandon it on account of bad weather, but it was subsequently recovered. At the foot are two large bronze sphinxes (perforated during the Great War by fragments from an aerial bomb).

The **Belgian Monument** commemorates the hospitality shown by people of this country to Belgians during the War.

Passing under Waterloo Bridge we note the fine river front of Somerset House (p. 190) and reach another of the series of Embankment Gardens. Here is the *Temple Station* of the District Railway. To the east is the tasteful little building originally designed by the late J. L. Pearson for use as the Astor Estate Office, and now the **Incorporated Accountants' Hall.** It is surmounted by a gilded caravel.

Nearly opposite the western boundary of the City (marked by a tablet) is moored **H.M.S. President,** the headquarters of the London Division of the Royal Naval Volunteer Reserve. Though small, it has the longest pay list in the Navy, as the names of officers serving at the Admiralty or engaged on special service at home or abroad are borne on its books. Across the road are pleasant glimpses of **Temple Gardens** (p. 197), but on our present round we will return to the Strand by one of the streets northward, or by the steps at the foot of Essex Street.

At No. 5, Strand Lane, a narrow passage at 163, Strand, is a genuine antiquity, the **Roman Bath,** one of the few relics of the Roman period in London. It has a continual flow of spring water and is about 15½ ft. long, 6½ ft. wide, and 5 ft. deep. *The Bath may be seen on weekdays between* 10.30 *and* 5; 6*d. When closed apply at St. Clement Danes Church.*

We shall regain the Strand close to **Australia House** (p. 189) and **St. Clement Danes Church,** at the eastern termination of Aldwych. The church was erected in 1681, from the designs of Wren, on the site of a much earlier building, traditionally said to have been the burial-place of Harold Harefoot and other members of the Danish colony settled here in Saxon times. The tower contains the famous old peal mentioned in the nursery rhyme: "Oranges and Lemons, said the bells of St. Clement's." The pulpit was carved by Grinling Gibbons. Above it hang the flags of Australia and New Zealand, in commemoration of War-time associations; on the south side is the Danish flag, in allusion to the foundation of the church.

Outside the east end of the church is a bronze **Statue of Dr. Johnson,** who regularly attended service at St. Clement Danes, his pew in the north gallery being indicated by a brass plate. He is further commemorated by a memorial window.

At the western end of the church is the **Gladstone Memorial,** of bronze, designed by the late *Sir Hamo Thornycroft, R.A.*

In Houghton Street is the **London School of Economics,** a branch of London University. Between Aldwych and the Law

Courts stands what is left of **Clement's Inn,** an ancient Inn of Chancery in the garden of which Falstaff and Shallow "heard the chimes at midnight."

The Royal Courts of Justice.

Plan II. L. 7.
Nearest Stations.—Aldwych (Piccadilly Tube) and Temple (District Railway).

The Royal Courts of Justice, generally called the "Law Courts," extend back to Carey Street. The style is what is known as Monastic Gothic, and the building, exclusive of site, cost little short of a million pounds, most of which was provided out of unclaimed funds in Chancery. The principal entrance, facing the Strand, has a fine recessed archway, flanked by towers in which are the entrances to the public galleries of the various Courts. There are nineteen of these, serving the King's Bench, the Chancery, and the Probate, Divorce and Admiralty Divisions and the Court of Appeal. These, however, proved insufficient, and four new courts were erected in 1911–13 at a cost of about £100,000. The Courts are entered by way of the mosaic-paved *Central Hall*, which is 238 ft. long and 80 ft. high, and has a fine rose window in the gable. Here is the marble statue of *Sir William Blackstone* presented to the Bar of England by the American Bar Association in 1924. Only barristers and solicitors and persons connected with the cases are allowed in the body of the Courts and in the Central Hall, but anyone may ascend the steps in the towers and take a seat in the public galleries. The Central Hall is shown to the public during vacations. The Judges' entrance is at the back, in Carey Street.

On the west side is a pleasant stretch of greensward, thrown open in the daytime, alongside which we may pass to the steps leading up to **Carey Street,** where is the **Bankruptcy Court,** with which no reader will desire to be too closely acquainted. Serle Street leads onward to **Lincoln's Inn Fields** (Plan II. L. 7), almost the largest of London's "Squares," the magnificent plane trees of which afford grateful shade on a summer day. (Tennis courts, 1*s*. 6*d*. per hour ; bookable three days in advance.) The gardens were laid out by Inigo Jones early in the seventeenth century, and were long a noted resort of duellists. Lord William Russell was executed here in 1683. A tablet under the summer-house in the centre marks the spot, but according to the late Sir G. L. Gomme it is inaccurately placed. Most of the houses are now occupied by solicitors, but at one time this was the most fashionable place of residence in London, and several of the existing mansions were built for members of the nobility. Tablets commemorate several notable residents. No. 58 was for some years occupied by Dickens's biographer, Foster, and in *Bleak*

House is introduced as the office of the ill-fated Tulkinghorn. In the north-west corner is *Newcastle House*, a historic building that has recently undergone skilful internal reconstruction.

On the south side are the **College of Estate Management** and the **Land Registry,** and the **Royal College of Surgeons,** erected in 1835 from the designs of Barry. It contains the museum of anatomy founded by John Hunter, the famous surgeon, who died in 1793. (*Visitors are admitted on the personal introduction or written order of a member, or on application to the secretary, on Mondays, Tuesdays, Wednesdays and Thursdays between* 10 *and* 4 *in winter, and* 10 *and* 5 *in summer. The Museum is closed during September.*) The collection, which has been greatly augmented since Hunter's death, occupies five large rooms, and is one of the most remarkable in the world. Some of the exhibits are decidedly gruesome. In the large room are contrasted the skeleton of Byrne, the Irish giant, 7 ft. 7 in. high, and that of Caroline Crachami, who died when ten years of age, having attained the height of only 20 in. There are numerous skeletons of animals, and cases illustrating nearly all the dreadful ills that flesh is heir to. The library contains 50,000 volumes.

In the north-east corner of Lincoln's Inn Fields is the **Institute of Auctioneers and Estate Agents,** a very attractive modern building. At No. 13 is **Sir John Soane's Museum** (Plan II. L. 7), *open free from* 10.30 *to* 5 *on Tuesdays, Wednesdays, Thursdays and Fridays from March to August inclusive. Also Thursdays and Fridays in October from* 10.30 *to* 5, *November* 10.30 *to* 4. *At other times apply personally or by letter to the Curator. Catalogues* 1s. *and* 6*d.*

The Museum contains the fine collection of books, manuscripts, and Egyptian and Oriental antiquities formed by Sir John Soane, the architect who designed the Bank of England and who commenced life as a mason's son. One of the most important features is the alabaster sarcophagus, found in 1817, of Seti I. (1350 B.C.), the father of Rameses the Great. The collection of pictures, statuary, etc., includes the eight originals of Hogarth's *Rake's Progress*, and works by Reynolds, Turner, Canaletto, Watteau, etc. This interesting collection should certainly be seen.

Opposite, and within the gardens, is a memorial seat to *Margaret MacDonald* (d. 1911), wife of Mr. Ramsay MacDonald, the first Labour Premier in this country—one of the few London memorials to women other than queens.

To the east of the square is **Lincoln's Inn** (Plan II. L. 7), another of the four great Inns of Court. The others are Gray's

Inn, Holborn (p. 168), and the Inner and the Middle Temple (p. 197). These four "societies," governed by Benchers, alone have the power of "calling to the bar." Prior to the erection of the present Law Courts, the Court of Chancery held its sittings here. Entering by the picturesque gateway from Lincoln's Inn Fields, we have on the left the **Library** of red brick, built in 1845. In the Hall is a large fresco entitled "A School of Jurisprudence," executed gratuitously by G. F. Watts. It has recently been restored. The collection, founded in 1497, is the largest and finest law library in London, containing over 70,000 volumes and a number of valuable MSS. bequeathed by Sir Matthew Hale and others. Passing the pleasant gardens (note the fine wrought-iron gates), we come to the **Chapel,** erected from the designs of Inigo Jones in 1623, and containing some good stained-glass windows and wood carvings. The **Hall** dates from 1506, and recent very thorough restoration—amounting almost to rebuilding—has revealed the original work, long covered with plaster and stucco. Readers of Dickens will like to recall that here was heard the case of Jarndyce *v.* Jarndyce.

The Gatehouse opening on to Chancery Lane was built in 1518 by Sir Thomas Lovell, whose arms appear above, together with those of Henry VIII. and Henry de Lacy, Earl of Lincoln. The gateway was restored in 1899. Close to the gateway, a tablet on the wall of No. 24, Old Square, recalls the residence of John Thurloe, Cromwell's Secretary of State.

Chancery Lane (Plan II. L. 7) connects Fleet Street with Holborn. The upper part of the western side is overlooked by the somewhat dingy offices of Lincoln's Inn (and see p. 196). Near the Fleet Street end is the **Law Society's Institution.** The fine Tudor building on the opposite side of the Lane is the **Public Record Office.** (*The public are freely admitted to the Museum containing the more famous treasures, between* 2 *and* 4 *p.m. daily, except Saturdays and Sundays. Organized parties at other times by arrangement. Search rooms open* 10 *to* 4.30 ; *Saturdays* 10 *to* 2.) Here are stored in fire-proof rooms the state papers and records formerly kept in the Chapter House of Westminster Abbey, the Rolls Chapel, and other places. Documents prior to 1801 and records of Government departments may be inspected gratis by holders of students' tickets ; for others there is a small search fee. The collection includes among other interesting MSS. the original volumes and ancient covers of *Domesday Book*, most of the documents connected with the "Gunpowder Plot," including the warning sent to Lord Mounteagle, and Wellington's report from the battle of Waterloo. The Museum occupies the site of the old Rolls Chapel ; several monuments are still to be seen.

South of the Record Office is **Clifford's Inn,** one of the most lovely and peaceful corners in London until in 1935 the greater part of the site was covered by a modern block of offices. The old Hall remains, however, and contains the Library and Museum of the *British Optical Association.*

To the north of the Record Office is the street known as Bream's Buildings, with the **Birkbeck College,** founded in 1824 as the Birkbeck Institute, the evening classes at which have been, and are, a priceless boon to thousands of busy City workers. Near the Holborn end of Chancery Lane, Southampton Buildings provide another entrance to **Staple Inn** (p. 169). This street leads also to the **Patent Office,** where inventions and trade marks are registered. The excellent library (over 100,000 vols.), rich in scientific works, journals, transactions, etc., both British and foreign, may be used by anyone on signing the visitors' book (*week-days,* 10–9). **Fetter Lane** (Plan II. M. 7), to the east, running approximately parallel with Chancery Lane, though hardly an inviting thoroughfare, has some interesting associations. It is variously said to derive its name from the *faitours,* or beggars, once infesting it, and a colony of *feutriers* (felt-makers or saddlers). Dryden and Otway, the poets, at one time lived here, and here John Gerard (1545–1612) had his herbal garden. He was a surgeon as well as superintendent of the gardens of William Cecil, Lord Burghley. He was one of the first (according to his *Herball* of 1597) to experiment with "Turkey wheat" (American maize), sweet potatoes, Jerusalem artichokes, not to mention his interest in tulips, which were also natives of "Turkey" in his day. The **Moravian Chapel,** almost opposite the Record Office and approached by a long passage, is more than 150 years old. The *Royal Scottish Corporation* building boasts an unusual luxury among city offices—a front garden.

We regain our main line of route in Fleet Street, but it will be advisable to retrace our steps for a few yards westward to the spot opposite the Law Courts where a monument in the roadway marks the site of the old **Temple Bar** (Plan III. L. 8). This famous portal to the City, which callous Londoners allowed to be carted away to private grounds at Theobald's Park, Cheshunt, was built by Wren in 1670, and was long used for the exhibition of conspirators' and criminals' heads, notably those who were "out" in 1745. It had, however, more pleasing associations. As one writer well says :—

"The shadow of every monarch and popular hero since Charles II.'s time rested for at least a passing moment at the old gateway. Queen

Photochrom Co., Ltd.,] [*Tunbridge Wells.*

THE TEMPLE CHURCH.

H. Felton,] [*London.*

PUMP COURT, TEMPLE.

Walter Scott,] [*Bradford.*

MIDDLE TEMPLE LANE.

Will F. Taylor,] *[London.*

MIDDLE TEMPLE HALL.

Herbert Felton,] [*London.*

THE BANK OF ENGLAND.

Anne passed here to return thanks at St. Paul's for the victory of Blenheim. Here Marlborough's coach ominously broke down in 1714, when he returned from his voluntary exile. George III. passed through Temple Bar, young and happy, the year after his coronation; and again, when old and almost broken-hearted, he returned thanks for his partial recovery from insanity; and that graceless son of his, the Prince Regent, came through the Bar in 1814, to thank God at St. Paul's for the downfall of Bonaparte. Queen Victoria sued for admission to the City at Temple Bar on November 9th, 1837, when she attended the Lord Mayor's banquet after her accession."

It is strange that a king should have to ask for admission to his own capital, yet such is the real significance of Temple Bar and other points on the city boundary. In accordance with ancient custom, it is still the practice whenever the Sovereign visits the City in state for the Lord Mayor to receive him here, at Holborn Bars, or at the boundary on the Embankment (p. 192), and to tender the sword of state, which His Majesty is expected to return immediately. A small reproduction of the old gateway hangs before a neighbouring restaurant. The present ugly monument is usually known as the "Griffin," though, as a matter of heraldic fact, the supporters of the City arms are dragons—held by some calumnious individuals to typify the rapacity of the citizens. Adjoining the Law Courts we have the *Branch Bank of England*, designed by Blomfield; while on the south side is *Child's Bank*, the successor of the building where the fair but frail Nell Gwynne kept her account, and which figured as "Tellson's" in Dickens's *Tale of Two Cities*. At the entrance to the Inner Temple, facing the foot of Chancery Lane, is No. 17, Fleet Street, with a projecting upper storey. The house was built in 1610. On the first floor is a chamber known as **Prince Henry's Room,** *open free week-days* 10 *to* 5 *April to September*; *and* 10 *to* 4 *during the rest of the year.* It is believed to have been used as the Council Chamber of the Duchy of Cornwall. In view of the interest attached to the house, the London County Council, with the assistance of the Corporation, purchased the building in 1900, when it was on the point of demolition, and restored the premises at a total cost of £30,000.

The Temple

(Plan III. L. and M. 8)

is one of the most interesting places in London. Between busy Fleet Street and the broad Embankment are a venerable church, Gothic halls, piles of stately buildings, quadrangles, spacious lawns, trees and flower gardens, and a shady nook where plays a little fountain close to rockeries and flowers. The Temple has the flavour of a university town, mingled with associations of the old Crusading times and the literary history of the eighteenth century. "It is the most elegant spot in the metropolis," wrote Charles Lamb, who was born in Crown Office Row. "What a cheerful, liberal look hath that portion of it which, from three sides, overlooks the greater garden—that goodly pile 'of building strong, albeit of Paper hight,' confronting, with massy contrast, the lighter, older, more fantastically shrouded one, named of Harcourt, with the cheerful Crown Office Row (place of my kindly engendure) right opposite the stately stream which washes the garden-foot with her yet scarcely trade-polluted waters . . . a man would give something to have been born in such places."

In 1185 the Knights Templars, that remarkable Order which so successfully combined the priestly and the military characters, removed from Holborn to the banks of the Thames, and built the famous Church. After the abolition of the Order, in 1312, Edward II. gave the property to Aymer de Valence, Earl of Pembroke, whose tomb may be seen in Westminster Abbey. On his death the knights of the rival Order of St. John of Jerusalem—the Hospitallers—became possessed of the property, and in 1346 leased it to the doctors and students of the law, who have ever since, with characteristic tenacity, retained it. In 1609 James I. abandoned his rights in favour of the corporations of the Inner and Middle Temple. The Inner Temple was so called to distinguish it from the Outer Temple, beyond the City boundary, the Middle Temple being between the two. The Outer Temple has long ceased to have any official recognition, though the name is still applied to a block of offices adjoining Temple Bar. The heraldic device of the Inner Temple is a winged horse (*Pegasus*), that of the Middle Temple the holy lamb (*Agnus Dei*). Wags have it that "the lamb sets forth the innocence; the horse the expedition of the lawyers."

The Temple Church.

Open daily, except Mondays, 10 to 1, 2 to 4.
Sunday Services at 11 and 3 (except Aug. and Sept.). The music is very fine. The public are admitted, without an order, so far as space permits.

There are two parts, the characteristic "Round Church" of the Templars, of which there are only four examples in this country, and the Early English Choir. The former, 58 ft. in diameter, was built by the Templars and consecrated by Heraclius, Patriarch of Jerusalem, in 1185. It is in the Transition-Norman style. The choir dates from 1240. The Norman porch, by which the church is entered, is much admired: it has recently been restored. The tiled pavement, with the oft-repeated emblems of the Temple, the painted ceiling and the nine tombs of Crusaders, with recumbent figures in full armour, are the chief features of the interior. Most of the stained-glass windows are modern. In the stair leading up to the circular triforium is a small penitential cell with slits through which the choir is seen. In this narrow prison disobedient Templars were confined ; and there is a grim tradition that those who had broken their vows were here starved to death, while day by day the services of the church were chanted in their ears. The standing of the church is peculiar. It is private—the joint property of the Inner and Middle Temple corporations (whose emblems, the winged horse and the lamb, decorate the ceiling of the choir) —and exempted from episcopal jurisdiction by a Papal Bull. The rector, known as "the Master," holds office not by reason of induction or institution, but by virtue of Letters Patent issued by the Sovereign. Within the church are memorials of John Selden (1654) and Richard Hooker (1660), but more frequently visited is the **Grave of Oliver Goldsmith** (1774), outside the church, to the north of the choir. Poor Noll wrote many of his best works and died at No. 2, Brick Court (second floor), marked by a memorial. His neighbour below (first floor) was Sir Wm. Blackstone, of the *Commentaries*. Thackeray rented chambers for a time in the same block. The **Master's House,** close to the church, has had many distinguished occupants.

The **Inner Temple Hall** (1870) was designed by Smirke. Adjoining is the **Inner Temple Library,** a Gothic building (1862) containing about 70,000 volumes, including the Petyt collection, bequeathed in 1707 by a former keeper of the Tower records.

Middle Temple Hall, in which the benchers and students dine (at the call of an ox horn, 3 ft. long and dated 1786), was built in 1572, and has a magnificent oak roof, richly carved, and a fine oak screen. Among several royal portraits is a replica of the equestrian figure of Charles I. by *Van Dyck*. On the dais at the end of the Hall, Shakespeare is believed to have acted in *Twelfth Night* early in 1602. The long table that stands here, made from an oak in Windsor Park, was the gift of Queen Elizabeth to the Benchers. Upon it she is said to have signed the death-warrant of Mary, Queen of Scots. The smaller table was constructed from the timbers of Drake's ship, **The Golden Hind.** When the Hall is not in use, visitors can gain access freely at reasonable hours by pulling the bell at the entrance.

The **Middle Temple Library** (50,000 vols.) is housed in a beautiful Gothic building nearer the river.

It is very restful to stroll for a while through the various courts and quadrangles, with their interesting associations. It was in **Fountain Court** that Ruth Pinch, of *Martin Chuzzlewit*, was accustomed to meet her brother Tom, "with the best little laugh upon her face that ever played in opposition to the fountain and beat it all to nothing." The old fountain familiar to Dickens was removed many years ago. Of the host of eminent names, legal and otherwise, associated with the Temple, we need only mention Raleigh, Pym, Ireton, Beaumont, Wycherley, Burke, Sheridan, Moore and Cowper. Dr. Johnson had rooms in Inner Temple Lane, the modern Johnson's Buildings marking the site; and Charles Lamb, as we have seen, was born in Crown Office Row. A fountain and statue on the lawns overlooking the Embankment commemorate his connection with the Temple. An interesting survival is the old wigmaker's shop in the Cloisters. Wigs have been made on this spot for at least 400 years.

The pleasant **Temple Gardens,** formerly reaching right down to the river, but now separated from it by the Embankment, have been rendered immortal by Shakespeare in *Henry VI., Part I*, as the scene of the quarrel between Plantagenet and Somerset, when the white and red roses—those fatal emblems of civil war—were plucked and adopted as badges. Appropriately, a *Temple Rose Show* is held each summer in the gardens.

From the quiet of the Temple with its stately buildings and green lawns it is but a step to the bustle of—

Fleet Street,

(**Plan** II. L. and M. 7)

famous the world over as the journalistic centre of London. In or near it are the offices of nearly all the great newspapers and periodicals, where hosts of busy toilers are at work both day and night. The name is, of course, derived from the old *Fleet River* (now debased to the rank of a common sewer, of which the last portion flows below Farringdon and New Bridge Streets) which flowed from Hampstead to Holborn and entered the Thames at Blackfriars. Readers of Pope's *Dunciad* will recall the not very pleasant references—

"To where Fleet Ditch, with disemboguing streams
Rolls the large tribute of dead dogs to Thames."

and again—

"Sons of a day! just buoyant on the flood,
Then numbered with the puppies in the mud."

Fleet Street itself, owing to successive widenings, is almost entirely modern, but the explorer has only to turn into any of the quaintly-named courts and byways on either side to find an abundance of Queen Anne and Georgian houses.

On the north side is **St. Dunstan's Church,** erected 1831–3. Some monuments from the church which formerly occupied the site are preserved within, including a brass of 1530. Note the beautiful lantern tower, very similar to the famous Boston "Stump." The projecting clock was returned to the church in 1935 after having for some years adorned St. Dunstan's Lodge,

Regent's Park—that same house which during the War became famous as headquarters of work among blinded men. A little knot of sightseers generally waits to see the clubbed giants strike the quarter-hours. The figure of Queen Elizabeth over the school door on the east side of the church formerly adorned the old Lud Gate on Ludgate Hill. The church was immortalized by Dickens in *The Chimes*, and has associations with Isaak Walton, of *Compleat Angler* fame, who "resided for some years in Fleet Street, at the corner of Chancery Lane (west side), and, between 1652 and 1664, was overseer of the poor and a sidesman and vestryman of this parish." The memorial window was erected by the principal angling associations. A monument close to the railings commemorates *Lord Northcliffe*.

On the opposite side is *Gosling's Bank* (Barclays), the windows bearing the sign of the old "Three Squirrels," where Warren Hastings, Clive, Pope, Samuel Richardson, Camden, Ellenborough, Sir Philip Francis, and many other famous men kept their accounts. The *Cock Tavern* displays as sign a gilded chanticleer, the original of which, carved by no less a hand than that of Grinling Gibbons, is preserved inside.

Fetter Lane has already been noticed (p. 196).

Crane Court, on the north side of Fleet Street, witnessed the first meeting of the Royal Society. In **Wine Office Court** is the celebrated *Old Cheshire Cheese*, always associated with Johnson and Goldsmith. American visitors in particular like to find their way to this quaint old hostelry—still with the pristine simplicity of wooden benches and sanded floor—to try its noted beef-steak puddings (Wednesdays). At No. 9, Wine Office Court, is the *City Women's Club*. No. 7 is **Dean Wace House,** the headquarters of the National Church League. A tablet on No. 17, **Gough Square,** beyond the head of the Court, marks the house where Dr. Johnson lived from 1748 to 1758, and where he toiled over his great Dictionary. The house has been carefully restored to its eighteenth-century condition, and may usually be inspected (10 *to* 4.30 *or* 5), together with a number of MSS., autographs, first editions, etc., of great interest to Johnsonians. The Great Cham died in Bolt Court, hard by.

Whitefriars Street and **Bouverie Street,** now given over to printers and their myrmidons, lead down to the former Alsatia, so vividly described by Scott in *The Fortunes of Nigel*. On the left of Fleet Street is the magnificent new building of the *Daily Telegraph* and the new home of the *Daily Express*. *T. P. O'Connor* (1848–1929) is fittingly commemorated by a bronze bust on the wall of *Chronicle House*.

In **Salisbury Square,** Richardson, the father of the English novel, carried on his printing business; and here, as we may without immodesty remind the reader, is **Warwick House,** the headquarters of Messrs. Ward, Lock & Co., Limited, the publishers of this Guide and of a hundred and thirty similar volumes dealing with holiday resorts in this country and abroad, of the *Windsor Magazine*, Mrs. Beeton's cookery books, and numerous children's books and other works. In this Square, too, are the offices of the **Church Missionary Society.** Close at hand rises the steeple (223 ft. high) of **St. Bride's Church** (*open daily* 12 *to* 3), rebuilt by Wren in 1680—one of the finest specimens of the Italian style in England. In the central aisle is the flat tombstone of Samuel Richardson. Lovelace, the author of "Stone walls do not a prison make," and "I could not love thee, dear, so much, Loved I not honour more," was buried in the old church, destroyed during the Great Fire. By reason of its memorials to literary men the church has been called "the Cathedral of Fleet Street." Among the entries in the register of christenings is one recording the baptism of Samuel "the son of John Peapis and his wife Margaret," on 3rd March, 1632–3. It is now generally accepted that the infant was no other than Samuel Pepys of the immortal *Diary*, and that he first saw the light in a house in Salisbury Court. In a house, now demolished, overlooking the churchyard, John Milton lived.

Bride Lane leads round the church to the **St. Bride Foundation Institute,** containing a general lending and reference library, free to persons resident or employed in the western portion of the City; halls; baths, etc. To the south, Bridewell Lane recalls the old **Bridewell,** a palace (*vide* Shakespeare's *Henry VIII.*) presented by Edward VI. to the City authorities and afterwards used as a house of correction for recalcitrant City apprentices and other misdemeanants. Bridewell Hospital was afterwards united with Bethlem or "Bedlam."

Any of the streets hereabouts would bring us down again to the Embankment, east of Temple Gardens. In this locality are a number of imposing buildings and blocks of offices; it is almost another Fleet Street, so numerous are the newspaper and publishing premises. Overlooking the Embankment is **Sion College,** founded in 1630 and containing a library of over 110,000 volumes, especially rich in theological works. The **City of London School,** for boys, faces the river; the girls' school is in Carmelite Street. In John Carpenter Street is the **Guildhall School of Music,** maintained by the Corporation of London to provide high-class musical instruction at moderate fees. There are about 140 professors and over 3,000 pupils. Close at hand, in Tudor Street, are the headquarters of the **Institute of Journalists.**

Blackfriars Bridge

is the widest and busiest road bridge in London. More than 41,000 vehicles and over 60,000 pedestrians pass this busy corner every day. **Subways** for pedestrians pass beneath the roadways.

The bridge takes its name from the monastery of the Black Friars, founded early in the thirteenth century, on the north bank of the river. In 1450 Henry VI.'s Parliament assembled in the monastery, and three-quarters of a century later it was the scene of the court held by Wolsey and the Papal Legate to try the divorce case of Henry VIII. and Katherine of Aragon, a scene that lives for ever in the pages of Shakespeare's *Henry VIII*. At the northern end of the Bridge is the *Blackfriars Station* of the District line with the *St. Paul's Station* of the Southern Railway adjoining.

At this point the Fleet River flowed into the Thames, and interesting relics of old quays, etc., were excavated during the erection of the huge building on the opposite corner—the headquarters of the many activities associated with Messrs. Lever Bros., Ltd.

Turning northward up **New Bridge Street** we reach **Ludgate Circus** (Plan II. M. 7), at the eastern termination of Fleet Street and the foot of Ludgate Hill. A fine architectural opportunity was missed when this Circus was constructed, and people of taste have never ceased to deplore the indifference which permitted the railway bridge to be carried right across the only clear approach to St. Paul's Cathedral. Many people will look with interest on the *Edgar Wallace Memorial* tablet, at the corner of Fleet Street and St. Bride Street. **Farringdon Street,** leading northward to King's Cross, covers the old Fleet River (p. 200). On the east side, on a site partly occupied now by the Memorial Hall, stood for many generations the infamous **Fleet Prison** for debtors, rendered immortal by Dickens as the scene of the incarceration of Mr. Pickwick. Sir Walter Besant's *Chaplain of the Fleet* gives some vivid pictures of life in this foul den at another period. The **Memorial Hall,** long the headquarters of the Congregational body, was built in 1874 in memory of the "fidelity to conscience" of the 2,000 ministers ejected from the Church in 1662 by the Act of Uniformity.

THE CITY.

"I pray you, let us satisfy our eyes with the memorials and the things of fame that do renown this City."—*Twelfth Night.*

FOR the exploration of the City proper (for boundaries, see plan on pp. 40–41) we can hardly choose a better starting-point than the triangular spot in the very heart of London commonly spoken of as—

The Bank.

(**Plan** III. N. 8.)

The significance of the name should not go unnoticed, for although "the Bank" originally implied solely the Bank of England, the neighbourhood is now so closely packed with British and foreign banks and financial organizations as to merit the designation "The Bank of the World." That this is no empty phrase will be appreciated by all who have followed the powerful influence of "The Old Lady of Threadneedle Street" (i.e. the Bank of England) in the solution of post-war financial problems throughout the World.

Both above and below ground this is a busy spot—although a recent census showed eleven places in London that were even busier. Here converge no fewer than seven of the most important thoroughfares, each filled from morn till night with an unending stream of omnibuses, motors, carts, cyclists and pedestrians. A recent official count gave an average at the Bank of over 3,000 vehicles an hour; while underground over 600 trains a day bring people to or from this busy centre. Here may be seen, better than anywhere else, that stirring spectacle of the policeman with uplifted arm which nearly always moves the wonder and admiration of visitors from abroad. No fewer than 20 per cent. of the City police force are continually engaged in the regulation of traffic. Yet what could more convincingly demonstrate the power of law and order in His Majesty's capital than the simple statement that the average daily effective strength of the City force is only about 1,100 men?

Even with the aid of the Belisha Beacons (p. 47) it requires dexterity of no common order to get across the roadways in safety, and pedestrians, especially strangers, are strongly advised to make use of the **Subway.**

Walter Scott,] [Bradford.

THE BANK OF ENGLAND AND THE ROYAL EXCHANGE.

[*L.M.S.*

THE GUILDHALL.

The Subway also gives access to the **Bank Stations** of the Central London and the Morden-Edgware Lines.

The Bank of England

(**Plan** III. N. 8)

occupies the whole of the four-acre area between Threadneedle Street, Princes Street, Lothbury and Bartholomew Lane. The accommodation of the original one-storey building having become inadequate, a new and lofty structure has been raised within the fortress-like walls with which Sir John Soane surrounded the site, and which have a solidity calculated to inspire confidence in the breast of the most timid investor. It will be observed that, for purposes of security, they are entirely windowless, all the rooms being lighted from interior courts; but even a Raffles who succeeded in passing this barrier would be baffled at the extraordinary series of defences surrounding the vaults, which include concentric walls of steel and concrete, enormously strong, between which armed guards patrol day and night. To make assurance doubly sure the establishment is guarded at night by a detachment of the Guards, whose daily arrival and departure gives an element of variety to the motor-ridden streets of the City. That these precautions are not unnecessary may be inferred from the fact that there are generally at least 160 million pounds in gold and silver in the vaults. During the daytime (9 to 3) persons having business, and even the public generally, are allowed to pass through the various rooms, but to get "behind the scenes," and see the intricate processes of printing bank-notes and weighing sovereigns and bullion, a special permit (rarely granted) from the Governor or Deputy-Governor is necessary.

The Bank was founded in 1694, and, although generally regarded as a national institution, is really a private corporation, doing the ordinary business of a bank as well as exercising its exclusive privileges in the printing, issue and cancellation of bank-notes, the registration of stock transfers, payment of dividends, etc. Notes of a value of £5 and upwards paid in are at once cancelled, but are not actually destroyed until a period of five years has elapsed.

Opposite the Bank, in the angle formed by Threadneedle Street and Cornhill, is—

The Royal Exchange.

Plan III. N. 8.
Admission.—The interior court is open (free) daily to all, except on certain afternoons.

This is the third building of the kind which has occupied the site. The first Exchange, founded by Sir Thomas Gresham, and opened by Queen Elizabeth in 1571, fell a victim to the Great Fire of 1666; and a similar fate overtook its successor in 1838. The present building, designed by Tite, was opened by Queen

Victoria in 1844. The steps of the Royal Exchange are one of the places from which a new sovereign is always proclaimed on his accession. In front stands a memorial, designed by Sir Aston Webb, P.R.A., to London troops who fell in the Great War. Close by is an equestrian *Statue of the Duke of Wellington* (riding without stirrups) by Chantrey. The interior of the Exchange is a large quadrangular court, with a tessellated pavement which formed part of Gresham's building and, like the pavements of several City churches, was spared by the Fire. The court was originally planned into " walks " patrolled by the various merchants. But the "Silkman's " walk has vanished as completely as those of the Salters and the Barbadoes, and except for some tallow and grease business about 4 p.m. on Wednesdays, but little Exchange business is done here. The ambulatory is decorated with a famous set of 32 spirit-varnish **Frescoes** by distinguished artists. The visitor is strongly advised not to miss seeing these pictures—anyone may go in. The pictures are plainly labelled, the subjects relating to the history and development of London.

The hall also contains statues of Queen Victoria, Queen Elizabeth, Charles II., and Connor's bust of Abraham Lincoln. As already remarked, the exchange business of London has long outgrown this hall and the brokers have migrated to the Baltic and other Exchanges.

The Royal Exchange has a famous peal of **Bells,** recast in 1921. They play English, Scottish and Irish melodies at 9, 12, 3 and 6 p.m.

Recent rebuilding has transformed the appearance of this once familiar corner of London. The Royal Exchange and the Mansion House remain as relics of an age which loved Classic porticoes; all around are soaring examples of the new architectural spirit, and the conjunction of styles raises some interesting points for architectural students.

The Mansion House.

Plan III. N. 8.

Admission.—The Egyptian Hall, etc., are shown (circumstances permitting) to visitors making previous application by letter addressed to the Lord Mayor's Secretary.

This, the official residence of the Lord Mayor, is the last of the trio of public buildings overlooking this " hub " of the City. It was built between 1739 and 1753, mainly, it is said, from fines levied on stalwart Nonconformists. It has a fine Corinthian portico, from the platform of which official announcements are often made. The chief room is the *Egyptian Hall*, where the somewhat lavish hospitality expected from London's chief citizen is exercised. The Lord Mayor receives a salary of £10,000 a year, but if rumour speaks correctly, he is generally out of pocket at the end of his year of office. To the left of the entrance is the *Lord Mayor's Police Court.*

On the corner formed by King William Street and Lombard Street stands the Church of **St. Mary Woolnoth,** rebuilt in 1716 by Hawksmoor, a pupil of Wren. John Newton, joint author with Cowper of the *Olney Hymns,* was once rector, and was buried here with his wife, but their remains were removed in 1893 to Olney. Beneath the church run the Morden-Edgware and Central London Tubes, the *Bank Station* harmonizing with the church.

Indecision is fatal at this busy spot, for the loiterer is likely to be swept off his feet, but with so many diverging thoroughfares it is not easy to make up one's mind which to traverse first. Let us turn westward along the Poultry and Cheapside to St. Paul's Cathedral and Ludgate Hill, and so join the last route of our West End section.

ROUTE IX—CHEAPSIDE—GUILDHALL—GENERAL POST OFFICE—ST. PAUL'S CATHEDRAL—LUDGATE HILL—OLD BAILEY—QUEEN VICTORIA STREET —CANNON STREET.

On the right of the **Poultry** (Plan III. N. 8) are the magnificent new headquarters of the *National Provincial* and the *Midland Banks,* the latter designed by *Sir Edwin Lutyens* and rightly described as a masterpiece. The street in its modern aspect gives little indication of its former character, when the old Chepe was from end to end an open market. This and neighbouring thoroughfares still bear the names of the commodities once displayed for sale in them. On the north side are Milk Street, Wood Street, Ironmonger Lane and Honey Lane, and to the south is Bread Street. The name of **Cheapside** (Plan II. N. 7) is an obvious derivation from the Anglo-Saxon *ceapian,* to sell or bargain. Though less than a quarter of a mile in length, Cheapside is one of the most important city thoroughfares, and is lined with shops. Jewellers, tailors and hosiers especially favour it. A tablet on Nos. 40–41 marks the site of the old *Cheapside Cross.* In **Old Jewry,** on the right, are the headquarters of the **City Police** (see p. 33). The name recalls a synagogue built by Jews who were subsequently driven farther east. Close at hand, with main entrance in Prince's Street, is **Grocers' Hall,** the headquarters of the old and wealthy Grocers' Company, or "Pepperers." At the corner of Ironmonger Lane is the **Mercers' Hall,** rebuilt in 1884. The Mercers are the richest of the City Livery Companies, having an annual income exceeding £110,000.

At **King Street** we turn rightward for—

The Guildhall.

Plan II. N. 7.
Admission.—The Great Hall is open all day and may be freely seen. The Art Gallery and the Museum are open from 10 to 4 or 5. The Library and News Room are open daily from 10 to 6.
Nearest Stations.—Bank (Central London, and Morden-Edgware Line), Moorgate (Metropolitan, etc.), Mansion House (District).

This famous civic palace is chiefly associated in the popular mind with the great banquet on Lord Mayor's Day (November 9), when important political pronouncements are frequently made by members of the Government. It has been the scene of some of the most stirring episodes in our history. Nearly every crowned head in Europe—when crowned heads were more common—was fêted within these walls; and many of our leading statesmen, soldiers and sailors have here been honoured with the freedom of the City—an honour esteemed second only to honours received from the hands of the Sovereign. As we cross the Yard a good view is obtained of the fine fifteenth-century porch. Until 1910 the east wing bore no sort of resemblance to the west wing, but this has now been remedied, and the entire south front appears according to the eighteenth-century design of George Dance, R.A. The Guildhall, begun about 1411, was partly destroyed by the Great Fire in 1666, but it has recently been discovered that the existing Hall contains much more of the original work than was generally believed. The **Great Hall** is used for the election of the Lord Mayor and Sheriffs and members of Parliament for the City, and for many civic and political gatherings. In the gallery at the west end are the famous wooden figures known as *Gog* (left) and *Magog* (right). They are 14 ft. 6 in. high, and were carved by one Captain Richard Saunders in 1708. Formerly wickerwork figures of these unprepossessing individuals were carried in Lord Mayors' processions. The window at the eastern end was given by the people of Lancashire as an acknowledgment of the City's benevolence during the great Cotton Famine of 1862–5. The other windows represent scenes from the history of the City. A restoration of the walls in 1909 resulted in the discovery of a fifteenth-century window in the south-west corner. The fine open timber roof is modern (1865). Ranged round the hall are monuments to Wellington, Nelson (inscription by Sheridan), Chatham (inscription by Burke), Wm. Pitt, and Lord Mayor Beckford, and there are also memorials and colours associated with regiments connected with the City. In the north-west corner are standard measurements of a foot and a yard, and let into the floor of the hall are plates marking a chain (66 ft.) and 100 feet.

Beyond the richly decorated **Council Chamber** is the **Aldermen's Court Room,** with a painted ceiling by Thornhill.

The **Guildhall Library,** founded in 1423, is maintained as a free library by the Corporation, and *may be used by anyone over 16 years of age signing the visitors' book at entrance* (*open daily* 10 *to* 6). The principal library is a magnificent hall in Tudor style, 100 ft. long and 50 ft. high, with six book-lined bays on either side. The roof, with arched ribs, the stained-glass windows, and the fine chimney-pieces merit special attention. On state occasions the Lord Mayor receives distinguished guests in this room. The Library comprises over 200,000 volumes and 15,000 important MSS., being, as one would expect, especially rich in works on London and Middlesex. The catalogue is arranged on the " card " system. A well-furnished **Newspaper and Directory Room** adjoins.

Many valuable old prints, badges, medals, coins, etc., are arranged in cases along the corridors, and at the head of the stairs leading down to the Museum is a collection of clocks, watches, etc., belonging to the Clockworkers' Company.

The **Museum,** below the Library, may be entered directly from Basinghall Street. It contains a most interesting collection of antiquities and curiosities associated with the City, including Roman remains, quaint old shop and tavern signs and autographs of distinguished men. The **Crypt,** divided into east and west portions, formed part of the fifteenth-century Guildhall.

The **Corporation Art Gallery** (*admission, see p.* 208) is usually entered from Guildhall Yard, of which it forms the eastern side. The permanent collection includes a number of oil and water-colours by Sir John Gilbert, R.A.; the Gassiot bequest of more than a hundred British and foreign pictures; several portraits by Reynolds, and a number of busts. Plaques erected by the City Corporation remind us that the Guildhall Chapel stood here from 1299–1822, and Blackwell Hall from 1356–1820.

On the opposite side of the Yard is the *Guildhall Police Court.* In Guildhall Buildings is the *City of London Court.*

The **Irish Chamber** is the headquarters of the Irish Society, actually a highly important committee of the City Corporation. It is entirely independent in its jurisdiction. The Corporation appoints it, but has no further control over it, as its powers are defined by statute. Its function is to administer the City's Irish estates—a relic of the part taken by London in the " plantation of Ulster " 300 years ago. These are mainly in Coleraine and, as the name itself suggests, Londonderry. Under the society's charter the whole of its revenue, which is large, must be spent in those districts.

At the corner of Guildhall Yard stands the Church of **St. Lawrence Jewry,** built by Wren in place of one destroyed by the Great Fire. A stained-glass window commemorates Sir Thomas More, who was born in Milk Street hard by (p. 211). In the vestry, with its finely-painted ceiling, are carvings by Grinling Gibbons. For more than two centuries the Lord Mayor and Corporation have attended service here on Michaelmas Day, prior to the election of a new Lord Mayor. The weather vane takes the form of a gridiron, in allusion to the legendary history of St. Lawrence.

Gresham Street (Plan II. N. 7) runs from the north-west corner of the Bank of England to St. Martin's-le-Grand along a course roughly parallel to Cheapside. The first turning on the right is Aldermanbury. The Church of **St. Mary, Aldermanbury,** contains the tomb of the infamous Judge Jeffreys. Milton was married here in 1656 to his second wife, though his spell of happiness was of short duration. In the churchyard is a memorial to Herminge and Condell, who acted with Shakespeare and edited the first folio edition of the plays. Nearly all the offices and warehouses hereabouts are tenanted by firms connected with the wholesale drapery trade; a notable exception being the *Chartered Insurance Institute*.

Westward along Gresham Street at the corner of Basinghall Street is **Gresham College,** founded under the will of Sir Thomas Gresham, and rebuilt in 1913. Near the Post Office end is the **Goldsmiths' Hall,** rebuilt from Hardwick's designs in 1835. The hall contains notable pictures of sovereigns, and a goblet out of which Queen Elizabeth is said to have drunk at her coronation. The "hallmark" of the Company, a leopard's head, is familiar to all fortunate enough to possess gold plate or ornaments. At the corner of Gresham Street and Wood Street is the **Haberdashers' Hall.** This Company, with an income of £60,000 a year, has done much for education.

Returning now to Cheapside, we note on the south side the famous **Bow Church,** or, to give its full name, the Church of St. Mary-le-Bow.

A person born within the sound of Bow Bells is a "Cockney," or Londoner pure and simple. It was the sound of Bow Bells, if we are to believe tradition, that lured the runaway apprentice, Dick Whittington, back from Highgate, to be Lord Mayor of London. In 1905, after a long interval of disuse, the *Whittington Chimes* were restored, from a setting provided by Sir Charles V. Stanford. The church was rebuilt by Wren after the Great Fire, the steeple, 235 ft. high, being generally considered his masterpiece. Many authorities, indeed, regard it as the finest Renaissance campanile in the world. Recently the church has undergone thorough restoration. Below the church is a *crypt* (3*d*.), showing Roman, Saxon and Norman work. It forms a series of "bows," or arches, and the ecclesiastical court which formerly met here became in consequence known as the Court of Arches (now removed to the Sanctuary, Westminster). The tablet on the west wall relating to John Milton was removed from the Church of All Hallows, Bread Street, on its demolition.

A tablet on the block of business premises at the corner of **Bread Street** and Watling Street, surmounted by a bas-relief, reads: "Milton, born in Bread Street in 1608, baptized in All Hallows Church, which stood here, *ante* 1878." In the now-demolished fane of St. Mildred's, Cannon Street, a few yards to the south, Shelley was married to Mary Godwin on December 30th, 1816.

In **Milk Street,** north of Cheapside, almost opposite Bread Street, Sir Thomas More was born in 1480. At the corner of Wood Street and Cheapside still flourishes the famous **Plane Tree** referred to by Wordsworth in "Poor Susan." At the corner of Foster Lane is **Saddlers' Hall,** with **St. Vedast's Church** (Wren's) to the north. In **Old Change,** to the south, is **St. Augustine's Church** (Wren's again), of which the Rev. R. H. Barham, author of the facetious *Ingoldsby Legends*, was rector at the time of his death.

Several important thoroughfares converge at the west end of Cheapside. **Aldersgate Street** (Plan II. N. 7), with its memories of Milton and John Wesley, runs northward to the Metropolitan station of the same name, and is thence continued as the **Goswell Road,** of Pickwickian associations, to the *Angel* (now a Lyons restaurant) at Islington (see p. 228). The southern part of Aldersgate Street is known as **St. Martin's-le-Grand,** a name familiar in all quarters of the globe as the headquarters of our great postal system. The name is a relic of a wooden church dedicated here in 1050.

The General Post Office.

Plan II. M. and N. 7.
Nearest Stations.—St. Paul's (Central London Tube), Aldersgate Street and Barbican (Metropolitan), Mansion House (District).

The enormous and ever-growing postal business of London is carried on in no fewer than nine extensive blocks of buildings. The famous old building on the east side of Aldersgate Street, with Ionic portico and clock, erected in 1825–9 on the site of the church of St. Martin's-le-Grand, was demolished in 1912–13, and the site is now occupied by fine modern offices. The extensive block opposite, erected in 1870–3, forms the C.T.O. Building, the greater part being appropriated by the Telegraph Department and the engineering staff. Adjoining is **Headquarters Building,** which contains the offices of the Postmaster-General and the administrative staff. **King Edward Building** occupies part of the site of the old Bluecoat School. Here London E.C. district and foreign letters are sorted and despatched, and all the ordinary work of a district post office is carried on. The *Public Hall* (entrance in King Edward Street) for the sale of stamps, despatch of telegrams, etc., is *open from* 6.45 *a.m. to* 9 *p.m. Poste Restante* on left. An interpreter is in attendance. In front of the building appropriately stands a *Statue of Rowland Hill,* pioneer of the "penny post."

Faraday Building, in Queen Victoria Street (p. 222), is used by the Telephone Department. Other huge postal buildings are at Mount Pleasant, where inland letters and parcels are dealt with; Kensington (Savings Bank); Manor Road, Holloway (Postal and War Savings); Cornwallis Road (Money Orders); and Studd Street, N. (stores).

Post Office "Tube" Railway. An interesting underground railway carries parcels and other matter from the G.P.O. to Paddington on the one hand and Whitechapel on the other. The trains are electrically driven and automatically controlled, and thanks to many ingenious loading devices 30,000 mail-bags are transmitted daily. It is computed that the railway relieves street congestion to the extent of 2,400 van miles every day.

The unsuccessful "atmospheric" railway, built years ago to convey mails between the G.P.O. and Euston, has now entered on a useful career, sections of its tunnel forming a channel for innumerable telegraph and telephone wires.

Particulars of the London postal, telegraphic and telephonic arrangements will be found on pp. 34–5.

The G.P.O. Headquarters Building partly shuts in a small open space formerly the graveyard of the Church of **St. Botolph Without,** but now familiarly known as the **Postmen's Park.** By the happy suggestion of G. F. Watts, R.A., a cloister was erected here, in which are placed from time to time tablets commemorative of acts of heroism, especially in humble life. The great artist is himself commemorated by a small statuette. A tablet on the railings overlooking Aldersgate Street commemorates the evangelical conversion of John and Charles Wesley, which occurred in this neighbourhood in 1738.

In Shaftesbury Place, Aldersgate Street, is the magnificent Hall of the **Ironmongers' Company.**

Disregarding **Newgate Street** (p. 231) for the while, we will turn into **St. Paul's Churchyard,** the north side of which is closed to the passage of vehicles. Here are some noted drapery establishments, both wholesale and retail. We can enter St. Paul's by the North Porch, but it will be better first to pass round to the western end in order to gain a good idea of the exterior.

[*Daily Herald.*

ST. PAUL'S CATHEDRAL, A DISTANT VIEW FROM THE RIVER.

WEST FRONT, ST. PAUL'S CATHEDRAL.

Photochrom Co., Ltd.,] *[Tunbridge Wells.*

THE NAVE, ST. PAUL'S CATHEDRAL.

F. Frith & Co., Ltd.,] [*Reigate.*

THE CHOIR, ST. PAUL'S CATHEDRAL.

St. Paul's Cathedral.

Plans II. and III. M. and N. 7 and 8.

Admission.—The Cathedral is open daily from 9 to 5, or 6 in summer, but visitors are, of course, expected to refrain from walking about during service time (see below). The nave, choir, transepts and east end can be viewed without charge. Tickets must be obtained (9 a.m. to 3.30 p.m., 4.45 to 5.30 p.m.) at the office adjoining the South Transept for the Crypt, *6d.*, and the Library, Whispering Gallery and Stone Gallery, *6d.*; persons desirous of proceeding further to the Golden Gallery (*1s.*) and the Ball (*1s.*) must obtain tickets from the keeper of the Stone Gallery.

Services.—*Week-days.*—Holy Communion 8 a.m. in Chapel of St. Dunstan; Matins, 10 a.m. in Nave. Short Service, in Chapel of St. Dunstan, 1.15 p.m. (During Lent, Saturdays excepted, this service is held in the Nave and commences with a short address.) Evensong (Choral), 4 p.m.

Sundays.—Litany, in Chapel of St. Dunstan, 7.45 a.m. Holy Communion, in Chapel of St. Dunstan, 8 a.m. Matins, Holy Communion (Choral), with Sermon, 10.30. Evensong (Choral) with Sermon, 3.15 p.m. Second Evensong and Sermon (musical portion, Chants and Hymns), 7 p.m.

On Christmas Day, Good Friday and Ascension Day the services are as on Sundays, except that there is no second Evensong on Christmas and Ascension Days, and on Good Friday there is no 7.45 a.m. Litany, but the Three Hours' service (12–3) is held.

On ordinary Saints' Days and Holy Days there is a sermon at Evensong.

Nearest Stations.—St. Paul's (formerly Post Office) (Central London Tube). Blackfriars or Mansion House (District), Blackfriars (formerly St. Paul's) (Southern Railway).

Many **bus routes** also pass St. Paul's Cathedral.

Principal Dimensions.—Length, including portico but not steps, 515 ft.; interior, 479 ft.; width across transepts from door to door, 250 ft.; nave and aisles only, 102 ft. Height from pavement to top of cross, 365 ft.; height of inner dome, 225 ft.; diameter, 102 ft.; height of western towers, 221 ft. The golden ball is 6 ft. in diameter, and will hold comfortably ten persons.

Historical Note.—Opinions are generally agreed that the present Cathedral is at least the third to occupy the site, more probably the fourth or fifth. Tradition even speaks of a Temple of Diana long before the introduction of Christianity. Early in the seventh century, probably A.D. 607, we find Ethelbert, King of Kent, rearing what for those days must have been a stately fane, and endowing it with, among other gifts, the manor of Tillingham in Essex: a manor, it is interesting to note, still in the possession of the Dean and Chapter, constituting probably the most ancient tenure in the country. This structure, after various vicissitudes, was destroyed by fire in 1087, shortly after the Norman Conquest. Its successor, immediately commenced but not completed for upwards of two centuries, is still referred to as **Old St. Paul's.** Colossal as is the present building, Old St. Paul's was even larger, having a length of 586 ft., while the spire, destroyed by fire in 1561, was 489 ft. in height (some authorities say 520 ft.). On the north-east side of the present choir, close to Cheapside, stood until 1643 old **St. Paul's Cross,** so often referred to in the history of the Reformation period. In 1910 a monument was erected close to the spot.

In the gardens on the south side of the Cathedral are exposed some remains of the old Cloisters and of the Chapter House. Others were discovered in 1912 as far distant as the north side of Paternoster Row.

Old St. Paul's fell to somewhat base uses in its later days, the nave becoming a public promenade and a place of assignation for all sorts of doubtful characters, while a theatre was actually erected against the outer walls. Under Charles I. extensive restoration, in which Inigo Jones was the leading spirit, took place, but the Commonwealth Parliament appropriated the funds, and Cromwell stabled his troopers' horses in the nave. In 1666 came the Great Fire and Wren's opportunity. He had already, as Assistant-Surveyor-General of His Majesty's Works, submitted a scheme for the repair and adaptation of the old building, but the Fire gave him an almost clear ground to work upon. He was, however, unfortunately hampered throughout by an officious Committee. A model of his original design is still preserved in the Cathedral. It is simply marvellous that while engaged on this stupendous undertaking Wren was yet able to build almost simultaneously upwards of thirty other City churches, no two of which are alike in conception or detail, though all bear an exact and harmonious relation to the great central building. The Cathedral was begun in 1675, opened for service in 1697, and completed in 1710, Wren receiving all through the not very princely salary of £200 a year. The necessary funds (estimated at about a million pounds, or five times that sum in present values) were raised, except for a comparatively small amount, by taxes on coal and wine entering the Port of London. In Wren's old age, we are told, he retired to Hampton, but once every year insisted upon being carried to a spot beneath the dome where he could contemplate the work of his hands. He died in 1723, at the ripe old age of ninety-one. *Lector, si monumentum requiris circumspice*—" Reader, if thou seekest his monument look around," tersely says the tablet over his tombstone.[1]

Unfortunately the opposition to Wren's plans appears to have included bad faith on the part of the builders, and the pillars supporting the Dome, instead of being built of solid stone, were merely faced with ashlar and filled with rubble—a deception which a few years ago developed alarming results, the Dome having shown increasing signs of insecurity. Recent very skilful restoration has, it is hoped, averted any further subsidence. The task occupied five years and involved the consolidation of the piers with metal rods and with liquid cement injected under pressure ; and the encircling of the Dome by an enormous chain of rustless steel, 30 tons in weight and 450 yards long. Not the least notable feature of the work is the manner in which it has secured the safety of the Dome without in the slightest degree altering its appearance.

Exterior.

The Cathedral is built entirely of Portland Stone, on the plan of a Latin cross, a form which expands easily to the eye of a

[1] This inscription is repeated over the north door.

spectator, and exhibits its beautiful combinations at one view. A modification of the simple cross is made at the western end by projections northward and southward, forming St. Dunstan's Chapel and the Chapel of the Order of St. Michael and St. George. The flanking bell towers serve the purpose of elongating the west front and giving it more importance, but the chapels can only be regarded as excrescences. Wren would have had a Greek cross (i.e., a cross having four equal arms), with a huge central dome supported by eight pillars, but he was overruled by the Court party, who feared that such a building would be unsuited to the Roman Catholic ritual they hoped to see re-established. In general appearance St. Paul's bears a marked resemblance to St. Peter's at Rome, but is, of course, much smaller. Though essentially a Gothic building, its character is almost entirely masked by Classic details, Wren's openly expressed intention being "to reconcile as near as possible the Gothic to a better manner of architecture." The exterior columns and coupled pilasters consist of two orders, the lower Corinthian, the upper Composite. This upper wall is little more than a screen to hide what in a Gothic church would be the flying buttresses, but it is of sufficient solidity to form an essential part of the system of abutments by which the thrust of the dome is resisted.

The **Western Façade,** looking down Ludgate Hill, has a width of 180 ft., with a double portico, on the pediment of which is a bas-relief by Bird, representing the conversion of St. Paul. On the apex stands a colossal statue of St. Paul, with St. Peter on his right and St. James on his left. In the north tower is a peal of twelve bells, presented by various City Companies and hung in 1878 (the tenor weighs 62 cwt., the note being B flat); in the south, or clock tower, is *Great Paul*, the largest bell in England. It weighs nearly 17 tons, and is over 9½ ft. in diameter. It is rung for five minutes daily at one o'clock and is used as the five-minute service bell on Sundays. The *Clock* face is 17 ft. in diameter. The copper hands, specially shaped to resist wind and snow, have lengths of 9 ft. 6 in. and 5 ft. respectively. The clock strikes on three old bells, the biggest, on which the hours are sounded, weighing 5¼ tons. This bell (cast *temp*. Edward I., and formerly hung in New Palace Yard, Westminster) is always tolled on the occasion of the death of the Sovereign, the Archbishop of Canterbury, the Bishop of London, the Dean of St. Paul's or the Lord Mayor. In the first case the tolling continues for two hours, in other cases for one hour.

Close to Ludgate Hill stands a [1] *Statue of Queen Anne*, the removal of which London would bear with equanimity. The

[1] The original statue, by Bird, of which this is a modern copy, provoked the wits of the day, one of whom, taking advantage of the fact that facing it there stood a much-frequented tavern, produced the following couplet, which greatly tickled the popular fancy—

"Brandy Nan, Brandy Nan, you're left in the lurch,
Your face to the gin shop, your back to the church."

well-fed and remarkably tame pigeons here are generally surrounded by an admiring crowd.

At the foot of the twenty-two steps leading up to the doorway may be seen a slab inscribed, " Here Queen Victoria returned thanks to Almighty God for the sixtieth anniversary of her accession, June 22, 1897."

Passing now round to the south porch (Cannon Street side), we see that the double portico of the western front is repeated. The five statues of apostles replaced in 1900 the weather-beaten effigies erected by Bird. In the pediment will be noted a phœnix, with the motto " Resurgam." It is said that when Wren was marking out the ground, he sent a man to bring a stone from a heap of charred remains of the old Cathedral to indicate where the centre of the dome should be. The stone thus brought happened to be part of an old gravestone with this single word upon it. Regarding this as a good omen, Wren adopted the word as his motto.

Both externally and internally the great **Dome** is the most imposing feature of the Cathedral, though, as we have said, a distant view is necessary to appreciate its majesty. Many visitors do not realize that the dome is really double, the true dome (that seen from the inside) being much lower than the outer. Between the inner dome (brick) and the outer dome (wood covered with lead) is a hollow cone of brickwork supporting the lantern and the ball and cross.

Interior.

The amount of internal decoration contemplated by Wren is a point that has been much discussed, but it is hard to believe that he intended these vast spaces to be entirely unadorned, though it is only in our own generation that the work of enrichment has been seriously undertaken. To the left on entering is the **Chapel of All Saints,** or the **Kitchener Memorial Chapel.** Prominent on the floor is a recumbent effigy of the Field-Marshal, by *Reid Dick*. On either hand are statues of St. Michael and St. George, given by the nursing services. A receptacle in the north wall contains the Roll of Honour of the Royal Engineers. The two large silver candlesticks before the altar were formed from medals belonging to men of the London Rifle Brigade who lost their lives in the war.

Beyond is **St. Dunstan's Chapel,** where the early morning services are held. It has a Salviati mosaic, representing the Three Marys at the Sepulchre. In the opposite (south) aisle is the **Chapel of the Order of St. Michael and St. George.** The Order is a Colonial one, being conferred only for distinguished service beyond the seas. At the western end is a modern throne, of oak and lime, in accordance with the Grinling Gibbons work in the Cathedral. The central seat is that of the Sovereign ;

on either side are the stalls of the Grand Master and the Chancellor of the Order. From these diverge the oak stalls of the Knights Grand Cross of the Order, each overhung by a silk banner emblazoned with his personal arms.

St. Paul's is second only to Westminster Abbey in the number of its **Monuments** to the mighty dead. We can only indicate a few. In the north aisle are monuments of *Lord Leighton, P.R.A.* (1896), *General Gordon* (killed at Khartoum, 1885). On the adjacent pier is a marble bust of *Lord Roberts* (1832–1914). The gallant Field-Marshal rests in the Crypt. In an arch between nave and aisle is the *Wellington Monument* by Alfred Stevens, the upper portion tardily completed from an unfinished sketch in 1912. On the inner side of the easternmost pillars of the nave are G.F. Watts's "Time, Death and Judgment" and his "Peace and Goodwill." Against a pillar in the south aisle is *Holman Hunt's* "Light of the World," a larger replica of the earlier rendering of the same subject in the chapel of Keble College, Oxford. Some of the most interesting monuments are in the **Transepts.** In the North Transept are monuments to a number of admirals and generals. In the South Transept are more generals and admirals, including the fine monument of *Nelson*, by Flaxman. A mural monument commemorates *Captain Scott* and his gallant companions of the South Pole Expedition, 1912.

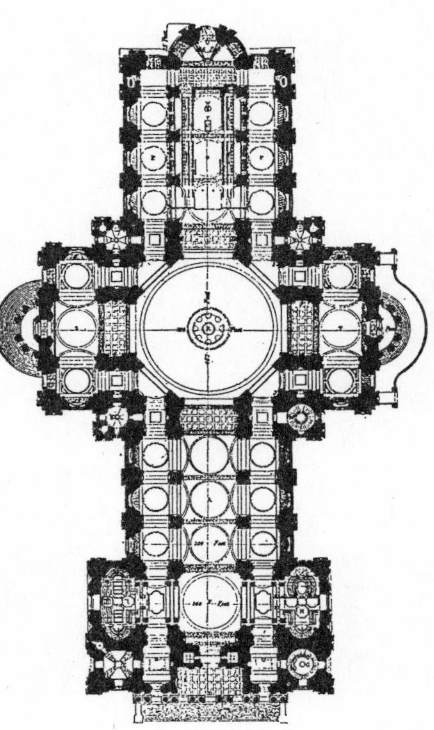

GROUND PLAN OF ST. PAUL'S CATHEDRAL.

Standing under the Dome one realizes the great dimensions of the structure. The highest part of the inner dome is 218 ft.

above the floor; the windows seen through the opening are nearly 300 feet, and are above the outer dome. The ceiling of the inner **Dome** is adorned with eight paintings by Thornhill, representing scenes from the life of St. Paul. In the niches above the Gallery are statues of the Fathers of the Church, while the spandrels between the great arches are covered by eight large mosaics representing apostles and prophets. *G. F. Watts* was responsible for St. Matthew and St. John on the north side; St. Mark and St. Luke were designed by *A. Brittan*; the four prophets were the work of *Alfred Stevens*. In accordance with Wren's intentions, the "quarter domes," at a lower level, have been decorated in mosaic by *Sir William Richmond, R.A.*, the subjects being the Crucifixion, the Entombment, the Resurrection and the Ascension.

On the right of the **Choir** is the **Pulpit**,[1] of marble, with a large sounding-board. The wonderfully rich choir stalls and the organ case were carved by *Grinling Gibbons*. The **Reredos**, of white Parian marble, is flanked by an open colonnade. The sculptures represent the Incarnation and Life of our Lord. The niche over the pediment is occupied by figures of the Virgin and Child, St. Paul and St. Peter, with the risen Saviour above, at a height of over 60 ft. from the ground. The frieze bears the inscription, *Sic Deus dilexit mundum* ("So God loved the world"). The two bronze candlesticks are copies of those at St. Bavon's, Ghent, said to have been in Old St. Paul's. The **Organ**, one of the finest in the world, is divided, the keyboard being placed on the north side, and the entire instrument is fitted with electric action. It has 5 manuals, 116 stops and 5,055 pipes, and was reconstructed by Willis in 1872, 1900 and 1930. It still incorporates pipes from the original organ built in 1695 by "Father" Smith. The splendid gates on either side of the altar are reproductions of older work; those leading to the apse were designed by that great artist *Tijou* and made of Sussex iron. The apse and the vaulting and walls are decorated with richly-coloured **Mosaics** by *Sir William Richmond*. The chief panels of the apse represent our Lord enthroned, with recording angels on either side. In the choir the most notable decorations are those of the three "saucer-domes," or cupolas, representing three days of creation, beginning at the west with Beasts, and continuing with Fishes and Birds.

Tickets for the **Crypt** must be obtained at the office at foot of Library staircase in the south aisle of nave (see p. 213). The Crypt extends beneath the entire church. Here lie the remains of most of those whose monuments appear in the Cathedral. The portion of the Crypt beneath the Choir is known as **Painters' Corner**, and contains either the graves or memorials of *Sir Joshua Reynolds, Sir Benjamin West, Sir Thomas Lawrence, J. M. W.*

[1] It is said that the preacher who hopes to be heard in St. Paul's must always turn rightward and preach at Lord Melbourne's tomb in the north aisle; but this has to some extent been corrected by microphones.

Turner, John Opie, Lord Leighton, Sir John Millais, Holman Hunt, Sir L. Alma-Tadema, Melton Prior, William Blake and other famous artists. Of even greater interest to many is the plain black marble slab beneath the last window recess of the south aisle, marking the **Grave of Sir Christopher Wren.** Above is the tablet bearing the often-quoted epitaph already referred to (p. 214). The east end forms the **Church of St. Faith,** used for the anniversary services of various societies. It contains a few mutilated monuments from Old St. Paul's. The place of honour immediately under the centre of the dome is occupied by the **Grave of Nelson.** The coffin was made from the mainmast of the French flagship at the Battle of Aboukir, *L'Orient.* The Italian sarcophagus was constructed by order of Cardinal Wolsey for his own interment. The **Tomb of Wellington** consists of a great block of porphyry resting on a granite base. The funeral car (cast from captured cannon) on which the Duke's remains were brought to the Cathedral stands at the extreme west end of the crypt. Close to Wellington's tomb are the graves of *Admiral Earl Jellicoe* (d. 1935) and of *Admiral Earl Beatty* (d. 1936), and a memorial of *Lord Charles Beresford* (d. 1919). In "Field-Marshals' Corner" rest the remains of three other great soldiers, *Field-Marshal Viscount Wolseley* (d. 1913), *Field-Marshal Earl Roberts, K.G.* (d. 1914), and *Field-Marshal Sir Henry Wilson* (assassinated 1922). Here, too, are mural tablets to *Field-Marshal Sir Evelyn Wood,* to *Florence Nightingale,* and to "*Lawrence of Arabia*" (d. 1935), and a bronze bust of *George Washington,* presented by the Sulgrave Institution of America in 1921.

By the 143 steps of the Library Staircase (*for admission see* p. 213) we reach the triforium, a gallery running above the south aisle to the **Library,** which is immediately over the Chapel of the Order of St. Michael and St. George (p. 216). Here are shown a number of interesting autographs and ancient MSS., portraits, seals, etc. Among them is a promise signed by Charles II, of £1,000 a year towards the rebuilding fund. Needless to say, there is no record of the receipt of the money. Next the visitor will be directed to the **Whispering Gallery,** which runs round the interior of the dome. A slight whisper against the wall on one side is distinctly audible on the other, a distance in a straight line of more than 100 ft. A further dark and narrow flight leads up to the **Stone Gallery,** encircling the foot of the outer dome. From this on a clear day a magnificent view over London is gained, though the prospect is, of course, not so extensive as that from the **Golden Gallery,** above the dome and at the foot of the lantern. Those who desire to see the Golden Gallery and the Ball must take tickets from the attendant in the Stone Gallery. The **Ball** is 6 ft. in diameter and will hold ten or twelve persons. The height from the pavement to the top of the Cross is 365 ft. The ball and cross were renewed in 1821. Those who succeed in reaching the Stone Gallery have ascended 375 steps, while the few who attain the sublimity of the ball have 627 heavenward steps to their credit.

St. Paul's has been the scene of many **Thanksgiving Services** of national importance. Queen Elizabeth rejoiced with her people at the overthrow of the Armada, and in 1702 Queen Anne publicly returned thanks for Marlborough's victories in the Low Countries and for the destruction of the Spanish fleet at Vigo. In 1704 the visit was repeated in gratitude for the victory of Blenheim. In more recent times we may recall the national thanksgiving in 1872 for the recovery from serious illness of King Edward VII., then Prince of Wales. In 1897 Queen Victoria took part in a solemn service at the foot of the steps in gratitude for the completion of a reign of sixty years, an event recorded by an inscription in the pavement. On June 8th, 1902, King Edward VII. and Queen Alexandra returned thanks for the restoration of peace in South Africa, and on the following 28th October for the recovery of the former from the sudden illness which delayed his Coronation. The Cathedral was also the scene of several very impressive services of national supplication during the War. On July 6th, 1919, King George V. and Queen Mary attended a great Peace Thanksgiving service at the close of the hostilities with Germany; their Majesties were here again in June, 1930, at the services celebrating the restoration of the Cathedral, and on May 6th, 1935, they came to St. Paul's for the Thanksgiving Service which formed the central act of the Silver Jubilee celebration.

Dean's Yard, in the south-west corner of St. Paul's Churchyard, leads past the **Deanery** to the **Choir House** in Great Carter Lane. **Doctors' Commons,** where marriage licences are issued by the Bishop of London's Registry, survives in name only. In Bell Yard, to the south, is a tablet recording the site of "the Bell, Carter Lane," whence Richard Quiney wrote the letter to Shakespeare, dated October 25, 1598, now in the Birthplace Museum at Stratford, the only letter extant addressed to the poet.

Cannon Street, at the south-east corner of the Churchyard, is referred to on p. 223; at this end the most notable feature is **Cordwainers' Hall,** rebuilt in recent years. Not everyone is aware that a cordwainer is a shoemaker, the name being indirectly derived from Cordovan, or *cordwain,* leather.

Paternoster Row (Plan II. M. 7), a narrow lane behind the north side of St. Paul's Churchyard, was long known the world over in connection with the book trade, but only three or four important publishing houses now have their headquarters here, the majority having migrated westward. But Paternoster Row has several excellent retail and "second-hand" shops, and is still an important distributing centre of the trade. Near at hand are Amen Corner, Ave Maria Lane, Creed Lane, and Godliman Street, all suggestive of the former exclusively ecclesiastical aspect of the locality.[1] In **Panyer Alley,** a short passage

[1] **Sermon Lane,** however, derives its name from the shere-moniers—men who cut the silver discs ready for stamping in a mint which stood near by; and "Godliman" is probably "Godelmynger"—a kind of cordwain.

near the eastern end of the Row, may be seen a tablet, with relief figure of a boy seated on a "panier," or basket, with this inscription:—

"When ye have sought the City round,
Yet still this is the highest ground.
August the 27, 1688."

The honour, however, more probably belongs to Cornhill.

At the western end of Paternoster Row is **Warwick Lane**; the building on the left, with terra-cotta bas-reliefs by *Tinworth*, is the **Cutlers' Hall.**

A section of **Old London Wall** may be seen by courtesy of the Oxford University Press at their premises in Warwick Square.

Stationers' Hall, near the foot of Paternoster Row, is the hall of the Stationers' Company, the members of which, unlike members of most City Companies, have generally some actual connection with the trade from which they take their name. Formerly all books published in Great Britain had to be registered here before copyright proceedings could be taken, but the passing of the Copyright Act of 1911 rendered this unnecessary, mere publication now securing copyright in the British Empire for a period of twenty-five years from the author's death, and, under certain conditions, for a further period of twenty-five years. Among the treasures of the Company are some very early registers—that of 1569 including "a boke intituled Ewclide," then first translated into English—and the composing stick used by Benjamin Franklin when working at a press in London.

Ludgate Hill (Plan II. M. 7) rises steeply from Ludgate Circus to St. Paul's. King Lud, after whom the hill is generally believed to be named, is regarded by all modern historians as mythical. A tablet on **St. Martin's Church** (Wren's) marks the site of the Old Lud Gate (see p. 70); and outside St. Dunstan's, Fleet Street (see p. 201), is a statue of Elizabeth which at one time stood over the Gate.

Old Bailey (Plan II. M. 7), of unhappy memories, connects Ludgate Hill with Newgate Street. The name is derived from the situation of the original building in the bailey of the old City wall. Here stood for many years the gloomy Newgate Prison, demolished in 1902–3. Numerous relics of the old prison, such as whipping-blocks, leg-irons, etc., can be seen in the Museum at the Guildhall (p. 209), and others are in the London Museum (p. 123). On the more northerly part of the site is the **Central Criminal Court,** opened in 1905, an imposing block erected at a cost of a quarter of a million pounds to replace the former inconvenient and dingy Sessions House.

The building was designed by *E. W. Mountford.* On the Old Bailey front the old stone of the prison was utilized as far as possible. Over the main entrance is a sculptured group by F. W. Pomeroy, A.R.A., representing the Recording Angel, supported by Fortitude and Truth. A conspicuous feature of the structure is the copper-covered dome, 195 ft. high, surmounted by a large bronzed figure of Justice. The building can be viewed on *Tuesdays and Fridays,* 10 *to* 4 (when the sittings of the Court permit), on application to the Keeper. Tickets of admission to important trials can generally only be obtained from one of the Sheriffs or Aldermen. The public galleries are entered from Newgate Street.

From the south side of Ludgate Hill a labyrinth of lanes would bring us down to Queen Victoria Street and the river. In Water Lane is the **Apothecaries' Hall,** dating from 1670. A tablet recalls that here stood the monastery of Blackfriars, built in 1278.

Queen Victoria Street (Plan III. M. and N. 8) runs diagonally from Blackfriars Bridge (p. 203) to the Bank, a distance of about two-thirds of a mile. Near its foot is the office of *The Times,* extending back to Printing House Square, in which, during the Stuart period, stood the King's printing-house. The newspaper is produced on the spot where stood the Blackfriars Playhouse, with which Shakespeare was so intimately connected. Almost opposite is **Blackfriars Station** (formerly *St. Paul's*) (Southern Railway), from which, at a lower level than Queen Victoria Street, **Upper Thames Street,** with its wharves and warehouses, follows the north bank of the river to London Bridge. Chaucer first saw the light in Thames Street, close to the present railway arch, in 1340. One of the docks still retains the name of **Castle Baynard,** an important fortress sometimes used as a royal residence and rendered famous by Shakespeare in *Richard III.* Its name is given to one of the City wards. Continuing up Queen Victoria Street, we have on the left the Church of **St. Andrew-by-the-Wardrobe,** rebuilt by Wren after the Fire. The quaint affix is explained by the fact that the office of the King's Great Wardrobe was formerly in the vicinity. Adjoining is the " Bible House " of the **British and Foreign Bible Society,** with a library containing a unique collection of copies and translations of Holy Scripture in many languages. Opposite is the **London Auction Mart,** the headquarters of London auctioneers. **Faraday House** bears little external evidence of its interest and importance: yet from here, or by means of connections made in this building, one can telephone to practically any part of the world as easily as to another part of London. Then on the left we reach the **Heralds' College,** or College of Arms, incorporated and endowed by Richard III. in 1484. The house was rebuilt as it stands after the Great Fire. The office of Earl Marshal and head of the College is hereditary in the person of the Duke of Norfolk. The College comprises the three kings of arms—Garter, Clarenceux and Norroy—six heralds and four pursuivants. In addition to their ceremonial functions, the Heralds regulate the bearing of arms, and preserve and trace pedigrees, genealogies, etc. On the south side of the street is **St. Benet's Church** (Wren's), now used as a Welsh church; and on the north is **St. Nicholas Cole Abbey,** the first of the City churches rebuilt by Wren.

At the *Mansion House Station* of the District Railway Queen Victoria Street crosses **Cannon Street** (Plan III. N. 8), and thence continues to the Bank. At the corner of Cannon Street and Queen Street is the *London Chamber of Commerce.* A short distance to the east are **Cannon Street Stations** (Southern and District Railways). A tablet in the church of **St. Michael Royal,** College Hill, commemorates the burial-place of "Sir Richard Whittington, four times Lord Mayor of London, 1396–1419." The building dates only from 1690, the Church known to "Dick" having perished in the Fire of 1666; but the position of the tomb is shown on the south side of the altar, near the organ. Nowadays it is doubted whether the "Sir" was more than a courtesy title (there is no official record of a knighthood); and learned historians go so far as to contradict the ballad's assurance that Dick was Lord Mayor of London. (See also p. 21.)

In Dowgate Street is **Skinners' Hall,** with a fine series of historical paintings by *Frank Brangwyn, R.A.* In the wall of **St. Swithin's Church,** Cannon Street, may be seen the famous **London Stone,** supposed, though considerable difference of opinion exists on the subject, to have been the *milliarium* of the Roman Forum in London, from which distances along the great highways were reckoned. In **St. Swithin's Lane** are the **City Carlton Club** and **New Court,** the latter the headquarters of the great house of Rothschild, with **Salters' Hall** adjoining. **St. Mary, Abchurch,** another of Wren's churches, has cupola paintings by Thornhill and carvings by Grinling Gibbons. In **Walbrook,** just behind the Mansion House, is **St. Stephen's Church,** generally considered one of Wren's masterpieces. The most notable feature is the cupola, "a kind of probationary trial previous to the architect's greater dome of St. Paul's." Here, in the family vault, lies Sir John Vanbrugh, the famous architect upon whom was penned the witty epitaph : " Lie heavy on him, earth, for he laid many a heavy load on thee."

We have now regained our starting-point at the **Bank** (p. 204).

ROUTE X.—MOORGATE—CITY ROAD—LONDON WALL—CRIPPLEGATE—THE CHARTERHOUSE — THE MARKETS — CLERKENWELL — SMITHFIELD—NEWGATE STREET—HOLBORN VIADUCT.

Starting again from the Bank, we walk northward along **Prince's Street,** the whole of the east side of which is occupied by the Bank of England. **Gresham Street** (p. 210) runs off to the left, but we will keep northward along **Moorgate** to the old City boundary, still known as London Wall. Just beyond, with entrance in Moorfields, is the *Moorgate Station* of the Metropolitan Railway, serving also as the terminus of the L.M.S. (Midland) and L.N.E.R. (Great Northern) City services, and close at hand are stations on the *Morden-Edgware Tube* and the Metropolitan Line, serving the Finsbury Park area of North London. A tablet on No. 75, Moorgate marks the site of the old gate from which the thoroughfare takes its name.

Were we to follow Moorgate northward we should pass on the right **Finsbury Circus,**[1] with pretty gardens forming an ideal setting for the bowling green. On the left of the City Road, just beyond **Finsbury Square,** are the headquarters and drill ground of the **Honourable Artillery Company,** generally known as the H.A.C., the oldest military body in the kingdom. The corps was formed in 1537, under the title of the Guild or Fraternity of St. George, and from it were always selected the officers of the City Trained Bands. It rendered magnificent service during the War, and its ranks furnished a large number of officers for the Regular Army. The " Troop of Colour " is held annually in July. In the museum are many torn and tattered flags, suits of old armour, portraits, etc. The Ancient and Honourable Artillery Company of Boston (Mass.), the oldest corps in America, was founded in 1638 by emigrant members of the H.A.C. Close at hand are the headquarters of the **London Rifle Brigade,** another famous City regiment.

To the north is **Bunhill** (Bonehill, see p. 190) **Fields Cemetery,** for more than two centuries the chief burial-place of Nonconformists. A little to the south of the central walk is the **Tomb of John Bunyan,** with recumbent figure erected in 1862 ; while to the north of the walk is an obelisk in memory of **Daniel Defoe,**

[1] Finsbury Circus and Square are sometimes confused by strangers with the suburb of **Finsbury Park,** several miles to the north, where there is an important junction of the Underground Lines with the Great Northern (L.N.E.R.) lines.

subscribed for by youthful readers of *Robinson Crusoe*. Here, too, are buried Isaac Watts, the hymn-writer; the redoubtable Susannah Wesley, mother of John and Charles Wesley; John Owen; Henry, Richard and William Cromwell, descendants of the Protector; and William Blake, the poet-artist. In the Friends' Burial-Ground adjoining is the **Grave of George Fox,** the founder of the Society. In **Bunhill Row** Milton wrote the greater part of *Paradise Lost*, and here he died (1674). A warehouse (No. 124) now occupies the site (tablet).

On the east side of the City Road stands **Wesley's Chapel** (Plan II. O. 6), the "Cathedral of Methodism." The first stone was laid by John Wesley in 1777, and here he preached during the later years of his life. He is buried in the graveyard behind. In front is his statue, a centenary memorial, and in the chapel are tablets in memory of his mother and his brother Charles. Adjoining the Chapel is **Wesley's House,** part of which is now used as a Museum (*open week-days* 10–1, 2–4; *admission* 6*d*.).

At the corner of City Road and Old Street (there is little to justify the name) is St. Luke's Hospital; close by is the famous **Moorfields Ophthalmic Hospital.** Here too is the *Leysian Mission House* (Methodist).

This is a digression, however. We will assume that the visitor, on reaching **London Wall** (Plan II. N. and O. 7), turns left (westward) and follows approximately the course of the old city wall (see p. 69), a long section of which is exposed to the view of the passer-by in the disused churchyard of St. Alphage, near the top of Wood Street. The old porch of **St. Alphage** (the church was demolished in 1919), on the south side of London Wall, serves as a chapel for private prayer. Here are preserved some memorials removed from the church, including one to Sir Rowland Heyward, Lord Mayor in 1570 and again in 1590, including his two wives and sixteen children. Near the top of **Wood Street**—the headquarters of wholesale haberdashery—is the Church of **St. Giles, Cripplegate** (Plan II. N. 7), known the world over as the burial-place of John Milton. The poet was born in the neighbouring ward of Bread Street on the 9th December, 1608 (see p. 211). (*The Church is open daily* 10 *to* 5; *Saturdays* 10 *to* 1; *entrance in Fore Street.*) The building dates from the end of the fourteenth century, and was fortunate in escaping the great fire which swept this quarter in 1897, just as it escaped the greater Fire of 1666.

Close to the north door is a bronze **Statue of Milton,** with an appropriate quotation from *Paradise Lost*. The poet is further commemorated by a bust against the south wall of the nave, and a stone tablet let into the floor near the chancel marks approximately the place of his interment (d. 1674, aged 66).

The entry in the parish register of that date reads: "John Milton, gentleman, Consumption, chancel, 12 (November)." Other noteworthy features are the window (next to the Milton bust) commemorating Edward Alleyn, the founder of Dulwich College (p. 260), the quaint oval window at the east end, and the Grinling Gibbons carving on the pulpit and font. Oliver Cromwell and Elizabeth Boucher were married in this church on August 22nd, 1620. Other worthies here interred were Foxe, author of the *Book of Martyrs*; Frobisher, the explorer; and Speed, the topographer. In the south-west angle of the Churchyard, at some distance from the passage railing, may be seen another fragment of the old London wall—a circular bastion, dwarfed by the warehouses which tower above it.

In Monkwell Street is the **Barbers' Hall,** originally the Hall of the Barber-Surgeons, the precursors of the modern Royal College of Surgeons. The Hall contains a reputed Holbein and a portrait of Inigo Jones by Van Dyck.

In Jewin Street, Milton lived for a while. **Milton Street,** to the east, leading from Fore Street to Chiswell Street, is the "Grub Street" of literary tradition. Its modern name (dating from 1830) is not, as is commonly supposed, a tribute to the poet, but to a builder of the same name, who included the street in his sphere of operations. In Golden Lane, slightly to the north, is the **Cripplegate Institute** and **Library.** Passing along the **Barbican**—another reminder of the old fortified wall—we cross **Aldersgate Street** (p. 211), and turn left at the station to Charterhouse Square, on the north side of which stands that mellow institution, the **Charterhouse** (Plan II. M. 6), considered by Sir W. Besant "the most beautiful and most venerable monument of old London."

On applying at the porter's lodge (*Mon., Wed. and Fri.*, 3 *to* 5; 1*s*.) visitors are shown round by a guide. The name is a corruption of Chartreuse. The original Carthusian Monastery was founded for twenty-four monks in 1371, and after the Dissolution became the property successively of Sir Edward (afterwards Lord) North and the Duke of Norfolk, each of whom built a residence for himself. Queen Elizabeth and James I. both resided here for some days. In 1611 the property was purchased by "good old Thomas Sutton," Queen's Master of Ordnance, and endowed as a school for forty poor boys and a hospital for eighty poor men. The foundation for "poor brethren" still exists as of yore, though financial depreciation has necessitated a reduction of numbers. No one will visit this place without calling to mind Thackeray's dear old Colonel Newcome, who was one of the "poor brethren." The *Gatehouse* dates from the sixteenth century; the upper part was rebuilt about 1700. On the right of the *Entrance Court* will be seen the façade of the house built by the Duke of Norfolk about 1565. The *Great Hall*, in which such of the brethren as are able dine daily and where the Founder's Day Dinner mentioned by Thackeray in *The Newcomes* is held, is one of the finest Elizabethan rooms in existence. It was built early in the sixteenth century, the minstrels' gallery, screens and wood panelling being added about sixty years later by the Duke of Norfolk, by whose directions, too, the roof was probably raised and the four upper windows were inserted. The *Scholars' Hall*, used by the boys of the old foundation, is now the brothers' library. It was built by the Duke of Norfolk towards the end of the sixteenth century, partly from the materials of the earlier monastic buildings. The Chapel is reached by way of a *Cloister*, with memorials of Thackeray, Leech, Havelock, John Wesley, Roger Williams (the founder of Rhode Island), and other old scholars. The *Chapel* was altered by the monks early in the sixteenth century, and further altered by the Sutton Trustees in 1614. Its most notable feature is the elaborate monument of Thomas Sutton, the founder. Visitors are admitted to the services (week-days, 9.30 and 6; Sundays, 11). In the Master's Lodge are portraits by Kneller and others. The curfew is rung each night at 9, the number of strokes corresponding with the number of brethren resident at the time.

The **Charterhouse School**—of which Steele, Addison, Wesley, Havelock, Grote, Leech, Thackeray and other famous men were scholars—was transferred in 1872 to Godalming.

Close at hand is a long range of buildings used as the **Metropolitan Meat Market** (p. 30), west of which are the Poultry, Fish, Fruit and Vegetable Markets, lining Farringdon Street.

It is worth while to turn for a few yards up **St. John Street,** an unattractive thoroughfare running northward from the Meat Market to Islington. Almost immediately we have on the left *St. John's Lane*, spanned by that interesting relic of the old priory of the Knights of St. John of Jerusalem, **St. John's Gate** (Plan II. M. 6), built by Prior Docwra in 1504. The Order was suppressed by Henry VIII., and in the reign of Edward VI. Lord Protector Somerset pulled down most of the Priory buildings, and carted away the materials to help in the construction of Somerset House. In the rooms over the Gate the *Gentleman's Magazine* first saw the light. The rooms and the modern hall adjoining are occupied by the Order of St. John in England and by its foundation, that useful society the *St. John Ambulance Association*. To view the rooms it is necessary to write the Secretary of the Order. Permission is usually given for Saturday afternoons. Near the gate stands an old-world smithy; Smithfield's horse-drawn traffic provides plenty of work. In St. John Square, north of the gate, is **St. John's Church,** the Norman crypt of which formed part of the Priory Church. A short distance to the west is Clerkenwell Green, with the

Sessions House of the County of London. The densely-populated neighbourhood of **Clerkenwell** is mostly occupied by watch-makers and metal-workers. Towards the northern end of St. John Street is the **Northampton Institute.**

The historic **Sadlers' Wells Theatre** was reopened, after re-building, in January, 1931. Shakespeare and opera are presented at popular prices, in conjunction with the productions at the "Old Vic" (see p. 257). The **"Angel,"** a busy tramway and omnibus centre, takes its name from the sign of a tavern which, repeatedly rebuilt, overlooked the cross-roads for centuries. Its modern successor is a restaurant owned by Messrs. Lyons. A short distance along **Upper Street** is the **Agricultural Hall,** the scene of important cattle shows and trade exhibitions. **Islington** may still be "merrie," as in Gilpin's day, but if so it very successfully disguises the fact. A notable feature is the great **Metropolitan Cattle Market,** reached by way of the Caledonian Road (see p. 30).

At Islington we are in close touch with the busy northern suburb of **Finsbury Park** (not to be confused with Finsbury *Circus* in the City). The Park is much used for cricket, football, etc. A mile or so farther north is **Alexandra Palace** (*open daily, 10 to dusk*). This great building, finely situated on Muswell Hill, was, after a chequered career, acquired in 1901 for the public use, and is controlled by a board of Trustees representing various local authorities. The grounds, comprising over 160 acres, command fine views of London and the country to the north, and contain a boating lake, cycling track, swimming baths, etc. The *Great Hall* has a very fine organ, recently restored at a cost of some £8,000. Adjoining is the *Alexandra Park Racecourse*. The most interesting modern development, however, is the adoption of part of the Palace for television transmissions by the B.B.C.

Returning to Charterhouse Street, we cross the **Meat Markets,** covering an area of nearly ten acres, to the open space still known as **Smithfield** (Plan II. M. 7), or "smooth field," an ancient jousting ground outside the City walls. The name of **Giltspur Street,** leading into Newgate Street, is an obvious reminder of the same picturesque period. In most minds, however, Smithfield has more sombre associations. Here, as the **Martyrs' Memorial** on the wall of St. Bartholomew's Hospital records, forty-three Protestants in the reign of Mary suffered death at the stake. It was at Smithfield, moreover, that Sir William Walworth, Lord Mayor, according to the traditional story, struck down Wat Tyler. For centuries the annual "Bartlemy Fair" was the occasion of popular revels of a far from dignified description. On the south side is **St. Bartholomew's**

THE CHARTERHOUSE: CLOISTER—DINING-HALL—THE CHAPEL.

RAHERE'S TOMB, ST. BARTHOLOMEW'S CHURCH.

[Dixon Scott.

LONDON BRIDGE.

[H. Joel.

THE BALTIC EXCHANGE.

[H. Joel.

LLOYDS: "THE ROOM"
(Under the Cupola is the famous Lutine bell.)

Hospital, commonly known as "Bart's," the oldest institution of the kind in England.

The Hospital originally formed part of an Augustinian Priory founded in 1123 by Rahere, the minstrel and favourite of Henry I, whose tomb we shall see in the church hard by. On the suppression of the monasteries Henry VIII. refounded the hospital and restored a great part of its former revenues, in grateful acknowledgment of which fact his statue still stands over the west gate, having figures of a sick man and a cripple on either side. The older quadrangular edifice was erected by Gibbs in 1730–3. Part of the site of Christ's Hospital was acquired in 1902 in connection with a rebuilding scheme, and the first new block, the casualty and out-patients' department, was opened in 1907. Endowments provide an income of about £60,000 a year, which is well employed in the relief of some 9,000 in-patients and an enormous number of out-patients. About 60,000 surgical and medical cases are treated annually. There is a convalescent home in connection at Swanley. The Medical School has long enjoyed a reputation second to none. Harvey, who discovered the circulation of the blood, Richard Owen, the anatomist, Abernethy, and many other famous physicians, have taught at "Bart's." In the Governor's Hall are portraits of famous physicians and surgeons by Kneller, Reynolds, Lawrence, Millais, Luke Fildes, and others. The paintings on the staircase, depicting the Good Samaritan and the Pool of Bethesda, were executed gratuitously by Hogarth. The Hospital, like all similar institutions in London, is in urgent need of further funds to meet the increased cost of maintenance.

East of the Hospital, in Little Britain, a picturesque Elizabethan half-timbered **Gateway** marks the entrance to the Church of **St. Bartholomew the Great** (Plan II. M. 7), the oldest church standing in London, if we except the chapel in the Tower. No visitor should miss seeing this fine Norman building (*open free daily from* 9.30 *to* 12.30, 2 *to* 5. *Admission to cloister and crypt,* 6*d.*). Services, see p. 20.

Like the Hospital, the Church was founded by Rahere in 1123, but the edifice we see is merely the choir and a small portion of the nave of the original Priory Church. The Early English nave, destroyed by Henry VIII., occupied the site of the graveyard, as can be seen by the remains. Through the exertions of several enthusiastic Rectors and others the church has been restored in recent years, at a cost of upwards of £60,000, and most of the encroachments which defaced and circumscribed it removed. The *Lady Chapel* at the east end, with its handsome wrought-iron screen, was long used for commercial purposes; in it Benjamin Franklin served a year as a journeyman printer. Its last tenant was a fringe manufacturer. The north transept was actually used as a blacksmith's forge. The best view of the church as a whole is from under the organ gallery looking east. Another pleasing vista is that looking westward through the massive Norman columns of the choir. On the north side of the choir is the *Tomb of Rahere* (d. 1143), with a richly decorated early Perpendicular canopy (*c.* 1405). The body is still above ground, immediately beneath the figure. On either side of the recumbent effigy is an Augustinian canon in his habit, holding an open Bible and pointing to Isaiah li. 3. The passage, beautifully appropriate to Rahere's work in draining the horse market site in Smithfield, and founding a church and hospital on the spot where formerly stood the gallows, runs, " He will comfort all her waste places; and He will make her wilderness like Eden, and her desert like the garden of the Lord." In the triforium opposite is *Prior Bolton's Window* with his rebus, Bolt-in-tun. In the south ambulatory is another fine monument to Sir Walter Mildmay (1589). He was founder of Emmanuel College, Cambridge, Chancellor of the Exchequer to Queen Elizabeth, and one of the commissioners who tried Mary, Queen of Scots. The *Crypt*, the vaulting of which has been renewed, was originally a bone crypt. Later it became a wine and coal cellar; it is now used as a mortuary chapel. The most recent object of reclamation has been the *Cloister* (Early English), long used as stables.

In the churchyard is observed annually on Good Friday a curious ceremony in accordance with which twenty-one aged widows of the City of London pick sixpences from a certain flat tombstone covering the remains of a lady who many years ago is said to have left a sum of money for the purpose.

Hogarth was baptized in St. Bartholomew's Church in 1697, though the record of the fact was made in the wrong book. He was born in the adjoining **Bartholomew Close.**

Proceeding in the direction of Newgate Street, we pass between huge buildings of the **General Post Office** (p. 211), and have on our right the fane of **Christ Church.**

Like nearly all the City churches, it was the work of Wren though the lower part contains many traces of the earlier monastery church, notably the marble pavement of the sanctuary. In one part of the flooring the effect of the Fire on the marble can be clearly seen. In the porch are several memorials of officials and others, removed from Christ's Hospital in 1905 on the demolition of that building. Particular attention should be paid to the marble font, for the carving is believed to be by Grinling Gibbons. It is certainly characteristic, and would appear to be an almost solitary example of his work in stone. The pulpit and part of the reading-desk were undoubtedly carved by him. The richly-decorated organ is a fine mellow instrument beloved by musicians. It has responded to the touch of both

Handel and Mendelssohn. In the chancel are six carved panels, representing the Apostles and the Last Supper, said to have been taken from a ship of the Spanish Armada. Richard Baxter, the celebrated Nonconformist, and Lawrence Sheriff, the founder of Rugby School, are buried here. The "Spital Sermon," preached on the second Wednesday after Easter, is attended by the Lord Mayor in state, in accordance with ancient custom. It was formerly given at the old Spital Cross, Spitalfields, and there is record of one discourse which attained such a length that the civic dignitaries in desperation requested the preacher to "print the rest." When published, the sermon filled 230 pages! Another annual function is the attendance of the Blue-Coat boys (see below) on St. Matthew's Day. They are afterwards regaled at the Mansion House, each boy receiving a gold or silver coin according to his standing in the school. The Blue-Coat School or **Christ's Hospital,** founded by Edward VI. in 1552, on the site of a monastery of the Grey Friars adjoining Christ Church, was in 1902 removed to new buildings near Horsham.

The greater part of the site is now occupied by the King Edward VII. block of the General Post Office (p. 211), the remainder by the new buildings of St. Bartholomew's Hospital.

Following **Newgate Street** (Plan II. M. 7) westward, we may take note that at No. 87, now a refreshment depôt, Sir Henry Irving served for some time as a publisher's clerk (tablet). On the left is the curved façade of the **Central Criminal Court** (p. 221). On the right is **St. Sepulchre's Church,** one of the bells of which was always tolled until 1890 on the occasion of an execution at Newgate. At an earlier period, when Tyburn (p. 155) was the place of execution, it was the considerate custom at this church to present a bunch of flowers to each criminal who passed along to his doom. In a glass case on the north wall is a handbell formerly rung outside the condemned cell at Newgate, at the midnight preceding execution, to the accompaniment of the rhymed admonishment of which a copy is also shown. The church was almost rebuilt in the seventeenth century, the best features being the fine porch and the heavily pinnacled square tower. The organ was built in 1677 by Renatus Harris. On the south side of the choir is buried the redoubtable *Captain John Smith,* "sometime Governour of Viginia and Admirall of New England." Roger Ascham (1515–1568), author of the *Schoolmaster,* also lies here. Below the courtyard of the Post Office, immediately east of St. Sepulchre's Church, is a well-preserved bastion of the old **Roman Wall** of London (see p. 69). To view it write for permission to the Secretary, General Post Office.

Westward of the churchyard begins **Holborn Viaduct** (Plan II. M. 7), spanning the old Holborn Valley, through which formerly ran the river Fleet (p. 200). Before the construction of the iron bridge over Farringdon Street, the steep Holborn Hill was one of the most dangerous parts of London. The Viaduct is much longer than is generally supposed—over a quarter of a mile—buildings lining the approaches to the bridge across **Farringdon Street** (p. 200) (reached by steps). At the east end is **Holborn Viaduct Station** (Southern Railway—S.E. & C. section). The **City Temple,** west of Farringdon Street, tersely tells its history on a tablet affixed to one of the outer walls. It has had two famous ministers in the persons of Dr. Parker (d. 1902) and the Rev. R. J. Campbell. **St. Andrew's Church,** formerly approached by steps, but now below the level of the road, was rebuilt by Wren in 1686. The Church has many interesting associations. The registers record the burial of Thomas Chatterton (August 28, 1770), and the christening on July 31st, 1817, at the age of twelve, of Benjamin Disraeli, afterwards Lord Beaconsfield. Hazlitt was married here in 1808, Charles Lamb acting as best man.

At **Holborn Circus** (Plan II. M. 7), in which stands a poor equestrian *Statue of the Prince Consort,* we reach the eastward limit of Route No. VI. (p. 169). Here are *Wallis's* and *Gamage's* stores. **Hatton Garden,** running northward from the Circus to Clerkenwell Road, and **Ely Place,** a *cul-de-sac* immediately to the east, stand on the site of the famous palace of the Bishops of Ely, where John of Gaunt, father of Henry IV., died in 1399. Says Gloucester in Shakespeare's *Richard III.* :—

> "My lord of Ely, when I was last in Holborn,
> I saw good strawberries in your garden there;
> I do beseech you send for some of them."

Later the palace was occupied by Sir Christopher Hatton, Lord Keeper to Queen Elizabeth. Hatton Garden is the centre of the world's diamond trade, and also contains the London offices of many of the leading manufacturers of pottery. The only portion of the palace which escaped the Fire has been restored, and now forms **St. Etheldreda's Church,** Ely Place, the only pre-Reformation church in London that has been restored to the Roman Catholic worship. The building is two-storied, and both the Chapel itself and the Undercroft should be seen. The church is thought by some to date from the Saxon period. The tracery of the east and west windows—the former said to be the largest east window in London, as it is certainly the most beautiful—the oak roof, and the cloister, in which fig-trees still flourish, make this quiet nook, in the heart of the great City, a place of exceptional interest. **Ely Place** is itself of great interest, being private property and exempt from Corporation jurisdiction. A gold-braided porter preserves the dignity and order of the place, and at night, when the gates are closed, he reassures those within with a mediæval "Fine night, all's well."

ROUTE XI.—THREADNEEDLE STREET—BISHOPSGATE—BETHNAL GREEN MUSEUM—GEFFRYES' MUSEUM—LIVERPOOL STREET—BROAD STREET —THE STOCK EXCHANGE—LOTHBURY.

From the Bank we turn this time along the quaintly-named **Threadneedle Street,** skirting the northern side of the Royal Exchange. Note the cleverly designed building of the *Eagle, Star and Dominions Assurance Company.* The red granite building in Old Broad Street, on the left, is the **Stock Exchange** (see p. 236). On the right of Threadneedle Street, beyond Finch Lane, is **Merchant Taylors' Hall,** the largest of those belonging to the London Livery Companies. The Company, incorporated in 1327, has an income of £50,000 a year. The present hall, in which are royal portraits by Reynolds and others, dates from 1671, its predecessor having perished in the Great Fire, the crypt alone being spared. **Bishopsgate,** taking its name from the old Bishop's Gate (a tablet marks the site), is a continuation northward of Gracechurch Street.

Nearly opposite Threadneedle Street is the *Bank of Scotland,* a corporation only a year younger than the Bank of England.

Bearing to the left we reach, a few yards beyond the Bank of Scotland, the short thoroughfare known as Great St. Helen's and giving access to **St. Helen's Church** (*open daily* 11.30 *to* 4, *except Saturdays*), unrivalled among City churches for the spaciousness of its interior.

The church occupies part of the site of a very ancient nunnery founded, if tradition is to be believed, in memory of Helena, mother of Constantine. The demolition of buildings in St. Helen's Place in 1922 exposed remains of a building of Saxon date, and another believed to be Roman. There were also revealed some arches of the nunnery. On obtaining a ticket at the church (1 or 2 persons, 1*s.*; up to 5 persons, 2*s.* 6*d.*, etc.) those interested may inspect these remains. The present church, dating in part from the thirteenth century, and consisting of a nave divided into two aisles by pillars and pointed arches, was judiciously restored by J. L. Pearson in 1893, at the expense of some of the City companies. On account of its many memorials of illustrious Londoners, St. Helen's is frequently termed the "Westminster Abbey of the City." The most notable monuments are those of Sir Thomas Gresham, Sir Julius Cæsar (not the invader of Britain, but a Master of the Rolls of James I.'s time), Sir John Crosby (d. 1475), of Crosby Hall, and his lady, and Sir Wm. Pickering. A memorial window in the northern aisle, or Nun's Choir, was erected in 1884, on the probability that a William Shakespeare assessed for rates in the parish in 1598 was the poet. The church has recently been restored.

Spanning the entrance to St. Helen's Place is a magnificent modern building erected for the Hudson's Bay Company (note the decorative allusions to trading: the building as a whole should be viewed from across the street). In St. Helen's Place is the **Leathersellers' Hall,** a modern building beneath which is the crypt of the old St. Helen's Nunnery. Near at hand is **St. Ethelburga's Church,** one of the oldest and smallest in London, fortunate in escaping the Great Fire. This church was long famous for the shops which masked its front; but these projected into the busy pavement and were demolished in 1933. Windows commemorate Henry Hudson and his companions, who received Holy Communion in the church before setting out in the *Hopeful,* 1607. A tablet on the house at the corner of Camomile Street marks the site of the former *Bishop's Gate,* erected by Bishop Erkenwald in Saxon days. On the left is the Church of **St. Botolph Without,** where Keats was baptized in 1795, its graveyard now laid out as a garden. Here stands a Memorial Cross, erected in 1916 and inscribed "In Memoriam. Officers and men of the Honourable Artillery Company who died in the Great War." Other sides are inscribed to Lord Kitchener, J. T. Cornwell (the youthful hero of Jutland), and "Our Brave Dead of Bishopsgate."

It is curious that **Houndsditch,** leading eastward through an unmistakably Jewish quarter to Aldgate, has a church of St. Botolph at each end. The name is a reminder of the old ditch without the City wall. The Sunday morning "old clo'" sales in this locality form one of the most curious spectacles of "Living London."

Were we to continue northward up Bishopsgate past **Liverpool Street Station** (see p. 236), we should shortly reach **Shoreditch,** passing on the way the **Bishopsgate Institute,** opened in 1894, and partly built by means of the surplus funds of a bequest left in 1481 to provide flannel petticoats for poor old women. The library, available to all persons resident or employed in the eastern part of the City, contains about 45,000 volumes.

An excusable, but not at first sight alluring, divagation from this point would be by motor-omnibus along Bethnal Green Road to the Bethnal Green Museum.

Bethnal Green Museum.

Plan II. Q. 5.
Access.—Trams and omnibuses pass the door.
Admission.—Open free daily; Monday and Thursday, 10 a.m. to 10 p.m.; other week-days, 10 a.m. to 5 p.m.; Sunday, 2.30 to 6 p.m.

This branch of the Victoria and Albert Museum was established in 1872 as a local museum for East London. The building is part of the old temporary structure which composed the original South Kensington Museum, and it is thus in direct descent from the Great Exhibition of 1851.

The exhibits include a good collection of water-colour and oil paintings, some of great value, and collections of costumes, furniture, textiles, ceramics and glass, birds, etc. A section of the Museum is arranged with a view to the special needs of children, who form a considerable proportion of its normal visitors. Recently the establishment has been enriched by the library of the late Paul Konody, the art critic.

Old Ford Road, to the north of the Museum, leads in half a mile to **Victoria Park,** the principal playground of East London, occupying over 200 acres and having a boating lake.

Shoreditch Church (St. Leonard's) is of great interest to Shakespearians on account of its records and memorials of James Burbage, Richard Tarleton, Will Somers, Spenser ("slain" by Ben Jonson), etc. Note also the old stocks and whipping-post. The name of **Curtain Road,** to the west, recalls the fact that here stood two of the earliest theatres in London: "The Theatre," which preceded the more famous *Globe* at Southwark as the scene of Shakespearian productions, and the Curtain Theatre. A tablet marks the site of the former, and a window in St. James's Church (facing the site of the "Curtain") recalls the Shakespeare associations of the somewhat dingy Curtain Road of to-day.

In Kingsland Road, half a mile or so beyond Shoreditch Church, is the **Geffrye Museum,** a small but interesting collection of furniture and old woodwork housed in the tree-shaded hospital founded by "Sir Rob. Geffryes, Knt., Alderman and Ironmonger." Formerly known as the Ironmongers' Almshouses, the buildings were bought by the L.C.C. and converted into a museum in 1914. (*Open till* 6 *p.m., week-days from* 11 *a.m., Sundays from* 2 *p.m. Closed Mondays, except Bank Holidays.*)

A great part of the west side of Bishopsgate at its northern end is occupied by **Liverpool Street Station** (Plan II. O. 7), the terminus of the Great Eastern section of the London and North-Eastern Railway. Adjoining Liverpool Street Station on the west is **Broad Street Station** (Plan II. O. 7), the terminus of the electrified North London line (L.M.S.—for Willesden Junction, Richmond, Watford, etc.). Below ground are the Liverpool Street Stations of the Metropolitan and Central London Railways. In Eldon Street is the Roman Catholic Church of **St. Mary, Moorfields.**

Neither **New Broad Street** nor **Old Broad Street,** leading southward to the Bank, have any apparent right to their name, though the soaring blocks of offices make the thoroughfare appear narrower than it is. In Old Broad Street (No. 19) is the **City of London Club,** frequented principally by bankers and merchants. At the eastern end of **London Wall** (p. 225) is **Carpenters' Hall.** The Church of **All Hallows-on-the-Wall** has its foundations in the old Roman wall, and the vestry perpetuates the outline of a bastion. The present church dates from 1764, but there was a church here before the Conquest. Throgmorton Avenue leads down to **Throgmorton Street,** generally crowded by bare-headed individuals of varying degrees of frivolity, whose presence betrays the whereabouts of that important institution, the **Stock Exchange** (Plan II. O. 7), in Capel Court. Only members are admitted to the building, but as not a little business is done "in the street," strangers may derive a certain edification from observing the solemnity with which matters of high finance are conducted. "Jobbers" deal in particular securities only; "brokers" act as intermediaries between jobbers and the public. Members are not allowed to advertise. Persons who do so are "outside brokers," not amenable to the stringent rules and regulations of the "House." In Throgmorton Street is the **Drapers' Hall,** with garden attached, a luxury indeed on such a site. The hall dates in part from 1667. To the north, in Austin Friars, is the **Dutch Church,** originally part of an important Augustinian Friary, which came into the hands of Henry VIII. at the Dissolution and was granted by the boy king, Edward VI., in 1550, "to the Dutch nation in London, to be their preaching place," a purpose it has ever since served. The building was fortunate in escaping the Great Fire, and has some ancient monuments. It is said to have the largest floor-space of any City church, St. Paul's Cathedral excepted. **Lothbury,** in which are the offices of some of the principal financial magnates, skirts the north side of the Bank of England. St. Margaret's Church, Lothbury, has a magnificent screen, while **Bartholomew Lane,** on the east, will bring us back to our starting-point.

ROUTE XII.—CORNHILL—GRACECHURCH STREET—LEADENHALL STREET —ALDGATE—WHITECHAPEL—FENCHURCH STREET—MARK LANE.

Another " spoke " radiating from the Bank is **Cornhill** (Plan III. N. and O. 8), having on its south side the striking new premises of *Lloyds Bank*. Farther east is **St. Michael's Church,** rebuilt by Wren after the Fire, and restored by Sir G. G. Scott. It has a fine Gothic tower, modelled on Magdalen Tower, Oxford, and a pulpit carved by Grinling Gibbons. The organ of **St. Peter's Church,** almost next door, was several times played by Mendelssohn, and in the vestry his autograph is treasured. The church was founded, according to an ancient tablet in the vestry, by " Lucius, the first Christian king of this land then called Britaine." Many remains of Roman London have been discovered hereabouts, and authorities place here the site of the Roman forum.

Gray, author of the famous *Elegy*, was born at No. 41, Cornhill (tablet). At the intersection **Gracechurch Street** (Plan III. O. 8) leads southward to London Bridge (p. 242). The peculiar name recalls a herb or grass market, at one time held in the yard of the demolished St. Benet's Church, hence known as the " Grass Church." Here Cornhill ceases, and its eastward continuation becomes **Leadenhall Street.** On the right is **Leadenhall Market,** for vegetables, poultry, etc. Until a few years ago dogs, cats, etc., were also shown, the last-named in steady demand for long voyages in rat-haunted ships and for warehouses. It is interesting in the circumstances to recall that the ground on which the market stands was given to the City by Dick Whittington. On this side of Leadenhall Street is the huge new headquarters of **Lloyd's,** where obliging " underwriters " will quote a premium for every imaginable form of risk. The institution takes its name from the old Lloyd's Coffee House, in Lombard Street, where seventeenth-century shipowners were accustomed to forgather. Lloyd's signal stations are dotted all round our coasts. For many years Lloyd's was located in the Royal Exchange, but in 1928 the great organization moved to this fine new building. *Lloyd's Register of British and Foreign Shipping* (see p. 241) is a separate undertaking, mainly concerned with the classification of vessels. The phrase " A1 at Lloyd's " is derived from the sign for wooden vessels of the highest class. The highest class of steel and iron vessels are registered 100 A1.

At the foot of **St. Mary Axe,** over the name of which antiquaries still wrangle, is **St. Andrew Undershaft** (*open daily* 12 *to* 2).

The church derives its name, according to Stow, from a long shaft, or Maypole, higher than the church steeple, which used to be set up opposite the south door. The Puritans declared the inoffensive shaft an idol, and had it "raised from the hooks whereon it had rested for two-and-thirty years, sawn in pieces and burnt." At the end of the north aisle is the alabaster monument of Stow (d. 1605), the chronicler of London, who is shown at his writing-table, with a real pen in hand. The pen, it is said, has been stolen over and over again, under the impression that it was the identical pen with which the *Chronicles* were written.

In St. Mary Axe, too, is the **Baltic Mercantile and Shipping Exchange,** the headquarters of merchants, shippers, brokers, etc., trading mainly in grain and similar products. Like Lloyd's, it sprang from a famous old coffee-house.

Continuing along Leadenhall Street, we have on the left the Church of **St. Katherine Cree** (*open daily* 12 *to* 2), rebuilt, except the Gothic tower, by Inigo Jones in 1631. In allusion to its dedication, it has a Catherine-wheel window. Holbein, the artist, is said to have been buried here in 1543. When the body of the church was rebuilt in 1630, one of the old pillars was left *in situ*. It now only shows 3 ft. above ground, the rest of it—15 ft.—being beneath the surface; a silent evidence of how much the ground has risen in the City. The "lion sermon," to commemorate the escape of a Lord Mayor of Charles I.'s time from the jaws of a lion in Africa, and a "flower sermon," the idea of which has been adopted far and wide, are annually preached in this church.

We are now at **Aldgate** (Plan II. O. 7), the site of a former City portal, Ale-gate, or All-gate (i.e., open to all), having beyond it one of the "without" wards—Portsoken, "the field beyond the gates." A plaque on Aldgate Post Office recalls that Chaucer lived in a house over Aldgate during 1374. Many a facetious debtor has attempted to right himself by a "draught (draft) on Aldgate Pump." Hereabouts, as a glance at shop signs and passing faces betrays, is the Jewish quarter of the Metropolis. Turning to the left, we pass close to St. James's Place, in which is the **Great Synagogue,** the Hebrew cathedral of London. At the corner of Houndsditch (p. 234) is the Church of **St. Botolph, Aldgate,** with a spacious open churchyard (among the graves is that of William Symington, one of the pioneers of steam navigation). In the church is preserved, though it is rarely shown, a somewhat ghastly relic—the supposed head of the Duke of Suffolk, beheaded on Tower Hill in 1554. The **Minories,** on the right, is an unattractive thoroughfare leading southward to the Tower of London. At the foot of Church Street is the quaint little Holy Trinity Church, now the St. Botolph Institute. It formerly belonged to an abbey of Minoresses, or nuns of St. Clare—hence the name of the main street. The church is also sometimes alluded to as " the Mumbling Church " a name which has been explained by reference to the exemption the church enjoyed from episcopal authority in matters ecclesiastical. It claimed the right to marry all comers without banns or licence. Many clandestine marriage ceremonies, therefore, were doubtless mumbled over there. American visitors are interested in the monuments to the Legge family (Earls of Dartmouth), with which George Washington was connected. One contains a representation of the Stars and Stripes. During the rebuilding of Nos. 15 and 16, **America Square,** near the Minories, in 1908, a splendidly preserved section (60 ft.) of the **Roman City Wall** was unearthed. No. 14 was the home, early in the nineteenth century, of Baron Meyer de Rothschild, the founder of the English branch of the great financial house. To the west of the Minories is **Jewry Street,** in which is the **Cass Technical Institute.** Another massive fragment of the old wall has been incorporated in the basement of Roman House at the bottom of this street. (See also p. 251).

Continuing along Aldgate, we have on the left **Middlesex Street** (formerly *Petticoat Lane*), famed for its open-air market on Sunday mornings.

From here the District Line runs for two miles beneath the Whitechapel and Mile End Roads to form a junction with the Tilbury and Southend line (L.M.S.R.) at Barking. Following **Whitechapel High Street,** we shortly have on the right **Commercial Road,** leading to Stepney, Limehouse, and the East and West India Docks. Here stands the **Sailors' Palace,** the headquarters of the successful work for seamen carried on in nearly all the ports of the world by the British and Foreign Sailors' Society. In Stepney Causeway, a short distance west of Stepney Station, are the administrative headquarters of **Dr. Barnardo's Homes** (Plan III. R. 8), caring for a huge family of destitute children, numbering about 8,000. Visitors desiring further information, or to inspect the various branches, should apply to the General Secretary for a *Guide to Visitors.*

In **Commercial Street,** leading northward from Whitechapel High Street, is **St. Jude's Church,** which has been for many years a centre of sweetness and light in a sordid district. **Toynbee**

Hall, adjoining, has long been an important educational centre, where University graduates have grappled at first hand with the problems of poverty and shared the lives of East End dwellers. Close at hand is the **Whitechapel Art Gallery** (Plan II. P. 7). A free Library and Museum adjoin.

In the **Whitechapel Road,** about half a mile beyond the Art Gallery, is the **London Hospital,** with accommodation for nearly 1,000 in-patients and an army of out-patients. The Hospital was founded in 1759. At the back is the large church of **St. Philip, Stepney.** Cambridge Road, on the left, would take us northward to the **Bethnal Green Museum** (p. 235). At the corner of this road, and at the beginning of the spacious **Mile End Road,** are the **Trinity Almshouses,** for seamen and their wives and widows, a picturesque group little altered since their establishment by Trinity House in 1696. No. 88, Mile End Road, marked by a tablet, was the residence of that dauntless navigator, Captain Cook. In the rear of the Beth Holim, at 253, Mile End Road, is a secluded little burial ground granted to the Jewish fraternity in London by Cromwell in 1657. It will be noticed that **Mile End** is just about a mile from the old City wall, a fact to which it doubtless owes its name. **Stepney Green,** on the south side of Mile End Road, leads obliquely to **St. Dunstan's,** the parish church of Stepney, a fine Perpendicular building, with registers dating back to 1568. It contains several tombs of fifteenth- and sixteenth-century worthies, including Sir Henry Colet, father of Dean Colet of St. Paul's.

Another is the well-known "fish and ring" monument to Dame Rebecca Berry, who was long supposed to be the heroine of the ballad called "The Cruel Knight and the Fortunate Farmer's Daughter." According to the story—a curious variant of that of St. Mungo, which gave rise to the "fish and ring" in the Glasgow arms—a knight was passing a cottage when he heard the cries of a woman. His knowledge of the occult sciences warning him that the child then born was destined to be his wife, he attempted unsuccessfully to encompass the death of the child, in order to escape this ignoble alliance. When she had grown to woman's estate he took her to sea with the intention of drowning her. Relenting of his purpose, he cast a ring into the sea and commanded her never to see his face again unless she could produce the ring. The woman became a cook, and, finding the ring in a cod-fish, married the knight.

Towards the eastern end of Mile End Road is the **People's Palace** (Plan II. R. and S. 6), the outcome of a suggestion in Sir Walter Besant's *All Sorts and Conditions of Men*. The funds were mainly provided by the trustees of Mr. Barber Beaumont and by the Drapers' Company. The Palace is also known as the East London College (affiliated to London University), and is the centre of much useful educational work. Following upon a fire, the Palace has been rebuilt and is now thoroughly well equipped.

We have wandered rather far from the city, however, and

must beg the reader to put on the magic slippers and return at a bound to **Aldgate** (p. 238). Varying our outward route, we will regain the Bank by way of **Fenchurch Street** (Plan III. O. 8). In Lloyd's Avenue, on the south side, is the fine building of **Lloyd's Shipping Registry,** with beautiful friezes and marbles. **Fenchurch Street Station** is the terminus of the former London, Tilbury and Southend Railway (now part of the London, Midland and Scottish system), and is also used by the Great Eastern section of the L.N.E.R. The *London Tavern*, a modern building with statues, at the corner of Mark Lane and Fenchurch Street, occupies the site of the old "King's Head," where Queen Elizabeth dined immediately after her release from the Tower in 1554. Some relics of the Virgin Queen are preserved within.

Steps in front of the station lead down to Hart Street, where is **St. Olave's Church** (*open* 12 *to* 3.30), one of the seven surviving City churches of the score or so that escaped the Fire. The dedication refers to St. Olaf of Norway (995–1035). The present building dates from the middle of the fifteenth century, and contains many quaint old monuments and brasses, some of which were removed from neighbouring fanes on their demolition.

It is chiefly interesting, however, as "our owne church" of Samuel Pepys, the diarist (1633–1703). He and his wife are buried here, as a modern memorial in the south aisle recalls. His association with the parish arose from the fact that he was Secretary to the Admiralty, the Navy Office at that period being in Crutched Friars. St. Olave's owed its preservation from the Fire to Pepys himself, it being at his suggestion that men were brought from the dockyards to blow up surrounding houses and thus stay the conflagration. The parents of Joseph Chamberlain were married here in 1835. Every year, on Trinity Monday, the Master and Brethren of Trinity House attend service at St. Olave's. It is also the official church of the Clothworkers' and Ironmongers' Companies.

Crutched Friars is a crooked street deriving its name from a former monastery of the Friars of the Holy Cross. Commercial as is all this quarter now, it is to be remembered that when the Court was in residence at the Tower, the nobility and gentry had mansions hereabouts and the great religious houses gave it an ecclesiastical importance hard indeed to realize to-day.

Mark Lane (a corruption of *Mart Lane*), connecting Fenchurch Street with Great Tower Street, is the distributing centre of the corn trade, the dealers on market days, chiefly Mondays, meeting in the two **Corn Exchanges,** the old building dating from 1827, the new hall from 1881. Mark Lane has been described as "the cradle of the British Navy," the Navy Office, or Admiralty, having been here until 1656, when it was removed to Crutched Friars, and subsequently westward. **Mincing Lane,** running parallel on the west, is the centre of the wholesale tea trade. Mark and Mincing Lanes and the streets thereabouts are also the headquarters of the wine trade, and the whole locality is honeycombed with vaults. The **Clothworkers' Hall,** half-way down Mincing Lane, seems somewhat out of place in such a locality. One of the Company's most treasured possessions is a loving cup presented by Pepys, who was Master in 1677.

Continuing along Fenchurch Street, we cross Gracechurch Street (p. 237) and enter **Lombard Street** (Plan III. N. and O. 8), generally considered the richest street in the world. On either side massive banks display plates bearing names we would gladly be more familiar with, and some hang out "signs" in the approved mediæval style. On the north side are two of Wren's churches, *St. Edmund King and Martyr* and *All Hallows.* The latter is about to be demolished.

In Post Office Court is that useful institution the **Bankers' Clearing House,** where cheques having a face value of thousands of millions change hands every year. The name of the street is an obvious reminder of the old Lombard moneylenders. Pope was born in Plough Court in 1688. At the western end of the street is **St. Mary Woolnoth,** already referred to (p. 207).

ROUTE XIII.—KING WILLIAM STREET—LONDON BRIDGE—THE TOWER—TOWER BRIDGE—THE DOCKS.

Now let us complete our rambles from the Bank by following **King William Street,** named after "our sailor king," in a south-easterly direction to London Bridge, whence we can turn eastward to the Tower and the Docks. Across the road is the *Monument Station* (Underground), and in Fish Street, to the east, is the **Monument** itself (Plan III. O. 8). London has thousands of monuments, and many of far greater significance than this one ; but by Londoners the column before us is invariably referred to as "The Monument." It is a fluted Doric column, 202 ft. high, erected by Wren to commemorate the Great Fire of 1666, which broke out in Pudding Lane close by, and destroyed property valued at over ten million pounds (p. 71). Wren's original intention was to fit the monument with lenses and convert it into a huge telescope. Persons desirous of so doing may, on payment of threepence, ascend (*week-days only*) to the "caged" gallery near the top. The view is sublime, but the steps are 311. The cage is designed to protect would-be suicides from themselves. The gilt urn, like Moses's bush, burns but is not consumed.

London Bridge (Plan III. N. 8) dates from 1831, and was designed by John Rennie. Considerably over 20,000 vehicles and more than 110,000 foot passengers cross it every day.

The Thames at this point narrows to 900 ft., but is much wider both above and below. The bridge is a granite structure of five arches, having a length of 928 ft. and a width of 65 ft. The span of the central arch is 152 ft. Until after the middle of the eighteenth century, London Bridge afforded the only means of crossing the Thames hereabouts except by boat. The predecessor of the present structure was more like a street than a bridge, being lined on both sides with houses and having fortified gates at each end. These gates were more often than not garnished with human heads.

From the east side of the bridge is gained a fine view of the busy **Pool,** so admirably rendered in the pictures of Vicat Cole, W. L. Wyllie, Chas. Dixon and others. *Adelaide House* towers above the bridge on the east. Below the west side is **Fishmongers' Hall.** The Fishmongers, incorporated so long ago as the reign of Edward I., are one of the wealthiest of the great companies. The King and the Prince of Wales are freemen. On the staircase is a statue of "Brave Walworth, knight, Lord Mayor," who slew rebellious Tyler; and the actual dagger is also shown, though it is quite erroneous to suppose, as many do, that this is the object which figures in the City arms. As a matter of fact, the heraldic emblem is not a dagger at all, but the blunt-pointed sword of St. Paul, the patron saint of London, and the City authorities so represent it on all official documents.

The northern approach to London Bridge spans **Lower Thames Street,** a decidedly "fishy" thoroughfare—if a road which is perpetually blocked can be called a thoroughfare—skirting the north bank of the Thames between London Bridge and the Tower. Just below the bridge, at the foot of Fish Street Hill, is the Church of **St. Magnus the Martyr,** rebuilt by Wren after the Fire. Here are buried the remains of Miles Coverdale, author of the first complete translation of the Bible. We are now in the somewhat unsavoury locality of **Billingsgate,** which has been almost from time immemorial the principal fish market of London. To be seen at its best (or worst), the Market should be visited shortly after the opening at 5 a.m. An interesting feature of the river are the **Dutch eel boats,** which have enjoyed the right of mooring here ever since the days of Queen Elizabeth. Adjoining is the **Custom House,** the fine river front of which,

488 ft. long, is an imposing feature in the view from London Bridge. Opposite, at the corner of St. Mary-at-Hill, is the **Coal Exchange,** with a tower over 100 ft. high. Among the curiosities shown here are the remains of a Roman bath, and a sword in the City arms made of wood of a mulberry tree said to have been planted by Peter the Great when learning shipbuilding in this country. In Idol Lane is the church of **St. Dunstan-in-the-East,** rebuilt in the early part of last century to replace a building designed by Wren, of which the steeple remains, being by common consent the most graceful in London. In Rood Lane, close by, is the interesting church of **St. Margaret Pattens,** rebuilt by Wren in 1687. Its canopied pews are unique in London, and it has some noteworthy pictures. Some pattens in a case hint at the origin of the name.

We turn now into **Great Tower Street,** the eastward continuation of **Eastcheap.** Nearly opposite *Mark Lane Station* is the church of **All Hallows, Barking,** so called not because it is in Barking, which is 7 miles distant, but because it was founded by the nuns of Barking Abbey, a figure of whose first Abbess, St. Ethelburga, may be seen in the porch. The pulpit and font cover were carved by Grinling Gibbons. The registers record the baptism of William Penn on October 23rd, 1644; he was born on the east side of Tower Hill (see below). In 1911 the Pennsylvania Society of New York erected a bronze tablet in the church in commemoration of the fact. Remains of Roman London have been discovered below the church and in the crypt is a model of Roman London. Recently the undercroft has been rebuilt, and the south-east portion of the church is being developed as a Mariners' Chapel.

All Hallows is the Guild Church of the **"Toc H"** movement; and in the Chapel of Cœur de Lion are preserved the Lamp of Maintenance lit by King Edward VIII., when Prince of Wales, in 1922, the sword of Edmund Street, etc. Renovations in 1924 disclosed a stone slab which was thought by some to have covered the "Lion Heart" of Richard I., that monarch having built here a chapel for the reception of his heart. But the relic is generally believed to be at Rouen.

We have now reached **Tower Hill,** as interesting a spot historically as any in the City. Here has been erected the **Merchant Navy Memorial,** unveiled by H.M. Queen Mary in 1928. Slightly to the north-west, on the lawn of Trinity Square gardens, is a slab of granite paving with the inscription, "Site of ancient scaffold. Here the Earl of Kilmarnock and Lord Balmerino suffered, 18th August, 1746." These were almost the last

THE TOWER OF LONDON.

[Dixon Scott.

Aerofilms, Ltd.,]

THE PC

Southwark Bridge is at the foot of the picture, Lond

[*London.*

LONDON.

ge in the centre and Tower Bridge towards the top.

THE TOWER BRIDGE.

persons in England to be beheaded (the honour of being the last belongs to Lord Lovat, 1747).

Were the list to be a full one a stone of enormous dimensions would be required. This was the place of public execution; only a few "privileged" persons were executed in the privacy of the Tower itself (see p. 248). A less dismal association is the fact that "at his father's house on the east side of Tower Hill, up a court adjoining the City Wall," William Penn, the founder of Pennsylvania, was born in 1644.

From the foot of the hill a passage leads to the **Tower Pier,** whence steamers start for Southend, Margate, etc., and other steamers and also motor launches ply to and from Greenwich and Westminster.

THE TOWER.

Plan III. O. 8.

Admission.—The Tower is open daily, except Sundays, from 10 to 6 (Oct. 1st to April 30th, 10 to 5). Tickets for admission must in all cases be obtained from the Office adjoining the principal entrance on Tower Hill. *The issue of these tickets ceases an hour before the time of closing.*

Fees.—The fees for all accessible parts total 1*s.* 6*d.*, viz. Vaults and Armouries of White Tower, 6*d.* (free on Saturdays and Bank Holidays); Jewel House, 6*d.*; Bloody Tower, 6*d.*; children between the ages of 3 and 14 half price. Any ticket, including the free ticket issued for admission to the Armouries on Saturdays, etc., admits gratis to the Beauchamp Tower and, at stated hours, to the Salt, Broad Arrow and Martin Towers and to certain rooms in the Byward Tower. The Chapel of St. Peter ad Vincula can also be seen by persons accompanied by a warder. (On Saturdays it is closed at 3.30 p.m.)

Nearest Station.—Mark Lane (District).

The fortress, including the **Moat,** now drained and used as a drill and playground, occupies an irregular pentagon of about 18 acres, the circuit of the outer walls being nearly two-thirds of a mile. Only a small portion is within the City boundary.

Historical Note.—Tradition has it that a fortress stood here in Roman times. In 1078 William the Conqueror built the great central keep, or White Tower, for the purpose of protecting and overawing the City. His architect was Gundulph, Bishop of Rochester, and the work bears a marked resemblance to that of Rochester Castle. The keep first became known as "La Tour Blanche" in the reign of Edward III., possibly, as some authorities contend, because it was at that time whitewashed. The inner wall, with its thirteen towers, was added by William Rufus, the moat by Richard I. Henry III. made extensive additions and surrounded the whole by a second wall, with rounded bastions on the north side, and towers commanding the river.

In viewing the Tower, it must be borne in mind that it has served the three purposes of a fortress, a palace, and a prison. Several of the Norman and Plantagenet kings were glad of its protection. Four foreign kings were detained here: King John the Good of France, after his overthrow by the Black Prince at

Poitiers; and three Scots kings, Baliol, David II. after the battle of Neville's Cross, and James I. of Scotland. The most touching of all Tower memories is, of course, the murder, in 1483, of the young king Edward V. and his brother, the Duke of York, at the instigation of Gloucester, afterwards Richard III. Some bones, supposed to be theirs, were found beneath the staircase leading to the second floor of the White Tower, and were interred, by order of Charles II., in Westminster Abbey. A plate in the wall marks the place where the bones were found, but now that the entrance to the White Tower is made from the north, this spot is no longer shown. The Tudor sovereigns made fairly frequent use of the Tower as a residence, but it can have been little to the taste of Elizabeth, some of whose early years were spent here as a prisoner. James I. and Charles II. were crowned from here; but the Tower has long ceased to have any special association with royalty, except from the fact that it serves as a place of custody for the Crown jewels.

We enter by wooden gates on the site of the **Lion Gate,** and obtain our tickets from the office on the right. The Ticket Office is on the site of the old **Lion Tower,** so named from the royal menagerie maintained here down to 1834, which gave rise to the expression about visitors coming to London "to see the lions."

Passing under the **Middle Tower** (*temp*. Henry III.), we cross a stone bridge over the Moat and reach the **Byward Tower,** giving access to the Outer Bail or Ward. Before this we shall probably encounter one or two magnificent specimens of the famous **Beefeaters,** or Wardens of the Tower, whose picturesque uniform has remained unchanged since the reign of Edward VI. Byward comes from *by-word,* the word that alone could get you by, or pass-word, as we should say to-day. Down to early Plantagenet times the Court of Common Pleas was held inside the Tower, and litigants and others who had the right to attend were given the pass-word. The most interesting feature within the Tower is the windlass for raising and lowering the portcullis.

Passing under the Byward Tower, we see on the left the **Bell Tower,** where the Princess Elizabeth was imprisoned. On the western wall that connects this tower with the **Beauchamp Tower** is the Prisoners' Walk, along which the Princess took exercise. Farther along the south front, on the right, overlooking the river, is **St. Thomas's Tower,** with the wide archway of the **Traitors' Gate** beneath it. It was by this gloomy water passage that State prisoners entered the Tower, some of the most notable being Sir Thomas More, Anne Boleyn, Lady Jane Grey, and the Duke of Monmouth. Opposite is the **Bloody Tower** (see also p. 250) with its portcullis, almost the only survival of the kind in working order. Through the little window above it, Archbishop Laud leaned out to bless Thomas Wentworth, Earl of Strafford, on his way to execution. Below this archway, accord-

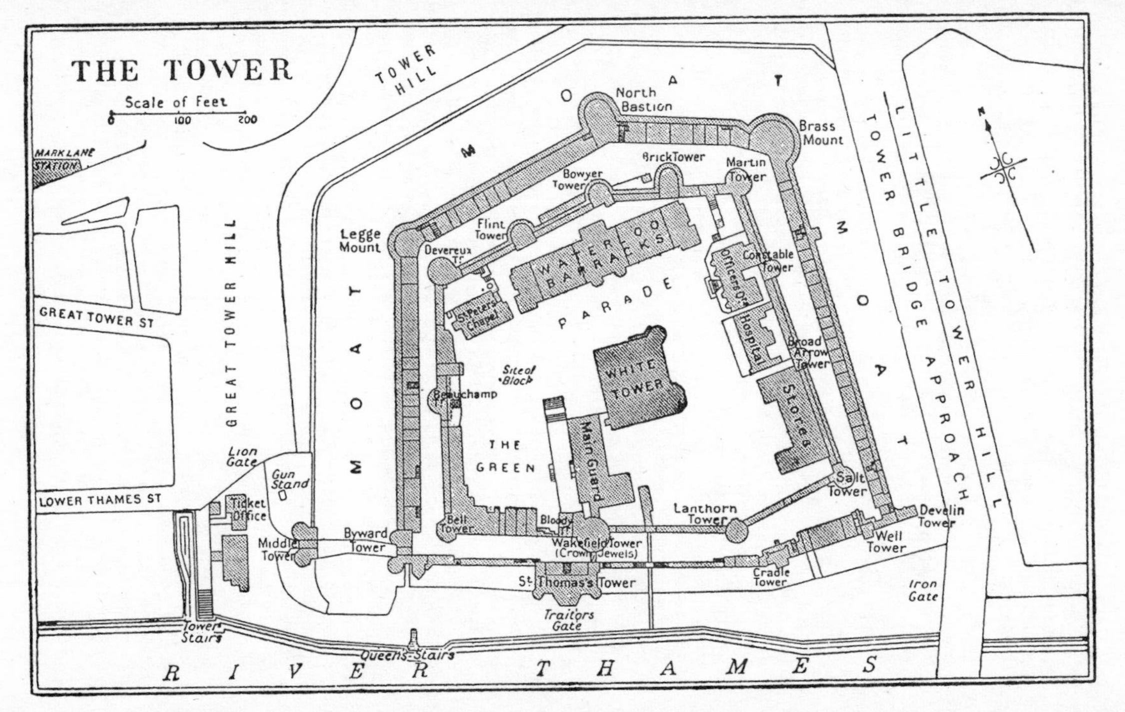
THE TOWER
Scale of Feet
0
100
200
MARK LANE STATION
TOWER HILL
GREAT TOWER ST
GREAT TOWER HILL
LOWER THAMES ST
Lion Gate
Gun Stand
Ticket Office
Middle Tower
Byward Tower
Tower Stairs
Queens Stairs
RIVER THAMES
MOAT
Legge Mount
North Bastion
Brass Mount
Brick Tower
Bowyer Tower
Martin Tower
Flint Tower
Devereux Tr.
St. Peters Chapel
WATERLOO BARRACKS
PARADE
Officers Qrs
Constable Tower
Hospital
Broad Arrow Tower
WHITE TOWER
Stores
Site of Block
Beauchamp
THE GREEN
Main Guard
Bell Tower
Bloody Tr.
Wakefield Tower (Crown Jewels)
St. Thomas's Tower
Traitors Gate
Lanthorn Tower
Salt Tower
Cradle Tower
Well Tower
Develin Tower
Iron Gate
TOWER BRIDGE APPROACH
LITTLE TOWER HILL

ing to Sir Thomas More, was the first burial-place of the little Princes. Later, he tells us, Richard III. "insisted on their resting in a better place, when a priest of Sir Thomas Brackenbury took them up, and buried them in such secrecy, as by the occasion of his death, which was very shortly after, no one knew it." This secret place we know now was in the White Tower, below St. John's Chapel, consecrated ground at that time. The staircase beneath which the bones were found was not built in the time of Richard III.

We pass between the Bloody Tower and the Traitors' Gate and then turn through the next gate in the Inner Curtain Wall, on the left, and have before us the **White Tower** (entrance on farther side). This, the central and oldest portion of the fortress, is a nearly square building, measuring 118 ft. from east to west, and 107 ft. from north to south. At the corners are turrets, three square and one circular. The walls in the lower part are 15 ft. thick, decreasing to 11 ft. in the upper storey. At the south-east corner are the ruins of the **Wardrobe Tower.** In this was embodied part of the **Roman Wall,** which is still visible. To the right is the **Salt Tower,** with a dismal dungeon in which, for some time, gunpowder and saltpetre were stored—hence, probably, the name. Prisoners also occupied the dungeon and other parts of the tower and have left inscriptions on the wall. The **Broad Arrow Tower** was also a dreaded prison throughout the troublous times of Elizabeth and Mary.

At the north-east corner of the Inner Ward is the **Martin Tower.** It consists of two storeys and dates from Henry II.'s reign, but it has been considerably modernized. The upper floor is reputed to be a haunt of the ghost of Queen Anne. Until 1841 the Crown Jewels were kept in this Tower—it was here that Colonel Blood made his famous attempt to steal them—but in that year a fire broke out and the regalia were rescued with such hazard that it was considered advisable to remove them to quarters less exposed to danger.

Entering the White Tower by an external stairway, we find ourselves on the lower floor of the **Armouries,** which comprise an extensive and valuable collection founded by Henry VIII. Generally speaking, the earlier arms and armour are on the top floor, while the lower floor contains the later weapons, Indian armour and personal relics, but a strictly chronological arrangement is not possible. The collection includes very few pieces prior in date to the fifteenth century. In a vault at the farther end of the floor we are on are exhibited an execution block, headsman's axes, gibbet, etc. Here were confined Sir Walter Raleigh, after his return from Guiana, Sir William Wallace, Guy Fawkes, and other notabilities. It will be noted that all this part is actually above ground, and the dungeons in their present state hardly suggest their old-time terrors. From this floor we ascend a winding staircase in the thickness of the wall to the middle floor, in an angle of which is the **Chapel of St. John,** one of the most perfect specimens of Norman architecture extant. It has lately been restored, and cunningly-placed lights display its features to advantage. When the Kings of England lived in the Tower this was their private Chapel. Here "Bloody Mary" was married by proxy to Philip of Spain, and here her unfortunate rival, Lady Jane Grey, prayed the night before her execution. Wat Tyler dragged the Archbishop of Canterbury from the altar of St. John's Chapel to death upon Tower Hill. On a higher floor the King's Council met, and it was here that Richard III. said to Lord Hastings: "Dost thou answer me with an if? By St. George, I will not dine until thy head is cut off." This chamber witnessed, too, the deposition of Richard II., from which, as Shakespeare shows, so many subsequent tragedies sprang.

From the Chapel we pass to the upper floors of the Armouries and then descend by many steps to the **Vaults.** Here are exhibited a number of ancient mortars and other curios, including a fine sculpture of the Lion of St. Mark and relics of the *Royal George*.

Leaving the White Tower and turning left, we cross the Green, with its ravens, to the Beauchamp Tower. To the north of the path is the **Site of the Scaffold,** paved with granite by order of Queen Victoria. Here were beheaded Lord Hastings (1483), Anne Boleyn (1536), the Countess of Salisbury, the "last of the Plantagenets" (1541), Catharine Howard (1542), Viscountess Rochford (1542), Lady Jane Grey (1554), and the Earl of Essex (1601). Anne Boleyn was beheaded with a sword, the others by axe. All were buried in the gloomy **Chapel of St. Peter ad Vincula,** as were also most of the celebrated persons beheaded on Tower Hill (p. 244). Well does Macaulay say of the chapel cemetery: "In truth, there is no sadder spot on earth than this." The Chapel may be viewed on application, and the public are admitted to the 11 a.m. Sunday service.

Eastward of the Chapel of St. Peter are the **Waterloo Barracks,** but these and other portions of the Tower in use for military purposes are not shown.

The **Beauchamp Tower,** on the west side of Tower Green, and forming part of the inner wall, is one of the most interesting portions of the fortress. Built by Edward III., it was long a place of confinement for prisoners of rank, and its inner walls are covered with inscriptions left by these unhappy mortals. A large number of the glass-protected inscriptions in the principal room on the first floor have been dexterously transferred from other parts of the building.

On the south side the Green is overlooked by the **King's House,** formerly the Lieutenant's lodgings, in the council room of which Guy Fawkes and his fellow-conspirators were examined by torture. This building was the scene of Lord Nithsdale's famous escape in female disguise (1716). Adjoining it is the house of the Gentleman Gaoler, from one of the windows of which Lady Jane Grey saw her husband led out to slaughter from the Beauchamp Tower, and his headless body brought to the Chapel, while the scaffold was even then being prepared for her own death.

A doorway in the south-east corner of the green leads to the first floor of the **Bloody Tower** (see also p. 246). On the right, immediately on entering, will be observed the apparatus for raising and lowering the ancient portcullis. In this tower Sir Walter Raleigh spent the first years of his second imprisonment, that lasted twelve years, and here began his *History of the World*. The walls bear carvings by prisoners. Cranmer and Ridley were confined here, also Judge Jeffreys, who drank himself to death within these walls. Ascending to the room on the second floor, reputed to be the scene of the murder of the Princes, we can pass out on to the Prisoners' Walk, wherefrom Sir Walter Raleigh would acknowledge the cheers that reached him from passing vessels.

Leaving the Bloody Tower, we descend the steps in front to the **Inner Bail,** and turn rightward to the **Wakefield Tower,** which was built by William Rufus and was originally called the Record Tower, sometimes the Hall Tower. Its present name is derived from the battle of Wakefield, as a result of which it was crowded with Yorkist prisoners. With equal propriety it might be renamed the Culloden Tower, having been crowded with rebels of '45. Henry VI. is said to have been stabbed by Richard Crookback in its little eastern chapel. But for many the chief interest of this tower is as the repository of the **Crown Jewels.** The large circular apartment has in the centre a double case of steel. The blazing crowns, sceptres, swords, etc., are all labelled and can be plainly seen when the crowd is not great. Among them is the Imperial State Crown. It contains about 3,200 diamonds, pearls, etc., and weighs nearly 2½ lb. The crown is surmounted by a diamond cross beneath which is placed one of the famous "Stars of Africa," presented to King Edward VII. by the Transvaal in 1908. The diamond is oblong in shape, weighs 309 3/16th carats, and can be detached when desired and worn by the Queen as a brooch and pendant. The second "Star" (egg-shaped) is even larger, weighing 516½ carats. It is, in fact, the largest diamond in the world. It is placed in the King's sceptre, but, like the sister jewel, can be removed if desired. The case also contains the Imperial Crown worn by King George V. as King-Emperor at Delhi in December, 1911; St. Edward's Crown, worn by the King at his Coronation; the State Crown worn by Queen Mary at the Coronation; and the orb, anointing spoon, state sword, and other Coronation regalia. The massive "salt-cellars" are a remarkable feature of the collection. In the recesses are cases containing insignia of the various knightly orders, state trumpets, etc.

Between the Moat and the river is a broad **Gun Wharf,** with seats, affording a pleasant and interesting outlook. For the **Tower Pier** see p. 245.

The **Tower Bridge** (Plan III. O. 9), opened 1894, was built by the City Corporation at a cost of a million and a half pounds.

The bridge has several novel features, one being the raised footway, 142 ft. above high water, reached by stairs in the Gothic towers, though this footway is generally closed ; the other, the twin bascules, or leaves, which are raised to allow the passage of large vessels. A bell is rung when the " elevation " is about to take place, which happens about fourteen times daily. The central span is 200 ft. long ; those on either side, with chain suspension, 270 ft. each. The designers were Sir Horace Jones and Sir J. Wolfe Barry. About 5,000 vehicles and more than four times that number of pedestrians use the bridge daily. An interesting survival of the early days of the Bridge is the neighbouring tug, riding at anchor but with steam up and ready to go to the assistance of any vessel in difficulties and threatening the bridge. The maintenance of the tug (which annually costs £2,821) was one of the conditions under which sanction was given for the erection of the bridge, but in the course of 40 years it has hardly been used.

The northern approach road to the Tower Bridge passes close to that interesting national institution, the **Royal Mint** (Plan III. P. 8). For permission to view, it is necessary to apply by letter about three weeks in advance to the Deputy-Master, stating number of party (must not be more than six), date of intended visit, etc. (*No admission during August or on Saturdays.*) The machinery employed for coinage purposes is of a most interesting character. Notes have replaced gold coins, but more silver and bronze pieces are minted than ever before. A recent annual average (including Colonial issues) was 221 million coins.

In Trinity Place, on the eastern side of Tower Hill, is a splendid section of the **Roman City Wall,** and beside it, in the wall of an electric sub-station, is a reproduction of a Roman memorial stone discovered here in 1936.

To the north of the Tower, in Trinity Square, is **Trinity House,** the headquarters of the Trinity Brethren, a corporation controlling lighthouses and buoys round the British coast, licensing pilots, and generally supervising navigation. The corporation was founded in 1515, and incorporated by Henry VIII. in 1541, under the style of " The Guild or Fraternity of the most Glorious and Undividable Trinity and of St. Clement in the parish of Deptford Strond." It consists of a Master, Deputy-Master, 24 Elder Brethren, and a number of Younger Brethren. Within may be seen, on written application, an interesting collection of pictures, busts, personal relics, etc. The magnificent block opposite is the headquarters of the **Port of London Authority.** Externally, the predominant feature is the massive tower, rising above a fine portico of Corinthian columns, and the building is in every way worthy of the world's greatest port.

The Docks.

During the summer the Port of London Authority organize highly popular cruises through the Docks, commencing from Tower Pier. For details see current announcements.

The long chain of Docks, extending from the Tower Bridge to beyond North Woolwich, with the Surrey Commercial Docks on the south side, and important outposts at Tilbury, hardly arrest attention in this vast Metropolis as they would elsewhere. But the miles of quays, the colossal warehouses, the vast basins filled with shipping of every description, provide a sight calculated to stir the blood of the most phlegmatic of Englishmen. Apart from the cruises, the best way to gain a general idea of the extent and importance of London's docks is to take a launch from Westminster Pier either to Greenwich or Woolwich. The return may be made by water or it may be varied by bus or railway.

One-third of the imports and one-fourth of the exports of the United Kingdom pass through the port. The docks were formerly owned by a number of joint-stock companies, but under the Port of London Act, 1908, the Port of London Authority was constituted. Nearly twenty million pounds have already been expended on Dock improvements, and in 1936 a further development scheme estimated to cost £12,000,000 was put in hand. There are now 45 miles of quayage, and in addition to the warehouses and sheds at the docks there are others up-town, capable of storing enormous quantities of goods. A visitor, unless under expert guidance, is likely to experience some difficulty in finding his way through these intricate mazes. In any case, the warehouses, cellars and other really interesting features can only be seen by persons armed with the necessary permit from the authorities. The London, St. Katherine, and the East and West India Docks are within easy reach of the City; the Royal Victoria and Albert and King George V. Docks and the Tilbury Dock may be reached by trains from Fenchurch Street. Buses and trams also serve the various docks. But, as already stated, apart from the special cruises *through* the Docks, the best impressions of London's shipping are obtained from a steamer or launch going up or down river.

Proceeding from the Tower Bridge, we have first **St. Katherine Dock,** covering a land area of 13 acres, and a water area of 10 acres; and next the **London Docks** (Plan III. P. and Q. 8 and 9), covering a land area of 66 acres and a water area of 34 acres. The warehouses can store about a quarter of a million tons of goods, and the gangways of the wine vaults are said to be nearly thirty miles in length. In addition to wine, wool, ivory, spices, coffee, etc., are mostly brought to the London Docks, which comprise the *Eastern* and *Western Docks*, the *Shadwell Basin*, and the more southerly *Wapping Basin*. To the north of the London Docks lies St. George's Street, a modern name which hardly disguises the former notorious Ratcliff Highway. From Wapping station the **Thames Tunnel** (Plan III. Q. 9), 1,200 ft. long, the first of a number of such undertakings, burrows beneath the river to Rotherhithe. It is used by the Underground Railway. Easy communication for vehicles and pedestrians between the north and south of the river is provided by the **Rotherhithe Tunnel,** constructed by the London County Council at a cost of upwards of two million pounds and opened in 1908. It runs obliquely under the Thames, the northern approach road beginning near Stepney Station, and the southern approach road at Lower Road, near Rotherhithe Station. The tunnel and its approaches are about a mile and a quarter in length. The extensive **Surrey Commercial Docks** and **Canal** occupy a combined land and water area of 455 acres on the curved peninsula between the Pool and Limehouse Reach. They are principally used for timber, grain and Canadian produce.

About midway between the London and the West India Docks is the Limehouse Basin of the **Grand Union Canal,** a useful waterway which makes a circuit of North London (we have already seen it at the Zoo), traverses the Midlands and eventually unites the Thames with the Mersey at Liverpool, though few cargoes make the entire journey. Between this and the river is Limehouse Causeway, often visited as **Chinatown,** where little knots of Chinese seamen can always be observed, and the lodging-houses and eating-places bear signs of which few Britishers know the meaning. The **West India Docks** (Plan III. T. and U. 9) occupy the northern portion of the **Isle of Dogs,** a tongue of land which here causes the river to make a wide sweep southward to Greenwich, and then northward again to Blackwall. The West India Docks occupy about 240 acres. To the south are the **Millwall Docks.** Here is a huge Granary, the finest in London, with a capacity of 24,000 tons—alas, only a week's supply for the hungry Metropolis. For **Greenwich** see p. 265. Here is the **Greenwich-Millwall Tunnel,** for foot passengers only. At **Blackwall** are the **East India Docks** (67½ acres), not nearly so large as their western neighbours. Hereabouts is the **Blackwall Tunnel** (Plan III. V. 9), providing free communication for pedestrians and vehicles between Blackwall and East Greenwich. The tunnel is 6,200 ft. long, but only about a fifth of it is actually under the bed of the river. Immediately to the east of the East India Docks is Bow Creek, where the *River Lea* finds an outlet to the Thames. Beyond are the **Royal Victoria, Royal Albert** and **King George V. Docks,** extending parallel with the river for three miles, and with a combined water area of 245 acres. There are 12¾ miles of quays. The water is maintained by a powerful electrical pumping installation at a depth of from 28 to 39 ft. Here are great warehouses for tobacco and frozen meat from Australia, New Zealand and South America. To accommodate the last-named trade are enormous Cold Stores which are capable of storing half a million carcases.

To provide accommodation for the largest modern steamships the **King George V. Dock** was constructed in 1921, south of the Royal Albert Dock. This is 4,500 feet long and 700 feet wide; it has a water area of nearly 65 acres and a quayage of over 2 miles. There is also a large dry dock 750 ft. in length and 100 ft. wide, capable of accommodating the largest liners. The cost of this improvement, executed by the Port of London Authority, exceeded £4,000,000.

Some sixteen miles farther down the river are the extensive **Tilbury Docks,** with a land area of 725 acres and a water area of 104½ acres. Tilbury is mainly a transit dock, offering special facilities to the large Far Eastern and other liners and to smaller craft bringing perishable cargo. As the river is here very deep, the largest ships can come up to the lock entrance at practically any time. The Port of London Authority in 1930 opened the Tilbury Passenger Landing Stage, which is available for liners at all states of the tide, day or night. A well-appointed Hotel adjoins the docks, commanding from its windows an unrivalled outlook on shipping, an average of over a thousand sea-going vessels passing it every week in the year.

Tilbury Fort was constructed by Henry VIII. for the defence of the Thames. Here Queen Elizabeth reviewed her troops in 1588, when the Armada invasion was threatened, using the memorable words, " I know I have the body of a weak, feeble woman, but I have the heart and stomach of a king, and a king of England too."

SOUTH LONDON.

ROUTE XIV.—THE BOROUGH—ST. SAVIOUR'S CATHEDRAL—IMPERIAL WAR MUSEUM—LAMBETH PALACE—BATTERSEA PARK—DULWICH GALLERY.

COMPARED with London north of the Thames, the south, or Surrey side, has little to interest the visitor. The districts adjoining the river are almost entirely industrial; while the outer regions like Camberwell, Clapham, Brixton, etc., though by no means without their amenities, are little more than dormitories for people employed in the City.

One part of South London that no visitor who has read his Dickens, or has any regard for historical associations, will care to overlook, is that known as the **Borough.**

Crossing London Bridge (p. 243), we have on our left the approach road to the **London Bridge Stations** (Plan III. O. 9); and on the right the broad stone steps which give access to—

St. Saviour's Cathedral.

(**Plan** III. N. 9. **Services,** see p. 20.)

Though restored in recent years, the building is one of the oldest and most interesting in London. Portions of the Norman nave, dating from the early part of the twelfth century, were incorporated by Blomfield in the new nave, erected 1891–6. The choir and Lady Chapel were built by Peter de Rupibus about 1207. James I. of Scotland was here wedded to the niece of Cardinal Beaufort. But the chief interest of the church lies in its literary associations, some of the most notable names in English literature having been connected with the parish of Southwark. John Gower, the friend of Chaucer, Edmund Shakespeare, brother of the poet, and Massinger and Fletcher, the dramatists, were buried here; as was also Lawrence Fletcher, joint lessee with Shakespeare and Burbage of the Globe Theatre, Bankside. John Harvard, founder of the famous University in the States, was baptized here on the 29th November, 1607, his father being then a churchwarden. To mark the tercentenary of his birth, the Chapel of St. John, north of the chancel, was in 1907 restored by "sons and friends of Harvard University," and a memorial window inserted. There are also memorial windows to most of the worthies named above, as well as to Chaucer, Bunyan, and others. Also commemorated are the Protestant martyrs who, during Mary's reign, were tried in the Lady Chapel (which—a kitchen in Elizabethan times—has recently been restored). There is a fine *Memorial of William Shakespeare,* whose theatre, the Globe, stood close at hand.

Adjoining the church is the **Borough Market,** for fruit and vegetables; westward is **Southwark Bridge,** rebuilt 1921. The northern end is dominated by **Vintners' Hall,** a fine modern building. On the south side of Park Street, near the Bridge, a memorial marks the site of the **Globe Playhouse** of Shakespeare's time.

On the opposite side of the Borough High Street, St. Thomas Street leads to **Guy's Hospital** (Plan III. N. 9), founded in 1721 by the miserly bookseller, Thomas Guy.

Continuing down the Borough High Street, we pass the site of the *Talbot* or *Tabard Inn,* from which the Canterbury Pilgrims were accustomed to set out, as described by Chaucer. The old *Tabard* was burnt down in 1873. Lower down is the successor to the *White Hart,* where Mr. Pickwick first encountered the jovial Sam Weller. Between Nos. 75 and 77 the *George Inn,* with its dormer roofs and its quaint inner courtyard and galleries, still reminds us of these old-world hostelries. In the graveyard of **St. George's Church,** at the corner of Great Dover Street, are the graves of many generations of debtors confined in the now demolished *Marshalsea Gaol,* immortalized in *Little Dorrit* and commemorated by a tablet in the churchyard. In **Lant Street,** nearly opposite the Church, the irrepressible Bob Sawyer lodged with Mrs. Raddle while acquiring the status of a "saw-bones" at Guy's.

The southward continuation of Borough High Street is **Newington Causeway,** at the end of which is the **Elephant and Castle.** Six important thoroughfares meet here, and it is one of the busiest of London's tram, bus and tube centres. A few yards to the south, in Newington Butts, is the **Metropolitan Tabernacle,** the successor of a larger structure built to accommodate the immense congregations attracted by the preaching of Charles Haddon Spurgeon.

In Walworth Road is the **Cuming Museum,** with relics of London and Londoners of the past. (*Week-days,* 12–8.30; *Saturdays, from* 10 *a.m.; Sundays,* 6–9. *Free.*)

St. George's Road, close by, will bring us to the former **Bethlem Hospital,** or **Bedlam,** built in 1812–15 to replace the famous "Old Bedlam" in Moorfields, founded so long ago as 1247, the oldest charitable institution for the treatment of the insane in the world. The hospital has moved into the country, having outgrown its site, and the buildings now house—

The Imperial War Museum.

Plan III. M. 10. Plans of Museum, see p. 259.
Access.—Nearest tube station—*Lambeth North; Waterloo* and *Elephant and Castle* are slightly more distant. Westminster is about 10 minutes' walk from the Museum. Buses, etc., crossing Westminster Bridge nearly all pass within a short distance of the Museum; and most of the buses crossing Blackfriars and London Bridges are also useful—in the former case get off at St. George's Circus; in the latter at Elephant and Castle.
Open free daily, except Good Friday and Christmas Day, from 10 a.m. to 4, 5 or 6 on weekdays, and from 2 p.m. on Sundays.

The Museum was founded as a memorial of the effort and sacrifice made by the men and women of the Empire during the Great War of 1914–1918.

The general arrangement of the collections is best understood by reference to our plans of the Museum (see p. 259). Apart from the Reference Sections (which include a Library of close on 60,000 volumes dealing with all aspects of the War and a quarter of a million photographs), the main feature of the Museum is its picture galleries, totalling about 5,000 works of art. The remaining exhibition galleries are devoted to trophies, relics, models, etc., of naval, military and aerial interest.

At the junction of St. George's Road with the Westminster Bridge Road stands **St. George's Roman Catholic Cathedral** (Plan III. M. 10), designed by Pugin, and opened in 1848, but still wanting its central tower. Here Cardinal Wiseman was enthroned as first Archbishop of Westminster. A few yards to the west, at the corner of Westminster Bridge Road and Kennington Road, is **Christ Church,** built to replace the old Surrey Chapel, rendered famous by the preaching of Rowland Hill. The tower and spire were built with American contributions as a memorial of Lincoln, the stonework being appropriately ornamented with the stars and stripes.

At **St. George's Circus** (Plan III. M. 10) the roads from Blackfriars, Waterloo, Westminster and Lambeth Bridges all meet.

The Waterloo Road would bring us in a few minutes to **Waterloo** (Plan III. L. 9, see p. 60), the terminus of the South-Western section of the Southern Railway. The fine entrance archway is a memorial of railwaymen fallen in the War. Opposite the station is the **Union Jack Club,** for soldiers and sailors, founded as a memorial of men of both services who lost their lives in the South African and Chinese Wars. At the corner of New Cut is the **"Old Vic."** Here opera (in English) and Shakespeare are played to crowded houses, and the "masses" demonstrate time and again that they have as keen an appreciation of good drama and music as any West End audience.

From St. George's Circus a bus or tram will take us to **Lambeth Palace** (Plan III. L. 10), near Lambeth Bridge.

This mellow Tudor pile, for nearly seven centuries the London residence of the Archbishops of Canterbury, can only be visited by permission, but the **Library,** with its 30,000 printed books and 14,000 MSS., is *open daily, on Mondays, Wednesdays, Thursdays and Fridays from* 10 *to* 4 *or* 4.30 (*Tuesdays,* 10 *to* 1 *only*), *save for about six weeks from the end of August.* The part actually occupied by the Archbishop was rebuilt by Archbishop Howley in 1834. The most interesting portions of the older building are the *Gatehouse* built by Cardinal Morton in 1499; the *Lollards' Tower,* erected by Archbishop Chicheley about 1450; the *Chapel,* built by Archbishop Boniface in 1245, but with a modern roof; the *Great Hall,* used as the Library, the work of Archbishop Juxon, who attended Charles I. on the scaffold; and the *Guard Room,* with portraits of archbishops by Reynolds, Lawrence, Herkomer, and others. In the gardens are some luxuriant fig-trees, said to have been brought from Spain, and planted by Cardinal Pole, Legate to the court of Queen Mary.

Ten acres of the grounds are maintained for public use under the name of the **Archbishop's Park.** Adjoining the south gateway of the Palace is **St. Mary's Church,** containing the graves of six archbishops. It has a fine Perpendicular tower.

In one of the windows is a representation of a pedlar and his dog, commemorating the bequest to the church of a piece of land by a pedlar who had been sheltered by the priest. The receipts from the land amounted at first to 2*s.* 8*d.* per year, but when the London County Council found it necessary to acquire the "Pedlar's Acre" in connection with their new County Hall, they had to pay the handsome sum of £81,000.

Opposite the Palace the river is crossed by the rebuilt **Lambeth Bridge,** at the far end of which Thames House and the headquarters of *Imperial Chemical Industries* are well seen. The new headquarters of the **London Fire Brigade** (see p. 26) are among the finest in the world. We can either cross the river by the bridge, or follow the **Albert Embankment** (p. 78) to Westminster Bridge, passing the series of seven detached buildings serving as **St. Thomas's Hospital** (Plan III. L. 9 and 10). Or from Lambeth Bridge we could continue westward in the direction of Battersea Park. As we approach Vauxhall Bridge the **Tate Gallery** (see p. 117) is well seen across the water. The road bridge beneath **Vauxhall Station** (Southern Railway: S.W. section) leads to **Kennington Oval,** the headquarters of the Surrey C.C. and the scene of many county matches. Beyond, bordering the main road to Clapham, is **Kennington Park,** formerly Kennington Common, the scene of the Chartist assembly in 1848.

Battersea Park, one of the largest and most attractive of South London pleasure grounds, adjoins the south bank of the river, almost opposite Chelsea Hospital. It is 198 acres in extent,

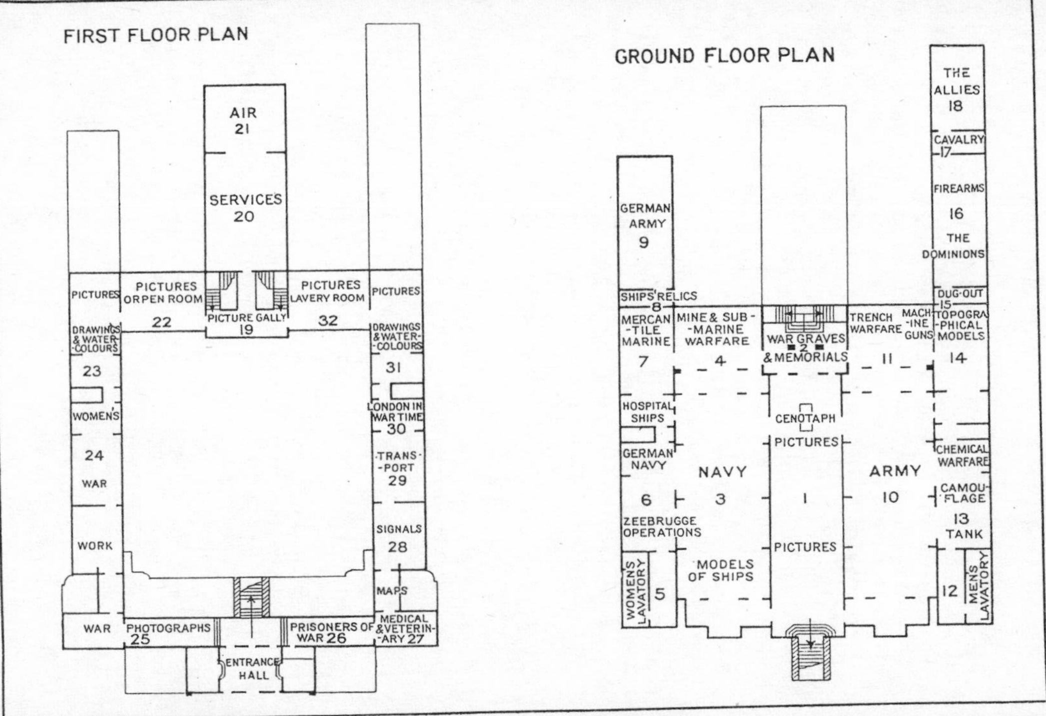

THE IMPERIAL WAR MUSEUM.

and includes a large expanse of water and a well-kept *Sub-tropical Garden.* Near the east end of the Park the river is crossed by the **Chelsea Suspension Bridge** (rebuilt 1935–7), and at the west end by the **Albert Suspension Bridge.**

For **Chelsea** and its many interesting associations, see p. 181.

One or two other features of South London not included in the above route demand mention. The most important is the **Dulwich College Picture Gallery,** about half-a-mile from North Dulwich Station (Southern Railway, S.E. section, or by bus by way of Red Post Hill). Entrance in Gallery Road. Most of these important and valuable works of art (originally bought as the nucleus of a projected National Gallery of Poland) were bequeathed to the College in 1811 by Sir Francis Bourgeois, R.A. *The Gallery is open free daily from* 10 *to* 4, 5, *or* 6, *Sundays* (*April to September*) *after* 2. It contains two well-known works by *Murillo,* and is strong in Dutch and Flemish masters, including *Cuyp, Wouverman, Rembrandt, Van Dyck,* and the two *Teniers.* There are also examples of *Gainsborough, Reynolds,* and other British masters. **Dulwich College** was founded in 1619 by Edward Alleyn, the actor, and is a large and flourishing institution.

An interesting survival in this locality is the *Toll Gate* across the road near Dulwich College.

Hardly more than a mile farther south is the site of the **Crystal Palace,** that monument of the Great Exhibition of 1851 and of the skill of Sir Joseph Paxton. The Palace, alas, was gutted by fire in December, 1936.

Popular open spaces in this locality are **Dulwich Park** (72 acres), famous for its spring show of rhododendrons and its rock garden, **Peckham Rye** (115 acres) and **Brockwell Park** (127 acres). At 100, London Road, adjoining Lordship Lane Station, is the **Horniman Museum** (*open daily, except Tuesdays,* 11 *till dusk, Sundays from* 2), containing many articles of historical and archæological interest, collections of insects, carved furniture, enamels, armour, and toys.

Clapham Common is an open space of 220 acres. **Tooting Common,** to the south-east, contains nearly 150 acres. **Tooting Bec** is so called as having been a dependency of the famous Abbey of Bec, in Normandy.

John Ruskin spent the earlier part of his life at Denmark Hill and Herne Hill, a fact which is commemorated by the name of **Ruskin Park,** on the west side of Denmark Hill. Adjoining is **King's College Hospital.**

ST. SAVIOUR'S CATHEDRAL, SOUTHWARK.

Topical,] [*London.*

THE IMPERIAL WAR MUSEUM.

MILTON'S COTTAGE, CHALFONT ST. GILES—GREENWICH HOSPITAL AND THE NATIONAL MARITIME MUSEUM—GREENWICH OBSERVATORY.

Valentine & Sons, Ltd.,] *[Dundee.*

HIGH BEACH, EPPING FOREST.

ON HAMPSTEAD HEATH.

TRIPS FROM TOWN.

THE nearer suburbs encircling London will not, as a rule, arouse enthusiasm ; but once the stranger has passed this middle belt, no matter whether he goes north, south, east or west, he will find within the compass of an easy excursion innumerable places of beauty and historic interest. All we can do, in the limited space at our command, is to set out in alphabetical order a few particulars of the places most likely to attract, together with the facilities for reaching them. Several of the large tourist firms arrange day and half-day tours from London, combining rail, motor or steamer, etc., as well as luncheon and tea, at inclusive rates (see also p. 31). The "country services" of the buses and the Green Line coaches are also useful in this connection. Strangers desirous of spending an evening in beautiful surroundings without incurring a long journey should not overlook the easy access provided by the "Tubes" and electric railways to such spots as Hampstead Heath and Ken Wood, Richmond and Kew, etc. On certain days in each week during the summer the railway companies issue day and half-day excursion tickets at reduced fares to most of the places mentioned below, and throughout the year cheap week-end tickets are obtainable. The trips are usually advertised in the newspapers.

For the benefit of motorists we add a note of the road routes to the more distant resorts.

Ashridge Park.

Admission.—The Gardens are open on Saturdays, Sundays and public holidays from 2 p.m. Fee 1*s.* ; children 6*d.*

Rail to Berkhamsted (L.M.S.) station from Euston ; thence walk over Berkhamsted Common, or by bus (about 2½ m.).

Road viâ Edgware and the Watford by-pass to Berkhamsted.

Motor Coach to Berkhamsted from Victoria, Hyde Park Corner or Marble Arch.

Ashridge Park, formerly the seat of Lord Brownlow, was, with some 150 acres of charming grounds, in 1928 presented by the late Mr. Urban Broughton to the Conservative Party as a memorial of Mr. Bonar Law. The donor's intention was "to preserve for the nation an historic site and a stately building ; to establish a centre where all grades of Conservatives can find a curriculum suited to their requirements, and to give enjoyment to the public by admitting it to the gardens once a week."

A further 300 acres of the Park have been acquired as a

permanent open space, making, with **Berkhamsted Common** (lovely with gorse and bracken and beech woods) and **Ivinghoe Beacon** (with fine views), a total open space of more than 2,000 acres under the care of the National Trust.

Barnet.

Train (L.N.E.R.) from Kings Cross or Finsbury Park stations to *New* Barnet. Or by bus.

Road Route via Finchley and the Great North Road (13 m.) to Station Road, *New* Barnet. Green Line coaches from Victoria, Marble Arch, King's Cross, etc.

To Londoners Barnet is known as a pleasant northern suburb; historians know it on account of the Battle of Barnet (1471) where Warwick was slain. Recently the place has acquired new interest in the **Abbey Folk Park and Museum** at Park Road, New Barnet (*open weekdays only*, 11 *to* 8, *or dusk if earlier*). Admission to all sections, 1*s*. 3*d*. This, the first open-air museum in England, includes a "Prehistoric" Village of seven huts, a thirteenth-century tithe-barn Church, a sixteenth-century Witch's cottage, a Smithy, Farriers, Wheel-wrights, a series of twelve old-time "Shops," an Ethnographical section; African village, Chinese Temple of Initiation, etc. In addition there are collections of Prehistoric, Roman and Mediæval, Tudor and Stuart remains: ancient stained glass, MSS., furniture, period rooms and Victorian by-gones, carriages, etc. Altogether, 44 show buildings and 42,000 objects are on view.

An excursion to Barnet may well be combined with a visit to Hatfield or St. Albans (see pp. 270, 273).

Brighton.

Electric trains from London Bridge or Victoria (Southern Railway), 51 miles. The expresses do the journey in an hour. Day and half-day excursions are run.

Road Route, viâ Westminster Bridge, Brixton, Streatham, Croydon by-pass, Red Hill, Crawley and Pyecombe ($51\frac{1}{2}$ miles).

Motor Coaches run from and to London daily throughout the year. See announcements in newspapers.

With its five miles of sea front, its magnificent hotels and shops, and many facilities for amusement, Brighton is never likely to lose its hold on the affections of Londoners. The principal features are the fine promenades, the Piers, the Pavilion (built by the Prince Regent, afterwards George IV.), the Aquarium and the great Sports Stadium; but Brighton is less interesting in itself than as a background against which to view the extraordinary and diversified crowds which flock there, especially at week-ends and on Bank Holidays. A favourite excursion is that to the Devil's Dyke, high up on the spacious South Down range. Our *Guide to Brighton* should be consulted for fuller information.

Burnham Beeches (Bucks).

Rail (G.W.) from Paddington (21 m.). Or by London and North-Eastern Railway (Marylebone) to Beaconsfield.

In connection with certain trains buses run between Slough and Beaconsfield, viâ Stoke Poges and Farnham Royal, through tickets being issued to cover motor and the rail journey to and from London. In summer there are also conveyances from Slough Station to Burnham Beeches. As Burnham Beeches Station is a mile and a half from the woods, and there is no public conveyance, it is usually more convenient to book to Slough. Burnham Beeches are included with Maidenhead and other Thames resorts in many circular trips from Town.

Buses.—The service from Hounslow to Windsor passes through Slough.

Coaches.—" Green Line " coaches in summer direct to Burnham Beeches from Trafalgar Square and Hyde Park Corner.

Road Route, viâ Chiswick, the Great West Road and the Colnbrook by-pass to Slough; or viâ Acton, Hanwell, Uxbridge and Farnham.

Londoners are indebted to the City Corporation for the preservation and maintenance of this magnificent pleasure-ground, comprising over 400 acres of the finest sylvan scenery in England. In autumn especially, when the trees are all " in russet mantle clad," the place is one of great beauty. The pollard beeches are generally considered the finest in the world. In 1921 the late Viscount Burnham presented an additional 65 acres as a memorial of his father, the first Lord Burnham, whose work for journalism is commemorated in the name **Fleet Wood.** About midway between Slough and Burnham Beeches (say two miles from either) is **Stoke Poges,** the scene of Gray's famous *Elegy*. The red-brick tomb of the poet's mother, in which he was himself interred, will be seen close to the south wall of the church.

Chalfont St. Giles (Bucks).

Rail (Metropolitan) from Baker Street, or L.N.E.R. from Marylebone, to Chalfont and Latimer station, from which the village is about 3 miles distant. Or from Marylebone or Paddington to Seer Green, Gerrard's Cross (whence buses run to Chalfont St. Giles) or Beaconsfield.

Road Route, viâ Harrow, Pinner and Rickmansworth, or viâ Uxbridge. Green Line coaches from Oxford Circus and Baker St. Station to Chalfont viâ Hayes and Uxbridge.

This prettily placed village is visited on account of **Milton's Cottage,** where *Paradise Lost* was finished and *Paradise Regained* commenced. It stands at the end of the village, on the left. (*Admission 6d., or 3d. each for a party.*) It has been altered but little since the poet's time. Beautifully situated among beech trees about two miles to the south, and most conveniently reached by bus from Beaconsfield station (G.W.R.), is **Jordans,** the charming old Meeting House in the grounds of which rest the remains of William Penn, the founder of Pennsylvania, and his wife and children. A little above the Meeting House is the *Hostel*, with a barn containing timbers from the *Mayflower*.

Croydon Air Port.

Train to Croydon or Waddon (Southern Railway), thence by bus; or by bus direct. Passengers by the air liners are conveyed between the Air Port and Central London by special motors.

Croydon is the British headquarters of civilian commercial flying, with huge air-liners of various nationalities constantly arriving from and departing for the Continent, etc. For permission to enter the *Control Tower*, whence telephonic communication is maintained with aircraft *en route*, and to inspect the ingenious arrangements for direction-finding, etc., special application must be made; but visitors are admitted (6*d*.) to the roof overlooking the starting-point and are shown the hangars and aeroplanes, and the excursion is well worth making. Joy rides of short duration may be taken.

(For notes on other aerodromes see p. 67.)

Epping Forest.

Rail from Liverpool Street (L.N.E.R.). Chingford is the most popular approach, but the stations on the L.N.E.R. line at Loughton and Theydon Bois are also in touch with some of the most charming parts of the Forest. Cheap day tickets are issued.

Buses and Trams.—Several lines bring the Forest within easy reach of the central parts of London. Green Line coaches start from Portman Square, Baker Street Station and Liverpool Street.

Epping Forest, comprising 5,604 acres, is merely a "remainder" of the Great Forest of Waltham, which until a century or so ago reached almost to London. When successive encroachments bade fair in a short while entirely to obliterate the Forest, the Corporation of London intervened, and after expensive litigation succeeded in securing all the unenclosed portion for the use and enjoyment of the public for ever. The one-day visitor will be well advised not to lose touch with the central high road that runs right through the Forest, from Woodford, through Buckhurst Hill, to Epping, a distance from south to north of over ten miles. The finest part is generally considered to be *High Beach*, a little to the west of the point where the road to Loughton crosses the highway just referred to at the *Robin Hood Inn*. Tennyson resided here when he wrote *Locksley Hall*. The elevated spire of High Beach Church is the most serviceable of Forest landmarks. Near at hand is the *King's Oak Hotel*, a favourite resort of picnic parties. The most common trees are the oak, hornbeam, beech, and birch. **Gilwell Park,** in the words of the Chief Scout, is "the home and Mecca of the Boy Scout Movement."

About two miles south-east of Chigwell is **Hainault Forest.** Owing to nineteenth-century disafforestation only about a third of the 1,100 acres is woodland. A public golf course (18 holes) is maintained by the London County Council, where anyone may play for 1*s*. a round. Needless to add, it is besieged by players, especially on Saturdays and holidays.

Epsom (Surrey).

Rail from Waterloo (14½ m.), or from Victoria and London Bridge to *Epsom* Station (2 m. from Racecourse), 15¾ m. Or by Southern Railway (Brighton section) to *Epsom Downs* Station (16 m.).

The nearest station to the Racecourse is **Tattenham Corner,** reached from Charing Cross, Cannon Street and London Bridge Stations.

Road Route (14½ m.) viâ Clapham, Balham, Tooting, Merton and Ewell.

Motor Bus services from Morden Station. Green Line coaches from Victoria.

Epsom, with its delightful surroundings, is well worth a visit. The famous Racecourse is on Epsom Downs, about 500 ft. above sea-level. The **Derby** is run on a Wednesday at the end of May or the beginning of June, the **Oaks** on the following Friday.

Gravesend.

Gravesend, reached either by Southern Railway, or from Fenchurch Street or St. Pancras viâ Tilbury, is the entrance to the Port of London and the home of most of the Thames pilots. Pilotage in the London district is compulsory, with few exceptions, for vessels exceeding 60 tons burden engaged in the foreign trade. Gravesend men are generally considered the most skilful river boatmen in the world. With its opposite neighbour, **Tilbury** (p. 254), Gravesend is a favourite yachting station. Visitors from the United States will certainly find their way to the *Parish Church of Saint George*, to see the register containing the entry of the burial of the famous Indian Princess, Pocahontas, who did so much to befriend the early settlers of Virginia, and died at Gravesend in 1616 during a visit to this country. She is commemorated by two stained-glass windows, the gift of the Virginia Society of Colonial Dames of America.

Greenwich.

Steamers and Motor Launches provide the most pleasant and interesting way of travelling to and from Greenwich. The vessels start from and return to *Westminster Pier*, in the shadow of Big Ben. Fares about 1*s.* single, 1*s.* 6*d.* return. Many of the boats call also at Tower Pier (see p. 245).

Rail by Southern Railway (6½ m.), from Charing Cross to *Maze Hill*, a few minutes' walk from National Maritime Museum, by way of Park Place and Park Row.

Trams and buses from Blackfriars, Westminster Bridge or Waterloo.

Greenwich is of peculiar interest to visitors from Britain overseas, for under the old constitutional theory all the colonies were reckoned as part of the Royal manor of Greenwich. During the War of Independence it was gravely argued in the House of Commons that Americans could not reasonably complain of "taxation without representation," seeing that they were represented in Parliament by the Kent members.

Greenwich Hospital, a long range of buildings with an imposing frontage to the river, occupies the site of an old royal palace used as a residence by successive sovereigns from the early part of the fifteenth century to the time of the Commonwealth. Henry VIII. and his daughters Elizabeth and Mary were born here; and here the youthful Edward VI. passed away. Charles II. commenced to rebuild the palace, but completed only the west, or King Charles, wing, overlooking the river. Under William and Mary building was resumed, and in 1705 the edifice was converted into a hospital for superannuated seamen. It no longer serves this purpose. The Hospital was closed by Act of Parliament in 1869 and in 1873 the buildings were taken over by the Admiralty and converted into the Royal Naval College for the higher education of Naval Officers.

The buildings of the College comprise four blocks. In the south-eastern block, under one of the twin domes, is the **Chapel,** built by James Stewart (*open daily, except Fridays and Sundays*); and beneath the other dome is the **Painted Hall** (*closed during restoration*), built by Wren and decorated throughout with paintings by Thornhill.

NATIONAL MARITIME MUSEUM.

Admission.—Fridays, *6d.*; other days free. Open weekdays, 10–6; Sundays, 2.30 to 6. Closed on Good Friday, Christmas Eve and Christmas Day.
Entrance at junction of Park Row and Park Place.
Refreshment Room and Tea Garden, opening from the Navigation Room.

This Museum was founded by Act of Parliament in 1934 and comprises the Queen's House and the buildings erected at the beginning of the nineteenth century for the accommodation of the Royal Hospital School, which migrated to Suffolk in 1932.

The **Queen's House** was erected by Inigo Jones for Anne of Denmark, Queen Consort of James I. and subsequently completed for Henrietta Maria, the wife of Charles I. It is unique in that it was built over the road between Deptford and Woolwich. The Queen's bedroom has a painted ceiling and her sitting-room a ceiling carved in wood and richly gilt. Other rooms on the first floor have ceilings of unusual beauty, and on the south of the House is a loggia, originally designed for the Royal Family to show themselves to their subjects.

In the Queen's House are collected the portraits, battle-pieces and models illustrating the Navy from the time of Henry VIII. until the coming of William and Mary to Greenwich in 1689.

In the *Caird Buildings* note the marble Rotunda, designed by Sir Edwin Lutyens and Sir William Reid Dick, which commemorates Sir James Caird, to whom the Museum is indebted for the cost of its construction as well as for more than half of the exhibits. Beyond the Caird Rotunda is the *Library*, containing a unique collection of books and manuscripts, atlases and charts. On either side of the Rotunda are the Medal Room and the Seal Room.

A staircase constructed from the timbers of H.M. ships *Defence, Defiance, Ganges* and *Arethusa* leads to the Galleries, with an extraordinarily interesting collection of models and relics associated with Anson, Hawke, Cook, Howe, Duncan, St. Vincent and Nelson and their stirring times. It is quite impossible in the space at our disposal even to attempt to describe the contents of these rooms, which provide a wonderful illustration of the evolution of the British Navy.

In Church Street, close to Greenwich Park station, is the **Church of St. Alfege,** containing the tombs of General Wolfe (d. 1759) and Thomas Tallis, the 16th-century church musician.

South of the Hospital is **Greenwich Park,** a royal domain of 185 acres, laid out by Charles II. and commanding magnificent views Londonwards. Crowning a hill in the centre is the **Royal Observatory,** to which interested visitors are occasionally admitted on making written application to the Director. The time-ball descends precisely at 1 p.m. and the correct time is then telegraphed to all the most important towns. Visitors generally seek out the line marking the *Greenwich Meridian,* which crosses the path a few yards north of the Observatory gates. Greenwich Observatory originated in a desire to provide seamen with satisfactory data for determining their positions at sea and thus the Greenwich meridian became and remains of world-wide importance. Opposite the gates of the Observatory is a fine statue of *General Wolfe* by Professor Tait Mackenzie. It was presented to this country by the Canadian People.

Adjoining Greenwich Park on the south is **Blackheath** (267 acres), where Wat Tyler and Jack Cade marshalled their hosts, and where many a pretty highway robbery has taken place. Here, too, golf was introduced to an, at first, unappreciative Southron public by James I.

Hampstead Heath.

Nearest Stations.—Hampstead for south side, Golder's Green for north, both on the Morden-Edgware line; Hampstead Heath (L.M.S.).

Trams and Buses from Holborn, King's Cross, Hampstead Road, etc.

Hampstead Heath, with its broken heights, its grassy glades and furze-covered expanses, and its far-reaching views, is without exception the best of London's open spaces. The Heath proper comprises only 240 acres, but adjoining common lands increase the public area to 804 acres. On the north are the **Golder's Hill Estate** (36 acres), and **Waterlow Park** (29 acres), while to the east is **Parliament Hill** (267 acres). Also to the north is **Ken Wood,** with the mansion and the valuable collection of pictures and furniture formed by the late Lord Iveagh. (*The House is open weekdays* 10 *to* 5; *Sundays* 2.30 *to* 5; *earlier in winter. Admission* 1s. *on Wednesdays and Fridays*; *other days free.*) Close at hand also are the beautiful **Highgate Woods** (69 acres), maintained by the City Corporation. A magnificent view is gained from the *Flagstaff* (440 ft. above sea-level).

Well Walk, close to the High Street, takes its name from the famous spa so extensively patronized by " the quality " in the seventeenth and eighteenth centuries. Keats lodged here in 1817–18, and later lived at *Lawn Bank,* at the foot of Keats Grove. Lawn Bank, in the garden of which the *Ode to the Nightingale* was written, has been acquired by the public, and is now maintained as a Keats Memorial and Museum. *The Keats House is open* (*free*) *on Mondays, Wednesdays and Saturdays from* 10 *to* 6 *p.m., April to September* (*October to March,* 10 *to* 4 *p.m.*). *The Museum adjoining, containing a unique collection of relics of Keats and his circle, is open every weekday from* 10.30 *to* 8 *p.m. Both house and museum are closed on Sundays.*

In the graveyard of Hampstead Church are buried Sir J. Macintosh, the historian; Joanna Baillie; John Constable, some of whose most famous pictures were inspired by the locality; G. du Maurier (1896); and Sir W. Besant (1901). In the neighbourhood is the **Everyman Theatre** (repertory).

In Hoop Lane, off the Finchley Road, on the northern borders of Hampstead Heath, is the **Golder's Green Crematorium.**

Close at hand is the extensive **Hampstead Garden Suburb,** of interest as an example of successful town-planning.

Hampton Court.

Rail from Waterloo (Southern Rly.) to Hampton Court Station, 15 m. Or from L.M.S. and District Stations, viâ Richmond, to Teddington.
Motor Buses from Putney, Highgate, etc.
Rail and Trolley Bus.—To Hammersmith, by Underground, thence by trolleybus viâ Twickenham. Or by tram to Wimbledon, changing there to the trolleybus for Kingston and Hampton Court.
Coaches (Green Line) from Victoria and Hyde Park Corner.
Steamers run during the summer months (see announcements in newspapers) from Westminster Bridge to Hampton Court.
Admission.—The Gardens are open daily until dusk. Portions of the Palace are open daily 10 to 4, 5 or 6, Sundays from 2. To view the State Apartments, Chapel, Haunted Gallery and Great Hall a charge of 1*s.* is made on weekdays (Saturdays, 6*d.*; Bank Holidays and Sundays free; children half price.) The Great Kitchen and Cellars (3*d.*) and the Orangery (2*d.*) are open at the same hours as the State Apartments.

No visitor to London, however pressed for time, should fail to see the beautiful and stately palace built by Cardinal Wolsey

PLAN OF HAMPTON COURT MAZE.

for his own delight, and afterwards "presented"—not very willingly, we must believe—to his royal master, Henry VIII. It is the largest and in many respects the finest of all the royal palaces of England, though it has not been occupied by the sovereign since the time of George II. It contains about a thousand apartments, of which four-fifths are occupied by royal pensioners and other privileged persons; but the magnificent State Rooms, with their fine pictures, the Courts, and the charming gardens are open to all. In recent years several parts not formerly visible have been opened to the public, including the old moat and a fine battlemented bridge, built by Henry VIII. for his "owne darling," Anne Boleyn; the famous "Haunted Gallery"; and "My Lord Cardinall's Lodgynges." The "ghost" of the Haunted Gallery is supposed to be that of Catherine Howard, another of Henry's unfortunate "darlings."

The Palace is of red brick, now delightfully mellowed by time. Perhaps the finest portions of the original building are the **Great**

Gatehouse and the **Clock Court.** In the latter is the famous astronomical clock constructed for Henry VIII. The **Great Hall,** with its magnificent tapestries and wonderful timber roof (recently restored), was built by the same monarch. The **State Rooms,** surrounding the Fountain Court, were added for William III. by Sir Christopher Wren. The Palace was used as a residence by Henry VIII., Cromwell, the Stuart kings, William III., George I. and George II. Although some of the best of the paintings have been removed in recent years to other palaces, the collection still ranks as one of the finest in England. The celebrated "Hampton Court Beauties," by *Kneller*; and the "Windsor Beauties," of the Court of Charles II., by *Lely*, should be seen. The finest tapestries are the eight pieces in the Great Hall, illustrating the life of Abraham, and the copies of the famous Raphael cartoons, presented by Baron D'Erlanger.

In recent years the **Great Kitchen** and the **Tilt Yard** have become accessible to the public.

Notable features of the beautiful **Gardens** are the *Great Vine*,[1] planted in 1768; and the *Maze*, adjoining the Lion Gates, the intricacies of which can easily be threaded by one who bears in mind always to follow the hedge on the *right* when going in and the *left* hedge when coming out. In the Wren **Orangery** (*admission 2d.*) are nine large tempera paintings, by Andrea Mantegna, representing the triumph of Julius Cæsar. Opposite the eastern façade of the Palace is the **Long Water** (nearly ¾ of a mile long), constructed by Charles II. The **Home Park** (600 acres) is bounded on all but the western side by the Thames It is open to the public.

Opposite the **Lion Gates** is the principal entrance to **Bushy Park,** a royal demesne of over 1,000 acres, noted for its tame deer. The famous *Chestnut Avenue*, the flowering of which during May lures crowds of sightseers, stretches right across the Park to Teddington, the vista broken only by the *Diana Fountain*. Many of the trees are over 200 years old.

Harrow-on-the-Hill.

Rail from Baker Street (Met.) or Marylebone, 9½ m. Other routes are by Bakerloo Tube, joining the L.M.S.R. line at Queen's Park, or by District and Piccadilly Lines to *South Harrow Station*. Also from Euston or Broad Street.

Road Route viâ Maida Vale, Cricklewood, Hendon and Kenton. Green Line coaches from Victoria and Marble Arch.

Harrow is chiefly visited for the famous **School,** founded in 1571 by John Lyon, a yeoman of the parish. It rivals Eton in the affections of the aristocracy. Among distinguished scholars may be mentioned Lord Byron, Sheridan, Sir Robert Peel, Palmerston and Cardinal Manning. The view from the churchyard terrace (400 ft. high), from the Peachey tomb (now

[1] An offshoot of this vine in the Royal Gardens at Windsor, planted in 1775, has long since outgrown its parent.

protected by an iron casing), on which Byron used to lie outstretched, is very extensive. The finely-placed *Church*, consecrated in 1094, with its Norman tower, is also of great interest (*open all day*).

Hatfield (Herts).

Rail from King's Cross, 17¾ m. Also from Moorgate and Broad Street, changing at Finsbury Park.

Road Route viâ Highgate, Finchley, Barnet and Potter's Bar. Green Line coaches from Victoria, Marble Arch and Baker Street Station.

Admission.—The house is generally shown, in the absence of the family, on Wednesdays and Thursdays between 2 and 5 p.m., from Easter Monday to 1st August, on application to the Housekeeper. Also on Easter Monday, Whit-Monday, and August Bank Holiday. No order is required for parties of fewer than twelve. The Park is open to inhabitants of Hatfield. Picnics are not allowed.

Hatfield House, the historic home of the Cecils, was built by the first Earl of Salisbury, who exchanged Theobald's Park with James I. for this estate. It is a lovely Jacobean building of mellow red brick, containing many works of art and historical relics. The *Church*, just outside the Park, is a large and richly-adorned building, in the Decorated style. The *Salisbury Chapel*, where the late Marquess and many of his family repose, is on the north side of the chancel, and the Victorian statesman is commemorated by a bronze statue outside the main gates of the Park.

Henley.

Rail from Paddington (G.W.), 35¾ m.

Also by Messrs. Salter Bros.' Saloon **Steamers** from Kingston (p. 273).

Road Route viâ Hammersmith, Chiswick, the Great West Road, Slough and Maidenhead; or (a prettier route) viâ Uxbridge, Beaconsfield, Bourne End and Marlow.

This pleasant little town is one of the most popular centres for river scenery. During **Regatta Week** (beginning of July) accommodation is at a premium. See our *Guide to the Thames* for details.

Kew Gardens.

Rail to either Kew Bridge (L.M.S. and S.R.) or Kew Gardens (Underground) Stations. The former station is about ten minutes' walk from the principal, or northern, entrance; from the latter it is five minutes' walk to the Victoria Gate.

Steamers during summer from Westminster Bridge (see announcements).

Motor Buses from Hammersmith, Kensington, etc., pass three entrances.

Trolley Buses from Hammersmith or Shepherd's Bush to Kew Bridge.

Admission.—The Gardens are open daily from 10 a.m. to 8 p.m. or dusk; until 8.30 p.m. on Saturdays, Sundays and Bank Holidays, June—August. Closed on Christmas Day. The Hot-houses are not opened until 1, except on students' days, when they are open also from 10 to 11.45 a.m.

Fee, one penny (Bank Holidays free); *6d.* on Students' Days (Tuesdays and Fridays, except Good Friday and Tuesdays following Bank Holidays).

Photography and Sketching is permitted in the gardens on payment of *3d.*; otherwise apparatus, cameras, etc., must be left at the entrance.

Refreshments (teas and light luncheons) are served at the Pavilion near the Temperate House.

Motors may be parked near the main entrance, near Kew Green.

The **Royal Botanic Gardens** combine the attractions of a delightful open space of nearly 300 acres with those of a museum. The visitor may wander at will through what is practically a lordly park, with every species of tree, shrub and flower plainly labelled for his edification. The grounds comprise stately avenues and sequestered walks, lakes and ponds, palm-houses and conservatories, gorgeous flower-beds, rockeries, museums and classic temples, and a large herbaceous ground. The most important features are the large *Palm House*, kept always at

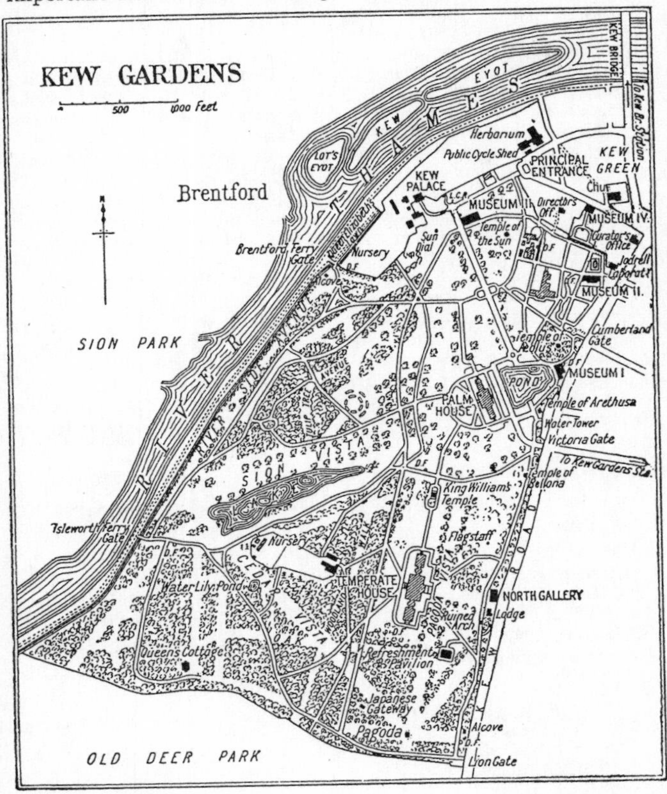

a temperature of 80°, the *Temperate House*, the four *Museums*, the *Herbarium*, and the *North Gallery*. Other houses are devoted to tropical aroids, tropical ferns, filmy ferns, succulents, begonias, orchids, water-lilies, alpine plants, etc. Always delightful, Kew should be seen also at such seasons as "bluebell time," or when the masses of rhododendrons or daffodils are in bloom.

Among other works of universal importance carried out at Kew was the raising from seeds specially brought from Brazil —at that time the world's sole source of rubber supply—of the 1,000 plants with which the rubber industry was introduced into the Malay Peninsula and Ceylon. Kew was also instrumental in introducing the almost indispensable quinine plant from South America into India.

A touch of quaintness is given to the southern end of the Gardens by the **Chinese Pagoda,** 165 ft. high, and its neighbour, a **Japanese Gateway** which is an exact copy of the gate of the great Buddhist Temple of Nishi Hongwanji. A notable addition to the Gardens is a **Flagpole** of Douglas fir from Vancouver island, presented by the Government of British Columbia. Said to be the tallest in the world, it is 215 ft. in height and weighs 18½ tons. In the northern part of the grounds, close to the main entrance, is **Kew Palace** (*admission 3d.; open* 1 *to* 6; *Tuesdays and Fridays,* 10 *to* 6), a favourite residence of George III.; many relics of his family may be seen here. Queen Charlotte died here in 1818. On the left of the large lake as one proceeds towards the river are the secluded grounds of the Queen's Cottage, an enclosed path through which is open to the public. The large building on the Middlesex side of the river is *Sion House,* a seat of the Duke of Northumberland. (The Lion came from Northumberland Avenue—see p. 76).

On **Kew Green** stands the brick church of *St. Anne,* dating from 1714. Gainsborough, the artist (d. 1788), is buried in the churchyard.

Maidenhead.

Rail from Paddington (G.W.), 24½ m. *Taplow* station, on the Bucks side, is equally near the river.

Motor Buses connect Maidenhead with Windsor and with Henley.

Road Route (28 m.) viâ Hammersmith, the Great West Road and Slough.

Charming river scenery, especially the reach below the lovely wooded grounds of **Cliveden. Boulter's Lock,** the busiest lock on the Thames, provides an interesting spectacle in the season at all hours of the day, but especially on a fine Sunday. See our *Guide to the Thames.*

Richmond.

Rail (Southern—S.W.) from Waterloo (9¾ m.); or from Broad Street. Also by District Railway.

Buses.—There are several services of motor omnibuses. Green Line coaches from Victoria and Hyde Park Corner.

Steamboats in summer (see announcements).

No place in the environs of London is more attractive than Richmond, delightfully situated on the slope of a hill overlooking the Thames on the Surrey side. It is an uphill walk of about a mile from the station to the beautiful *Terrace Gardens,* from which is gained that matchless **View** of woodland, water and tranquil pasture-land that poets and painters have vied with each other in depicting. By the acquisition of the Petersham meadows in the foreground and of the Marble Hill estate across the river at Twickenham, this view is now secured to the public for all time. Occupying the site and perpetuating the name of the historic hotel is the *Star and Garter Home* for Disabled Soldiers and Sailors, a beautiful building forming the Women's Memorial of the Great War. **Richmond Park,** 2,358 acres in extent and between ten and eleven miles in circumference, was first enclosed by Charles I. The Park is one of the most popular resorts of Londoners, and during week-ends and on public holidays the stream of motors on the principal thoroughfares is unending. Large herds of fallow and red deer roam the Park. The public *Golf Courses* are exceedingly popular. Nearly in the middle are the *Pen Ponds*, covering 18 acres, a favourite resort of skaters. (Richmond also boasts an indoor ice rink.) The *White Lodge* was the residence before her marriage of Queen Mary, and was in 1894 the birthplace of King Edward VIII. The house figures, like Richmond Hill, in Scott's *Heart of Midlothian. Pembroke Lodge* was the seat of Lord John Russell.

The Richmond " Maids of Honour," it may be well to explain, are a kind of sweet cheese-cake.

South of Richmond, and reached from it by a pleasant walk either along the picturesque tow-path or through the Park, is the Royal Borough of **Kingston,** with Hampton Court Palace on the opposite bank of the river. At Kingston may be seen, enclosed by railings, the *Coronation Stone*, on which Athelstan and other Saxon kings were crowned. The stretch of river between Richmond and Kingston is very popular with boating parties. Kingston is the starting-point of Messrs. Salter Bros.' well-known steamers to Henley and Oxford. See our *Guide to the Thames*.

St. Albans (Herts).

Rail from St. Pancras or King's Cross; or from Euston or Broad Street, viâ Watford (L.M.S.R.).

Bus Service from Golder's Green.

Road Route (20 m.) viâ Marble Arch, Cricklewood, Hendon, Edgware and Elstree; or (21 m.) viâ Great North Road to Barnet. Green Line Coaches from Victoria Hyde Park Corner and Marble Arch.

This ancient city, the *Verulamium* of the Romans, and the burial-place of the great Francis Bacon, Viscount St. Albans, is well worth a pilgrimage from London. The **Cathedral** boasts one of the longest naves in England (275 feet), and is a mixture of the Norman, Early English and Decorated styles, not too happily restored by the late Lord Grimthorpe. Bacon's tomb is in *St. Michael's Church*, parts of which are even older than the Abbey. Recently extensive and valuable excavations have revealed many features of the Roman Verulamium. The quaint round tavern known as *The Fighting Cocks* proudly claims to be the oldest inhabited house in England.

Southend and Westcliff.

Rail from Fenchurch Street (35¾ m.), from Liverpool Street (41½ m.) and St. Pancras (42 m.).
Steamer from London Bridge during summer; *see* newspapers.
Road Route (about 45 m.) viâ Tottenham or Leyton to Woodford, where begins the Southend Road, affording a clear run right to Southend.

Southend shares with Brighton the advantage of being sufficiently near to London to be available as a place of residence for City men. The tide recedes so far that the Pier has a length of a mile and a half.

The Surrey Hills.

Access.—The Southern Railway issues cheap tickets to the principal centres, available for return from a different station from that at which the rail is left on the outward journey; in many cases the available stations lie on either side of very beautiful tracts. In addition to the Southern Railway (South-Western and Brighton sections) **Motor Buses** and the Green Line Coaches run to the hills from Town, but as much of the journey is through tram-lined suburban highways this is not recommended as a means of approach if a good train service is available. There are also day or half-day **Motor-Coach Tours.** (See p. 31.)

The choicest features of the country immediately south of London are comprised in the chalk range running east and west some 10 to 15 miles from Town. On the northern edge the chief starting-points for exploration are **Epsom** (see p. 264), **Leatherhead, Banstead** and **Purley.** Along or near the southern edge of the range are such famous beauty-spots as **Guildford, Box Hill** (**Dorking**) and **Leith Hill** (965 ft.), the two latter with wonderful views across the Sussex Weald. Box Hill has been acquired for the nation and placed under the National Trust.

The Thames.

A large and rapidly growing number of Londoners find their principal recreation on the Upper Thames, the river of pleasure *par excellence*. To quote the late Sydney Crossley :—

"In point of real beauty, one questions whether the surroundings of the Thames are surpassed in the world. Grander scenery than that offered by Mapledurham, Cliveden, Marlow, Sonning, or the woods of Wytham is, of course, to be found in many places. But where is the simple rustic beauty of the Thames to be found elsewhere? Certain spots, occasional reaches, there may be on other rivers which rival certain reaches on it, but one knows of no single stream which presents such an endless variety of changing beauties as does the Thames. And there is something exceptionally English about it all. There is no single spot on the Thames that could be situated anywhere but in England."

To the average Londoner, the lower reaches by Richmond, Kingston, Molesey and Windsor are more familiar than the parts more particularly referred to above, but the Great Western Railway renders the whole stream up to and even beyond Henley available for a day, or even a half-day's boating or fishing. Those who merely wish to see the river in leisurely and pleasant fashion cannot do better than avail themselves of the excellent steam launches run daily in summer by Messrs. Salter Bros. between Kingston and Oxford. Two days are required for the entire trip, but passengers can board or leave the boats at any lock or stopping place. **Motor-Coach Trips** embrace some of the choicest scenery of the Thames Valley, and many allow time for a short boating excursion.

For a full description of the Thames and its many beauty spots, and for details as to excursions, see the *Guide to the Thames* in this series, containing specially-drawn charts of the river.

Waltham Abbey.

Rail from Liverpool Street or St. Pancras (12¾ m.) to Waltham Cross station.
Buses to Waltham Cross, connecting with a local service to Waltham Abbey. Green Line Coaches from Oxford Circus.
Trams from Finsbury Park and Stamford Hill.

This ancient Abbey, situated on the Lea, about three miles from the western border of Epping Forest, was founded by the Saxon Harold, and here he knelt to pray before setting out for the fatal field of Hastings. The nave has been restored, and is now used as the parish church. **Waltham Cross,** a mile west of the Abbey, was erected by Edward I., like Charing Cross and others, to mark the places where the body of Queen Eleanor rested on its way from Grantham to London.

Whipsnade.

Access.—Rail from St. Pancras (L.M.S.) to Luton, completing the journey by bus. It is well to enquire as to services before leaving London. Motor coaches, etc., from London.
Admission daily, including Sundays, from 10 a.m. to " lighting-up time." Adults, 1*s.*, children, 6*d.*
Refreshments can be obtained at Whipsnade.

The " Country Zoo " belonging to the Zoological Society and organized in connection with the Zoological Gardens in Regent's Park (p. 152) provides one of the most popular trips from Town. It is an area of 500 acres on the Chiltern Hills and the general intention is to develop it " as a Park in which wild animals will have more space and freedom than in London, and also as a sanctuary for British wild birds and plants." Strangers should bear in mind that at Whipsnade the animals are not caged, but roam in large enclosures ; field glasses are therefore very useful.

Windsor and Eton.

Rail (G.W.) from Paddington (21¼ m.), or from Waterloo (25¾ m.).
Omnibuses from Hounslow. Green Line Coaches from Trafalgar Square.
Road Route (22½ m.) viâ Hammersmith, Chiswick, the Great West Road, Staines and Old Windsor (there are many alternative routes).

Windsor Castle.

Admission.—When the Court is not in residence and for about a fortnight beforehand (*see* newspapers), the *State Apartments* and the *Queen's Doll's House* (entrance on North Terrace) are generally open to the public every week-day except Friday, from 11 to 3, Nov. 1 to March 31 ; until 4, April 1 to May 31, and during October ; 11 to 5, June 1 to September 30. Adults are charged 1*s.*, children 6*d.* (proceeds devoted to local charities). Parties are conducted by official guides. For the Queen's Doll's House the fee is 6*d.* The *Albert Memorial*

Chapel and the *Round Tower* are open on the same days and at the same hours as the State Apartments, except that the Chapel is closed between 1 and 2 p.m. daily and the Round Tower is closed during the winter. The *Curfew Tower* can be seen any day on application to the keeper at the Tower at the back of the Horse Shoe Cloisters. *St. George's Chapel* may be viewed any week-day (except Fridays) between 11 a.m. and 4 p.m. The Chapel is usually closed during part of August and part of September. The western portion of the *North Terrace* is open to the public every day; the east end (from which the East Terrace Gardens are seen) whenever the State Apartments are open. Guides are available to conduct visitors round the *Precincts* any week-day, 10–5 in summer; 10–4 winter. Apply at Henry VIII's Gateway.

Windsor Castle, famous the world over as the residence of the British Sovereign, was founded by William the Conqueror, and has been extended and altered by nearly every succeeding monarch. Under Queen Victoria no less a sum than £900,000 was expended in this way, and King Edward VII. carried out an extensive rearrangement and embellishment of the interior.

Even when the State Apartments are not accessible (see above) the visitor will find plenty to occupy and interest him. The Castle comprises two main portions, the **Lower Ward,** in which are St. George's Chapel, the Albert Memorial Chapel, the Horse Shoe Cloisters, and the residences of the Knights of Windsor and others; and the **Upper Ward,** in which are the State Apartments, the King's Private Apartments (scarcely ever shown), and the south wing, in which the royal guests and visitors are accommodated. Between the two portions is the massive **Round Tower,** which should be ascended for the sake of the extensive view over the Thames Valley. The Castle is nearly a mile in circumference.

Passing under **Henry VIII.'s Gateway,** we have before us **St. George's Chapel,** a beautiful example of the Perpendicular style, begun by Edward IV. and completed by Henry VIII. In the richly-decorated Choir, with its fan-vaulting, are the stalls of the Knights of the Garter. A subterranean passage leads to the Tomb House, constructed by order of George III., below the Albert Memorial Chapel. Here lie the bodies of George III., George IV., William IV., George V. and other royal personages.

The **Albert Memorial Chapel,** originally intended by Henry VIII. for his own mausoleum, and afterwards presented to Cardinal Wolsey, was restored and sumptuously decorated by Queen Victoria in memory of the Prince Consort. The Chapel can only be seen from the barrier.

The **State Apartments,** in which foreign sovereigns visiting His Majesty are accommodated, are entered from the North Terrace. They are beautifully furnished, and are hung with priceless pictures by Rubens, Rembrandt, Van Dyck, and others. Much of the carving was done by Grinling Gibbons. The **Waterloo Chamber,** used for banquets and theatrical performances, is entirely hung with portraits of persons associated with the close of Napoleon's military career.

Adjoining the entrance to the State Apartments is that to the

HAMPTON COURT: THE GATEHOUSE—THE PAGODA, KEW GARDENS—RUINS AT VIRGINIA WATER.

[*Sport and General.*

HENLEY REGATTA.

[*P. G. Luck.*

THE THAMES, FROM RICHMOND HILL.

[*Dixon Scott.*

WINDSOR CASTLE, FROM THE RIVER.

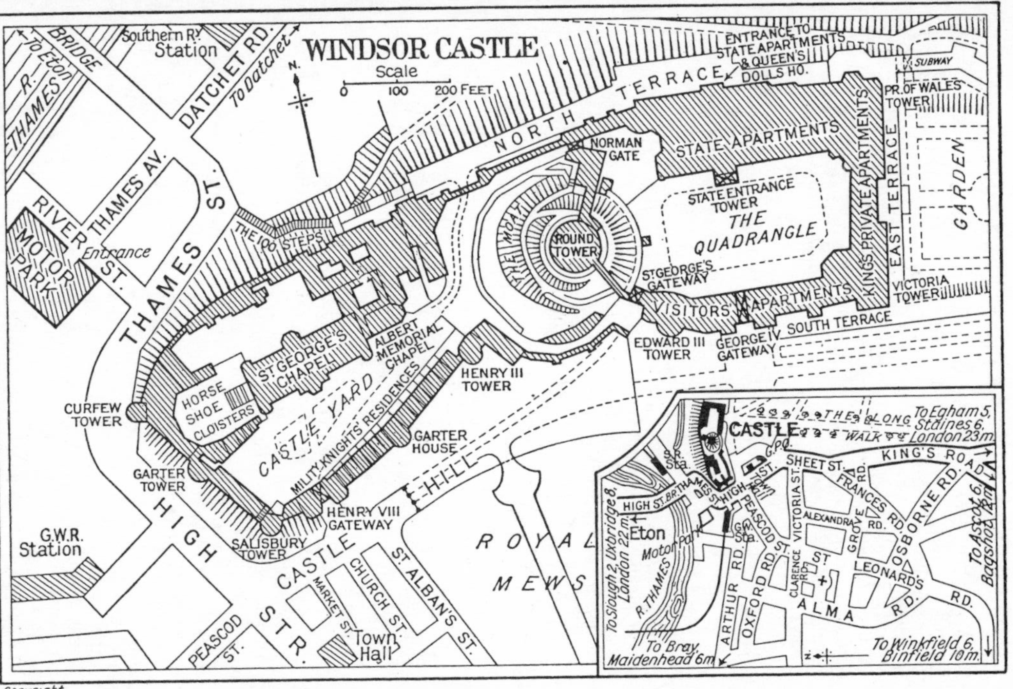

WINDSOR CASTLE
Scale
0
100
200 FEET
N.
To Eton
R. THAMES
BRIDGE
Southern Ry. Station
DATCHET RD.
To Datchet
THAMES AV.
RIVER ST.
Entrance
MOTOR PARK
THAMES ST.
THE 100 STEPS
NORTH TERRACE
ENTRANCE TO STATE APARTMENTS & QUEEN'S DOLLS HO.
SUBWAY
PR. OF WALES' TOWER
NORMAN GATE
STATE APARTMENTS
STATE ENTRANCE TOWER
THE QUADRANGLE
KING'S PRIVATE APARTMENTS
EAST TERRACE
GARDEN
ROUND TOWER
THE MOAT
ST. GEORGE'S GATEWAY
VICTORIA TOWER
VISITORS' APARTMENTS
SOUTH TERRACE
EDWARD III TOWER
GEORGE IV GATEWAY
ST. GEORGE'S CHAPEL
ALBERT MEMORIAL CHAPEL
HENRY III TOWER
HORSE SHOE CLOISTERS
CASTLE YARD
MILITY. KNIGHTS' RESIDENCES
CURFEW TOWER
GARTER HOUSE
GARTER TOWER
HILL
HENRY VIII GATEWAY
SALISBURY TOWER
G.W.R. Station
HIGH STR.
CASTLE
ROYAL MEWS
PEASCOD ST.
MARKET ST.
CHURCH ST.
ST. ALBAN'S ST.
Town Hall
CASTLE
THE LONG WALK
To Egham 5, Staines 6, London 23m.
G.P.O.
S.R. Sta.
SHEET ST.
KING'S ROAD
HIGH ST.
BR.
THAMES ST.
HIGH ST.
Town Hall
FRANCES RD.
OSBORNE RD.
To Ascot 6, Bagshot 12m.
Eton
G.W. Sta.
PEASCOD ST.
VICTORIA ST.
ALEXANDRA RD.
GROVE RD.
To Slough 2, Uxbridge 8, London 22m.
Motor Park
R. THAMES
ARTHUR RD.
OXFORD RD.
CLARENCE RD.
ST. LEONARD'S RD.
ALMA RD.
To Bray, Maidenhead 6m.
To Winkfield 6, Binfield 10m.
N.
Copyright.

Queen's Doll House, which, in juvenile minds at any rate, rivals the State Apartments themselves in interest. The House is a wonderfully exact model of a twentieth-century house, building, furniture and equipment being on the scale of one-twelfth.

The **Home Park,** immediately adjoining the Castle, comprises about 400 acres, and is bordered on three sides by the Thames. Close to Frogmore House is the **Royal Mausoleum,** where rest the bodies of Queen Victoria and the Prince Consort (*open free to the public once a year only, on Whit-Mondays, from* 11–4). If possible, a drive should be taken through **Windsor Great Park,** which stretches southward from the Castle for upwards of five miles, and comprises 18,000 acres. Motorists are allowed only on the 3-mile long Queen Anne's Ride, but otherwise there are few restrictions. One of the finest views in England is that of the Castle from Snow Hill, at the southern end of the **Long Walk.**

Virginia Water is at the southern end of the Great Park, and may be directly reached from London by Southern Railway to Virginia Water station (about 1½ miles distant). Coaches and buses also run from Windsor and from Staines and London. The route from London is by the Great West Road, Staines, Egham.

The *Lake* (artificial) covers an area of about 150 acres, and is rather more than two miles long. The *Ruins*—genuine antiquities—were brought from Tripoli and re-erected in 1825.

Eton, immediately opposite Windsor, on the Bucks side of the river, is gained by crossing the bridge. The famous **College,** founded in 1440 by Henry VI., includes among its pupils, past and present, many of the greatest names in English history. The boys number about a thousand. Both School and Chapel can generally be seen on application.

Woolwich.

Rail from Charing Cross, Cannon Street and London Bridge to Woolwich Arsenal station (10 m.). Trams and buses from Westminster and Blackfriars Bridge.

Visitors of British nationality desirous of seeing **Woolwich Arsenal** must obtain an order from the War Office, Whitehall. The Arsenal covers 600 acres, and employs, even in normal times, several thousand men. Some of the operations, particularly those in the Gun Factory, are of great interest.

Southward is **Eltham,** with the banqueting hall and other remains of a Palace of Plantagenet and Tudor kings. Henry V. spent Christmas at Eltham Palace after his victory at Agincourt, and Henry VIII. and Queen Elizabeth passed several years of their childhood here. Extensive restorations have recently been carried out. The Great Hall (*open free on Thursdays ; summer* 11–7, *winter* 11–4) has a fine hammer-beam timber roof, rivalled only by that in the Hall of the Middle Temple. The moat, crossed by a fifteenth-century bridge, and the ancient houses close by, combine to make Eltham Palace a scene of captivating interest and beauty.

INDEX

Where more than one reference is given, the first is the principal.

For Banks, Bridges, Churches, Clubs, Docks, Hospitals, Libraries, Music Halls, Monuments, Parks, Railway Stations, Railways, Theatres, *see* lists under those headings.